Communications in Computer and Information Science   **925**

Commenced Publication in 2007
Founding and Former Series Editors:
Phoebe Chen, Alfredo Cuzzocrea, Xiaoyong Du, Orhun Kara, Ting Liu,
Dominik Ślęzak, and Xiaokang Yang

More information about this series at http://www.springer.com/series/7899

Kang Li · Jianhua Zhang
Minyou Chen · Zhile Yang
Qun Niu (Eds.)

Advances in Green Energy Systems and Smart Grid

First International Conference on Intelligent Manufacturing
and Internet of Things and 5th International Conference on Computing
for Sustainable Energy and Environment, IMIOT and ICSEE 2018
Chongqing, China, September 21–23, 2018
Proceedings, Part III

Springer

Editors
Kang Li
The University of Leeds
Leeds
UK

Jianhua Zhang
North China Electric Power University
Beijing
China

Minyou Chen
Chongqing University
Chongqing
China

Zhile Yang
Shenzhen Institute of Advanced Technology
Chinese Academy of Sciences
Shenzhen
China

Qun Niu
Shanghai University
Shanghai
China

ISSN 1865-0929 ISSN 1865-0937 (electronic)
Communications in Computer and Information Science
ISBN 978-981-13-2380-5 ISBN 978-981-13-2381-2 (eBook)
https://doi.org/10.1007/978-981-13-2381-2

Library of Congress Control Number: 2018953020

This Springer imprint is published by the registered company Springer Nature Singapore Pte Ltd.
The registered company address is: 152 Beach Road, #21-01/04 Gateway East, Singapore 189721, Singapore

Preface

This book constitutes the proceedings of the 2018 International Conference on Intelligent Manufacturing and Internet of Things (IMIOT 2018) and International Conference on Intelligent Computing for Sustainable Energy and Environment (ICSEE 2018), which were held during September 21–23, in Chongqing, China. These two international conference series aim to bring together international researchers and practitioners in the fields of advanced methods for intelligent manufacturing and Internet of Things as well as advanced theory and methodologies of intelligent computing and their engineering applications in sustainable energy and environment. The new conference series IMIOT is jointly organized with the well-established ICSEE conference series, under the auspices of the newly formed UK-China University Consortium in Engineering Education and Research, with an initial focus on intelligent manufacturing and sustainable energy.

At IMIOT 2018 and ICSEE 2018, technical exchanges within the research community took the form of keynote speeches, panel discussions, as well as oral and poster presentations. In particular, two workshops series, namely the Workshop on Smart Energy Systems and Electric Vehicles and the Workshop on Communication and Control for Distributed Networked Systems, were held again in parallel with IMIOT 2018 and ICSEE 2018, focusing on the two recent hot topics of the integration of electric vehicles with the smart grid, and distributed networked systems for the Internet of Things.

The IMIOT 2018 and ICSEE 2018 conferences received 386 submissions from over 50 different universities, research institutions, and companies from both China and UK. All papers went through a rigorous peer review procedure and each paper received at least three review reports. Based on the review reports, the Program Committee finally selected 135 high-quality papers for presentation at the IMIOT 2018 and ICSEE 2018. These papers cover 22 topics and are included in three volumes of the CCIS series, published by Springer. This volume of CCIS includes 30 papers covering 5 relevant topics.

Located at the upstream Yangtze basin, Chongqing constitutes the most important metropolitan area in the southwest of China. It has a glorious history and culture and serves as a major manufacturing center and transportation hub. Chongqing is also well-known for its spicy food and hotpot, attracting tourists and gourmets from around the world. In addition to academic exchanges, participants were treated to a series of social events, including receptions and networking sessions, which served to build new connections, foster friendships, and forge collaborations. The organizers of IMIOT 2018 and ICSEE 2018 would like to acknowledge the enormous contribution of the Advisory Committee, who provided guidance and advice, the Program Committee and the numerous referees for their efforts in reviewing and soliciting the papers, and the Publication Committee for their editorial work. We would also like to thank the editorial team from Springer for their support and guidance. Particular thanks are of course due to all the authors, as without their high-quality submissions and presentations the conferences would not have been successful.

Finally, we would like to express our gratitude to our sponsors and organizers, listed on the following pages.

September 2018

Fusheng Pan
Shilong Wang
Mark Price
Ming Kim Lim
Kang Li
Yuanxin Luo
Yan Jin

Organization

Honorary Chairs

Fusheng Pan   Chongqing Science and Technology Society/Chongqing University, China
Shilong Wang   Chongqing University, China
Mark Price   Queen's University Belfast, UK

General Chairs

Ming Kim Lim   Chongqing University, China
Kang Li   Queen's University Belfast, UK

Advisory Committee Members

Erwei Bai   University of Iowa Informatics Initiative, USA
Zhiqian Bo   China Xuji Group Corporation, China
Tianyou Chai   Northeastern University, China
Phil Coates   Bradford University, UK
Jaafar Elmirghani   University of Leeds, UK
Qinglong Han   Swinburne University of Technology, Australia
Deshuang Huang   Tongji University, China
Biao Huang   University of Alberta, Canada
Guangbin Huang   Nanyang University of Technology, Singapore
Minrui Fei   Shanghai University, China
Sam Ge   National University of Singapore, Singapore
Shaoyuan Li   Shanghai Jiaotong University, China
Andy Long   University of Nottingham, China
Dong Yue   Nanjing University of Posts and Communication, China
Peter Taylor   University of Leeds, UK
Chengshan Wang   Tianjin University, China
Jihong Wang   University of Warwick, UK
Xiaohua Xia   Petoria University, South Africa
Yulong Ding   University of Birmingham, UK
Yugeng Xi   Shanghai Jiaotong University, China
Sarah Supergeon   University College London, UK
Derong Liu   University of Illinois, USA
Joe Qin   The Chinese University of Hong Kong, Hong Kong, China
Savvas Tassou   Brunel University London, UK
Qinghua Wu   South China University of Technology, China
Yusheng Xue   China State Grid Electric Power Research Institute, China
Jiansheng Dai   King's College London, UK

I-Ming Chen	Nangyang Technological University, Singapore
Guilin Yang	Institute of Advanced Manufacturing Technology, Ningbo, China
Zhuming Bi	Indiana University Purdue University Fort Wayne, USA
Zhenyuan Jia	Dalian University of Technology, China
Tian Huang	Tianjin University, China
James Gao	University of Greenwich, UK
Weidong Li	Coventry University, UK
Stan Scott	Queen's University Belfast, UK
Dan Sun	Queen's University Belfast, UK

International Program Committee

Chairs

| Yuanxin Luo | Chongqing University, China |
| Yan Jin | Queen's University Belfast, UK |

Local Chairs

Xuda Qin	Tianjin University, China
Fuji Wang	Dalian University of Technology, China
Yingguang Li	Nanjing University of Aeronautics and Astronautics, China
Adam Clare	University of Nottingham, UK
Weidong Chen	Shanghai Jiaotong University, China
Rui Xiao	Southeast University, China
Furong Li	Bath University, UK
Min-Sen Chiu	National University of Singapore, Singapore
Petros Aristidou	University of Leeds, UK
Jinliang Ding	Northeastern University, China
Bing Liu	University of Birmingham, UK
Shan Gao	Southeast University, China
Mingcong Deng	Tokyo University of Agriculture and Technology, Japan
Zhengtao Ding	The University of Manchester, UK
Shiji Song	Tsinghua University, China
Donglian Qi	Zhejiang University, China
Wanquan Liu	Curtin University, Australia
Patrick Luk	Cranfield University, UK
Guido Maione	Technical University of Bari, Italy
Chen Peng	Shanghai University, China
Tong Sun	City University London, UK
Yuchu Tian	Queensland University of Technology, Australia
Xiaojun Zeng	The University of Manchester, UK
Huaguang Zhang	Northeastern University, China
Shumei Cui	Harbin Institute of Technology, China
Hongjie Jia	Tianjin University, China
Youmin Zhang	Concordia University, USA

Xiaoping Zhang   University of Birmingham, UK
Peng Shi   University of Adelaide, Australia
Kay Chen Tan   National University of Singapore, Singapore
Yaochu Jin   University of Surrey, UK
Yuchun Xu   Aston University, UK
Yanling Tian   University of Warwick, UK

Organization Committee

Chairs

Congbo Li   Chongqing University, China
Minyou Chen   Chongqing University, China
Adrian Murphy   Queen's University Belfast, UK
Sean McLoone   Queen's University Belfast, UK

Special Session Chairs

Qian Tang   Chongqing University, China
Xin Dai   Chongqing University, China
Johannes Schiffer   University of Leeds, UK
Wenlong Ming   Cardiff University, UK

Publication Chairs

Zhile Yang   Chinese Academy of Sciences, China
Jianhua Zhang   North China Electric Power University, China
Hongjian Sun   Durham University, UK
Trevor Robinson   Queen's University Belfast, UK

Publicity Chairs

Qingxuan Gao   Chongqing University, China
Junjie Chen   Southeast University, China
Brian Falzon   Queen's University Belfast, UK
Ben Chong   University of Leeds, UK

Secretary-General

Yan Ran   Chongqing University, China
Dajun Du   Shanghai University, China
Rao Fu   Queen's University Belfast, UK
Yanxia Wang   Queen's University Belfast, UK

Registration Chairs

Guijian Xiao   Chongqing University, China
Shaojun Gan   Queen's University Belfast, UK

Program Committee Members

Stefan Andreasson	Queen's University Belfast, UK
Andy Adamatzky	University of the West of England, UK
Petros Aristidou	University of Leeds, UK
Vijay S. Asirvadam	Universiti Teknologi Petronas, Malaysia
Hasan Baig	University of Exeter, UK
Lucy Baker	University of Sussex, UK
John Barry	Queen's University Belfast, UK
Xiongzhu Bu	Nanjing University of Science and Technology, China
Jun Cao	University of Cambridge, UK
Yi Cao	Cranfield University, UK
Xiaoming Chang	Taiyuan University of Technology, China
Jing Chen	Anhui University of Science and Technology, China
Ling Chen	Shanghai University, China
Qigong Chen	Anhui Polytechnic University, China
Rongbao Chen	HeFei University of Technology, China
Weidong Chen	Shanghai Jiaotong University, China
Wenhua Chen	Loughborough University, UK
Long Cheng	Chinese Academy of Science, China
Min-Sen Chiu	National University of Singapore, Singapore
Adam Clare	University of Nottingham, UK
Matthew Cotton	University of York, UK
Xin Dai	Chongqing University, China
Xuewu Dai	Northeastern University, China
Li Deng	Shanghai University, China
Mingcong Deng	Tokyo University of Agriculture and Technology, Japan
Shuai Deng	Tianjin University, China
Song Deng	Nanjing University of Posts and Telecommunications, China
Weihua Deng	Shanghai University of Electric Power, China
Jinliang Ding	Northeastern University, China
Yate Ding	University of Nottingham, UK
Yulong Ding	University of Birmingham, UK
Zhengtao Ding	University of Manchester, UK
Zhigang Ding	Shanghai Academy of Science and Technology, China
Dajun Du	Shanghai University, China
Xiangyang Du	Shanghai University of Engineering Science, China
Geraint Ellis	Queen's University Belfast, UK
Fang Fang	North China Electric Power University, China
Minrui Fei	Shanghai University, China
Dongqing Feng	Zhengzhou University, China
Zhiguo Feng	Guizhou University, China
Aoife Foley	Queen's University Belfast, UK
Jingqi Fu	Shanghai University, China
Shaojun Gan	Queen's University Belfast, China
Shan Gao	Southeast University, China

Xiaozhi Gao	Lappeenranta University of Technology, Finland
Dongbin Gu	University of Essex, UK
Juping Gu	Nantong University, China
Zhou Gu	Nanjing Forestry University, China
Lingzhong Guo	Sheffield University, UK
Yuanjun Guo	Chinese Academy of Sciences, China
Bo Han	Xi'an Jiaotong University, China
Xuezheng Han	Zaozhuang University, China
Xia Hong	University of Reading, UK
Guolian Huo	North China Electric Power University, China
Weiyan Hou	Zhengzhou University, China
Liangjian Hu	Donghua University, China
Qingxi Hu	Shanghai University, China
Sideng Hu	Zhejiang University, China
Xiaosong Hu	Chongqing University, China
Chongzhi Huang	North China Electric Power University, China
Sunan Huang	National University of Singapore, Singapore
Wenjun Huang	Zhejiang University, China
Tan Teng Hwang	University College Sedaya International University, Malaysia
Tianyao Ji	South China University of Technology, China
Yan Jin	Queen's University Belfast, UK
Dongyao Jia	University of Leeds, UK
Jongjie Jia	Tianjin University, China
Lin Jiang	University of Liverpool, UK
Ming Jiang	Anhui Polytechnic University, China
Youngwook Kuo	Queen's University Belfast, UK
Chuanfeng Li	Luoyang Institute of Science and Technology, China
Chuanjiang Li	Harbin Institute of Technology, China
Chuanjiang Li	Shanghai Normal University, China
Dewei Li	Shanghai Jiao Tong University, China
Donghai Li	Tsinghua University, China
Guofeng Li	Dalian University of Technology, China
Guozheng Li	China Academy of Chinese Medical Science, China
Jingzhao Li	Anhui University of Science and Technology, China
Ning Li	Shanghai Jiao Tong University, China
Tongtao Li	Henan University of Technology, China
Weixing Li	Harbin Institute of Technology, China
Xiaoli Li	Beijing University of Technology, China
Xin Li	Shanghai University, China
Xinghua Li	Tianjin University, China
Yunze Li	Beihang University, China
Zhengping Li	Anhui University, China
Jun Liang	Cardiff University, UK
Zhihao Lin	East China University of Science and Technology, China
Paolo Lino	University of Bari, Italy
Bin Liu	University of Birmingham, UK

Chao Liu	Centre national de la recherche scientifique, France
Fei Liu	Jiangnan University, China
Guoqiang Liu	Chinese Academy of Sciences, China
Mandan Liu	East China University of Science and Technology, China
Shirong Liu	Hangzhou Dianzi University, China
Shujun Liu	Sichuan University, China
Tingzhang Liu	Shanghai University, China
Wanquan Liu	Curtin University, Australia
Xianzhong Liu	East China Normal University, China
Yang Liu	Harbin Institute of Technology, China
Yunhuai Liu	The Third Research Institute of Ministry of Public Security, China
Patrick Luk	Cranfield University, UK
Jianfei Luo	Chinese Academy of Sciences, China
Yuanxin Luo	Chongqing University, China
Guangfu Ma	Harbin Institute of Technology, China
Hongjun Ma	Northeastern University, China
Guido Maione	Technical University of Bari, Italy
Marion McAfee	Institute of Technology Sligo, Ireland
Sean McLoone	Queen's University Belfast, UK
Gary Menary	Queen's University Belfast, UK
Gillian Menzies	Heriot-Watt University, UK
Wenlong Ming	Cardiff University, UK
Wasif Naeem	Queen's University Belfast, UK
Qun Niu	Shanghai University, China
Yuguang Niu	North China Electric Power University, China
Bao Kha Nyugen	Queen's University Belfast, UK
Ying Pan	Shanghai University of Engineering Science, China
Chen Peng	Shanghai University, China
Anh Phan	Newcastle University, UK
Meysam Qadrdan	Imperial College London, UK
Donglian Qi	Zhejiang University, China
Hua Qian	Shanghai University of Engineering Science, China
Feng Qiao	Shenyang Jianzhu University, China
Xuda Qin	Tianjin University, China
Yanbin Qu	Harbin Institute of Technology at Weihai, China
Slawomir Raszewski	King's College London, UK
Wei Ren	Shaanxi Normal University, China
Pedro Rivotti	Imperial College London, UK
Johannes Schiffer	University of Leeds, UK
Chenxi Shao	University of Science and Technology of China, China
Yuntao Shi	North China University of Technology, China
Beatrice Smyth	Queen's University Belfast, UK
Shiji Song	Tsinghua University, China
Yang Song	Shanghai University, China
Hongye Su	Zhejiang University, China

Guangming Sun	Beijing University of Technology, China
Tong Sun	City University of London, UK
Xin Sun	Shanghai University, China
Zhiqiang Sun	East China University of Science and Technology, China
Wenhu Tang	South China University of Technology, China
Xiaoqing Tang	The University of Manchester, UK
Fei Teng	Imperial College London, UK
Yuchu Tian	Queensland University of Technology, Australia
Xiaowei Tu	Shanghai University, China
Gang Wang	Northeastern University, China
Jianzhong Wang	Hangzhou Dianzi University, China
Jingcheng Wang	Shanghai Jiaotong University, China
Jihong Wang	University of Warwick, UK
Ling Wang	Shanghai University, China
Liangyong Wang	Northeastern University, China
Mingshun Wang	Northeastern University, China
Shuangxin Wang	Beijing Jiaotong University, China
Songyan Wang	Harbin Institute of Technology, China
Yaonan Wang	Hunan University, China
Kaixia Wei	NanJing XiaoZhuang University, China
Lisheng Wei	Anhui Polytechnic University, China
Mingshan Wei	Beijing Institute of Technology, China
Guihua Wen	South China University of Technology, China
Yiwu Weng	Shanghai Jiaotong University, China
Jianzhong Wu	Cardiff University, UK
Lingyun Wu	Chinese Academy of Sciences, China
Zhongcheng Wu	Chinese Academy of Sciences, China
Hui Xie	Tianjin University, China
Wei Xu	Zaozhuang University, China
Xiandong Xu	Cardiff University, UK
Juan Yan	University of Manchester, UK
Huaicheng Yan	East China University of Science and Technology, China
Aolei Yang	Shanghai University, China
Dongsheng Yang	Northeastern University, China
Shuanghua Yang	Loughborough University, UK
Wankou Yang	Southeast University, China
Wenqiang Yang	Henan Normal University, China
Zhile Yang	Chinese Academy of Sciences, China
Zhixin Yang	University of Macau, Macau, China
Dan Ye	Northeastern University, China
Keyou You	Tsinghua University, China
Dingli Yu	Liverpool John Moores University, UK
Hongnian Yu	Bournemouth University, UK
Kunjie Yu	Zhengzhou University, China
Xin Yu	Ningbo Institute of Technology, Zhejiang University, China
Jin Yuan	Shandong Agricultural University, China

Jingqi Yuan	Shanghai Jiao Tong University, China
Hong Yue	University of Strathclyde, UK
Dong Yue	Nanjing University of Posts and Communications, China
Xiaojun Zeng	The University of Manchester, UK
Dengfeng Zhang	University of Shanghai for Science and Technology, China
Huifeng Zhang	Nanjing University of Posts and Communications, China
Hongguang Zhang	Beijing University of Technology, China
Jian Zhang	State Nuclear Power Automation System Engineering Company, China
Jingjing Zhang	Cardiff University, UK
Lidong Zhang	Northeast Electric Power University, China
Long Zhang	The University of Manchester, UK
Qianfan Zhang	Harbin Institute of Technology, China
Xiaolei Zhang	Queen's University Belfast, UK
Xiaoping Zhang	University of Birmingham, UK
Youmin Zhang	Concordia University, USA
Yunong Zhang	Sun Yat-sen University, China
Dongya Zhao	China University of Petroleum, China
Guangbo Zhao	Harbin Institute of Technology, China
Jun Zhao	Tianjin University, China
Wanqing Zhao	Cardiff University, UK
Xingang Zhao	Shenyang Institute of Automation Chinese Academy of Sciences, China
Min Zheng	Shanghai University, China
Bowen Zhou	Northeastern University, China
Huiyu Zhou	Queen's University Belfast, UK
Wenju Zhou	Ludong University, China
Yimin Zhou	Chinese Academy of Sciences, China
Yu Zhou	Shanghai Tang Electronics Co., Ltd., China
Yunpu Zhu	Nanjing University of Science and Technology, China
Yi Zong	Technical University of Denmark, Demark
Kaizhong Zuo	Anhui Normal University, China

Sponsors

Chongqing Association for Science and Technology, China
Shanghai University, China

Organizers

Chongqing University, China
Queen's University Belfast, UK

Co-organizers

Southeast University, Beijing Institute of Technology, Dalian University of Technology, Harbin Institute of Technology, Northwestern Polytechnical University, South China University of Technology, Tianjin University, Tongji University, Shanghai University, University of Birmingham, Cardiff University, University College London, University of Nottingham, University of Warwick, University of Leeds.

Contents – Part III

Energy Saving

Energy Storages

Power System Analysis

Clean Energy

Research on Refined Load Forecasting Method Based on Data Mining

Yawen Xi[1(✉)], Junyong Wu[1], Chen Shi[1], Xiaowen Zhu[1], Ran An[1], and Rong Cai[2]

[1] Electrical Engineering School of Beijing Jiaotong University, Haidian District, Beijing, China
16121551@bjtu.edu.cn
[2] ABB China Research Institute, Chaoyang District, Beijing, China

Abstract. Load forecasting is a basic work of power system dispatching. With the rapid development of smart grid technology, the accuracy of load forecasting is put forward by increasing demand. Fusion load, weather and other multi-sourced data, a refined load forecasting method of support vector machine (SVM) based on data mining is proposed. Firstly, the history load data is clustered and the operation days are divided into six categories. Then, the load data and weather data such as humidity and temperature are fused together, a refined load forecasting model based on data mining is proposed. And the parameters of the model are optimized globally. Forecasting the load of a prefecture-level city in Zhejiang Province in 2013, the load prediction error of sampling point and daily average load forecasting rate are used as indexes to evaluate the prediction accuracy, the prediction results show that the prediction accuracy of the support vector machine (SVM) refined load forecasting method based on historical data and real-time influencing factors proposed in this paper is significantly higher than that of the traditional load forecasting method.

Keywords: Load forecasting · Data mining · Support Vector Machines (SVM) Forecasting accuracy

1 Introduction

Load forecasting is an important basis for the safe and stable operation of power system and is also a basic work of planning and dispatching of power system. Traditional load forecasting methods include extrapolation, exponential smoothing, correlation analysis, regression analysis, time series, Kalman filter and gray system. Modern load forecasting methods include artificial neural networks [1], support vector machines [2, 3], wavelet transforms [4, 5], and fuzzy regression. Each method has unique advantages and obvious shortcomings. Applications of data mining technology to screen historical data and combine with the existing load forecasting method is a new trend of load forecasting.

Project Supported by ABB China Research Institute (No. ABB20171128REU-CTR).

© Springer Nature Singapore Pte Ltd. 2018
K. Li et al. (Eds.): ICSEE 2018/IMIOT 2018, CCIS 925, pp. 3–13, 2018.
https://doi.org/10.1007/978-981-13-2381-2_1

In literature [6], many factors that affect power system load fluctuation are fused by using multi-kernel function to build support vector machine forecasting model, the forecasting results show that this method can effectively improve the speed and accuracy of load forecasting. Literature [7] uses the load similarity date and meteorological similarity day as training samples to reduce the dimensionality of input variables and eliminate a large amount of redundant data. Literature [8] proposes a short-term intelligent combined forecasting method for power system based on the combination of gray model and support vector machine regression algorithm.

In this paper, firstly, the daily attribute law of load is tapped by using data mining technology, corresponding forecasting models are established for different attribute dates (different clustering categories) respectively, the load data and weather data such as humidity and temperature are fused as the input sample of a model. Next, the load data and weather data used in this paper come from a prefecture-level city in Zhejiang Province. Since Zhejiang Province is located in the southeast coastal zone and the summer rain and heat are in the same period, it is necessary to fully consider the local geographical location and climatic conditions, analyze the correlation between each influencing factor of the weather and the load, highlight the main weather factors and ignore the secondary weather factors so as to improve the prediction accuracy. Finally, the global search of c and g is carried out for the parameters of SVM to find the best parameters.

2 Data Collection and Preprocessing

2.1 The Processing of Bad Load Data

The processing methods for a single bad data: according to the smoothness of the load curves of the power system, the load data of the abnormal point is obtained from the average of the last load data and the next load data of this point. And the processing methods for continuous multiple bad data: according to the similar characteristics of the load curves of power system, trying to find a way to replace the similar load curve by the adjacent date of the neighborhood, and if it cannot be found, it will be eliminated directly.

2.2 The Interpolation Processing of Weather Data

The original load data is 96 sampling points a day, and the original weather data is 24 sampling points a day. In fact, support vector machines (SVM) need multi-point load data correspond to multi-point weather data when modeling. Therefore, the existing weather data needs to be interpolated preprocessing, this paper adopts triple spline interpolation.

2.3 The Quantization of the Type of Weeks and Holidays

This paper quantifies the type of weeks as A = {1, 2, 3, 4, 5, 6, 7}, and 1 to 7 corresponds to Monday to Sunday. And the holiday attributes are quantified as B = {0, 1, 2}, where 0 represents the holiday, and 1 represents the day after the holiday, and 2 represents other dates except these two types.

2.4 The Normalization of Sample Data

In this paper, the simple linear normalization is used, and the transformation formula can be calculated as follows:

$$y_i = \frac{x_i - x_{min}}{x_{max} - x_{min}} \tag{1}$$

In the formula, y_i is the input sample data after normalization processing, x_i is the input sample data after pretreatment, x_{min} is the minimum value in the sample after preprocessing, and x_{max} is the maximum value in the sample after preprocessing.

3 Analysis of Regular Characteristics of Load

3.1 The Regular Characteristics of Day Load

The typical daily load curve has two peaks of "morning peak" and "evening peak". The time of emergence of morning peak and evening peak is exactly the same with people's living rules and working hours, and the daily morning peak and evening peak are mostly fixed, which provides convenience for us to analyze user's power consumption rule. Typical daily load curve is shown in Fig. 1.

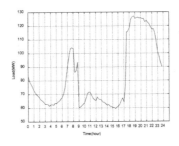

Fig. 1. Typical daily load curve

3.2 The Regular Characteristics of Week Load

The regular characteristics of week load is mainly manifested in the following two points: one is that the load curves of weekdays and weekends are roughly the same, the daily load curve has two peaks of "morning peak" and "evening peak". The second is that the load of the weekends is significantly lower than that of the weekdays, the reason is that the proportion of industrial load in the local load is relatively large, the factory will shut down on weekends, so the load will decrease. Taking the load data for the second week of 2011 in Zhejiang Province to analyze the regular characteristics of the week load, the red lines represent the load curves from Monday to Friday, the blue lines represent the load curves on weekends, as shown in Fig. 2.

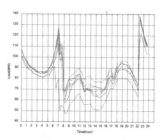

Fig. 2. Load curves in one week (Color figure online)

3.3   The Regular Characteristics of Holiday Load

The changes of load of different holidays is roughly the same, and it is not necessary to analyze all the holidays. Taking the load data of a certain region in Zhejiang Province in 2010, 2011 and 2012 as an example to draw the load curves of the National Day for three consecutive years, as shown in Fig. 3. It can be seen from the figure that the load curves of National Day in different years are roughly the same, and the load before and after the annual festival is significantly higher than that of the National Day.

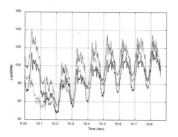

Fig. 3. Load curves during the National Day in 2010, 2011, 2012

4   Correlation Analysis of Load and Influencing Factors of Weather

In addition to the regular characteristics of load, the influence of the weather, such as temperature and humidity, on the load cannot be neglected [9]. The correlation degree between the influencing factors of weather and load is analyzed quantitatively. Pearson correlation analysis is used to analyze the correlation from two time dimensions. First, from the perspective of the whole year, the Pearson correlation analysis is carried out with the annual load and weather data of a certain region in Zhejiang Province in 2012, the results of quantitative analysis are shown in Table 1. From Table 1, it can be seen that the influence of temperature and humidity on load is larger than other factors.

Second, from a seasonal perspective, as Zhejiang Province is located in the southeast coastal area, belonging to the subtropical monsoon climate, rain and heat are over the same period. Pearson correlation analysis is conducted on the summer load and weather data of a certain region in Zhejiang Province in 2012, the quantitative analysis results are shown in Table 2. As can be seen from Table 2, the correlation between temperature, humidity and load is particularly significant in summer, that is, the effect of temperature and humidity on load is very large.

Table 1. Correlation analysis of annual load and its influencing factors in 2012

Correlation coefficient	Load
Temperature	0.476
Humidity	−0.382
Rainfall	0.040
The wind speed of two minutes	0.147
The wind direction of two minutes	0.003

Table 2. Correlation analysis of summer load and its influencing factors in 2012

Correlation coefficient	Load
Temperature	0.758
Humidity	−0.557
Rainfall	−0.115
The wind speed of two minutes	0.074
The wind direction of two minutes	0.083

In fact, in the summer of Zhejiang Province, the early summer is hot and humid with more rain. And the midsummer is sunny and hot with little rain, which is the hottest time of the year. That is, the correlation between summer rainfall and load is also strong, but the results of the analysis are not obvious. Therefore, taking the summer load and weather data in a certain region in Zhejiang Province in 2012 as an example, the weather conditions are classified to further analyze the correlation between summer rainfall and load. The results of the analysis are shown in Table 3.

Table 3. Correlation analysis of summer load and rainfall in 2012

Correlation coefficient	Load
Rainfall (Temperature around 23°, Humidity around 90%)	0.627
Rainfall (Temperature above 27°, Humidity below 85%)	−0.045

5 Establishing Support Vector Machine Load Forecasting Model Based on Data Mining

5.1 The Selection of Clustering Methods and Numbers

The basic clustering methods include clustering method based on partition, clustering method based on hierarchy, clustering method based on density and clustering method based on grid. The most commonly used clustering methods are k-means clustering and stepwise clustering. Because k-means clustering needs to specify the value of k in advance, and when the amount of data is not large, the initial grouping largely determines the result of clustering. And stepwise clustering can output the number of arbitrary specified clusters by generating the distance matrix. Therefore, this paper chooses the step clustering method based on Euclidean distance.

At present, there is no good method to select the number of clustering, only through continuous attempts. By the author's own attempt, when the number of clustering is selected to be 6, it is basically guaranteed that each clustering result contains a certain number of sample. The 6 categories are: weekdays, weekends, national legal holidays, and festivals other than the national statutory holidays (such as Christmas, etc.), the first day after the holidays and special days (such as the G20 Summit).

5.2 The Principle of Support Vector Machine

The basic principle of support vector machine [10–12] for load forecasting is that for the training samples set $\{x_i, y_i\}_{i=1}^{l}$, the input samples are $x_i \in R^n$, the output values $y_i \in R$ are corresponding to the input samples, l is the number of training samples. The goal of SVM [13] is to find the regression function from input space R^n to output space R:

$$y = f(x) = (\omega \cdot x) + b \tag{2}$$

In the formula, $\omega \in R^n$ is the weight, $x_i \in R^n$ are the input samples, and $b \in R$ is the threshold.

For linear regression problems, according to the statistical theory, SVM determines the regression function by minimizing the target, that is:

$$Min\left\{\tfrac{1}{2}\|\omega\|^2 + C \cdot \left[v\varepsilon + \tfrac{1}{l}\sum_{i=1}^{l}(\zeta_i + \zeta_i^*)\right]\right\}$$
$$s.t.((\omega \cdot x_i) + b) - y_i \leq \varepsilon + \zeta_i \tag{3}$$
$$y_i - ((\omega \cdot x_i) + b) \leq \varepsilon + \zeta_i^*$$
$$\zeta_i^* \geq 0, \varepsilon \geq 0$$

In the formula, ε is the non-sensitive loss function, ζ_i and ζ_i^* are the relaxation factors. For the constraint conditions, $\alpha_i^{(*)}$, α_i, η_i, $\eta_i^{(*)}$, $\beta \geq 0$, the regression function of SVM based on Lagrange algorithm is:

$$f(x) = \sum_{i=1}^{l} (\alpha_i^* - \alpha_i)k(x_i \cdot x) + b \tag{4}$$

In this paper, the radial basis function with relatively good prediction effect is selected as the kernel function of SVM [13–15].

5.3   The Selection of Best Parameters c and g by Cross Validation

Regarding the optimal selection of SVM parameters [16, 17], there is no internationally recognized a good uniform method, the commonly used method is to let c and g in a certain range of values, for the selected c and g, the training set is used as the original data set and the K-CV method is used to obtain the mean square error of the training set under this set of c and g.

The best parameters c and g chosen by K-CV are shown in Fig. 4.

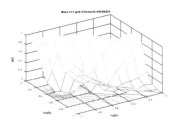

Fig. 4. Selection of the best parameters c and g by K-CV

As can be seen from Fig. 4, in the process of selecting the best parameters c and g, the c and g can be searched throughout the grid, so that the mean square error can fluctuate within a range of 0 to 1. The best pair of parameters selected by cross validation is: $c = 1$, $g = 2$.

6   Example Verification

6.1   Input the Sample Data

In this example, the load data and weather data such as temperature and humidity in a certain region in Zhejiang Province in 2012 are selected as training samples. With January 9, 2013 as the forecasting date, a corresponding support vector machine load forecasting model is established for the attribute of the forecasting day.

6.2   The Evaluation Indicators of the Prediction Result

Taking the sampling point load forecasting deviation rate E_i and the daily average load forecasting accuracy rate A_d as the evaluation indicators to measure the prediction effect, the formulas are as follows:

Sampling point load forecasting deviation rate E_i:

$$E_i = \frac{L_{i,f} - L_i}{L_i} \times 100\% \tag{5}$$

Table 4. The daily average load forecasting rate of various forecasting methods

Load forecasting methods	Weekday	Weekend	Holiday
ARMA	88.66%	86.55%	87.67%
Traditional SVM	93.57%	92.53%	92.45%
The method proposed in this paper	97.41%	97.24%	97.16%

In the formula, E_i represents the load forecasting deviation rate (%) at i moment, $L_{i,f}$ represents the load forecasting value (MW) at i moment, and L_i represents the actual load value (MW) at i moment.

Daily average load forecasting accuracy rate A_d:

$$A_d = (1 - RMSE) \times 100\% \tag{6}$$

$$RMSE = \sqrt{\frac{1}{n} \sum_{i=1}^{n} E_i^2} \tag{7}$$

In the formula, A_d represents the load forecasting accuracy (%), $RMSE$ represents the daily load forecasting bias root mean square, E_i represents 15-min load forecasting bias (%) at i moment, n represents the daily actual assessment points.

6.3   Results Analysis

Table 4 shows the load forecasting results of three typical operating days, that is, the daily average load prediction accuracy of three major load on weekday (2013.01.09), weekend (2013.02.16) and holiday (2013.06.12). And the prediction results are compared with the classical time series method and the traditional support vector machine load forecasting method.

As can be seen from Table 4, compared with the classical time series method and traditional SVM load forecasting method, the load forecasting method proposed in this paper that combines historical data and real-time influencing factors can improve the prediction accuracy by 5% to 10%.

Because of the limited text, this paper gives a detailed description of the load forecasting results for the weekday (2013.01.09). The comparison between the prediction results of the three load forecasting methods and the actual load is shown in Fig. 5.

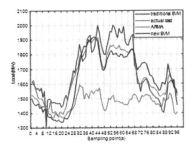

Fig. 5. Comparison between the prediction results of three kinds of load forecasting methods and the actual load

From the comparison of the four load curves in Fig. 5, whether the smoothness of the overall load curve or the predicted value of a single load point which is adopted the load forecasting method of support vector machine based on historical data and the real-time influencing factors proposed in this paper is much better than the traditional support vector machine load forecasting method and time series load forecasting method.

In order to compare the prediction accuracy of the three prediction methods more intuitively, as shown in Fig. 6, the curves in this figure show the absolute value of the load prediction bias of 96 sampling points adopting three different prediction methods.

From Fig. 6, it is clear that for the 96 sampling points load forecasting on January 9, 2013, which adopt the load forecasting method of support vector machine method based on historical data and real-time influencing factors, the absolute values of the load prediction deviation rates are mostly below 5%, and concentrate in the vicinity of 3%. The absolute values of the deviation rates of the 96 sampling points prediction methods of the traditional support vector machine are basically above 5%, which

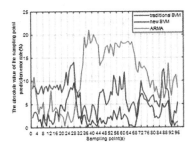

Fig. 6. Comparison of the absolute values of predicted deviations by three forecasting methods

concentrate near 8%. The absolute values floating range of the load forecast deviation rates of the 96 sampling points of the time series load forecasting method are larger, and the mean value is about 13%.

Through the example analysis, it verifies the effectiveness of the load forecasting method of support vector machine based on historical data and real-time influencing factors, which improves the prediction accuracy significantly.

7 Conclusion

In this paper, the load data, temperature, humidity and other weather data are fused to propose a load forecasting method of support vector machine based on data mining, conclusions are as follows:

(1) According to the multi-source information such as load and weather, using correlation analysis and clustering algorithm, the operation days are divided into several categories, and the prediction models are respectively established to effectively improve the accuracy of load forecasting.
(2) Global optimization of the core parameters of support vector machine can also improve the prediction accuracy.
(3) The results of a practical example show that compared with the traditional support vector machine and time series load forecasting method, the method proposed in this paper can improve the load prediction accuracy by about 5% to 10%.
     Due to the different load characteristics, geographical locations and weather conditions in different regions, the clustering results and model parameters obtained may not be the same. Therefore, load forecasting models must be adapted to local conditions which can effectively improve the accuracy of load forecasting.

References

1. Su, X., Liu, T., Cao, H., et al.: Short-term load forecasting method for multi-distributed BP neural network based on Hadoop architecture. Proc. CSEE **37**(17), 4966–4973+5216 (2017)
2. Luo, N., Zhu, Y., Du, C.: Application of support vector machine method in electric load forecasting. Power Syst. Technol. **31**(S2), 215–218 (2007)
3. Geng, Y., Han, X., Han, L.: Short-term load forecasting based on least squares support vector machine. Power Syst. Technol. **18**, 72–76 (2008)
4. Zhang, P., Pan, X., Xue, W.: Short-term load forecasting based on wavelet decomposition, fuzzy gray correlation clustering and BP neural network. Electr. Power Autom. Equip. 32 (11), 121–125+141 (2012)
5. Zu, X., Tian, M., Bai, Y.: Short term load forecasting method based on fuzzy clustering and function wavelet kernel regression. Electr. Power Autom. Equip. 36(10), 134–140+165 (2016)
6. Wu, Q., Gao, J., Hou, G., et al.: Short-term load forecasting support vector machine algorithm based on multi-source heterogeneous fusion of load factors. Autom. Electr. Power Syst. 40(15), 67–72+92 (2016)

7. Li, B., Huang, J., Wu, Y., et al.: A short-term load forecasting method based on fractal feature correction of meteorological similar days. Power Syst. Technol. 41(06), 1949–1955 (2017)
8. Tang, J., Liu, J., Yang, K., et al.: Short-term load combination forecasting by grey model and least square support vector machine. Power Syst. Technol. 33(03), 63–68 (2009)
9. Gao, Y., Sun, Y., Yang, W., et al.: Study on short – term forecast of meteorological sensitive load based on new human comfort. Proc. CSEE 37(07), 1946–1955 (2017)
10. Huo, J., Shi, T., Chang, J.: Comparison of random forest and SVM for electrical short-term load forecast with different data sources. In: IEEE International Conference on Software Engineering and Service Science, pp. 1077–1080. IEEE (2017)
11. Ye, N., Liu, Y., Wang, Y.: Short-term power load forecasting based on SVM, pp. 47–51 (2012)
12. Zhang, M.G., Li, L.R.: Short-term load combined forecasting method based on BPNN and LS-SVM. In: Power Engineering and Automation Conference, pp. 319–322. IEEE (2012)
13. Selakov, A., Ilic, S., Vukmirovic, S., et al.: A comparative analysis of SVM and ANN based hybrid model for short term load forecasting. 52(11), 1–5 (2012)
14. Liu, B., Xu, G.: Short-term power load forecasting based on LS-SVM. In: International Conference of Information Science and Management Engineering, pp. 311–314. IEEE Computer Society (2010)
15. Zhang, Q., Liu, T.: Application of SVM and wavelet neural network method for short-term power load forecasting. In: The International Conference on Computer and Automation Engineering, pp. 412–416. IEEE (2010)
16. Niu, D., Liu, D., Chen, G., et al.: Support vector machine models optimized by genetic algorithm for hourly load rolling forecasting. Trans. China Electrotech. Soc. 22(06), 148–153 (2007)
17. Xie, H., Wei, J., Liu, H.: Parameter selection and optimization method of SVM model for short-term load forecasting. Proc. CSEE 26(22), 17–22 (2006)

Water Level Control of Nuclear Power Plant Steam Generator Based on Intelligent Virtual Reference Feedback Tuning

Zhi Han[1], Hu Qi[2], Ling Wang[1(✉)], Muhammad Ilyas Menhas[1,3], and Minrui Fei[1]

[1] Shanghai Key Laboratory of Power Station Automation Technology, School of Mechatronics Engineering and Automation, Shanghai University, Shanghai 200072, China
{hanzhi,wangling,mrfei}@shu.edu.cn,
ilyasminhas75@yahoo.com
[2] Shanghai Power Construction Testing Institute, Shanghai 200031, China
[3] Department of Electrical Engineering, Mirpur University of Science and Technology, Mirpur A.K., Pakistan

Abstract. The steam generator is one of the most important equipment in nuclear power plants. The water level control of steam generators is a challenging problem due to its complicated characteristics. This paper studies a novel intelligent virtual reference feedback tuning method based on human learning optimization (IVRFTH) and applies it to the water level control, in which the optimal controller can be directly designed without knowing the mathematical model of the controlled object. The simulation results show that the developed IVRFTH surpasses the standard IVRFT method with the introduction of human learning optimization (HLO). As IVRFTH is easy to design the optimal controller without the model information, it is very promising for the engineering application.

Keywords: Intelligent VRFT · Human learning optimization · Steam generator
Water level control · Data-driven control

1 Introduction

The steam generator system in the nuclear power plant is a complex control system, which is non-linear and non-self-balancing [1]. The safe and stable operation of the steam generator is directly related to the normal operation of the nuclear power plant [2]. Gu proposed a novel control strategy in combination of active disturbance rejection technology with multimodel-based control, and the method can quickly eliminate interference under different load conditions, which can realize accurate dynamic control for the water level of steam generator [3]. Tan proposed a simple gain-predetermined water level control system, which has the advantages of simple structure and easy implementation [4]. Le proposed an adaptive backstepping method and designed a cascade control structure to reduce the influence of load disturbance in the feedwater flow on the water level control, which kept the steam generator water level safe [5].

© Springer Nature Singapore Pte Ltd. 2018
K. Li et al. (Eds.): ICSEE 2018/IMIOT 2018, CCIS 925, pp. 14–23, 2018.
https://doi.org/10.1007/978-981-13-2381-2_2

Besides, various advanced methods, such as fuzzy control [6] and neural networks control [7], were proposed.

However, due to its complex characteristics, it is still difficult for the safe and stable operation of the steam generator. Moreover, the modelling of the real system needs to be complemented by various empirical relationships. Consider that, a novel data-driven control method called IVRFT is integrated with Human Learning Optimization (HLO) has been proposed in the paper. In the presented IVRFT based on HLO method (IVRFTH), IVRFT [8] can design the controller directly by using a set of I/O data, which avoids the necessity of modelling and consequently significantly reduces the effort of the controller design and dodges the risk of degrading the performance of controllers caused by the error of the model. Then the introduction of HLO can efficiently find the optimal controller based on IVRFT and achieve the ideal control performance for the water level system.

The paper is organized as follows. The optimal controller design based on the IVRFTH is presented in Sect. 2. Then the IVRFTH is applied to the water level control of the steam generator and its performance is validated in Sect. 3. This paper is ended with the final conclusion.

2 Intelligent Virtual Reference Feedback Tuning Based on HLO

2.1 Intelligent Virtual Reference Feedback Tuning

Intelligent VRFT is an improved control method based on the standard VRFT and meta-heuristics [9, 10]. VRFT can design the controller through only a set of system I/O data without knowing the mathematical model of the controlled object [11].

The idea of VRFT is shown in Fig. 1.

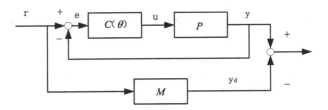

Fig. 1. Model reference scheme of VRFT.

The objective of VRFT is to design a controller to minimize the function given in Eq. (1).

$$J_{MR}(\theta) = \left\| \frac{P(z^{-1})C(z^{-1};\theta)}{1 + P(z^{-1})C(z^{-1};\theta)} - M(z^{-1}) \right\|_2^2 \tag{1}$$

Since the controlled object $P(z^{-1})$ is unknown, the objective function $J_{MR}(\theta)$ cannot be directly derived. Assume that a set of I/O data $\{u(t), y(t)\}$ $(t = 1, 2, \ldots L, L$ is the data length) of the controlled object is obtained from the field, then virtual input signal $e^{vir}(t)$ can be calculated given a reference model $M(z^{-1})$ as Eq. (2)

$$e^{vir}(t) = r^{vir}(t) - y(t) = M^{-1}(z^{-1})y(t) - y(t) \qquad (2)$$

where $M^{-1}(z^{-1})$ is the inverse of $M(z^{-1})$. An expected controller should generate u (t) when it is fed by $e^{vir}(t)$. The principle of VRFT, as shown in Fig. 2, is to identify the controller $C(z^{-1}; \theta)$ parameters by using the controller's virtual input and output signals so that the objective function, i.e. Eq. (3), is minimized.

$$J_{VRFT}(\theta) = \frac{1}{N} \sum_{t=1}^{N} \left\| u(t) - C(z^{-1}; \theta)e^{vir}(t) \right\|^2 \qquad (3)$$

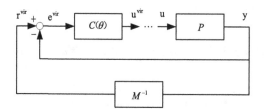

Fig. 2. Control principle of VRFT.

Obviously, in the objective function of VRFT, i.e. Eq. (3), there is no control performance indicator and it is not practical to design an optimal controller. However, as revealed by Fig. 1, the designed close-loop control system by VRFT approaches the reference model $M(z^{-1})$. Considering the widely used reference model in VRFT as Eq. (4)

$$M(z^{-1}) = \frac{(1 - A)z^{-1}}{1 - Az^{-1}} z^{-d} \qquad (4)$$

where A is the adjustable parameter, d is the time-delay. Inappropriate reference models will directly impair the performance of the final designed controller. If the parameter A value is too small, the VRFT method may fail; and if the A is too large, the dynamic response index of the system will become unsatisfactory. It is obvious that the controller designed with the reference model having a smaller A will have better dynamic performance when the VRFT is guaranteed to be valid.

Since the reference model and the controller interact with each other, and the small variation of the reference model parameter has the profound influence for the system, it is difficult to manually set an ideal reference model. Thus, IVRFT [8] is used to design the optimal controller, in which the objective function is re-defined as Eq. (5),

$$J_{IVRFT} = J_{VRFT}(\theta) + k \times A \tag{5}$$

where k is the weight of parameter A. To ensure that J_{vrft} plays a major role in this fitness function for the validness of VRFT, the k value should be small enough. The optimization of the objective function of IVRFT needs meta-heuristic algorithms [8]. Therefore, the choose of meta-heuristics in IVRFT is very important as it directly determines the performance of the designed controller.

2.2 Human Learning Optimization

Human Learning Optimization (HLO) was first proposed by Wang et al. [12]. The HLO algorithm is very simple to implement, and previous works show that it has superior optimization performance on various problems such as scheduling, deceptive problems [12–15]. Therefore, HLO is used to solve IVRFT to improve the control performance in this paper.

2.2.1 Initialization
HLO is a binary algorithm, and each bit represents a basic component of human knowledge to be learned. An individual in HLO can be coded as Eq. (6), and each bit is randomly initialized to 0 or 1.

$$x_i = \begin{bmatrix} x_{i1} & x_{i2} & \dots & x_{ij} & x_{iM} \end{bmatrix} \quad 1 \leq i \leq N, \ 1 \leq j \leq M \tag{6}$$

where x_i is the ith individual, N is the number of individuals in the group, and M is the dimension of the solution [12].

2.2.2 Learning Operators

(1) Random Learning Operator

People will constantly try new strategies to get better solutions. This process is often random because they do not know which strategy is better. Mimicking this random learning strategy, HLO performs the RLO as Eq. (7) to search new knowledge,

$$x_{ij} = Rand(0, 1) = \begin{cases} 0, 0 \leq r \leq 0.5 \\ 1, \quad else \end{cases} \tag{7}$$

where r is random number between 0 and 1.

(2) Individual Learning Operator

In the process of learning, humans consciously or unconsciously memorize and store useful experiences to guide the following research, which can improve the efficiency of learning when encountering the same or similar problems. HLO emulates this individual learning strategy of humans and implement ILO as Eqs. (8) and (9).

$$x_{ij} = ik_{ipj} \tag{8}$$

$$ikd_i = \begin{bmatrix} ikd_{i1} \\ ikd_{i2} \\ \vdots \\ ikd_{ip} \\ \vdots \\ ikd_{iT} \end{bmatrix} = \begin{bmatrix} ik_{i11} & ik_{i12} & \cdots & ik_{i1j} & \cdots & ik_{i1M} \\ ik_{i21} & ik_{i22} & \cdots & ik_{i2j} & \cdots & ik_{i2M} \\ \vdots & \vdots & & \vdots & & \vdots \\ ik_{ip1} & ik_{ip2} & \cdots & ik_{ipj} & \cdots & ik_{ipM} \\ \vdots & \vdots & & \vdots & & \vdots \\ ik_{iT1} & ik_{iT2} & \cdots & ik_{iTj} & \cdots & ik_{iTM} \end{bmatrix}, \ 1 \leq p \leq T \tag{9}$$

where ikd_i is the individual knowledge database (IKD) of the ith individual, and ikd_{ipj} is the jth bit of the pth best solution stored in the IKD. T represents the IKD size.

(3) Social Learning Operator

In a social environment, humans can significantly improve the learning efficiency by sharing knowledge. To improve the performance, HLO performs SLO as Eqs. (10) and (11) to simulate the social learning of humans,

$$x_{ij} = sk_{qj} \tag{10}$$

$$SKD = \begin{bmatrix} skd_1 \\ skd_2 \\ \vdots \\ skd_i \\ \vdots \\ skd_H \end{bmatrix} = \begin{bmatrix} sk_{11} & sk_{12} & \cdots & sk_{1j} & \cdots & sk_{1M} \\ sk_{21} & sk_{22} & \cdots & sk_{2j} & \cdots & sk_{2M} \\ \vdots & \vdots & & \vdots & & \vdots \\ sk_{q1} & sk_{q2} & \cdots & sk_{qj} & \cdots & sk_{qM} \\ \vdots & \vdots & & \vdots & & \vdots \\ sk_{H1} & sk_{H2} & \cdots & sk_{Hj} & \cdots & sk_{HM} \end{bmatrix}, 1 \leq q \leq H, \quad 1 \leq j \leq M$$

$$\tag{11}$$

where SKD denotes the social knowledge database (SKD), and skd_i represents the ith best knowledge saved in the SKD.

In summary, HLO generates new candidates by executing RLO, ILO, and SLO as Eq. (12):

$$X_{ij} = \begin{cases} RLO, & if \quad 0 < rl < pr \\ ILO, & if \quad pr < rl < pi \\ SLO, & if \quad pi < rl < 1 \end{cases} \tag{12}$$

where rl is a random number between 0 and 1. HLO performs RLO, ILO, and SLO, with the probability pr, $(pi\text{-}pr)$, and $(1\text{-}pi)$, respectively.

2.2.3   Updating of the SKD and IKD

After all the individual has completed the study, HLO calculates the fitness value of the new solution and update the IKDs and SKD. If the fitness value of the new candidate solution is better than the fitness value of the worst solution in the corresponding individual IKD, the new candidate solution is retained. The SKD is updated in the same way [12].

2.3   Water Level Control Based on IVRFTH

PID controllers are widely used in the nuclear power plants, and therefore this paper uses IVRFTH to design the optimal PID controller for the water level control.

The PID controller can be represented as Eq. (13) [8]:

$$u(k) = u(k-1) + K_p[e(k) - e(k-1)] + K_i e(k) + K_d[e(k) - 2e(k-1) + e(k-2)] \tag{13}$$

And it can be formulized as Eq. (14):

$$C(z^{-1}; \theta) = K_p + \frac{K_i}{1 - z^{-1}} + K_d(1 - z^{-1}) \tag{14}$$

Then the virtual output signal can be calculated as Eq. (15):

$$u^{vir}(z^{-1}) = [K_p + \frac{K_i}{1 - z^{-1}} + K_d(1 - z^{-1})] \times [\frac{1 - z^{-1}}{(1 - A)z^{-1}} z^{-d}]y \tag{15}$$

The parameterization is expressed as Eq. (16):

$$u^{vir}(z^{-1}) = \varphi^T(t)\theta = [\varphi_p(t) \quad \varphi_i(t) \quad \varphi_d(t)] \begin{bmatrix} K_p \\ K_i \\ K_d \end{bmatrix} \tag{16}$$

where $\varphi_p(t)$, $\varphi_i(t)$, $\varphi_d(t)$ are the coefficients of control parameters K_p, K_i, K_d, respectively. They are calculated as Eqs. (17)–(19):

$$\varphi_p(t) = \frac{1}{1 - A}[y(t + d + 1) - y(t + d)] \tag{17}$$

$$\varphi_i(t) = \frac{1}{1 - A}[y(t + d + 1)] \tag{18}$$

$$\varphi_d(t) = \frac{1}{1 - A}[y(t + d + 1) - 2y(t + d) + y(t + d - 1)] \tag{19}$$

With the collected I/O data, and the K_p, K_i, K_d and A given by HLO, the fitness of each controller, i.e. J_{IVRFT}, can be computed and used for the optimization of the controllers.

The procedure of IVRFTH is as follows:

Step 1:   Sample a set of input and output data $\{u(t), y(t)\}$;
Step 2:   Set the parameters of HLO;
Step 3:   Set the search ranges of K_p, K_i, K_d, and A;

Step 4:   Randomly generate the initial population, calculate the fitness function of each initial solution, and initialize the IKDs and SKD;

Step 5:   Execute the learning operators of HLO as Eq. (12) to generate new candidates;

Step 6:   Calculate the fitness of new candidates, and update the IKD and SKD;

Step 7:   Check whether the algorithm satisfies the termination condition; If the condition is reached, output the optimal solution found by HLO; otherwise, return to step 5.

3   Simulation and Analysis

When the nuclear power unit is in daily operation, the water level of the steam generator must be monitored and controlled so that it is within the operating limits. When the water level deviates from the set normal range, it will directly affect the safety and economic operation of nuclear power plant [3].

In the paper, IVRFTH is applied to control the water level system of steam generators as Eq. (20) [16]. Note that IVRFTH, as well as the standard VRTF and IVRFT, does not need any model information for the design of controller. The model here is only used to generate the input and output data for IVRFTH and evaluate the performance of the designed controllers later.

$$G(s) = \frac{0.0164}{8.6663s + 9.0234} e^{-9.0234s} \qquad (20)$$

To verify the performance of the IVRFTH, IVRFT [8], the Z–N method [17], and the model-based optimal PID controller design with HLO (MPID) are used for a comparison. The fitness function, as Eq. (21) [18], is adopted in MPID,

$$Fit = w_1 \times T_{up} + w_2 \times IAE + w_3 \times OS \qquad (21)$$

where T_{up} stands for the rise time, IAE stands for the integral of absolute error, and OS stands for the overshoot. w_1, w_2, and w_3 are the weights of rise time, IAE, and overshoot in the fitness function, respectively, and the values are set to 1, 1, 5000 as recommended in [8].

The control performance of all the methods are depicted in Fig. 3, and the performance indexes are shown in Table 1. The results show that the Z-N method cannot achieve an expected performance on the water lever control system. The studied IVRFTH has better performance than the standard IVRFT, which has faster rise time and smaller IAE. IVRFTH is a little inferior to MPID since the latter is designed with the perfect model and directly by using the performance criteria as the fitness function. However, the performance of IVRFT is very close to MPID and it is better than MPID with 1% model error. Considering a perfect model of steam generators is impractical to be constructed in real nuclear power plants, IVRFTH have its advantages in terms of the ideal control performance and ease of implementation.

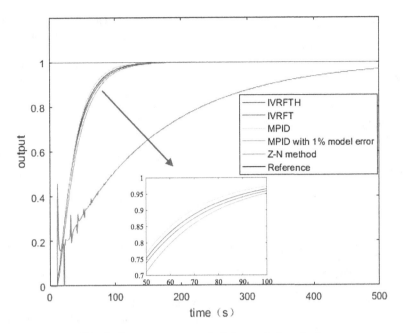

Fig. 3. Response curves of all the control methods

Table 1. Control performance of various water level control methods

Methods	T_{up}	IAE	OS
IVRFTH	58	36.44	0
IVRFT	59	37.62	0
MPID	56	35.34	0
MPID with 1% model error	61	39.03	0
Z-N	322	126.81	0

4   Conclusions

The water level control is a challenging problem for the steam generator operation in nuclear power plants due to its complex characteristics. The difficulty of modelling would cause significant performance loss for the model-based control methods in real applications. Therefore, IVRFTH is studied and applied to the water level control, which can directly design the optimal controller with a set of input and output data. The simulation results indicate that IVRFTH achieves better control performance with the introduction of HLO. Considering that IVRFTH can easily achieve the ideal control performance without model information, it is promising to be applied to water level control of the steam generator and other engineering objects.

Acknowledgments. This work is supported by National Natural Science Foundation of China (Grant No. 61633016 & 61703262), Key Project of Science and Technology Commission of Shanghai Municipality under Grant No. 16010500300 and 15220710400, Shanghai Sailing Program under Grant No. 16YF1403700, and Natural Science Foundation of Shanghai (No.18ZR1415100).

References

1. Li, C., Ye, J., Zhao, M.: Multi-model control for water lever of steam generator in nuclear power plants based on linear active disturbance rejection. Autom. Instrum. **32**(1), 46–50 (2017)
2. Zhang, Z., Hu, L.: Performance assessment for the water level control system in steam generator of the nuclear power plant. Ann. Nucl. Energy **45**, 94–105 (2012)
3. Gu, J., Ji, N., Sun, Y., Wang, D.: The multimodel-based active disturbance rejection control for water level of steam generator in nuclear power plants. J. Chin. Soc. Power Eng. **32**(5), 373–377 (2012)
4. Tan, W.: Water level control for a nuclear steam generator. Nucl. Eng. Des. **241**(5), 1873–1880 (2011)
5. Wei, L., Fang, F., Shi, Y.: Adaptive backstepping-based composite nonlinear feedback water level control for the nuclear U-tube steam generator. IEEE Trans. Control Syst. Technol. **22** (1), 369–377 (2014)
6. Thakur, A., Singh, H., Wadhwani, S.: Designing of fuzzy logic controller for liquid level controlling. Int. J. u-and e-Serv. Sci. Technol. **8**(6), 267–276 (2015)
7. Habibiyan, H., Setayeshi, S., Arab-Alibeik, H.: A fuzzy-gain-scheduled neural controller for nuclear steam generators. J. Ann. Nucl. Energ. **31**(15), 1765–1781 (2004)
8. Wang, L., Ni, H., Yang, R., et al.: Intelligent virtual reference feedback tuning and its application to heat treatment electric furnace control. Eng. Appl. Artif. Intell. **46**, 1–9 (2015)
9. Guardabassi, G., Savaresi, S.M.: Virtual reference direct design method: an off-line approach to data-based control system design. IEEE Trans. Autom. Control **45**(5), 954–959 (2000)
10. Formentin, S., Campi, M.C., Savaresi, S.M.: Virtual reference feedback tuning for industrial PID controllers. IFAC Proc. Vols. **47**(3), 11275–11280 (2014)
11. Campi, M.C., Lecchini, A., Savaresi, S.M.: Virtual reference feedback tuning: a direct method for the design of feedback controllers. Automatica **38**(8), 1337–1346 (2002)
12. Wang, L., Ni, H., Yang, R., Fei, M., Ye, W.: A simple human learning optimization algorithm. In: Fei, M., Peng, C., Su, Z., Song, Y., Han, Q. (eds.) LSMS/ICSEE 2014, Part II. CCIS, vol. 462, pp. 56–65. Springer, Heidelberg (2014). https://doi.org/10.1007/978-3-662-45261-5_7
13. Wang, L., Yang, R., Ni, H., et al.: A human learning optimization algorithm and its application to multi-dimensional knapsack problems. Appl. Soft Comput. **34**, 736–743 (2015)
14. Li, X., Yao, J., Wang, L., Menhas, M.I.: Application of human learning optimization algorithm for production scheduling optimization. In: Fei, M., Ma, S., Li, X., Sun, X., Jia, L., Su, Z. (eds.) LSMS/ICSEE 2017, Part I. CCIS, vol. 761, pp. 242–252. Springer, Singapore (2017). https://doi.org/10.1007/978-981-10-6370-1_24
15. Wang, L., Pei, J., et al.: A hybrid-coded human learning optimization for mixed-variable optimization problems. Knowl. Based Syst. **127**, 114–125 (2017)
16. Li, C., Ye, J., Zhao, M.: Two-degree-of-freedom model driving control of evaporator water level in nuclear power plant. Yunnan Chem. Technol. **43**(5), 55–60 (2016)

17. Åström, K.J., Hägglund, T.: Revisiting the Ziegler-Nichols step response method for PID control. J. Process Control **14**(6), 635–650 (2004)
18. Wang, L., Yang, R., Pardalos, P.M., et al.: An adaptive fuzzy controller based on harmony search and its application to power plant control. Int. J. Electr. Power Energy Syst. **53**, 272–278 (2013)

Characteristics Investigation for Hydro-Mechanical Compound Transmission in Wind Power System

GuoQin Huang[1,2(✉)], ShaQi Luo[1,2], Bo Hu[1,2], and Jin Yu[1,2]

[1] State Key of Laboratory of Mechanical Transmission,
Chongqing University, Chongqing 400044, China
huangguoqin@cqu.edu.cn
[2] College of Mechanical Engineering, Chongqing University,
Chongqing 400044, China

Abstract. Aiming at the problem of variable speed constant frequency (VSCF) in wind power system, a design scheme of power split type compound hydraulic mechanical continually variable transmission (HMCVT) used in wind power system is proposed. With variable speed input and constant speed output as the premise, the design scheme combines the characteristics of hydraulic high power density, stepless speed change and mechanical high efficiency by means of power split. Its static speed and efficiency properties are theoretical analyzed. Combined with the actual working conditions, the Matlab/Simulink software is used for modeling the HMCVT wind power system, dynamic simulation and analysis. Finally, the transmission test platform had been built, and the experimental data and simulation results are basically the same. The results show that the HMCVT wind power system can realize VSCF. Its dynamic characteristics are good, and efficiency can be stabilized at around 87%.

Keywords: Wind power generation · VSCF · HMCVT
Speed regulation characteristics · Efficiency

1 Introduction

The research and utilization of new energy has become the focus of attention all over the world. At present, the cost of wind power is close to the cost of thermal power generation. However, in the whole wind power industry, it is urgent to optimize the technology of wind power system to ensure that the initial cost and maintenance cost are reduced under the premise of high efficiency, sustainability and stability of the whole system [1].

Doubly fed VSCF wind power system has many shortcomings, such as large excitation current, high excitation loss, expensive electrical equipment and difficult to troubleshoot. Some scholars began to turn to the hydraulic transmission chain suitable for wind power system [2, 3], and put forward hydraulic circuits made up of hydraulic pumps and motors for the purpose of asynchronous power generation and voltage stabilization, but the efficiency was only 72.9%. The existing vehicle hydrostatic transmission is applied to the wind power generation system and the turbine [4].

© Springer Nature Singapore Pte Ltd. 2018
K. Li et al. (Eds.): ICSEE 2018/IMIOT 2018, CCIS 925, pp. 24–35, 2018.
https://doi.org/10.1007/978-981-13-2381-2_3

The drawback is the low efficiency. In order to make up for the low efficiency of the hydraulic circuit, a power diverting transmission system [5], which is composed of the mechanical branch and the servo branch, is put forward, but the cost of the servo motor is also high. In order to solve the problem of low efficiency of hydraulic loop, a mechanical-hydraulic transmission which can be used in wind power system is put forward, but the efficiency is still low in some stages [6]. In China, the input and output coupling transmission for wind power is proposed by Zhejiang University, but the speed range of the input coupling transmission is narrow [7].

The HMCVT proposed in this paper can be applied to wind power, and has achieved the following points:

1. VSCF. When the wind speed fluctuates, it adjusts the transmission ratio of the hydraulic branch by adjusting the displacement ratio e of the variable pump, so as to keep the output shaft speed constant. Based on the dynamic characteristics of the transmission, it is possible to reduce the capacity of the converter or even replace it.
2. High power and high efficiency. Based on the high power density of the hydraulic circuit and the high efficiency of the mechanical circuit, the efficiency of the HMCVT can reach 90%, and it is generally stable at about 87%, which is higher than the static pressure transmission and hydraulic torque converter.
3. The structure is compact. In view of the high power density of the hydraulic system, the HMCVT will be more compact than other transmission structures. And it is cheaper than power electronic converters.

2   Mathematical Modeling of HMCVT Wind Power System

2.1   Structure and Principle of HMCVT Wind Power System

Flowchart of HMCVT wind power system is shown in Fig. 1. The electronic components such as the rectifier are cancelled. The main principle of the work: by changing the displacement ratio of the hydraulic pump, the continuous adjustment of the transmission in a large range is realized, which means that the transmission can realize the variable speed input and the constant speed output.

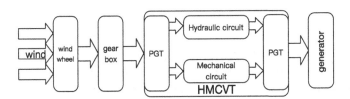

Fig. 1. Flowchart of HMCVT wind power system

The structure of HMCVT is shown in Fig. 2. It consists of an input shaft n_1, two planetary gear trains (PGT) A_1 and A_2, a hydraulic circuit and an output shaft n_0. There are 6 types of connection for each PGT. Therefore, the transmission system has 36 kinds of structure. The structure shown in Fig. 2 has the advantages of high efficiency, wide speed range and no power cycle.

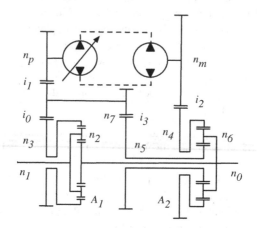

Fig. 2. Structure of HMCVT

In this system, the energy captured by the wind wheel flows into the HMCVT through the gear box. After the energy flows through the input PGT A_1, the energy flows into the hydraulic circuit and the mechanical circuit respectively. The energy is converged by the output PGT A_2 and the output shaft n_0 is kept at the constant speed.

2.2   Characteristics Analysis of HMCVT

The speed governing characteristic of HMCVT is defined as the ratio i_{HM} of the speed n_0 to the speed n_1, which varies with the displacement ratio e of pump to motor.

The relationship between the speed equation of the three components of the PGT and the HMCVT scheme shown in Fig. 2:

$$
\begin{cases}
n_1 + A_1 n_3 - (1+A_1)n_2 = 0 \\
n_5 + A_2 n_4 - (1+A_2)n_6 = 0 \\
n_4 = \frac{en_3}{i_0 i_1 i_2} \\
n_5 = \frac{n_3}{i_0 i_3}
\end{cases}
\tag{1}
$$

A_1 and A_2 are the characteristic coefficient of the two PGT. n_1 is the input shaft, n_2 is the output shaft, n_3 is the connection shaft, n_5 is the input shaft of the output PGT, n_6 is the output shaft of the output PGT, n_4 is the connection shaft.

The speed governing characteristic equation of the HMCVT can be deduced from the formula (1):

$$
i_{HM} = \frac{n_3}{n_1} = \frac{i_1 i_2 + A_2 e i_3}{(1+A_1)(i_1 i_2 + A_2 e i_3) - A_1(1+A_2)i_0 i_1 i_2 i_3}
\tag{2}
$$

By adjusting the displacement ratio e of the variable displacement pump and the quantitative motor, the stepless speed regulation function can be realized.

The efficiency of the HMCVT is defined as the ratio of output shaft power to input shaft power.

$$\eta_{HM} = -\frac{P_O}{P_I} = -\frac{M_O n_O}{M_I n_I} = -\frac{M_O}{M_I} i_{HM} \tag{3}$$

The efficiency characteristics of the HMCVT can be obtained from the formula (2) and (3).

$$\eta_{HM} = -\frac{M_O n_O}{M_I n_I} = -\frac{(1+A_1)(A_2 e i_3 + i_1 i_2 \eta_H) - A_1(1+A_2)i_0 i_1 i_2 i_3 \eta_H}{i_1 i_2 \eta_H + A_2 e i_3} i_{HM} \tag{4}$$

2.3 Mathematical Model of Hydraulic Circuit

The model of pump-controlled speed adjustment system should be based on the flow equation of the pump, and the continuous equation of the high pressure oil flow and the balance equation of the motor and the load, so as to establish the transfer function of the hydraulic circuit. The flow equation of the pump:

$$Q_p = D_p \omega_p - C_{ip}(p_h - p_l) - C_{ep}p_h \tag{5}$$

Where D_p is the output flow of the pump, ω_p is the pump input angle speed, C_{ip} and C_{ep} are the internal and external leakage coefficient of the pump, respectively. p_h and p_l are the pressure of high and low pressure cavity, respectively.

The flow continuity equation of the high pressure cavity of the system:

$$Q_p = C_{im}(p_h - p_l) + C_{em}p_h + D_m \frac{d\theta_m}{dt} + \frac{V_o dp_p}{\beta_e dt} \tag{6}$$

Where C_{im} and C_{em} are the internal and external leakage coefficient of the motor, V_o is the total volume of the pump and motor, p_p is the output pressure of the variable pump, β_e is the elastic modulus of the hydraulic oil, and D_m is the displacement of the hydraulic motor.

The balance equation between the motor and the load torque:

$$D_m(p_h - p_l) = J\frac{d^2\theta_m}{dt^2} + B_m\frac{d\theta_m}{dt} + G\theta_m + T \tag{7}$$

Where J is the moment of inertia of the motor, B_m is the viscous damping coefficient of the hydraulic oil, and T is the output torque of the motor.

Combined Eqs. (5)–(7), the transfer function of hydraulic circuit can be obtained after Laplace transform:

$$n_m = \frac{\frac{D_p n_p}{D_m} - \frac{C}{D_m^2}\left(1 + \frac{V_Q}{\beta_e C}s\right)T}{\frac{V_Q J}{\beta_e D_m^2}s^3 + \left(\frac{CJ}{D_m^2} + \frac{B_m V_Q}{\beta_e D_m^2}\right)s^2 + \left(1 + \frac{B_m C}{D_m^2} + \frac{G V_Q}{\beta_e D_m^2}\right)s + \frac{GC}{D_m^2}} \tag{8}$$

Where C is the total leakage coefficient of the pump controlled motor system, and n_p is the speed of the variable pump. Neglecting some minor factors and using the displacement ratio $e(s)$ as input, the transfer function of the system can be obtained:

$$\frac{n_m(s)}{e(s)} = \frac{n_p}{\frac{s^2}{\omega_c^2} + \frac{2\xi_c}{\omega_c}s + 1} \tag{9}$$

Where ω_c is hydraulic natural frequency, $\omega_c = \sqrt{\frac{\beta_e D_m^2}{V_o J}}$; ξ_c is damping ratio, $\xi_c = \frac{C}{2D_m}\sqrt{\frac{\beta_e J}{V_o}} + \frac{B_m}{2D_m}\sqrt{\frac{V_o}{\beta_e J}}$.

2.4   Wind Wheel Model

To study the transmission characteristics of the wind power system, the wind turbine must be modeled. The power absorbed by the wind wheel is determined by formula (10) [8]:

$$P = T\omega = \frac{1}{2}C_p\rho\pi R^2 v^3 \tag{10}$$

Where P is the power of the wind wheel, W; T is the output torque of the wind wheel, N·m; ω is the angular velocity of the wind wheel, rad/s; ρ is air density, kg/m³; R is the radius of the wind wheel, m; V is wind speed, m/s; C_p is the power coefficient of the wind wheel. Equation (11) can be obtained, because of $\lambda = R\omega/v$ (λ is tip speed ratio):

$$T = \frac{C_p}{2\lambda}\rho\pi R^3 v^3 \tag{11}$$

It is known that the cut-in speed of a wind wheel is $v_{\omega in} = 3.5$ m/s, the cut-out speed is $v_{\omega e} = 25$ m/s, and the speed range of wind wheel is 9.0–17.6 r/min [9]. The output characteristic of the wind turbine can be obtained by power coefficient in article [8] and formula (10) and (11). The output characteristics of the wind wheel can be obtained by interpolation method.

$$P = -12627n^4 + 861710n^3 - 21595379n^2 + 2365535898n - 957532875 \tag{12}$$

$$T = -120581n^3 + 8228726n^2 - 206220686n + 2258751445 - 9143765420/n \tag{13}$$

where n is the speed of the wind wheel, r/min.

3 Simulation and Analysis

3.1 Simulation of the HMCVT Model

The static characteristics of HMCVT are analyzed through theoretical models. In order to study its dynamic characteristics, computer simulation is an effective method. Using Matlab/Simulink software, modeling and dynamic simulation and analysis of HMCVT wind power system are carried out. The system model is shown in Fig. 3.

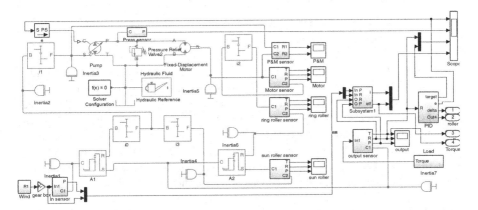

Fig. 3. Simulation model of wind power system

The 3D model of the transmission prototype is shown in Fig. 4, and the moment of inertia of each rotating part is derived by Inventor, and the inertial elements are added to the Simulink model.

Fig. 4. 3D model of transmission prototype

The Simulink model is composed of mechanical branch and hydraulic branch, taking into account the rotational inertia of the transmission, using the Proportion Integration Differentiation (PID) controller to adjust the displacement e in real time. For example, Fig. 5 is the block diagram of the control system.

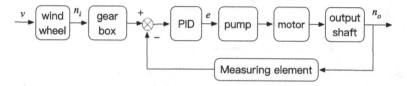

Fig. 5. Block diagram of control system

3.2 Static Simulation of HMCVT

Figure 6 is the speed regulation characteristic curve, in which the theoretical curve is obtained by formula (2). From Fig. 6, it can be seen that the range of i_{HM} is about 0.2–2.14 (about 10 times),with the change of e. The WD70-1500 wind power system with a capacity of 1.5 MW, its cut-in speed is $v_{\omega in} = 3.5$ m/s, and cut-out speed $v_{\omega e} = 25$ m/s, so the speed change is 7.14 times. Based on this speed regulation characteristic, the capacity of the converter can be reduced or even replaced completely, and the speed range of cut-in and cut-out can be widened simultaneously. The speed characteristics of the simulation are basically consistent with the theoretical speed governing characteristics. Due to the leakage of high pressure oil and viscous friction of the gear, the output shaft speed is slightly lower than the theoretical value, that is, the speed characteristic of the simulation is slightly lower than the theoretical value.

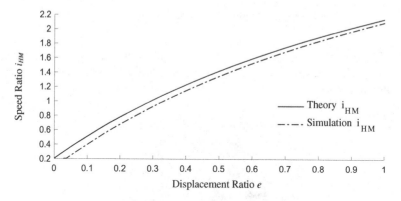

Fig. 6. Theory and simulation speed regulation characteristic curve

The efficiency characteristic curves are shown in Fig. 7, where the theoretical curve is obtained by formula (4). From the theoretical efficiency characteristic curve, it can be seen that the efficiency of HMCVT can keep around 87%, when the i_{HM} stay around 0.2–2.14. The efficiency of HMCVT is higher than that of torque converter 80% [3, 10].

In Fig. 7, simulation curves show that the efficiency of the theoretical analysis decreases with the increase of e, when the displacement ratio is between 0 and 0.27. The reason is that the hydraulic power diversion ratio increases with the increase of e, that is, the mechanical circuit power with high efficiency falls down, so the overall efficiency declines. However, in the theoretical analysis, the volumetric efficiency and

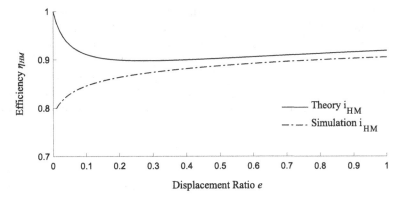

Fig. 7. Theory - simulation efficiency curves

the counter torque caused by load are not considered, so as to there are some different between theoretical and simulated analysis. In the simulation, when e is very low, the counter torque of the output shaft passes through the PGT A_2 to the hydraulic motor, which makes the motor have a reversal trend and hydraulic leakage, so there is a certain amount of energy loss at the motor. However, with the increase of e, the power of the hydraulic circuit increases gradually, and the load of the motor is constant, so the influence of the energy loss at the motor is gradually weakened, and the overall efficiency is gradually rising. When e is between 0.27 and 1, the simulated and theoretical efficiency are basically the same, and the efficiency increases slowly with the increase of e. The reason is that the hydraulic power diversion ratio decreases with the increase of e, that is, the mechanical circuit power with high efficiency rises, so the overall efficiency increases.

The static simulation results show that the simulation results of speed governing characteristics and efficiency curves are basically consistent with theoretical analysis conclusions. The speed regulation characteristic is not only wide and good linearity, but also easy to adjust and control speed. The volumetric efficiency and hydraulic leakage caused by reverse torque make simulation efficiency very low when e is very low. However, theoretical analysis does not consider hydraulic leakage. The overall development trend is still the same. The efficiency of the main work section is about 87%.

3.3   Dynamic Simulation of HMCVT Wind Power System

Taking 1.5 MW VSCF doubly fed induction generator as an example, the synchronous speed of generator is 1500 r/min, that is, output shaft $n_o = 1500$ r/min. The cut-in and cut-out of 1.5 MW typical wind power are 3.5 and 25 m/s. The wind speed of cut-in and cut-out are extended to 3.5 and 28 to test the performance of HMCVT wind power system. Wind speed data are provided by a company whose measuring time ranges from 21:00 to 13:00 the next day.

Figure 8 shows the dynamic characteristics of the generator's speed when the measured wind speed signals are input. At the initial stage of running, there are 1.8% fluctuations in 51 s. Then the wind speed fluctuates from the initial 3.5 m/s to 27 m/s, and the maximum peak is 28 m/s. The simulation results show that the fluctuation of the transmission shaft is kept within 0.57%, and the error is in 0.5 Hz to meet the standard of grid connected power generation. It shows that wind speed almost has no effect on speed of output shaft when the wind speed fluctuate between the cut-in and cut-out.

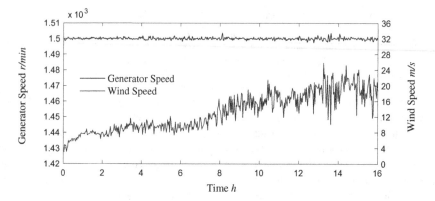

Fig. 8. Response curve of measured wind speed signal

Figure 9 is the efficiency curve of the measured wind speed signal. The efficiency of the whole system are about 88.32% in the low wind speed section (means 3.5–15 m/s), and about 85.95% in the high wind speed section (means 15–27 m/s). Because of the gradual increase of wind speed, i_{HM} of the transmission decreases, that is, e decreases, so the efficiency gradually decreases, which is consistent with the theoretical analysis results.

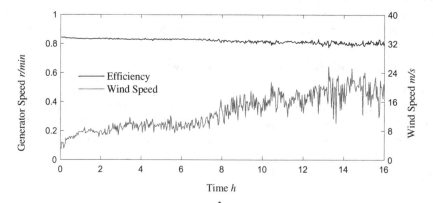

Fig. 9. Efficiency curve of measured wind speed signal

The simulation results of actual wind speed signals show that the system has good dynamic quality. The accurate control of rotating parts with large inertia still has a fast response speed, and its robustness is good in normal operation. Even if the wind speed fluctuates between 3.5 to 28 m/s, the output shaft can fluctuate within 0.57%, and the efficiency is stable at about 85.95–88.32%. All simulation results are consistent with the theoretical analysis conclusions.

3.4   Test and Study of HMCVT

Figure 10 shows a HMCVT test platform, the left is a driver, the middle is the HMCVT, and the right is dynamometer. The experiment mainly tests its speed regulation characteristics to verify the comprehensiveness and effectiveness of the simulation strategy.

Fig. 10. Transmission test platform

The experimental data were measured by the test platform. And the Simulink model of the hydraulic mechanical composite transmission was established by the same simulation strategy, and the speed regulation characteristic curve of the output coupling type was obtained as shown in Fig. 11. The experimental data are generally lower than the simulation results about 2.64%, because that the influence factors are not fully considered in the simulation, but the change trend is basically the same.

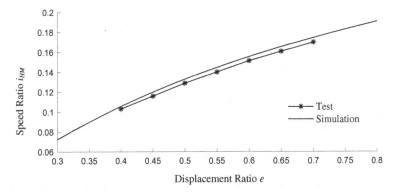

Fig. 11. Speed regulation characteristics

From the above, the simulation data of the hydraulic mechanical composite transmission is basically consistent with the experimental data. And the same simulation strategy are adopted in the HMCVT and the hydraulic mechanical composite transmission. It shows that the simulation strategy can simulate the real test environment effectively and comprehensively.

4   Conclusion

According to the actual working condition of the wind power system, the design of the HMCVT is put forward. Based on the principle of compound transmission, the theoretical analysis of the HMCVT is carried out. Modeling and dynamic simulation and analysis of HMCVT wind power system are carried out.

Theoretical analysis and simulation results show that the speed range of the transmission is large, and VSCF can be realized in the range of cut-in and cut-out wind speed. The maximum overshoot is 1.8%, which means that the dynamic characteristics are good. The engine speed can be stabilized at rated speed and the fluctuation is less than 0.5%, which means that the stability is good. The efficiency of HMCVT at low wind speed is about 88.32%, and the efficiency is about 85.95% at high wind speed.

This paper proves that the HMCVT can be used in wind power generation and has a good application prospect. Nevertheless, the reliability of system control is a complex problem for large inertial systems, which needs further study.

Acknowledgments. This paper is supported by the National Natural Science Foundation of China (No. 51375507).

References

1. Marques, A.B., Taranto, G.N., Falcao, D.M.: A knowledge-based system for supervision and control of regional voltage profile and security. IEEE Trans. Power Syst. **20**(1), 400–407 (2005)
2. Diepeveen, N.F.B., Laguna, A.J.: Dynamic modeling of fluid power transmissions for wind turbines. In: Proceedings of the EWEA Offshore 2011 Conference (2011)
3. Tița, I., Călărașu, D.: Wind power systems with hydrostatic transmission for clean energy. Environ. Eng. Manag. J. **8**(2), 327–334 (2009)
4. Silva, P., Antonio, G., Nicola, F., et al.: Performance prediction of a multi-MW wind turbine adopting an advanced hydrostatic transmission. Energy **64**(1), 450–461 (2014)
5. Xueyong, Z., Peter, M.: A novel power splitting drive train for variable speed wind power generators. Renew. Energy **28**(13), 2001–2011 (2003)
6. Shahaboddin, S., Dalibor, P., Amineh, A., et al.: Support vector regression methodology for wind turbine reaction torque prediction with power-split hydrostatic continuous variable transmission. Energy **67**(4), 623–630 (2014)
7. Chi, Z.: Matching investigation on wind turbine and hydrodynamic torque converter. Master, Harbin Institute of Technology (2010)
8. Chengdang, Z.: Research on the Power Control Technology for Wind Turbine with Hydro-mechanical Transmission. Master, Zhejiang University (2015)

9. Chunbao, L., Wenxing, M., Weiwei, M., et al.: Calculation and analysis of wind turbine transmission system based on hydrodynamic speed adjustment. J. Tongji Univ. (Natural Science) **41**(10), 1584–1588 (2013)

10. Chang, L.: Optimization of power matching on torque-converter with diesel engine for wheel Loader. Trans. Chin. Soc. Agric. Mach. **41**(11), 25–29 (2006)

A Novel Wind Power Accommodation Strategy Considering User Satisfaction and Demand Response Dispatch Economic Costs

Jie Hong, Xue Li[✉], and Dajun Du

School of Mechatronical Engineering and Automation, Shanghai University, Shanghai 200072, China
lixue@i.shu.edu.cn

Abstract. This paper is concerned with wind power accommodation strategy by considering user satisfaction and demand response dispatch economic costs. Firstly, price-based demand response dispatch economic costs model and user satisfaction model are established, which are incorporated into a multi-objective optimization model. Then, multi-objective function is transformed into single objective function by the normalized method, which is solved by the sequential quadratic programming method. Finally, simulation is operated on the modified IEEE-30 nodes distribution network, and simulation results show that the proposed strategy can successfully eliminate the wind fluctuations in a certain range.

Keywords: Price-based demand response · User satisfaction · Wind power fluctuation · User price elasticity coefficient

1 Introduction

Since the global energy shortage and the environmental pollution continue to aggravate, it is necessary to change the social energy structure [1]. To solve the problems, renewable energy has been employed rapidly [2,3], but the intermittent of renewable energy poses a challenge to the safe and stable operation of large-scale power grids. However, demand response as a highly-controllable virtual resource is an effective strategy for responding to renewable energy fluctuations. Thus, the paper focuses on demand response strategy to accommodate wind power fluctuations. With respect to the application of demand response technology for wind power accommodation, there exist some research results. For example, a real-time optimal scheduling model is established in [4], which aims at minimizing the dispatch economic costs on the power grid side. Based on the objective function of the lowest power cost and minimum load fluctuation, two phases demand response is constructed to optimize the user electricity

© Springer Nature Singapore Pte Ltd. 2018
K. Li et al. (Eds.): ICSEE 2018/IMIOT 2018, CCIS 925, pp. 36–45, 2018.
https://doi.org/10.1007/978-981-13-2381-2_4

consumption behavior in [5,6]. The demand response behavior of users to time-sharing price is analyzed by obtaining user load demand response matrix in [7].

The above researches are not concerned with dispatch economic costs and user satisfaction simultaneously when wind power accommodation strategies are developed. To solve the above problems, this paper is concerned with wind power accommodation strategy by taking the price-based demand response dispatch economic costs and user satisfaction into account. Then, multi-objective function is transformed into single-objective function by normalized method, and sequential quadratic programming method is used to acquire the amount of interactive response. Simulation confirms the feasibility and effectiveness of the proposed strategy.

The rest of this paper is organized as follows: price-based DR dispatch economic costs and user satisfaction model is given in Sect. 2. Section 3 presents demand response model and its solution method. Simulations are given in Sect. 4, following the conclusion in Section. 5.

2 Price-Based DR Dispatch Economic Costs and User Satisfaction Model

2.1 Price-Based DR Dispatch Economic Costs Model

According to the current electricity price or incentive mechanism, user changes their power consumption mode to better match the demand for power with the supply [9]. In general, demand response fall into two categories: price-based demand response and incentive-based demand response. The former refers to the customer changing the electricity consumption mode or the power demand according to the current nodal price. The latter refers to the DR implementing agency motivates users to reduce their loads when the reliability of the system is affected or the electricity price is high.

With respect to price-based demand response, the electricity price affects the customers' power consumption, which can guide the customer to use electricity more reasonably. After price-based demand response is carried out, the electricity price and load of each node maybe changed [4]. Thus, the corresponding changes (i.e., C_i) in electricity sales income on the power grid can be expressed by

$$C_i = P_{l,i} \times c_i - P_{l,i0} \times c_{i0}, \qquad (1)$$

where $P_{l,i0}$ and c_{i0} are the load and the electricity price of the ith node before demand response respectively, $P_{l,i}$ and c_i are the load and the electricity price of the ith node after demand response [10], and

$$P_{l,i} = \alpha_i c_i + \beta_i, \qquad (2)$$

where α_i, β_i are the price elasticity coefficients.

Next, the amount of demand response can be calculated by

$$\Delta P_{l,i} = P_{l,i0} - P_{l,i}. \qquad (3)$$

According to different price-based DR response modes, the unbalanced power of the system is distributed to a plurality of different DRs to get the expected amount of price-based DR involved in grid interaction. The corresponding price signal for different price-based DRs is given in [4], i.e.,

$$s.t. \sum_{i=1}^{N} \Delta P_{l,i} = \sum_{i=1}^{N_{wind}} \Delta P_{windi}, \tag{4}$$

where N, N_{wind} are the number of nodes and wind farms, and ΔP_{windi} is the wind power fluctuation.

Substituting (2) and (3) into (1), (1) can be re-written as

$$C_i = \frac{1}{\alpha_i} \Delta P_{l,i}^2 + \frac{\beta_i - 2P_{l,i0}}{\alpha_i} \Delta P_{l,i}. \tag{5}$$

Therefore, demand response dispatch economic costs can be calculated by the inverse of changes in grid side electricity sales income before and after demand response:

$$C_r = -C_i. \tag{6}$$

Demand response dispatch economic costs (6) will be employed in the following demand response model.

2.2   User Satisfaction Model

After the above price-based DR dispatch economic costs model is constructed, the impact of electricity consumption on the customers' lives is also considered. It reflects the users' comfortableness, which can be described by the satisfaction model [5], i.e.,

$$\begin{aligned} \max S, \\ S = \gamma_1 \varepsilon + \gamma_2 \theta, \\ \gamma_1 + \gamma_2 = 1, \end{aligned} \tag{7}$$

where ε is electricity comfort satisfaction, θ is electricity expenses satisfaction, S denotes user satisfaction, γ_1, γ_2 are the coefficients and balance the relationship between ε and θ. Furthermore, how to calculate ε and θ is given as follows:

(1) Electricity expenses satisfaction θ. Electricity expenses satisfaction is to reflect the user's attention to the electricity cost. It can be expressed as

$$\theta = 1 + \frac{\sum\limits_{i=1}^{N} (c_{i0} P_{l,i0} - c_i P_{l,i})}{\sum\limits_{i=1}^{N} c_{i0} P_{l,i0}}. \tag{8}$$

(2) Electricity comfort satisfaction ε. Except for the users' electricity expenses, the users' comfortableness is also considered importantly. It can be computed by

$$\varepsilon = 1 - \frac{\sum\limits_{i=1}^{N} |P_{l,i0} - P_{l,i}|}{\sum\limits_{i=1}^{N} P_{l,i0}}, \tag{9}$$

where N is the number of nodes.

3   Demand Response Model and Its Solution Method

3.1   Demand Response Model

Objective Function. Load demand response sets demand response capacity of each node with load is μ times of its own load, demand response capacity of node without load is not more than μ times the entire system load. According to the nodal price of the ith node at the tth instant. The spatial load response is based on the maximize user satisfaction and the minimize demand response dispatch economic costs. The model is as follows:

$$maxS, \\ \min \sum_{r=1}^{N} C_r, r = 1, 2...N_{RL}, \tag{10}$$

where S is user satisfaction; C_r is dispatch economic cost of the rth price-based demand response, and N_{RL} is the total number of price-based demand response.

Constraints. Constraints are divided into equality constraints and inequality constraints.

(1) Unbalanced power caused by the fluctuation of wind power is distributed to many nodes that participate in the demand response, i.e.,

$$s.t. \sum_{i=1}^{N} \Delta P_{l,i} = \sum_{i=1}^{N_{wind}} \Delta P_{windi}, \tag{11}$$

where N are the number of system nodes, N_{wind} is the number of wind farms, ΔP_{windi} is the amount of wind power fluctuation of the ith wind farm, and $\Delta P_{l,i}$ is the amount of interactive response of the ith node.

(2) Constraint of demand response capacity. It shows that the user-side demand response capability is limited to a certain extent, i.e.,

$$P_{Di}^{\min} \leqslant P_{Di} \leqslant P_{Di}^{\max}, \tag{12}$$

where P_{Di} is the load of the ith node; $P_{Di}^{\min}, P_{Di}^{\max}$ are the lower and upper bound of the load of the ith node after the demand response.

(3) Branch flow security constraints. After demand response, it must ensure that the flow of each branch is within the allowable safety range, i.e.,

$$P_{l,i\,\min} \leqslant P_{l,i} \leqslant P_{l,i\,\max}, \tag{13}$$

where $P_{l,i}$ is the power flow of the lth branch, $P_{l,i\,\min}$ and $P_{l,i\,\max}$ are the lower limit and the upper limit of the lth branch, respectively.

(4) Node voltage security constraints. After the demand response is carried out, the node load changes will cause the node voltage to change. In order to avoid the occurrence of node voltage threshold crossing, the node voltage after the demand response must be limited, i.e.,

$$U_{i\,\min} \leqslant U_i \leqslant U_{i\,\max}, \tag{14}$$

where U_i is the voltage of the ith node, $U_{i\,\min}$ and $U_{i\,\max}$ are the lower and upper limit of the node voltage of the ith node.

3.2   Multi-objective Optimization

In order to solve the above multi-objective optimization problem. The min-max normalization method is used to normalize two objective functions, and sequential quadratic programming method is used to acquire the amount of interactive response. The normalization method is as follows:

$$\min F = \sum_{i=1}^{m} w_i \left(\frac{f_i - f_{i\,\min}}{f_{i\,\max} - f_{i\,\min}} \right),$$
$$\sum_{i=1}^{m} w_i = 1, \tag{15}$$

where f_i is the objective function, $f_{i\,\min}$ and $f_{i\,\max}$ are the maximum and minimum values of the objective function, respectively. According to the order of magnitude difference between the maximum and minimum of satisfaction and the difference between maximum and minimum of dispatch economic costs, the normalized weight of satisfaction function is set to 0.01, and the weight of dispatch economic costs is set to 100.

3.3   Solution of the Model

It's known that demand response dispatch economic costs is a quadratic function of the amount interactive response, Therefore, the objective function and the constraint of the demand response are transformed into the objective function and the constraint with the amount of interactive response as a variable. Furthermore, the bi-objective function is transformed into a single-objective function by the above normalized method to solve the problem.

Transformation of the Optimization Model. Therefore, the above model is transformed into a model with the amount of interactive response $\Delta P_{l,i}$ as independent variable.

(1) Price-based DR dispatch economic costs

$$C_r = -\frac{1}{\alpha_i} \times \Delta P_{l,i}^2 - \frac{\beta_i - 2P_{l,i0}}{\alpha_i} \times \Delta P_{l,i}. \tag{16}$$

(2) Electricity expenses satisfaction. Substituting (2) and (3) into (8), (8) can be re-written as

$$\theta = 1 + \frac{\sum\limits_{i=1}^{N} \left(c_{i0}P_{l,i0} - \frac{1}{\alpha_i}(P_{l,i0} - \Delta P_{l,i})^2 + \frac{\beta_i}{\alpha_i}(P_{l,i0} - \Delta P_{l,i}) \right)}{\sum\limits_{i=1}^{N} c_{i0}P_{l,i0}}. \tag{17}$$

(3) Electricity comfort Satisfaction. Substituting (3) into (9), (9) can be re-written as

$$\varepsilon = 1 - \frac{\sum\limits_{i=1}^{N} |\Delta P_{l,i}|}{\sum\limits_{i=1}^{N} P_{l,i0}}. \tag{18}$$

(4) Demand response constraints. For nodes with loads: they can be flexibly increased or decreased on the original basis, i.e.,

$$-\mu P_{Di} \leqslant \Delta P_{l,i} \leqslant \mu P_{Di}, \tag{19}$$

For nodes without load: they can not reduce the load and can only increase the load on the original basis load, i.e.,

$$0 \leqslant \Delta P_{l,i} \leqslant \mu P_{Di}, \tag{20}$$

where μ is the capacity of demand response.

(5) Branch flow security constraints: since all nodes of the entire system participate in the demand response, they will have an impact on the flow of a branch, i.e.,

$$P_{l,i\,\min} \leqslant P_{l,i0} + \sum_{r=1}^{N} \Delta P_{l,i(j)} \leqslant P_{l,i\,\max}, \tag{21}$$

where $\Delta P_{l,i(j)}$ is the impact of nodes involved in price-based demand response on the lth branch from the ith node to the jth node, N is the number of price-based demand response.

The nodal price in the system is the Lagrange multiplier before the power flow equation in the optimal power flow model [8], so each nodal price can be obtained by solving the optimal power flow.

4 Simulation Example

The calculation model used in this example is an modified IEEE-30 nodes distribution network [10]. The entire solution process is shown in Fig. 1. Four equal-valued wind farms are connected to the 13th, 20th, 26th, 30th nodes, it is demonstrated in Fig. 2. The wind farm consists of 30 doubly-fed inductive wind generators, and each doubly-fed inductive wind turbine has a rated capacity of 600 KW.

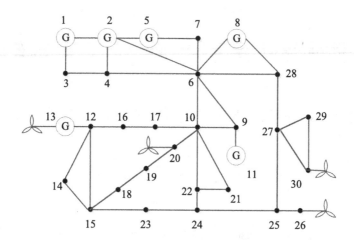

Fig. 1. Improved IEEE-30 power system Diagram

4.1 The Influence Analysis of Different Wind Power Fluctuation Coefficients

All nodal prices of the system are calculated every 3 h at a time interval, and the time 1 is taken as an example. The other times are similar. According to the user's degree of emphasis on two kinds of satisfaction, two kinds of satisfaction weights are set, e.g., the electricity comfort satisfaction degree weight is set to 0.1 and the electricity expense satisfaction rate is 0.9, respectively. The optimization results of two models are obtained under different wind power fluctuation conditions.

It can be found from Table 1 that when the fluctuation of wind power continued to increase, it basically remains stable at around 7% in model 1, it's better than that in model 2.

It can be seen from Fig. 3 that different nodes have different demand response elasticity coefficient and demand response capacity, different nodes have different the amount of interactive response.

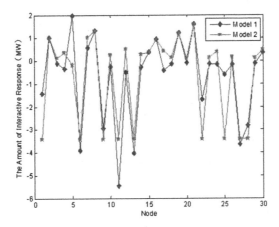

Fig. 2. Interactive response volume of each node of the two models

Table 1. Comparison of model 1 and model 2 results. (Note: wind power fluctuation coefficient(WPFC), wind power fluctuation(WPF), user satisfaction(US), DR dispatch economic cost(DRDEC), power grid income variation(PGIV).)

WPFC	WPF	US		DR DEC		PGIV	
		model 1	model 2	model 1	model 2	model 1	model 2
0.79	12.4	1.076	1.076	226.3	226.6	−226.3	−226.6
0.90	6.12	1.108	1.111	79.4	81.4	−79.4	−81.4
1.10	−6.12	1.152	1.181	−205.5	−196.8	205.5	196.8
1.26	−16.0	1.206	1.237	−427.6	−411.3	427.6	411.3
1.33	−20.0	1.219	1.238	−515.4	−478.4	515.4	478.4
1.41	−25.0	1.237	1.266	−623.5	−578.9	623.5	578.9
1.49	−30.0	1.262	1.295	−729.3	−680.1	729.3	680.1

According to Fig. 4, the load of each node compared with that before the demand response. The nodal prices such as the 1th, 6th, 11th, 25th, and 28th nodes in the entire system decrease significantly, and the corresponding node loads also increase.

4.2   The Effect Analysis of Different Capacity of Demand Response

It can seen that for model 2, as the capacity of demand response increases, the maximum degree of user satisfaction also increases, and the amount of power grid income variation on the grid side also increases in Table 2.

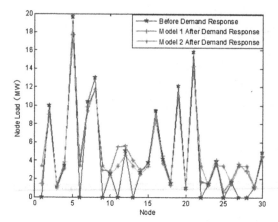

Fig. 3. Comparison of node loads for various nodes in the system before and after demand response

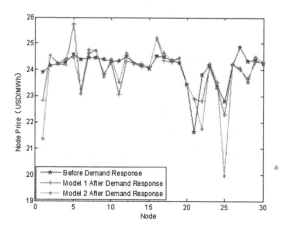

Fig. 4. Before and after demand response, the node electricity prices of each node in the system

Table 2. Comparison of model 1 and model 2 results.

DRC	WPF	US		DRDEC		PGIV	
		model 1	model 2	model 1	model 2	model 1	model 2
0.05	−20	1.1722	1.1872	−493.8	−480.9	493.8	480.9
0.10	−20	1.2198	1.2381	−515.5	−478.4	515.5	478.4
1.15	−20	1.2601	1.1971	−532.9	−372.5	532.9	372.5
1.20	−20	1.2946	1.2011	−546.6	−323.9	546.6	323.9

5   Conclusion

In this paper, a novel wind power accommodation strategy by taking the price-based demand response dispatch economic costs and user satisfaction into account is proposed. This strategy aims at minimizing scheduling cost and maximizing user satisfaction, then multi-objective function is transformed into single-objective function by normalized method, and sequential quadratic programming method is used to acquire the amount of interactive response. Finally, simulation results show that demand response capacity will have an effect on the elimination of wind fluctuations and the proposed strategy can successfully eliminate certain range of wind power fluctuations. In the future, the detailed classification of demand-side loads will be considered, and different demand response strategies will be made for different types of loads.

Acknowledgment. This work was supported in part by the National Science Foundation of China (Nos. 61773253). The Project of Science and Technology Commission of Shanghai Municipality (Nos. 15JC1401900, 17511107002, 14JC1402200).

References

1. Zeng, M., Wu, G.: Key problems and prospects of integrated demand response in energy internet. Power Syst. Technol. **11**(40), 3391–3398 (2016)
2. Dong C Y, Zhao J H.: From smart grid to energy internet: basic concepts and research framework. Autom. Electric Power Syst. **38**, 1–11 (2014)
3. Tian, S.L., Wang, B.B.: Key technologies of demand response in smart grid. J. Electric. Eng. **84**, 3576–3585 (2014)
4. Zeng, D., Yao, J.G.: Modeling price-based demand response optimization scheduling based on security constraints for wind power accommodation. J. Electric. Eng. **34**(31), 5571–5578 (2014)
5. Ding, W., Yuan, J.H.: Peak-valley time-share price decision model based on user price-based demand response and satisfaction. Autom. Electric Power Syst. **29**(20), 10 (2005)
6. Yan, L.W., Yu, C., Tan, Z.F.: Two-phase scheduling optimization model for wind energy source storage considering demand response. Power Grid Technol. **39**(5), 1287–1293 (2015)
7. Yan, L.W., Qin, C., Wu, H.L., et al.: Wind power electricity consumption stochastic optimal scheduling model considering multi-type demand response. Power Syst. Technol. **39**(7), 1839–1846 (2015)
8. Cao, J., Ma, H.Y., Liu, Y., et al.: Research on demand response strategy based on nodal price. Power Grid Technol. **40**(5), 1536–1542 (2016)
9. Hu, M., Xiao, J.W.: Distributed real-time demand response for energy management scheduling in smart grid. Int. J. Electric. Power Energy Syst. **1**(16), 233–245 (2018)
10. Hu, Y., Xiao, J.W., et al.: Hierarchical control strategy for residential demand response considering time-varying aggregated capacity. Int. J. Electric. Power Energy Syst. **1**(16) (2017)

Research on Operational Reliability of Digital Control Device of Nuclear Pressurizer Based on Dynamic Fault Tree

Hong Qian, Yaqi Gu$^{(\boxtimes)}$, Gaofu Yu, and Shanjin Wu

Shanghai University of Electric Power, Shanghai 200090, China
{qianhong.sh,Yaqi_acient}@163.com, {yugaofu002,
fragrantwu}@126.com

Abstract. The digital pressure control device of Pressurizer, which is equipped with the input Module of selecting median from four inputs, was used as the research object, then a fault tree including static part and dynamic part of the device is established. Next, the Method of Markov was used to analyze the dynamic part. The overall fault tree was analyzed according to the overall logic. And then the Bayesian method is used to obtain the current reliability index of the equipment based on the DCS operating data as input value of the fault tree. Finally own capability and the effect on entire device of input module of selecting median from four inputs is evaluated from the value of reliability and importance, the result shows that the input module is relatively highly optimized.

Keywords: The logic of selecting median from four inputs · Dynamic fault tree
Bayesian analysis · The evaluation of reliability · Digital control device of
nuclear pressurizer

1 Introduction

In the power plant control system, the input of analog quantity generally adopts the method of multi-point measurement and taking median value. Thermal power plant adopts the logic of selecting median from three inputs, such as the level measurement of the deaerator [1] and so on. In nuclear power plants, advanced nuclear reactors generally use the logic of selecting median from four inputs [2], the digital control device of Pressurizer, which is equipped with the above logic, was used as the research object in this article. There are two points to be analyzed, point one is the reliability of input Module of selecting median from four inputs, point two is about increased reliability of the entire control device after using the input module.

At present, there are many studies on reliability of digital control device, but most of them are based on historical data or factory data. In fact, the reliability index of equipment will change with the rise of running time, so the reliability evaluation based on the initial index value is inaccurate. Based on the operating data of DCS, Bayesian analysis is used to obtain more accurate reliability index in this article.

© Springer Nature Singapore Pte Ltd. 2018
K. Li et al. (Eds.): ICSEE 2018/IMIOT 2018, CCIS 925, pp. 46–57, 2018.
https://doi.org/10.1007/978-981-13-2381-2_5

Reliability analysis methods include failure mode and impact analysis, reliability block diagram, fault tree modeling and so on. Literature [3] verified the feasibility of Monte Carlo method in fault tree modeling and simulation of nuclear power plant safety system. Literature [4] used the method of MFM (multi-layer flow model) to analyze DCS of nuclear power plants. The fault tree was used in literature [5] to model nuclear power protection system. The above methods don't apply to the failure mode related to the sequence of failure of each device. The input module of selecting median from four inputs adds a backup channel compared with the three-input, the backup channel enters signal instead of failed preferred channel, but it only replaces one preferred channel to ensure accuracy, so the failure of the input module must be linked to the sequence of the failure of each channel. This article introduces a dynamic fault tree, which takes the sequence of failure into account.

2 The Configuration of Digital Control Device of Pressurizer

The function of Pressurizer is to maintain the primary circuit pressure of nuclear power at 15.5 MPa, so that the power plant will not encounter emergency shutdown and safety valve operation under the condition of normal load transients and the turbine dumping the entire load. Pressurizer control principle shown in Fig. 1.

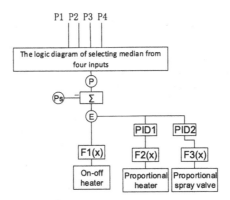

Fig. 1. Principle diagram of pressure control of pressurizer

According to Fig. 1, Digital Pressure Control device of Pressurizer is configured as follows, a pair of redundant controllers, a pair of redundant power, four input cards to avoid secondary faults and the six output cards. Hardware structure is shown in Fig. 2.

The on-site pressure signals P1/P2/P3/P4 are transfered to DPU via four input cards. Pressure signals processed is converted into control command in DPU and transfered to field devices via output cards. The logic of four-input is shown in Fig. 3.

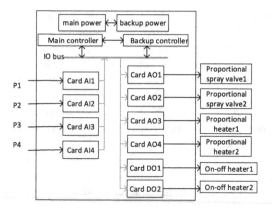

Fig. 2. Hardware structure of digital pressure control device of pressurizer

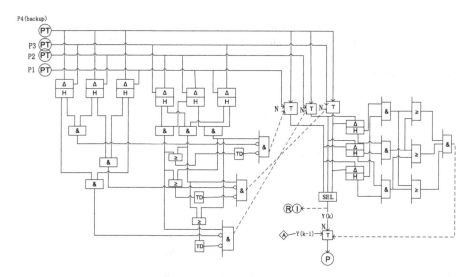

Fig. 3. The logic diagram of selecting median from four inputs

According to Fig. 3, the entire logic is divided into two parts of the backup channel access and two out of three decisions. The first part determines whether backup channel needs to be put in. First step is to determine whether there are deviation alarms for signal values of channels. Second step is to determine if the following conditions are true: one of the three preferred channels is detected a deviation alarm, backup channel and the other two preferred input channels aren't detected a deviation alarm, if these happen, the faulty channel is switched to the backup channel. The second part makes two out of three decisions for the final three channels. If there are deviation alarms in two or more channels, the input module is faulty and the operator inputs pressure measurement from the immediately preceding moment. Otherwise, the median of three channels or the average of two channels is output.

3   Bayesian Calculation of Failure Rate of DCS Equipment

3.1   The Reliability Index of DCS Based on Field Data

$Y_j(t)$ indicates the running status of device, which is obtained from the real-time database. t indicates running time of device. When $Y_j(t) = 1$, the equipment operates normally. When $Y_j(t) = 0$, the equipment fails, failure time $T_i|_{Y_j} = t$ that indicates the i-th fault time of device Y_j is recorded in days, months and years.

Mean Time Between Failures (MTBF) of the device is defined as (1).

$$MTBF|_{Y_j} = [\sum_{i=1}^{n} (T_{i+1}|_{Y_j} - T_i|_{Y_j}) + MTBF_0|_{Y_j}]/n \qquad (1)$$

In the formula, $MTBF_0|_{Y_j}$ indicates initial MTBF of device Y_j.

Failure rate is a common reliability index for engineer. It refers to the number of failures per unit time during operating, which is expressed as $\lambda = N/T$, where T is running time of the device, and N is the number of failures during T.

The tub curve can reflect the relationship of failure rate and running time. The DCS is considered to be in valid period in the article, so failure rate is constant and subject to exponential distribution, and $\lambda = 1/MTBF$ is true. The failure probability function of device is $F(t) = 1 - e^{-\lambda t}$, and the reliability function is $R(t) = 1 - F(t) = e^{-\lambda t}$.

3.2   Bayesian Estimation Method for Failure Rate of DCS Equipment

Bayesian method regards parameter to be estimated as a random variable of a prior distribution. According to prior distribution of parameters to be estimated and sample observation value, posterior distribution is obtained. The mathematical expectation of the posterior distribution is the Bayesian estimate of parameters to be estimated.

Given that DCS device complies with exponential distribution. Assuming that the MTBF of a device is known as 168900, the failure rate is 5.92×10^{-6}, it means that the device's prior information is (5.92, 1000000).

(1) Determine the conjugate prior distribution of failure rates for devices, it is the Gamma distribution, $\Gamma(\lambda|Z_0, \tau_0)$.
(2) Based on the properties of conjugate distribution and the Bayesian formula, the posterior distribution is obtained, it is $\Gamma(\lambda|Z_0 + Z_1 + \ldots + Z_n, T_0 + T_1 + \ldots + T_n)$ if there are n batches of field data (Zi, Ti) (i = 1, 2, ..., n).

(3) Calculate the value of point estimate for reliability R as formula (2).

$$R' = \left(\frac{\sum\limits_{i=0}^{n} T_i}{t + \sum\limits_{i=0}^{n} T_i} \right)^{\sum\limits_{i=0}^{n} Z_i} \tag{2}$$

Where t is the given task time. The posterior mean of failure rate is shown in (3).

$$\lambda_{Bayes} = \frac{N + \sum\limits_{i=0}^{n} Z_i}{T + \sum\limits_{i=0}^{n} T_i} \tag{3}$$

In the formula, T is the number of hours of the n + 1th operation of device and N is the cumulative number of failures in T hours.

4   Modeling Dynamic Fault Tree

Digital Pressure Control Device of Pressurizer includes controllers, power supplies, input and output modules. Any device failure will cause pressure control failure. Therefore, the relationship of them is OR logically.

Specific to each module, the power and the controller are configured redundantly. The relationship between the primary and the backup is AND logically. For actuators, such as spray valve and heater, output cards connected to different actuators are logically OR, and output cards connected to same actuators is logically AND.

The input module uses four parallel channels. First input module is considered to be faulty when there are two faults in the three final channels, which is represented by a 2/3 AND. Second according to Fig. 3, there are two failure modes for a single channel: one is that the preferred channel fails and the backup channel also fails. Two is that channel I2 or I3 has failed before channel I1 fails. The backup channel is used to replace channel I2 or I3, and it cannot replace two channels at the same time, so channel I1 must be faulty. The relationship between two failure modes is OR logically. It can be seen that failure mode two is related to the failure sequence of three preferred channels, so Priority AND Gate is introduced in the article. The fault tree model is shown in Fig. 4 based on the above analysis.

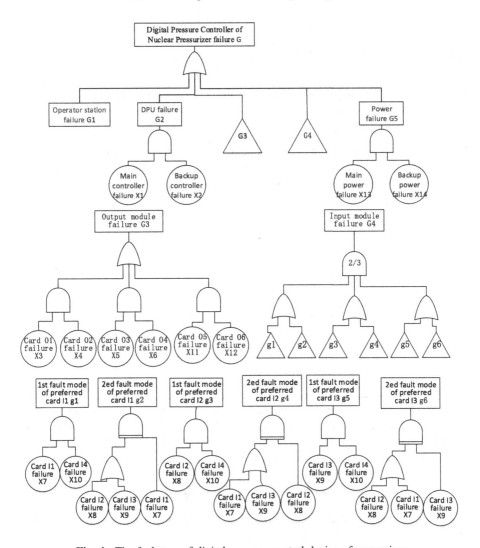

Fig. 4. The fault tree of digital pressure control device of pressurizer

5 Dynamic Fault Tree Analysis Based on Markov Process

5.1 Markov Process

If the transition probability is independent of the start time when a Markov chain X(t) transforms from state i at time u to state j at time u + t [6], the Markov chain is homogeneous, the transition probability is only related to time difference t. P_{ij} is used as the elements of the transition probability matrix P, so the transition rate matrix is A = P − U, where U is the same order identity matrix of P.

The equation of state is $P' = A * P$, where P is the column vector of the probability of each state and P' is the column vector of the probability derivative of each state. The failure probability can be obtained by solving the equation.

5.2 Qualitative Analysis of Dynamic Fault Tree Based on Markov Process

The failure mechanism of the priority AND gate is: when the basic events occur from left to right, the system output event is a fault, and if the basic event occurs from right to left, the output event is normal [7]. The priority AND gate is transformed functionally into Markov chain as shown in Fig. 5.

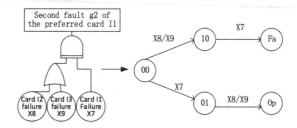

Fig. 5. Markov form of priority AND gate functionally

With the channel I1 fault as the top event, the state Fa corresponds to the occurrence of top event, the state Op corresponds to the nonoccurrence of top event, you can get two Markov chains as follows, 00—10—Fa/00—01—Op. Among them, "00" indicates that card I1, I2, and I3 are normal, "10" indicates that card I2 or I3 fails and card I1 is normal, and "01" indicates that the card I1 fails and I2 or I3 is normal.

5.3 Quantitative Analysis Based on Markov Dynamic Fault Tree

In this paper, assuming that the card failure rate is λ_4, the state transition diagram of the dynamic fault tree can be obtained as shown in Fig. 6.

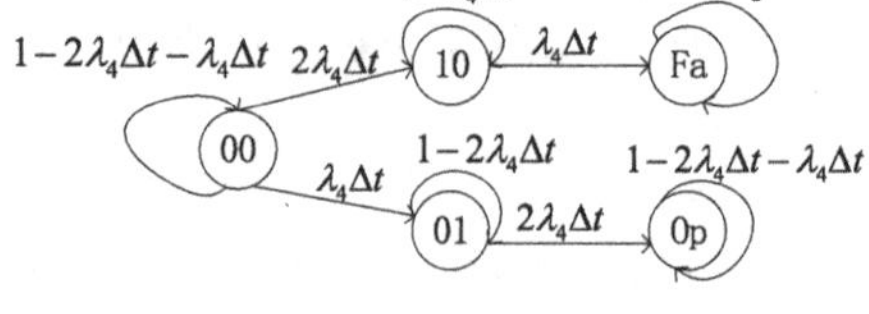

Fig. 6. State transition diagram of priority AND gate

According to Fig. 6, the state transition rate matrix is as (4),

$$A = \begin{bmatrix} -2\lambda_4 - \lambda_4 & 2\lambda_4 & \lambda_4 & 0 & 0 \\ 0 & -\lambda_4 & 0 & \lambda_4 & 0 \\ 0 & 0 & -2\lambda_4 & 0 & 2\lambda_4 \\ 0 & 0 & 0 & 0 & 0 \\ 0 & 0 & 0 & 0 & -2\lambda_4 - \lambda_4 \end{bmatrix} \tag{4}$$

The matrix of the differential equation $P' = A * P$ is shown in (5).

$$\begin{bmatrix} P_0'(t) \\ P_1'(t) \\ P_2'(t) \\ P_3'(t) \\ P_4'(t) \end{bmatrix} = \begin{bmatrix} -2\lambda_4 - \lambda_4 & 2\lambda_4 & \lambda_4 & 0 & 0 \\ 0 & -\lambda_4 & 0 & \lambda_4 & 0 \\ 0 & 0 & -2\lambda_4 & 0 & 2\lambda_4 \\ 0 & 0 & 0 & 0 & 0 \\ 0 & 0 & 0 & 0 & -2\lambda_4 - \lambda_4 \end{bmatrix} \begin{bmatrix} P_0(t) \\ P_1(t) \\ P_2(t) \\ P_3(t) \\ P_4(t) \end{bmatrix} \tag{5}$$

Let the initial condition be $[P_0(0) \quad P_1(0) \quad P_2(0) \quad P_3(0) \quad P_4(0)] = [1 \quad 0 \quad 0 \quad 0 \quad 0]$.

Using matlab to solve Eq. (7), the probability for g2 to occur is shown in (6),

$$p = \lambda_4/(2\lambda_4 + \lambda_4)e^{-(2\lambda_4 + \lambda_4)t} - e^{-\lambda_4 t} + 2\lambda_4/(2\lambda_4 + \lambda_4) = \frac{1}{3}e^{-3\lambda_4 t} - e^{-\lambda_4 t} + \frac{2}{3} \tag{6}$$

6   Reliability Evaluation of Pressurizer Digital Control Device

6.1   Digital Control Device of Nuclear Pressurizer Reliability Calculation

According to formula (8), combined with the logical relationship in Fig. 4, the failure probability of the input module G4 can be found as (7).

$$f_4(t) = \{1 - (e^{-\lambda_4 t} - \frac{1}{3}e^{-3\lambda_4 t} + \frac{1}{3}) \times [1 - (1 - e^{-\lambda_4 t})^2]\}^2$$
$$\times \{2(e^{-\lambda_4 t} - \frac{1}{3}e^{-3\lambda_4 t} + \frac{1}{3}) \times [1 - (1 - e^{-\lambda_4 t})^2] + 1\} \tag{7}$$

According to the logic relationship in Fig. 4, the failure probability of the static fault sub-block G3 can be obtained as (8).

$$f_3(t) = 1 - [1 - (1 - e^{-\lambda_3 t})^2]^3 \tag{8}$$

Finally, according to the logical relationship of the entire fault tree, the reliability of the Pressurizer digital control device can be found as (9).

$$F(t) = 1 - [1 - f_1(t)] \cdot [1 - f_2(t)] \cdot [1 - f_3(t)] \cdot [1 - f_4(t)] \cdot [1 - f_5(t)] \qquad (9)$$

In the (11), $f_1 = (1 - e^{-\lambda_1 t})^2$ represent operator station failure probability, $f_2(t) = 1 - 2e^{-\lambda_2 t} + e^{-2\lambda_2 t}$ represent controller failure probability, $f_3(t)$ represents output module failure probability, that is (8), $f_4(t)$ represents input module failure probability, that is (7), $f_5(t) = 1 - 2e^{-\lambda_5 t} + e^{-2\lambda_5 t}$ represent power failure probability.

6.2 Reliability Evaluation of Digital Control Device of Pressurizer

6.2.1 Analysis of Reliability Value

In this paper, the Digital Control Device of Pressurizer is configured for input module of selecting median from four inputs. Compared with three inputs, a backup card is added so that when one of three preferred cards fails, it can be switched to backup. When two cards fails, the first faulty card can be switched to backup card and only one input card fails finally, input module can still work normally. As for three inputs, if there are two faulty channels, input module fails. Both configuration schemes meet the single-failure principle, but the former is obviously more reliable. Next reliability analysis will be expanded from the quantitative point of view.

Table 1 shows the operation failure records of each DCS device. The initial MTBF and the initial failure rate of the known devices are shown in Table 2.

Table 1. Failure report

Device	Start time	Failure time
DPU	2008/10/10	2013/05/05
Power	2008/10/10	2013/08/08
Card O3	2008/10/10	2014/09/01

Table 2. Failure rate

Device	MTBF	Failure rate
DPU	3671428	2.72×10^{-7}
Power	1638461	6.1×10^{-7}
Input card	434782	2.3×10^{-6}
Output card	1836661	5.44×10^{-7}
Operator station	1369863	7.3×10^{-7}

According to online data of the equipment, the failure rate of each equipment is corrected by the method of Bayesian analysis in real time, it can be concluded as follows: operator station $\lambda_1 = 7.3 \times 10^{-7}$, controller $\lambda_2 = 2.8 \times 10^{-7}$, output card $\lambda_3 = 6.11 \times 10^{-7}$, input card $\lambda_4 = 2.3 \times 10^{-6}$, power $\lambda_5 = 6.5 \times 10^{-7}$.

Substituting the above data into the Eqs. (7) and (5), you can obtain the reliability versus time function of digital control device and the input module using the logic of selecting median from four inputs, and you can compare it with the three inputs. Figure 7 shows the comparison of the reliability of two input configurations.

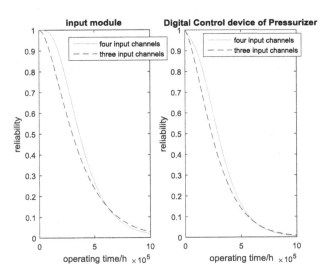

Fig. 7. Reliability comparison

It can be seen from Fig. 7 that after adding the common backup card, the reliability of the logic of selecting median from four inputs is significantly higher than before, and the reliability of the entire digital control device has also been improved.

6.2.2 Analysis of Importance Value

The degree of importance analysis is an important part of the reliability analysis. It is used to represent the contribution to the probability of occurrence of the top event when the cut set of a component or system fails. This paper uses probability importance to analyze reliability.

The importance of the bottom event is the difference in the probability of occurrence of the top event when the probability of the bottom event is 1 and 0 [8], which is shown in (10).

$$\Delta g_i(t) = g[1_i, F_i(t)] - g[0_i, F_i(t)] \tag{10}$$

The importance of the basic event reflects the degree of influence of occurrence of the basic event on the top event. It can be used to find weak points of the system and improve the reliability of system. At the same time, the lower the degree of importance, the lower possibility of the entire system failure caused by the component failure, it shows that the design is more optimized.

According to formula (10), the importance value of input cards can be calculated and recorded in Table 3.

Table 3. Comparison of importance value

Years of operation	The logic of selecting median from three inputs	The logic of selecting median from four inputs	
		Preferred card	Backup card
1	0.07074301	0.004156598	0.00424807
2	0.1328582	0.01609563	0.01671802
3	0.1871326	0.03480098	0.03657841
4	0.23429	0.05907566	0.06262562
5	0.2749956	0.08765473	0.09347692
6	0.3098607	0.1192886	0.1277146
7	0.339446	0.1528012	0.1639868
8	0.3642663	0.1871282	0.2010716
9	0.3847932	0.2213383	0.2379134
10	0.4014588	0.2546433	0.2736377
11	0.4146587	0.2863981	0.3075504
12	0.4247545	0.316095	0.3391279

According to Table 2, the importance value of the input card has been declined after adopting the logic of selecting median from four inputs compared with the former, it means that possibility of Pressurizer pressure control failure caused by single input card failure is declined, it proves that the logic of selecting median from four inputs is more highly optimized and increases reliability of the entire control device. In addition, as running time increases, the importance difference between two input schemes becomes smaller and smaller, because performance of card is degraded, the advantages logically are no longer significant, but in the first decade of operation, the optimization of the logic of selecting median from four inputs is much better than the three-input logic.

7   Conclusion

This paper mainly aims at the Control Device of Nuclear Pressurizer, uses the dynamic fault tree modeling to analyze and evaluate the reliability of logic of selecting median from four inputs, and studies the influence of the input logic on the reliability of overall device. For the switching relationship between preferred channel and backup channel, the priority AND gate are introduced. Then the dynamic fault tree is transformed into a Markov chain for quantitative calculation. The calculation result compared with the three-input logic show that the logic of selecting median from four inputs is superior to the three-input logic in improving reliability of system. In addition, this paper calculate current failure rate of devices by Bayesian considering operating data to make evaluation result more accurate.

Acknowledgments. This work was partially supported by Shanghai Science and Technology Committee (Grant No. 18020500900), National Natural Science Foundation of China (Grant No. 61503237), Shanghai Natural Science Foundation (Grant No. 15ZR1418300) and Shanghai Key Laboratory of Power Station Automation Technology (Grant No. 13DZ2273800).

References

1. Wang, Z.: Improvement of liquid level measurement method for deaerator. Forum Ind. Technol. **14**, 76–78 (2015)
2. Zhang, E.B.: Analysis of the implementation and characteristics of AP1000 regulator pressure automatic control logic. China Hi-Tech Enterp. **33**, 46–48 (2013)
3. Wang, X.K., Yang, X.H., Liu, G., et al.: Application of probabilistic safety assessment in nuclear power plant protection system. East China Electr. Power **38**, 725–729 (2010)
4. Chen, W.Q.: Research on Reliability Analysis Method of DCS in Nuclear Power Plant Based on MFM. Harbin Engineering University (2013)
5. Zhou, S.L., Liu, Y.Y., Du, W.: Reliability analysis of digital reactor power control system in nuclear power plant based on fault tree method. Nucl. Sci. Eng. **33**, 419–428 (2013)
6. Qian, H., Luo, J.B., Jin, W.J., et al.: Reliability evaluation of DEH system optimization based on dynamic fault tree. China Electr. Power **47**, 92–96 (2014)
7. Li, Y.F.: A New Method of Dynamic Fault Tree Analysis for Complex Systems and Its Application. University of Electronic Science and Technology of China (2013)
8. Kang, C.Z.: Research on Reliability Modeling and Evaluation of DCS in Thermal Power Plants. North China Electric Power University (2014)

Electric Vehicles

Research on Torsional Vibration Suppression of Electric Vehicle Driveline

Zhanyong Cao, Feng He[(⊠)], Huilin Li, and Zhu Xu

School of Mechanical Engineering, Guizhou University, Guiyang 550025,
Guizhou, China
fenghe-01@vip.sina.com

Abstract. In order to suppress the torsional vibration caused by electric vehicle low-damping characteristic, a driveline simulation model was constructed in Matlab/Simulink based on permanent magnet synchronous motor(PMSM) using vector control strategy. A fuzzy self-tuning PID controller was designed to improve speed feedback and robustness of motor controller. The results show that the dynamic characteristics of electric vehicle driveline can be revealed effectively by electro-mechanical coupling method. The application of fuzzy logic method to tune PID controller can contribute a lot to solve torque ripple problem caused by mutation load and mutation control signal.

Keywords: Electric vehicle · Vector control · Torsional vibration
Fuzzy self-tuning

1 Introduction

In order to improve the power efficiency of driveline, most electric vehicle cancels clutch and torque converter which is the damping parts of whole system comparing with traditional fuel vehicle. The experimental results show that sudden increase of motor torque will cause the shock of transmission shafts resulting in vehicle starting shaking [1]. For solving such torque ripple problems, researchers carried out a lot of research on torque transfer characteristics of electric vehicle driveline.

Zhang Lijun studied the shaking phenomenon of a hybrid electric vehicle when starting, the reason and control method of this vibration are put forward through road test and modeling experiment using finite element method [2]. Aiming at researching the abnormal noise of an electric vehicle driveline caused by sudden clutch joining, R Turnbull studied the effect of vertical load on the noise [3]. Ma proposed a torque ripple model of permanent magnet synchronous motor through bench test, and analyzed the mechanism of torque ripple by orders [4]. Considering that hybrid electric vehicle driveline removed clutch and torque converter, A kind of controller which can control the output torque of wheel is designed by Syed [5].

The powertrain of electric vehicle is different from that of fuel vehicle, and its mechanical part has low damping characteristic. Some scholars put forward that on the basis of synthetically considering the motor performance and vehicle application, the output torque ripple of motor can be restrained, the robustness of its control system can be improved, and the power output quality of driveline can be optimized [6].

© Springer Nature Singapore Pte Ltd. 2018
K. Li et al. (Eds.): ICSEE 2018/IMIOT 2018, CCIS 925, pp. 61–69, 2018.
https://doi.org/10.1007/978-981-13-2381-2_6

Aiming at optimizing the performance of motor control system, the torque ripple of electric vehicle driveline was restrained based on Matlab-Simulink, the torsional dynamics model of vehicle driveline was built, and the simulation experiment was carried out through studying the relationship between input resistance of driveline and intention of driver. A PID controller using fuzzy self-tuning method was designed, and the output curves of driveline using these controllers were compared and analyzed.

2   Torsional Vibration Model of Electric Vehicle Driveline

PMSM is the power source of electric vehicle powertrain. DC power is supplied from battery pack, and is converted to 3 intersections by the inverter to drive PMSM afterwards. After that, the output torque of motor is transmitted through transmission shaft to wheel. The torsional vibration simulation model of driveline is established by electro-mechanical coupling method. As shown in Fig. 1, the model includes two parts: electrical part and mechanical part.

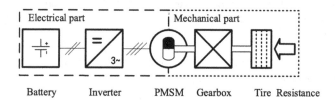

Fig. 1. Electric vehicle driveline

2.1   Vector Control Strategy for PMSM

In 3-phase coordinate system of PMSM, the rotor magneto-electric structure of synchronous motor is asymmetric, and the mathematical model is a set of nonlinear time - varying equations related to the instantaneous position of rotor, which is unfavorable for analysis and control of motor. Through Clark and Park transformations, equation can be transformed into d - q coordinate system.

The formulas of Clark transform and Park transform without zero sequence component are as follows:

$$\begin{bmatrix} i_\alpha \\ i_\beta \end{bmatrix} = \frac{2}{3} \begin{bmatrix} 1 & -\frac{1}{2} & -\frac{1}{2} \\ 0 & \frac{\sqrt{3}}{2} & -\frac{\sqrt{3}}{2} \end{bmatrix} \begin{bmatrix} i_A \\ i_B \\ i_C \end{bmatrix} \tag{1}$$

$$\begin{bmatrix} i_d \\ i_q \end{bmatrix} = \begin{bmatrix} \cos\theta & \sin\theta \\ -\sin\theta & \cos\theta \end{bmatrix} \begin{bmatrix} i_\alpha \\ i_\beta \end{bmatrix} \tag{2}$$

By means of Clark and Park coordinate transformation presented in Fig. 2, current in three-phase winding is equivalent to current in two-phase rotating winding, which can reduce coupling factor between parameters, simplify the mathematical model of system, and facilitate control and analysis of motor.

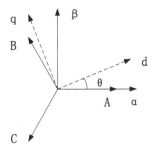

Fig. 2. Clark and Park transformation

Output torque of motor under d-q shafting is given by:

$$T_e = \frac{3}{2}p\left(\psi_f i_q + (L_d - L_q)i_d i_q\right) \tag{3}$$

Considering electric vehicle needs stable constant torque under starting condition, equation is obtained when $i_d = 0$:

$$T_e = \frac{3}{2}p\psi_f i_q \tag{4}$$

2.2 Torsional Dynamics Model of Driveline

Refer to an electric vehicle, the transmission ratio i is 3. 227, the radius of tire r is 25. 675 cm. The torsional vibration model of driveline is simplified to a second-order damped torsional vibration system. The two equivalent moment of inertia are electric shaft and main drive shaft [9], which is displayed in Fig. 3.

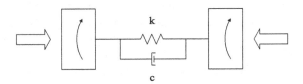

Fig. 3. Equivalent torsional dynamic model of driveline

Under high speed condition, driving resistance is mainly air resistance and rolling resistance.

$$F_{air} = \frac{1}{2} v_{vehicle}^2 C_d \rho A \tag{5}$$

$$F_f = G \cdot f \tag{6}$$

$$T_{re} = (F_{air} + F_f) \frac{r_{tire}}{i} \tag{7}$$

The model does not consider gear clearance, pavement response, tire deformation and other factors. The stiffness of spring k is 2000 N*m/rad and the damping coefficient c is 2500 N*m*s/rad.

Mathematical model of mechanical part is as follows:

$$
\begin{bmatrix} J_1 & 0 \\ 0 & J_2 \end{bmatrix} \begin{bmatrix} \ddot{\theta}_1 \\ \ddot{\theta}_2 \end{bmatrix} + \begin{bmatrix} c & -c \\ -c & c \end{bmatrix} \begin{bmatrix} \dot{\theta}_1 \\ \dot{\theta}_2 \end{bmatrix} \\
+ \begin{bmatrix} k & -k \\ -k & k \end{bmatrix} \begin{bmatrix} \theta_1 \\ \theta_2 \end{bmatrix} = \begin{bmatrix} T_e \\ -T_{re} \end{bmatrix} \tag{8}
$$

The natural frequencies of system are given by:

$$\omega_1 = 0, \ \omega_2 = \sqrt{k \left(\frac{1}{J_1} + \frac{1}{J_2} \right)} = 39.3 \, \text{Hz}$$

3 Fuzzy Self-tuning PID Controller

In order to improve the control performance of system, a fuzzy self-tuning PID controller is designed in the speed loop of motor controller.

3.1 Fuzzy Self-tuning PID Control Principle

Traditional PID controller has no self-tuning ability and can not adjust its parameters according to the change of external conditions. Fuzzy self-tuning PID controller, which can identify the variation of input variables and adjust parameters simultaneously, can be used to control more complex systems. By simulating the process of human brain and making full use of practical experience of operators, fuzzy control controller can adjust the parameters of PID controller online and control complex nonlinear system effectively.

A typical fuzzy PID control system is shown in Fig. 4.

Fuzzy PID controller takes deviation e, deviation change rate ec as input variable while using kp, ki and kd as output variables. Its working principle is based on traditional PID controller. According to the established fuzzy logic rules, input e and ec are treated with fuzzy processing and fuzzy operation respectively. The result of operation is sent into PID controller to realize the adjustment of PID parameters.

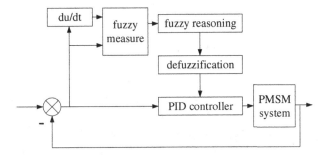

Fig. 4. Fuzzy PID controller

3.2 Membership Function and Fuzzy Rules

Through selection of quantization factor, basic domain of e, ec, kp and ki can be zoomed into fuzzy domain and the fuzzy sets is defined as {NB, NM, NS, Z0, PS, PM, PB}, corresponding to 7 vague words {negative big, negative median, negative small, zero, positive small, positive median, positive big}. The range of domain is [–3, 3], and the quantization level is {–3, –2, –1, 1, 2, 3}.

When setting PI controller parameters kp, ki, the relationship of them with deviations and deviations changing rate must be considered, and generally meet the following principles:

(1) when e is large, a large kp should be selected to achieve rapid response of system, and a small ki should be selected to reduce the overshoot of system by reducing its integral effect;
(2) when e and ec are at middle level, kp should be reduced appropriately, and the value of overshoot ki should be moderate to prevent excessive overshoot in system
(3) when e is small, it is necessary to increase kp and ki to reduce static error.

Based on above principles and after a lot of simulation debugging, the fuzzy rule table is obtained in Tables 1 and 2.

Table 1. kp fuzzy rule

e	ec						
	NB	NM	NS	ZO	PS	PM	PB
NB	PB	PB	PM	PM	PS	ZO	ZO
NM	PB	PB	PM	PS	PS	ZO	NS
NS	PM	PM	PM	PS	ZO	NS	NS
ZO	PM	PM	PS	ZO	NS	NM	NM
PS	PS	PS	ZO	NS	NS	NM	NM
PM	PS	ZO	NS	NM	NM	NM	NB
PB	ZO	ZO	NM	NM	NM	NB	NB

Tab. 2. ki fuzzy rule

e	ec						
	NB	NM	NS	ZO	PS	PM	PB
NB	NB	NB	NM	NM	NS	ZO	ZO
NM	NB	NB	NM	NS	NS	ZO	ZO
NS	NB	NM	NS	NS	ZO	PS	PS
ZO	NM	NM	NS	ZO	PS	PM	PM
PS	NM	NM	ZO	PS	PS	PM	PB
PM	ZO	ZO	PS	PS	PM	PB	PB
PB	ZO	ZO	PS	PM	PM	PB	PB

4   Simulation Results and Analysis

The power driveline model of electric vehicle is built based on Matlab-Simulink, as shown in Fig. 5. In driving mode, vehicle controller obtains the control value of vehicle motor by identifying driver's intention and chassis power. Because of complex road condition during vehicle driving, driver needs to operate accelerator pedal frequently, and the whole vehicle control system needs to satisfy driver's control feeling during acceleration. Consequently, the speed feedback and robustness of motor control system should be very reliable.

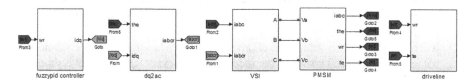

Fig. 5. Simulink model

Figure 6 shows the speed tracking of driveline model based on traditional PID speed loop and fuzzy self-tuning PID speed loop respectively. The target speed of model is simulated at 2000 r/m, and an additional interference of 100 N*m is set at 0. 1 s. The control system using fuzzy self-tuning PID has advantages of fast speed feedback and low overshoot. After interference, the tracking accuracy of fuzzy PID is lower than that of traditional PID due to wide basic domain of deviation E, but tracking speed of both is within allowable error range.

The control ability of traditional PID speed loop is invariant because of fixed value of KP and KI. If motor load changes, the output torque will fluctuate greatly. Figure 7 show the output torque of driveline. model based on fuzzy self-tuning PID and traditional PID in 0-2000 r/m acceleration process and additional interference respectively. Fuzzy self-tuning PID can obviously restrain torque ripple in case of vehicle load signal mutation. Its peak torque is 142 N*m, which is 17% less than that of traditional PID controller.

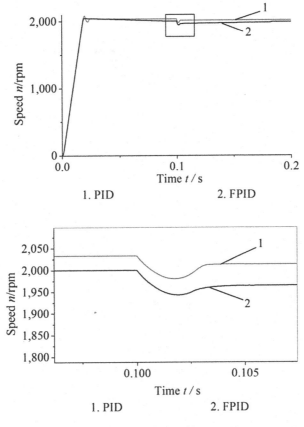

Fig. 6. Speed tracking

Figure 8 is phase current in motor controller. It can be seen that phase current distortion amplitude is smaller and attenuation is faster based on fuzzy self-tuning PID in case of control signal mutation at 0. 02 s and 0. 1 s.

FFT analysis is used to analyze the torque output data of system after 0. 1 s. The torque harmonic frequency on drive shaft is mainly concentrated in 0–100 Hz and 3700–4000 Hz. High frequency harmonic is generated by inverter switching signal in motor controller, while low frequency harmonic is generated by current distortion in controller. The output torque of model using fuzzy self-tuning PID is 2. 942 N*m at 40 Hz, which is only 78% of that of traditional PID model.

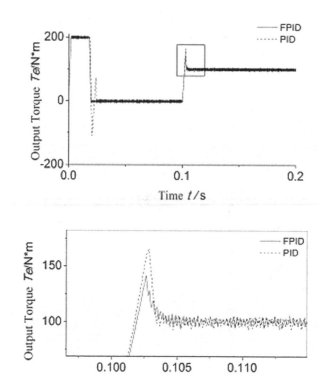

Fig. 7. Driveline output torque

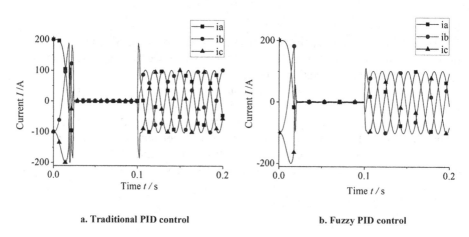

a. Traditional PID control   b. Fuzzy PID control

Fig. 8. Controller phase current based on traditional PID and Fuzzy PID

5   Conclusion

(1) Established simulation model effectively reflects the torsional vibration characteristics of electric vehicle power transmission system and provides a theoretical basis for further optimization of power output quality of transmission system.

(2) The design of fuzzy self-tuning PID controller can significantly improve speed feedback and robustness of motor controller, and improve the control performance of vehicle controller.

(3) The speed loop using fuzzy self-tuning PID can attenuate torque ripple caused by sudden change of load and control signal, reduce peak torque, and contribute a lot to solve the problem of torque ripple caused by electrical control.

References

1. Yu, P., Zhang, T., Wang, X., et al.: Powertrain torsional vibration of a central-driven pure EV. J. Vib. Shock **34**(10), 121–127 (2015)

2. Zhang, L.-J., Zheng, P., Meng, D.-J., et al.: Experimental study and control of longitudinal flutter during vehicle starting with motor drive mode for hybrid electric car. Automot. Eng. 35 (3), 212–218 (2013)

3. Turnbull, R., Miknas, O.R., Mohammadpour, M., et al.: Combined experimental and flexible multi-body dynamic investigation of high-energy impact-induced driveline vibration. Proc. Inst. Mech. Eng. Part K J. Multi Body Dyn. **231**, 181–193 (2016)

4. Ma, C., Zuo, S., Yang, D., et al.: Order feature analysis for torque ripple of permanent magnet synchronous motor for an electric vehicle. J. Vib. Shock **32**(13), 81–87 (2013)

5. Syed, F.U., Kuang, M.L., Ying, H.: Active damping wheel-torque control system to reduce driveline oscillations in a power-split hybrid electric vehicle. IEEE Trans. Veh. Technol. **58** (9), 4769–4785 (2009)

6. Wang, S., Kang, K., Zhong, Z., et al.: Overviews of torque ripple suppression method with permanent magnet synchronous motor used in electric vehicles. J. Power Supply **14**(5), 24–32 (2016)

7. Chen, Y., Zhang, D., Jiang, P.: Simulation analysis of vector control system for asynchronous motor in electric vehicles. J. Syst. Simul. **19**(16), 3761–3765 (2007)

8. Wang, C., Zhou, M., Guo, Q.: Vector Control AC Servo Drive Motor, pp. 1–20. Mechanical Industry Press, Beijing (1995)

9. Dost, P., Sourkounis, C., Agelidis, V.G.: On influence of deterministic and non-deterministic modulation schemes in two-level filter-less inverter performance driving a permanent magnet synchronous motor. In: Conference of the IEEE Proceedings of the Industrial Electronics Society, IECON 2013 (2014)

Exploring a Sustainable Business Routing for China's New Energy Vehicles: BYD as an Example

Yun Lin[1]([✉]) [iD], Jie Li[2] [iD], Xingjun Huang[1] [iD], Zhen Guo[1] [iD], Yi Sun[2] [iD], and Runzhi Zhang[1] [iD]

[1] College of Mechanical Engineering, Chongqing University, Chongqing 400030, China
linyun313@163.com
[2] School of Automotive Engineering, Chongqing University, Chongqing 400030, China

Abstract. The purpose of this paper is to explore the sustainable route of China's new energy vehicles with sustainable business model. It is based upon a case study of the new energy vehicles leader: BYD. In order to compare the different periods of business model of the example, business model canvas and triple layered business model canvas are proposed. Through the use of case studies drawn from real-world situations, BYD improve its technology to capture the market, innovate its business model to break the bottleneck. Other companies should learn from the merits of BYD's new energy vehicles development. The originality of the paper is that we compare the Business model canvas and Triple layered business model canvas and present a sustainable business approach, triple layered business model canvas, for new energy vehicle firms.

Keywords: Sustainability · China's new energy vehicles
Business model canvas · Triple layered business model canvas

1 Introduction

China is experiencing a rapid growth in new energy vehicles sales since 2000. Chinese government has issued several policies to encourage the production and purchase of new energy vehicles, planning to expand the new energy vehicles industry. However, it seems that private households have difficulties in finding new energy vehicles offerings sufficiently attractive. Therefore, it indicates business model innovations which are important complements to technology innovations should also be explored.

Business model innovation provides a potential way to re-conceptualize the purpose of the firm and the value creating logic, and rethink perceptions of value. As suggested by Stubbs and Cocklin [1] Porter and Kramer [2], the assertion is

K. Li et al. (Eds.): ICSEE 2018/IMIOT 2018, CCIS 925, pp. 70–80, 2018.
https://doi.org/10.1007/978-981-13-2381-2_7

that with careful business model redesign it is possible to more readily integrate sustainability into their business for mainstream businesses, design and pursuit sustainable business from the outset for new start-ups. Therefore, setting up a sustainable business model of China's new energy vehicles has been emerged as an important innovation.

This article uses the triple layer business model canvas (TLBMC) which builds on Osterwalder and Pigneur [3] original business model and allows for the incorporation of the triple bottom line in the process of business model design and innovation to communicate sustainable business model innovation of NEVs in China. Therefore, the study objectives are the following: establish the triple layer business model canvas on a specific firm, compare the original business model canvas and TLBMC, sum up the sustainable route for NEVs firms in China.

2   Methods

The method of this study sought to analysis sustainable business model by collecting existing cases and extracting necessary rules and conditions. We selected China's leader companies in the new energy vehicles industry-BYD as the exemplar case study. The steps proposed in Fig. 1 are followed below.

Fig. 1. Logic diagram

3   Results

The evolution of BYD's business model innovation has gone through two stages. The first stage is the fuel vehicle entering the market stage. The second stage is the new energy vehicle entering the market stage. As a result of the amount of information, we here summarize the business model canvas (Fig. 2)at the early stage and the three layer canvas (Figs. 3, 4 and 5) of BYD's new energy vehicles at the current stage.

Fig. 2. The business model canvas of BYD traditional fuel vehicles

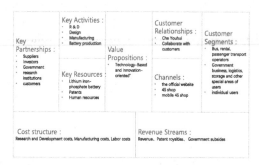

Fig. 3. The triple layered business model canvas's economic layer of BYD NEVs

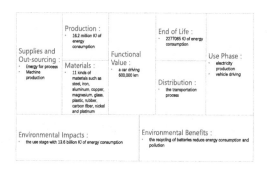

Fig. 4. The triple layered business model canvas's environmental layer of BYD NEVs

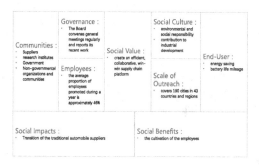

Fig. 5. The triple layered business model canvas's social layer of BYD NEVs

3.1   The Previous Fuel Vehicles Business Model

We believe that to describe a business model on economic layer can be done well by the nine modules, which demonstrate the logic of a company's searching for profit.

Customer segments. This module describes the different target groups and agencies a company wants to obtain and expect to serve. At early stage, When BYD enters the automotive industry, it uses the low-end car to make up for the gap in the market. The final customer of BYD's fuel car is the medium and low-end individual customer.

Value propositions. This module describes the provision of products and services that create value for a customer group. BYD insists on the talent as the fundamental management mode, with the imitation innovation as the technical path, with low cost and high quality as the competitive advantage.

Channels. This module describes how an organization can communicate and connect with its client base to convey its value proposition to them. BYD vehicles are available online and offline. And BYD innovate the new marketing model "mobile 4 S shop", which basically ensures the function of the "4S shop". Because of its special "mobile" nature, the sales and service will infiltrate to a wider Local.

Customer relationships. This module describes the model of a company's customer relationship established for a particular customer group. BYD establishes customer-centric development strategy, and establishes a car association to maintain customer relations. In addition, BYD provides an online community, set up Che Youhui for users to exchange knowledge.

Revenue streams. This module represents the cash earnings of an organization receives from each customer group. Early sales profit is the main source of income, gradually began to have a patent using income. BYD based on decomposition non-patented technology, has been widely used in the form of low cost high efficiency rapidly to own their own core technology, and apply for patent technology.

Key resources. This module describes the most important assets needed to ensure the smooth running of a business model. BYD implements humanistic management. In addition, BYD attaches great importance to technological innovation and has initiated "imitation innovation".

Key activities. This module describes the most important things that need to be done to keep your business model up and running. The main business includes the production of traditional fuel vehicles and related parts. BYD also improves the convenience and efficiency of automobile manufacturing by vertically integrating vertical supply chains while effectively reducing manufacturing costs.

Key partnerships. This module describes the network of suppliers and partners needed to keep a business model running smoothly. BYD's alliance with core suppliers to weaken the bargaining ability of suppliers. Safeguarding the rights and interests of investors has been a priority for BYD since its listing.

Cost structure. This module describes the full cost of running a business model. The costs of BYD are mainly by research and development costs, manufacturing costs, labor costs.

3.2   The New Energy Vehicles Business Model

The Business Model of BYD's New Energy Vehicles Based on Economic Layer. A sustainable business model on economic layer is based on the business model canvas. The TLBMC elements of the economic layer are used to describe the sustainable business model of BYD new energy vehicles.

Customer segments. BYD propose "bus electrification" strategy first to replace the traditional vehicles with new energy vehicle, and making bold innovations in the business model. Currently BYD's new energy vehicle products cover seven conventional fields including private vehicles, taxis, buses, coaches, logistics trucks, urban sanitation trucks, and construction trucks. What's more, the governments are also its target customers.

Value propositions. BYD always adheres to the "Technology-Based and Innovation-oriented" development philosophy. Currently BYD has established the Central Research Institute, the Auto Engineering Research Institute, the Electric Power Research Institute, the Truck and Special Vehicle Research Institute and the Light Rail Transit Research Institute, and has a total of approximately 20,000 sophisticated technical experts in hardware, software and testing.

Channels. BYD NEVs are still mainly sold through distributors. As the current company's new energy vehicle product categories are not yet abundant, BYD now uses BYD's traditional car sales channels.

Customer relationships. As in the early days, BYD provides an online community, set up Che Youhui for users. BYD also invested large sums of money each year for the club's integral reward program and riders' activities in all regions. Collaborate with customers to meet customer needs.

Revenue streams. The revenue of BYD new energy vehicles mainly come from two sides, one is sales revenue, the other is government subsides. The government provides strategic support to the NEVs industry through tariffs, subsidies and tax incentives. However, royalties are also part of the revenue streams.

Key resources. Based on the knowledge reserve of imitative innovation, BYD eventually leads to the path of independent innovation. As of 31 December 2016, BYD has accumulatively applied for 15,772 patents in China and 3,272 patents overseas. What's more, BYD adheres to the "people-oriented" principle in its human resources management, encourages employees to achieve technical innovation.

Key activities. BYD adhere to its own brand, independent research and development (R & D), with a complete industrial chain from R & D and design to create vehicles. The production of vehicles is still one of the key activities of BYD. With the development of new energy vehicles, battery production has become a major part of the new energy vehicle business.

Key partnerships. BYD seek to form a closed cycle for the suppliers' life cycle management and create an efficient, collaborative, win-win supply chain platform, and collaborate with customers to meet customer needs. What's more, BYD join research and technical cooperation with research institutions or academics. The government's subsidies and support for new energy vehicles have made BYD a partnership with the government.

Cost structure. Same as in the early days, the costs of BYD are mainly by research and development costs, manufacturing costs, labor costs. However, BYD invested more money to research and development design for new energy vehicles.

The Business Model of BYD's New Energy Vehicles Based on Environmental Layer. The environmental layer of the TLBMC builds on the life cycle perspective of environmental impact. The primary objective of the environmental layer of the TLBMC is to assess how the organization generates more environmental benefits than environmental impacts. BYD's first electric car, E6, was used as a research representative for data analysis.

Functional value. The functional value describes the focal outputs of a service (or product) of the organization being reviewed [4]. It simulates the functional unit in a life cycle assessment, which is a quantitative description of the service performance of the product system being investigated [5]. In this paper, the evaluation of the functional unit is a car driving 600,000 km. New energy vehicles throughout the life cycle of energy consumption and the main air pollutant emissions, including CO_2, NO_x, SO_x, CO, VOC, CH_4 [6].

Value propositions. BYD always adheres to the "Technology-Based and Innovation-oriented" development philosophy. Currently BYD has established the Central Research Institute, the Auto Engineering Research Institute, the Electric Power Research Institute, the Truck and Special Vehicle Research Institute and the Light Rail Transit Research Institute, and has a total of approximately 20,000 sophisticated technical experts in hardware, software and testing, who are engaged in the research and development in the areas of new materials, automobile, new energy and rail transit and actively promote the progress of the industry.

Materials. In the manufacturing process of the body material, 11 kinds of materials such as steel, iron, aluminum, copper, magnesium, glass, plastic, rubber, carbon fiber, nickel and platinum are considered. Assuming all steel are ordinary steel, all aluminum alloy is ordinary aluminum, copper, rubber, plastic and glass are regardless of model and species.

Production. The production component captures the actions that the organization takes to create value [4]. Using the GREET paint production, vehicle painting, vehicle assembly energy consumption, battery production energy consumption and emissions data, the total energy consumption of the automobile manufacturing stage are calculated synthetically. For BYD E6, 16.2 million KJ of energy consumption are produced during the car's manufacturing phase.

Supplies and out-sourcing. Supplies and out-sourcing represent all the other various material and production activities that are necessary for the organization to be functional, but not "core" [4]. For BYD E6, in the available data of the vehicle manufacturer, most of the impacts of supplies and outsourcing such as machines and energy were included in the use phase.

Distribution. Thus within the environmental layer, it is the combination of the transportation modes, the distances traveled and the weights of what is shipped which is to be considered. For BYD E6, distribution involves the shipment and packing of parts. In this paper, considering energy consumption and major air pollutant emissions in the manufacture, use and decommissioning phases of new energy vehicles, while consider the influence of the transportation process, mainly from the suppliers to the manufacturer, from the assembly line to the dealer, and from the consumers to the auto scrap yard [7].

Use phase. According to the "Mandatory Vehicle Scrapping Standards", the car travel 600,000 km that is scrapped standards, it is assumed that the car life cycle mileage of 60 million km, regardless of the length of time. For BYD E6, the use phase consists of two elements, electricity production and vehicle driving. The use phase generates 13.6 billion KJ of energy consumption, 97.4 million grams of CO_2,19.1 thousand grams of CO,48.1 thousand grams of SO_x,57.2 thousand grams of NO_x,157 thousand grams of dust,125 thousand grams of CH_4, and 8.33 thousand grams of VOC.

End-of-life. When the new energy vehicles reach the retirement age, some of the materials can be recycled after dismantling. Due to the lack of standard of car scrapping in China, the data of disassembly energy consumption is poor, so the data of GREET model is adopted that apart a 1360 kg of small passenger car required 1,476,090 KJ of energy consumption, dismantling a 2,098 kg of BYD E6 required 2,277,085 KJ of energy consumption.

Environmental impacts. The environmental impacts components extend the organizational impacts to include the organization's ecological costs [4]. For BYD E6, its environmental impacts can point to its largest contributor, the use stage with 13.6 billion KJ of energy consumption.

Environmental benefits. Environmental benefits refer to the amount of conventional pollutants and CO_2 emissions that can be reduced in the life cycle using alternatives. Compared to traditional fuel-powered vehicles, a unit of E6 can save fuel consumption by 14,120 litres, and reduce carbon dioxide emissions by 32 tons, sulfur dioxide emissions by 0.62 tons and nitrogen oxide emissions by 0.18 tons each year.

The Business Model of China's New Energy Vehicles Based on Social Layer. A key social aspect of TLBMC is to extend the original business model canvas through a stakeholder approach to both capture the interplay between stakeholders and the organization [4].

Social value. Social value reflects the aspect of an organization's mission, and its focus is more broadly to create benefits for stakeholders and society [4]. BYD strives to enhance the interest of government, shareholders, customers, employees, suppliers, partners and other stakeholders through innovative technology, products and management and sound commercial operation, seeking to earn the trust and respect of all stakeholders.

Employee. The employees' component provides a space to consider the role of employees as stakeholders in the core organization. BYD advocates "human-nurturing before goods-building" and emphases staff development. The quality and skills of staff are enhanced through training.

Governance. The governance component captures the organizational structure and decision strategy of an organization. The board convenes general meetings regularly and reports its recent work, supervises the overall operation and strategic development, and makes decision on the company's operation direction and investment plans; establish and complete a modern and standard organizational structure and enhance the efficiency and quality of investment decisions.

Communities. Economic relationships are built with business partners, while establishing social relationships with suppliers and local communities. BYD will train suppliers, in addition, BYD will organize seminars, join research projects and technical cooperation with research institutes. Not only cooperate with government, but also participate in community projects and non-governmental organizations meetings with non-governmental organizations and communities.

Social culture. The societal culture component recognizes the potential impact of an organization on society as a whole. BYD's strong corporate environmental and social responsibility and contribution to industrial development can be interpreted as a culture of accountability.

Scale of outreach. Scale of the outreach describes the depth and breadth of the organization's relationship with stakeholders over time. The global footprint of BYD new energy vehicles covers 190 cities in 43 countries and regions until February 29, 2016.

End-users. The end user is the "consumer" value proposition. For BYD, the end-user often happens to be the taxis, buses, coaches operators, government business, logistics, storage and transportation and other special areas of users, and low-end individual users. In the social canvas, BYD seeks to provide value by meeting the user's need in terms of energy saving and battery life mileage.

Social impacts. The social impacts partly solve the social cost of the organization. The development BYD new energy vehicles may impact on the relationship with the traditional automobile suppliers. Part of the traditional automobile suppliers is facing transition with the popularization of new energy vehicles.

Social benefits. Social benefits are the active social value creating aspects of the organization's action. BYD advocates "creation made man first" concept, pay attention to the cultivation of the employees, to improve the quality and skills of the staff.

4   Comparison and Discussion

4.1   Comparison of the Results

As shown in Fig. 6, the final results of the business models differ in various ways. Comparing to BYD fuel vehicles business model, the sustainable business model of new energy vehicles considers the environmental and social factor. The environmental layer supports the identification of opportunities to prevent pollution and reduce resource consumption through systematic analyses [5]. Based on the relationships of the stakeholders, the social layer stronger social benefits through the impact of strategic decision-making. Therefore, the sustainable business model provides three different interpretations. Furthermore, business strategies differ at different stages.

In contrast to the BMC of BYD fuel vehicles, where the customers are individual users, in the TLBMC of BYD new energy vehicles the combination of the mass market and public sector represent the impact of different actors on the business model. In addition, the use phase on the environmental layer includes some consideration of the client's material resource and energy saving though use. End user is the person in terms of energy saving and battery life mileage at present stage.

BYD, after imitative innovation, will eventually be able to move toward independent innovation. BYD has established three research and development systems: Shenzhen Academia Sinica, Electric Power Research Institute and Automotive Engineering Research Institute. For sustainable business model of

BYD NEVs, energy for process and machine production support the organization competitive advantage within the environmental layer. Similar to this, non-governmental organizations and communities are also considered for social value. Therefore, the sustainable business model of BYD NEVs not only consider "core" to the organization but also non-core to support the organization's value creation.

Fig. 6. Comparison of business model at different stages

4.2 Sustainability Implications of Case

The research has shown how BYD concretely put in place different business strategies at different stages. The case confirms that the correctness of the current sustainable business model to implement the sustainable development goals.

The case study demonstrates the applicability of the sustainable business model on the new energy vehicles, involving economic value, ecological value and social value. It also enables the other new energy vehicle firms to establish their business model in an effective and efficient way.

With the unprecedented speed at which customers' needs and behaviors are changing, a company's ability to rapidly adapt or generate innovative business models is critical to success. At present, new energy vehicles in the promotion period. The new energy vehicle firms should innovative ecological environment.

Besides, the case confirms that the sustainable business model is valuable for new energy vehicles firms. Analyzing the sustainable business model of new energy vehicles should emphasize adding value while reducing costs, reducing environmental pollution and increasing social benefits.

5 Conclusion

The objective of this paper is to analysis the China's new energy vehicles sustainable business model with the triple layered business model canvas. The case study confirms that the sustainable business model is valuable for new energy vehicles, and suggest that new energy vehicle firms should improve technology to capture the market, reduce the pollution and increase social benefits. The case study demonstrates the importance of innovation in order to find the suitable way of the new energy vehicles in particular period. What's more, the application of the TLBMC, a sustainable business model approach, in the case study demonstrate its applicability and efficacy. In contrast to BMC, the TLMBC offers a sustainable perspective on business model.

Acknowledgements. This work was supported in part by the National Social Science Fund of China (Grant No. 18BJY066), Fundamental Research Funds for the Central Universities (Grant No. 106112016CDJXZ338825), Chongqing key industrial generic key technological innovation projects (Grant No. cstc2015zdcy-ztzx60009), Chongqing Science and Technology Research Program (Grant No. cstc2015yykfC60002).

References

1. Robinson, J.: Squaring the circle? some thoughts on the idea of sustainable development. Ecol. Econ. **48**, 369–384 (2004)
2. Porter, M.E., Kramer, M.R.: The competitive advantage of corporate philanthropy. Harvard Bus. Rev. **80**(12), 57 (2002)
3. Osterwalder, A., Pigneur, Y.: Business Modell Generation. Willey, Hoboken (2010)
4. Joyce, A., Paquin, R.L.: The triple layered business model canvas: a tool to design more sustainable business models. J. Cleaner Prod. **135**, 1474–1486 (2016)
5. Rebitzer, G., Ekvall, T., Frischknecht, R.: Life cycle assessment part 1: framework, goal and scope definition, inventory analysis, and applications. Environ. Int. **30**(5), 701–720 (2004)
6. Gao, Y.B., Mao, X.Q., Yang, S.X.: Analysis and evaluation on energy conservation and emission reduction of new energy vehicles based on LCA. J. Environ. Sci. **33**(5), 1504–1512 (2013)
7. Liu, K.H.: Life Cycle Evaluation of BYD E6 Pure Electric Vehicle. Fujian Agriculture and Forestry University (2016)

Large-Scale Electric Vehicle Energy Demand Considering Weather Conditions and Onboard Technology

Simin Luo[1], Yan Tian[1], Wei Zheng[2], Xiaoheng Zhang[3],
Jingxia Zhang[3], and Bowen Zhou[3(✉)]

[1] Guangzhou Power Supply Bureau, Guangzhou 440100
Guangdong Province, China
81157183@qq.com, 498877376@qq.com
[2] State Grid Huludao Electric Power Supply Company, Huludao 125000,
Liaoning Province, China
zealweapon@163.com
[3] College of Information Science and Engineering, Northeastern University,
Shengyang 110819, Liaoning Province, China
1152707397@qq.com, 1101281415@qq.com,
zhoubowen@ise.neu.edu.cn

Abstract. Accurate knowledge of the state-of-charge (SOC) parameter estimated for electric vehicle (EV) batteries is of particular importance when calculating the EV energy demand. Many factors and methods have been proposed for SOC estimation. However, often methods focus on the battery itself rather than customer usage and related factors. This paper proposes a EV energy demand estimation method based on SOC, where onboard power electronics and weather conditions are considered. A practical mathematical model is proposed for large-scale EV provision in which a correction factor is included for calculation of actual maximum range. Typical values from real EVs and statistics are used to exemplify the model in a case study. The results presented in the paper indicate that with inclusion of weather factors and use of onboard technology, electricity consumption is greater and consequently the actual range of an EV is shortened and the EV energy demand is quantitatively increased.

Keywords: Electric Vehicle (EV) · State-of-Charge (SOC) · Energy demand
Weather condition · Onboard technology

1 Introduction

The state-of-charge (SOC) battery parameter provides a measured equivalent of the conventional fuel gauge for a battery electric vehicle (BEV) or plug-in hybrid electric vehicle (PHEV). The SOC indicates availability of the electric vehicle (EV) and helps customers manage their journeys, in much the same way as assessment of fuel in the tank. The remained SOC, also regarded as the initial SOC before charging, is one of the most important factors to determine the charging and discharging behavior of EVs. Many methods have been used to determine SOC since it cannot be measured directly [1].

© Springer Nature Singapore Pte Ltd. 2018
K. Li et al. (Eds.): ICSEE 2018/IMIOT 2018, CCIS 925, pp. 81–93, 2018.
https://doi.org/10.1007/978-981-13-2381-2_8

These methods can be grouped into three categories: electrochemistry-based, electric-based and a *practical* approach.

The electrochemistry- and electric-based methods can be considered as *detailed* approaches, meaning that several factors relating to battery chemistry and characteristics are considered. Electrochemistry methods [2–4] consider factors such as the types of electrolytes and electrodes, current density, ion concentration, and energy density. Electric-based methods [2–7] include battery parameters such as external voltage, current, temperature and efficiency. In both instances, SOC estimation is model-based requiring multiple inputs with a single (SOC) output.

Several other methods using, for example, the Thevenin Theorem [2], Neural Networks [5], Integral (Coulomb Counting Method) [6] and Kalman Filter [5, 7] are adopted for modelling.

In a practical approach, only the travel distance is considered [8, 9]. Thus, if SOC is assumed to drop linearly with distance, then after one day travel, SOC is reduced by $(1 - d/d_R)$, where d_R is the maximum range of the EV and d is the daily travel distance. A practical approach is considered a feasible basis for EV charging and discharging management in terms of sustainable power system operation and vehicle-to-grid (V2G) provision, since the number of factors – used in a more detailed method – is significantly reduced, thereby lessening the computational burden required for large-scale EV provision: a practical method need only consider the stochastic and intermittent characteristics of EVs, which includes the start charging time and initial SOC. Moreover, detailed approaches are usually adopted for individual EV SOC estimation. With large-scale EV integration, the accuracy and computational efficiency of detailed approaches require careful implementation, which may result in errors and time delays in a real-time context.

At present, EVs are characterized by: the maximum range (mi) and battery capacity (kWh); both are considered in Table 1. The maximum range is usually evaluated by practical testing, however onboard power electronics, device energy needs and weather conditions can impact energy consumption.

Table 1. Maximum range and battery size of EV

	Max range (mi)	Battery size (kWh)
Tesla Model S	300	85
Nissan Leaf	100	24
BMW i3	100	19
Mitsubishi i-MiEV	100	16
Ford Focus	100	23
Honda Fit	124	20
Volkswagen e-Golf	94	26.5
BYD e6	188	57
BYD Qin	125	35
DFM Venucia e30	109	24

Data from websites

It is apparent that onboard technology, such as air conditioning and entertainment devices, is often used to render a journey more flexible and pleasant. Usage of these electrical devices can dramatically reduce battery charge levels during travelling [10]. However, the mathematical impact is not clarified. Weather has previously been considered for renewable energy sources [11–13] and traditional vehicles [14], however limited work to date has discussed the impact of weather on EV SOC estimation. Leahy and Foley [14] provide a simple model which encompasses weather conditions however this has been discussed theoretically with no clear expression in a model. Jayaweera and Islam [15] have considered weather conditions in PHEV charging and discharging modelling, by arranging them in three categories: normal, moderate and severe. The weather categories are generated from a Gaussian distribution, but do not relate to actual and prevailing weather conditions. Wu et al. [16] explore the relationship between the driver's choice of "in-city routes" and local weather. The weather conditions are classified as clear, partly cloudy, cloudy, and rain. The data obtained is from real statistics but there is only one vehicle and the trips are only daily commutes. Several other papers [17–19] evaluate battery performance under different temperature conditions.

Therefore, it can be summarized from published work to date: (1) the use of onboard electronic devices and weather conditions are seldom considered; and (2) weather conditions are usually considered theoretically or ideally, which provides uncertainty.

This paper quantizes the impact of weather conditions and onboard consumption and estimates large-scale EV energy demand. A practical approach is adopted to determine the initial SOC after one day travel to indirectly estimate the energy demand. This paper is organized as follows: Sect. 2 discusses the quantization of weather conditions and onboard technology. Section 3 provides a mathematical expression for SOC, in which a maximum range is obtained. The probability density function (PDF) of initial SOC after one day travel is determined and typical values of influencing factors are presented. Finally, a case study is included in Sect. 4.

2 Quantization of Weather Conditions and Onboard Technology

2.1 Onboard Technology

In a conventional vehicle, onboard technology is powered by the vehicle battery, which is concurrently charged by the diesel or petrol fueled engine. In EVs however, all energy is supplied by the vehicle battery, including all system electronics, air conditioning, navigation aids and lights. Typical power requirements of various onboard electronic devices are listed in Table 2.

The total power consumed by electronic devices is expressed as,

$$P_{ele} = \eta_{AC}P_{AC} + \eta_{CD}P_{CD} + \eta_{Nav}P_{Nav} + \eta_{Scr}P_{Scr} + \eta_{ILi}P_{ILi} + \eta_{ELi}P_{ELi} \qquad (1)$$

Table 2. Power levels of typical onboard electronic devices

	Symbol	Power (kW)
Air conditioning	P_{AC}	3–5
CD player/Radio	P_{CD}	0.03–0.1
Navigator	P_{Nav}	0.02–0.2
Screen	P_{Scr}	0.05–0.2
Internal lights	P_{ILi}	>0.01
External lights	P_{ELi}	0.01–0.05

Data from websites

where η is the usage percentage of each device. The usage percentages can be obtained from statistics or real-time records.

2.2 Weather Conditions

It is apparent that people are more likely to use a car during rain or low temperatures [14]. Based on statistics and reasonable assumptions, day-ahead EV employment can be predicted using accurate weather forecasting, from which EV SOC after one day travel and EV capacity can be obtained.

In published work two parameters are frequently used to describe the probabilistic feature of EVs: the number of trips per day n; and the average travel distance per trip d_t. It is obvious that the daily travel distance d is the product of n and d_t. The probability density functions (PDF) of n and d_t are F_n and F_{dt}. However, there are two challenges in the application of F_n and F_{dt}:

(1) n and d_t are usually not independent variables under different weather conditions. When it is raining, people are more likely to travel by cars and public transport rather than bicycle, which leads to an increase in both n and d_t [14];
(2) There is lack of statistical data for n and d_t under different weather conditions. There is also little statistical data for d as well, but reasonable assumptions are made in the following discussions and case study.

Therefore, two parameters are proposed to describe weather under seven different conditions: (1) daily travel distance d and (2) daily average travel speed v_a. The PDF for d is periodic for weekdays and the weekend, as a consequence of the different trips. d is provided by the PDF as shown in Fig. 1, which is described as [8]

$$g(d; \mu, \sigma) = \frac{1}{d\sqrt{2\pi}\sigma} e^{-(\ln d - \mu)^2 / 2\sigma^2} \tag{2}$$

where μ is the $\log_e$ mean and σ is the standard deviation of the corresponding daily travel distance probability density distribution, $d > 0$.

Weather conditions include temperature, precipitation and wind. Typical values from UK statistics of these factors are listed in Table 3 [20]. Reasonable assumptions [21, 22] have been made due to lack of statistical data for some weather conditions.

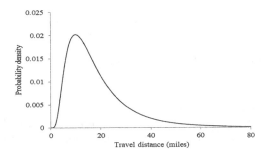

Fig. 1. PDF of daily travel distance

Table 3. Typical values of weather factor

	v_a (mi/h)	μ	σ
Normal day	18.42	3.20	0.6528
Low temperature	16.78	3.35	0.6499
High temperature	19.09	2.99	0.6584
Light precipitation	18.01	3.26	0.6523
Heavy precipitation	15.64	3.35	0.6499
Soft wind	18.15	3.22	0.6517
Strong wind	17.52	3.34	0.6505

μ and σ are not only affected by weather conditions but also by the statistical uncertainty. For example in 2008, the average (per annum) travel distance of private cars in Ireland was 16,376 km: in Dublin (capital city) travel distance was 12,886 km, while in more rural areas of the country, 17,241 km was the average travel [14]. Due to a lack of available statistical data, this paper has used published national statistical data for this case study.

3   A Customer-Based EV SOC Estimation Method

3.1   Mathematical Model

In this proposed method, a practical approach has been adopted in which it is not necessary to include the more extensive parameter set of detailed models. A practical consideration minimises computational burden (minimal parameterization), but importantly, provides a scalable solution in terms of large-scale EV integration and the necessity to develop information rapidly to reduce potential impacts on power system infrastructure through EV connection. Assuming that the capacity of EV battery packs is E_B, the SOC is estimated as,

$$\text{SOC} = (E_B - P_{tot} \cdot d/v_a)/E_B = 1 - (P_{tra} + P_{ele}) \cdot d/(v_a E_B)$$
$$= 1 - [E_B/(d_R/v_a) + P_{ele}] \cdot d/(v_a E_B) = 1 - (E_B/d_R + P_{ele}/v_a) \cdot d/E_B \qquad (3)$$
$$= 1 - (1/d_R + P_{ele}/v_a E_B) \cdot d = 1 - d/d_{RR}$$

where d_{RR} is the actual maximum range and $d_{RR} = 1/(1/d_R + P_{ele}/v_a E_B)$; P_{tra} is the average power consumption for traction; $P_{ele}/v_a E_B$ is the correction factor with respect to customer-based factors. E_B/d_R is the energy consumption of an EV travelling per unit distance; P_{ele}/v_a is the energy consumption of onboard technology and electronic devices per unit distance; $1/d_R$ is the SOC consumption of the EV travelling per unit distance; $P_{ele}/v_a E_B$ is also the SOC consumption of onboard technology and electronic devices per unit distance. In (3) the power loss is neglected and P_{tra} is assumed to be linear negative proportional to time.

3.2 Analysis of the Proposed Method

It is obvious that the longest possible travel distance for an EV is in the best interests of the user. However, while raw figures of available distance provide one measure of confidence for vehicle range, a more reliable basis for any confidence is accurate knowledge of battery capacity (cf. fuel remaining in the tank). Furthermore, accurate monitoring of onboard unit consumption can limit battery drain by load reduction or periodic connection. Thus, the problem can be considered as the minimization of the energy consumption (of onboard technology and electronic devices). The ratio of energy consumption of electronic devices with EV travelling is

$$\varepsilon = (P_{ele} d_R)/(v_a E_B) \qquad (4)$$

For a certain EV, P_{ele} is determined by statistics; d_R and E_B are determined by battery pack parameters; the other variable is daily average travel speed v_a. From (4) it can be determined that with a higher average travel speed, the ratio is smaller. Thus, taking into account (1), with less consumption, the ratio is smaller.

There are three variables in (3) which are P_{ele}, v_a and d, hence partial differentiation with respect to each variable renders,

$$\partial \text{SOC}/\partial P_{ele} = -d/v_a E_B \qquad (5a)$$

$$\partial \text{SOC}/\partial v_a = P_{ele} d/(v_a^2 E_B) \qquad (5b)$$

$$\partial \text{SOC}/\partial d = -(1/d_R + P_{ele}/(v_a E_B)) \qquad (5c)$$

Since all the parameters in (5a–5c) are positive, $\partial \text{SOC}/\partial P_{ele} < 0$, $\partial \text{SOC}/\partial v_a > 0$, and $\partial \text{SOC}/\partial d < 0$.

Therefore, as a brief conclusion, when onboard technology and device consumption is less, the daily average travel speed is higher and the daily travel distance is shorter. The longer the trip lasts, the longer the duration of power consumption by electrical loads, thus the higher the required energy by the electrical devices. In this work, it is assumed that the energy consumption by traction is independent on the vehicle's speed within the range given in Table 3. In comparison to raw estimates of travel distance, often based on vehicle manufacturer's specifications and published statistical data (e.g., Table 1) the effective travel distance of an EV will be shortened. It should also be noticed that battery degradation, which can influence battery capacity E_B, has not been included in this study, but its inclusion will be the subject of future work.

3.3 PDF of Initial SOC After One Day Travel

Taking (3) into (2), it can be derived that,

$$h(\text{SOC}; \mu, \sigma) = \frac{1}{d_{RR}(1 - \text{SOC})\sqrt{2\pi}\sigma}$$
$$\times \exp\left\{-[\ln(1 - \text{SOC}) + \ln(d_{RR}) - \mu]^2 \Big/ (2\sigma^2)\right\} \qquad (6)$$

The combined impact of multiple EV charging and/or discharging in a certain time interval at a certain power level can be modelled by (6) to provide a cumulative profile [23]. Time intervals and power levels can be determined by default values and the number of EVs calculated by optimization functions with certain objects considered.

Partial differentiation of (6) with respect to μ, σ, and d_{RR} are given in (7a–7c) below,

$$\frac{\partial h}{\partial \mu} = h \cdot \frac{\ln(1 - \text{SOC}) + \ln(d_{RR}) - \mu}{\sigma^2} = h \cdot \frac{\ln(d) - \ln(d_m)}{\sigma^2} \qquad (7a)$$

$$\frac{\partial h}{\partial \sigma} = h \cdot \frac{1}{\sigma} \cdot \left\{ \frac{[\ln(1 - \text{SOC}) + \ln(d_{RR}) - \mu]^2}{\sigma^2} - 1 \right\} = h \cdot \frac{1}{\sigma} \cdot \left\{ \frac{[\ln(d) - \ln(d_m)]^2}{\sigma^2} - 1 \right\}$$
$$\qquad (7b)$$

$$\frac{\partial h}{\partial d_{RR}} = h \cdot \frac{1}{d_{RR}} \cdot \left\{ \frac{\ln(1 - \text{SOC}) + \ln(d_{RR}) - \mu}{\sigma^2} - 1 \right\}$$
$$= h \cdot \frac{1}{d_{RR}} \cdot \left\{ \frac{\ln(d) - \ln(d_m)}{\sigma^2} - 1 \right\} \qquad (7c)$$

where d_m is the mean distance. Discussions of the influences of μ, σ, and d_{RR} on h are given in Table 4.

From Table 4 it can be determined that the PDF of battery SOC after one day travel is strongly affected by the parameters of this model as well as the initial SOC. Based on previous researches, the probabilities are calculated as the sum of the products of h and the number of EVs. However, the number of EVs is obtained by an optimization solution [25]. Moreover, the above parameters are usually calculated from statistics or defaults.

Table 4. Influences of the parameters in PDF

Conditions	Partial differential	Parameters changes	PDF changes
$d < d_m$	$\partial h / \partial \mu < 0$	$\mu \uparrow$	$h \downarrow$
$d > d_m$	$\partial h / \partial \mu > 0$	$\mu \uparrow$	$h \uparrow$
$d/d_m < e^{-\sigma}$ or $d/d_m > e^{\sigma}$	$\partial h / \partial \sigma > 0$	$\sigma \uparrow$	$h \uparrow$
$e^{-\sigma} < d/d_m < e^{\sigma}$	$\partial h / \partial \sigma < 0$	$\sigma \uparrow$	$h \downarrow$
$d/d_m < e^{\sigma^2}$	$\partial h / \partial d_{RR} < 0$	$d_{RR} \uparrow$	$h \downarrow$
$d/d_m > e^{\sigma^2}$	$\partial h / \partial d_{RR} > 0$	$d_{RR} \uparrow$	$h \uparrow$

$\uparrow$ and $\downarrow$ mean increasing and decreasing respectively.

4   Case Study

In this case study, a maximum travel distance of approximately 80 miles is assumed for EVs with a typical 25 kWh lithium-ion battery [24]. Thus, $d_R = 80$ mi and $E_B = 25$ kWh. Three cases are considered as follows:

(1) Case I: Normal day without usage of onboard technology or electronic devices;
(2) Case II: Normal day with limited use of onboard technology and devices;
(3) Case III: 10% usage of onboard technology and devices under different weather conditions as follows: III-A: Low temperature; III-B: High temperature; III-C: Light precipitation; III-D: Heavy precipitation; III-E: Soft wind; III-F: Strong wind;

4.1   Case I

In this case, $d_{RR} = d_R = 80$, $P_{ele} = 0$. The PDF of initial SOC after one day travel is shown in Fig. 2(a).

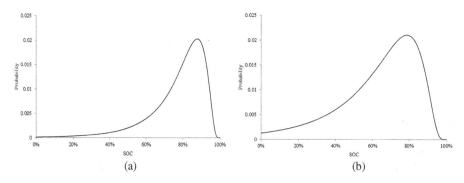

(a)   (b)

Fig. 2. (a) PDF of initial SOC in normal day, (b) PDF of initial SOC in normal day with onboard electronic devices in use

Figure 2 can be regarded as an SOC-axis reflection of Fig. 1 since it is simply calculated by $1 - d/d_R$. Figure 2 also demonstrates the discussion on (5c).

4.2   Case II

In this case, the power levels in Table 2 were set as moderate values. Thus, $P_{ele} = 4.28$ if η is assumed to be 100% for different devices. Then, $d_{RR} = 45.88$. The PDF of initial SOC after one day travel is shown in Fig. 2(b).

From Fig. 2(b) it can be seen that there is a slight curtailment when the SOC is small. The curtailment indicates that use of onboard technology and devices could significantly reduce the EV maximum range.

Figure 3 provides the trend of maximum ranges with the change of device usage, demonstrating the discussion in (5a). It is apparent that air conditioning consumes the greatest energy, if used throughout a trip; hence the vehicle distance is reduced to 60% of effective range. Other onboard devices, in comparison, have less impact on consumption rendering 4.6% reduction in vehicle range. Therefore minimizing the use of air conditioning in particular will limit the reduction of actual EV range.

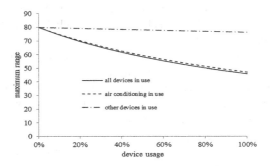

Fig. 3. Maximum range with device usage

4.3   Case III

Substituting the values in Table 3 into (3), (4) and (6), the PDFs of initial SOC under different weather conditions are obtained in Fig. 4.

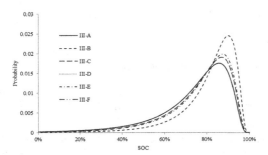

Fig. 4. PDFs under different weather conditions

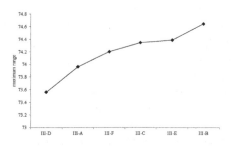

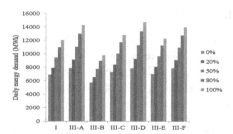

Fig. 5. Maximum ranges under different weather conditions

Fig. 6. Daily EV energy demand

Cases III-A, D and F have similar performances since the parameters do not vary significantly. In terms of actual weather conditions, it means that the travel patterns under low temperature, heavy precipitation and strong wind are similar. There are slight curtailments when the SOC is small, which can barely be seen from this figure. It will be illustrated in Fig. 5.

During light precipitation (Case III-C) and soft wind (Case III-E), the PDFs are close to the PDF in normal day due to similar travel patterns.

Case III-B shows that during high temperature there will be more capacity left in the EV battery based on the data in Table 3, meaning that people are more likely to use other transport to substitute EVs, which has the same conclusion in [14].

Figure 4 demonstrates the discussion in Table 4. The integrals of each curve in Fig. 4 are able to show the EV employment under various weather conditions. For example, the integral of Case III-B from 0% to 80% is smaller than that of Case III-A. It means that the initial SOC is higher when the temperature is higher, which also indicates that there is less EV use.

It should be noted that the different percentages of onboard technology and electronic device use are not related to different weather conditions in this case due to a lack of statistical data.

Figure 5 provides the maximum ranges under different weather conditions. Based on the data in Table 3, the cases are ordered with the increase of v_a also demonstrating the discussion in (5b), such that the effective travel distance rises with the increase of daily average travel speed.

4.4 Impact on EV Daily Energy Demand

The daily energy demand under different weather conditions with different levels of onboard technology and devices usage (0%–100%) is shown in Fig. 6. UK 2020 EV scale is considered [25].

From Fig. 6 it can be seen that EV energy demand increases with use of onboard technology and devices. In comparison with Fig. 6 it can be concluded that shorter effective range results in higher energy demand. Furthermore, both onboard technology and weather conditions influence EV daily demand, which consequently affect EV optimal charging and discharging [23].

5 Conclusions

The EV is considered a viable solution to offset excess consumption of fossil fuels for human transport. Many global countries are actively encouraging large-scale EV provision, though the most significant user concern is the actual range of commercial EVs. This paper connects the EV battery SOC with daily travel distance and estimates the EV energy demand by including customer-based factors, such as the level of onboard technology, electronic devices and prevailing weather conditions. The PDF of the initial battery SOC and actual maximum range of EV can be obtained. A correction factor is used in the SOC estimation method to include onboard energy consumption. Typical values of the parameters for PDFs under various weather conditions are given based on published statistics and basic assumptions of use. Moreover, the influence of basic onboard consumption patterns has also been analyzed.

The PDFs of the SOC under various weather conditions and the influences of customer-based consumption on EV maximum range have been exemplified in a case study. The results quantitatively show that with inclusion of onboard consumption, the actual travel range of an EV is reduced. Air conditioning in particular is a dominant onboard consumer and its use may reduce the maximum practical range to 60% of projected distance. Thus, minimizing air conditioning usage can extend the actual EV range. This paper has also established that a reduction in the use of onboard electronic devices, higher daily average travel speed, and a shorter daily travel distance will result in a higher (initial) SOC, thus providing a greater range thereafter.

The PDFs under low temperature, heavy precipitation and strong wind are similar, and the PDFs under light precipitation and soft wind are close to the PDF in a normal day. This is because the travel patterns under these weather conditions are similar. Furthermore, other transport is likely to be used to substitute EVs when outside temperatures are hot.

Both onboard technology and weather conditions influence EV daily energy demand. EV energy demand increases with use of onboard technology and devices. A shorter effective range results in higher energy demand.

Acknowledgments. This paper was supported by the National Natural Science Foundation of China (61703081), and Natural Science Foundation of Liaoning Province (20170520113).

References

1. Pop, V., Bergveld, H.J., Notten, P.H.L., et al.: State-of-the-art of battery state-of-charge determination. Meas. Sci. Technol. **16**(4), R93–R110 (2005)
2. Williamson, S.S.: Future charging infrastructures and energy management strategies for electric and plug-in hybrid electric vehicles. In: 2012 25th IEEE Canadian Conference on Electrical & Computer Engineering (CCECE), pp. 1–3. IEEE Press, New York (2013)
3. Erjavec, J.: Hybrid, Electric & Fuel-Cell Vehicles, 2nd edn. Delmar, New York (2013)
4. Stević, Z.: New Generation of Electric Vehicles. InTech, Rijeka (2012)
5. Liu, W., Xuan, Z., Jian, M.: A new neural network model for the state-of-charge estimation in the battery degradation process. Appl. Energy **121**, 20–27 (2014)

6. Xu, J., Mi, C.C., Cao, B., et al.: The state of charge estimation of lithium-ion batteries based on a proportional-integral observer. IEEE Trans. Veh. Technol. **63**, 1614–1621 (2014)
7. Zhang, C., Li, K., Pei, L., et al.: An integrated approach for real-time model-based state-of-charge estimation of lithium-ion batteries. J. Power Sources **283**, 24–36 (2015)
8. Zhang, P., Qian, K., Zhou, C., et al.: A methodology for optimization of power systems demand due to electric vehicle charging load. IEEE Trans. Power Syst. **27**, 1628–1636 (2012)
9. Cai, H., Du, W., Yu, X., et al.: Day-ahead optimal charging/discharging scheduling for electric vehicles in micro-grids. In: 2nd IET Renewable Power Generation Conference (RPG 2013), pp. 1–4. IET, London (2013)
10. Qi, Z.: Advances on air conditioning and heat pump system in electric vehicles – a review. Renew. Sustain. Energy Rev. **38**, 754–764 (2014)
11. Chukwu, U.C., Mahajan, S.M.: V2G parking lot with PV rooftop for capacity enhancement of a distribution system. IEEE Trans. Sustain. Energy **5**, 119–127 (2014)
12. Farghal, S.A., Tantawy, M.A., El-Alfy, A.E.: Optimum design of stand alone solar thermal power system with reliability constraint. IEEE Trans. Energy Convers. **EC-2**, 215–221 (2009)
13. Chien, J., Tseng, K., Yan, B.: Design of a hybrid battery charger system fed by a wind-turbine and photovoltaic power generators. Rev. Sci. Instrum. **82**, 095106 (2011)
14. Leahy, P.G., Foley, A.M.: Impact of weather conditions on electric vehicle performance. In: Proceedings of the Irish Transport Research Network Conference 2011, ITRN2011, Cork, pp. 1–4 (2011)
15. Jayaweera, D., Islam, S.: Risk of supply insecurity with weather condition-based operation of plug in hybrid electric vehicles. IET Gener. Transm. Distrib. **8**, 2153–2162 (2014)
16. Wua, X., Freeseb, D., Cabrerab, A., et al.: Electric vehicles' energy consumption measurement and estimation. Transp. Res. Part D Transp. Environ. **34**, 52–67 (2015)
17. Engvall, L., Cook, A., Khaligh, A.: A predictive trip-based method for state of charge maintenance in series PHEVs to boost cold weather efficiency. In: 2012 IEEE Transportation Electrification Conference and Expo (ITEC), pp. 1–6. IEEE Press, New York (2012)
18. Smith, R., Morison, M., Capelle, D., et al.: GPS-based optimization of plug-in hybrid electric vehicles' power demands in a cold weather city. Transp. Res. Part D Transp. Environ. **16**, 614–618 (2011)
19. Shams-Zahraei, M., Kouzani, A.Z., Kutter, S., et al.: Integrated thermal and energy management of plug-in hybrid electric vehicles. J. Power Sources **216**, 237–248 (2012)
20. Department for Transport: National Travel Survey 2012. https://www.gov.uk/government/publications/national-travel-survey-2012
21. National Grid: Historical Demand Data. http://www2.nationalgrid.com/UK/Industry-information/Electricity-transmission-operational-data/Data-explorer/
22. Tsapakis, I., Cheng, T., Bolbol, A.: Impact of weather conditions on macroscopic urban travel times. J. Transp. Geogr. **28**, 204–211 (2013)
23. Mahmassani, H.S., Dong, J., Kim, J., et al.: Incorporating weather impacts in traffic estimation and prediction systems. US Department of Transportation. FHWA-JPO-09-065, EDL# 14497 (2009)
24. Zhou, B., Littler, T., Foley, A.: Electric vehicle capacity forecasting model with application to load levelling. In: IEEE PES General Meeting 2015, pp. 1–5. IEEE Press, New York (2015)
25. European commission: Energy Roadmap 2050 Impact assessment and scenario analysis. SEC(2011) 1565 final (2011)

26. Zhou, B., Littler, T., Wang, H.: The impact of vehicle-to-grid on electric power systems: a review. In: IET Renewable Power Generation Conference 2013, pp. 1–4. IET, London (2013)
27. Cui, M., Ke, D., Sun, Y., et al.: Wind power ramp event forecasting using a stochastic scenario generation method. IEEE Trans. Sustain. Energy **6**(2), 422–433 (2015)
28. Cui, M., Zhang, J., Wu, H., et al.: Wind-friendly flexible ramping product design in multi-timescale power system operations. IEEE Trans. Sustain. Energy **8**(3), 1064–1075 (2017)
29. Cui, M., Zhang, J., Florita, A., et al.: An optimized swinging door algorithm for identifying wind ramping events. IEEE Trans. Sustain. Energy **7**(1), 150–162 (2016)

Siting and Sizing of Distributed Generation and Electric Vehicle Charging Station Under Active Management Mode

Weilu Shan[✉], Xue Li[✉], and Dajun Du

Shanghai Key Laboratory of Power Station Automation Technology, Shanghai University, Shanghai 200072, China
shanweilu2@shu.edu.cn, lixue@i.shu.edu.cn

Abstract. This paper is concerned with bi-level joint planning model of distributed generation (DG) and electric vehicle charging station (EVCS) siting and sizing under active management (AM) mode. Firstly, the joint planning model including DG and EVCS is established by taking the lowest annual comprehensive cost as the upper level objective. Then, the lower level model optimizes DG output curtailment by taking the uncertainty of load, EVCS charging load, and the intermittent DG output of wind farm and photovoltaic generator into account. According to the bidirectional interaction of upper and lower levels, the bi-level planning model is optimized by biogeography-based optimization (BBO) and primal-dual interior point method (PDIPM) respectively. Finally, simulation is operated on the revised IEEE-33 nodes distribution network, and simulation results show that the joint planning of DG and EVCS can obtain better planning scheme.

Keywords: Distributed generation (DG)
Electric vehicle charging station (EVCS)
Biogeography-based optimization (BBO) · Joint bi-level planning

1 Introduction

With the rapid development of the energy market and increasing attention to environmental protection, distributed generation (DG) and electric vehicle (EV) with clean advantages are playing an increasingly key role in the distribution network, which is the development trend of the power industry [1, 2]. A large number of DG and EV are accessed to distribution network, which present a severe challenge to the existing passive management model. Consequently, active management (AM) mode is proposed, where DGs and electric vehicle charging station (EVCS) are treated as part of the distribution network. However, it is necessary to study the joint optimal planning of DG and EVCS under AM mode.

Some research works have been proposed to the siting and sizing of DG and EVCS in the active distribution network (ADN). Considering the uncertainty of intermittent DWG, optimal planning of batteries in the ADN is presented, and the model is solved by a hybrid tabu search/particle swarm optimization (TS/PSO) algorithm [3]. It is

© Springer Nature Singapore Pte Ltd. 2018
K. Li et al. (Eds.): ICSEE 2018/IMIOT 2018, CCIS 925, pp. 94–104, 2018.
https://doi.org/10.1007/978-981-13-2381-2_9

assumed that DG can provide the critical loads of the distribution system by reallocating after some accident, and a hierarchical approach is proposed to assess the impact of changing of the distribution system in power system risk assessment [4]. The siting and sizing model of EVCS is established by taking lowest annual comprehensive cost as the objective considering the service radius of EVCS and environmental factors [5]. A cost-effective model is proposed to optimal the siting of EVCS, which can provide the best returns on investment while also meeting critical service requirements [6]. However, these studies are not concerned with the joint planning of DG and EVCS.

To solve these problems, a bi-level joint planning model of DG and EVCS siting and sizing under AM mode is established by taking the uncertainties of EVCS charging load, wind turbine generator (WTG), photovoltaic generator (PVG) and load into account. The upper planning aims at DG and EVCS joint planning with the goal of minimizing annual comprehensive cost, and the lower planning optimizes DG output curtailment. Furthermore, the upper and lower models are solved by biogeography-based optimization (BBO) and primal-dual interior point method (PDIPM), respectively.

The rest of this paper is organized as follows: the models of EVCS charging load, WTG, PVG, and load are given in Sect. 2. Section 3 presents the bi-level joint planning model and solution method for siting and sizing of DG and EVCS. Simulations are given in Sect. 4, following the conclusion in Sect. 5.

2 Modeling of EVCS Charging Load, WTG/PVG and Load

To describe the uncertainty of EVCS charging load, WTG, PVG and load, this paper divides 24 h a day into 24-time intervals for the accurate description of the input random variable and uses different models to describe the random variables.

2.1 EVCS Charging Load Model

According to the relevant experimental research, the charging and discharging power of EV can be approximately obeyed normal distribution [7], and the charge and discharge power can be expressed by normal distribution:

$$P_v \sim N(\mu_v, \sigma_v^2), \tag{1}$$

where P_v is the active power of EV charging demand; μ_v and σ_v^2 are the mean and standard deviation of the EV charging demand, respectively.

2.2 WTG/PVG and Load Models

Consider that the wind speed and light intensity are subjected to two parameters Weibull distribution [8] and beta distribution [9], PVG active power output P_{PVG} and WTG active power output P_{WTG} can be expressed as:

$$P_{PVG} = \begin{cases} P_{PVG,r}S/S_r, & S \leq S_r, \\ P_{PVG,r}, & S > S_r. \end{cases} \quad (2)$$

$$P_{WTG} = \begin{cases} 0, & v < v_{ci}, v > v_{co}, \\ \dfrac{v - v_{ci}}{v_r - v_{ci}} P_{WTG,r}, & v_{ci} \leq v \leq v_r, \\ P_{WTG,r}, & v_r < v \leq v_{out}. \end{cases} \quad (3)$$

where $P_{PVG,r}$ and $P_{WTG,r}$ are the rated output power of PVG and WTG, S_r is the rated light intensity, V_{ci} is cut-in wind speed, V_{co} is cut-out wind speed, V_r is rated wind speed.

The load can be described by normal distribution [10]:

$$P_{load} \sim N(\mu_p, \sigma_p^2), \quad (4)$$

where P_{load} is the active load, μ_p and σ_p^2 are the mean and standard deviation of the load, respectively.

3 Bi-level Planning Model and Solution for Siting and Sizing of DG and EVCS Under AM Mode

The main barrier for reaching the higher levels of DG in distribution network is the node voltage limit exceeding [11–13]. In order to overcome the above obstacle, two AM methods are used: (1) DG output controlling. The output of DG is adjusted by load at various times. (2) On-load-tap-changer (OLTC): OLTC maintains the network voltages within defined limits by actively changing the tap-changer setting at primary substation.

Then, a bi-level DG and EVCS siting and sizing joint planning model under AM mode is proposed, and the model takes the minimum annual comprehensive cost of DG and EVCS as the upper level planning objective. Furthermore, based on the siting and sizing of DG and EVCS, the lower level model optimizes DG output curtailment.

3.1 Upper Level Planning Model

The planning objective of the upper level model is shown as:

$$\min F_{total} = F_{inv,DG} + F_{inv,EVCS} + F_{OM,DG} + F_{OM,EVCS} + F_{loss} + F_{AM} - F_U, \quad (5)$$

where F_{total} is the annual comprehensive cost, $F_{inv,DG}$ and $F_{inv,EVCS}$ are the installation and investment cost of DG and EVCS, respectively, $F_{OM,DG}$ and $F_{OM,EVCS}$ are the annual operation and maintenance cost of DG and EVCS, F_{loss} is the annual active losses cost of the distribution network; F_{AM} is the cost of AM and F_U is the environmental subsidies of the renewable DG. $F_{inv,DG}, F_{inv,EVCS}, F_{OM,DG}, F_{OM,EVCS}, F_{loss}, F_{AM}$ and F_U can be calculated by:

$$F_{inv,DG} = \sum_{i \in N_{DG}} X_{inv,DG} w_{DG,i} \frac{r(1+r)^n}{(1+r)^n - 1}, \tag{6}$$

$$F_{inv,EVCS} = \sum_{i \in N_{EVCS}} (X^1_{inv,EVCS} + X^2_{inv,EVCS} w_{EVCS,i}) \frac{r(1+r)^n}{(1+r)^n - 1}, \tag{7}$$

$$F_{OM,DG} = 365 \sum_{t \in T} \sum_{i \in N_{DG}} X_{OM,DG} P_{DG,i,t} \Delta t, \tag{8}$$

$$F_{OM,EVCS} = 365 \sum_{t \in T} \sum_{i \in N_{EVCS}} X_{OM,EVCS} P_{EVCS,i,t} \Delta t, \tag{9}$$

$$F_{loss} = 365 \sum_{t \in T} X_{loss} P_{loss,t} \Delta t, \tag{10}$$

$$F_{AM} = 365 \sum_{t \in T} \sum_{i \in N_{DG}} X_{AM} P_{DG,i,t} \Delta t, \tag{11}$$

$$F_U = 365 \sum_{t \in T} \sum_{i \in N_{DG}} X_U P_{DG,i,t} \Delta t, \tag{12}$$

where N_{DG} and N_{EVCS} are DG and EVCS installation nodes, respectively; $X_{inv,DG}$ is the installation and investment cost of unit DG; $w_{DG,i}$ is the installation capacity at the candidate node i of DG; r is the discount rate, taking 10%; n is the economic life, taking 20 years; $X^1_{inv,EVCS}$ and $X^2_{inv,EVCS}$ are fix and variable investment cost of EVCS, respectively; $w_{EVCS,i}$ is the installation capacity at the candidate node i of EVCS; $T = 24h$; $X_{OM,DG}$ and $X_{OM,EVCS}$ are the operation and maintenance cost of unit of electricity by DG and EVCS; $P_{DG,i,t}$ and $P_{EVCS,i,t}$ are the charging load of the DG and EVCS at the candidate node i in period t; Δt is the time interval, taking $1\ h$; X_{loss} is the electricity price; $P_{loss,t}$ is the electricity losses in period t; X_{AM} is the AM cost of unit of electricity by DG; X_U is the environmental subsidies of unit of electricity by renewable DG.

The constraints of upper level planning model can be described as:

(1) DG penetration constraint:

$$\sum_{i \in N_{DG}} w_{DG,i} = \beta \sum_{j \in N_{node}} L_j, \tag{13}$$

$$w_{DG,i} = w_{WTG,i} + w_{PVG,i}, \tag{14}$$

where, $w_{WTG,i}$ and $w_{PVG,i}$ are the installation capacity at the candidate node i of WTG and PVG, respectively; β is the DG penetration; L_j is the load peak of the load node i.

(2) DG installation constraint:

$$w_{DG,i}\text{min} \leq w_{DG,i} \leq w_{DG,i}\text{max}. \tag{15}$$

(3) EVCS installation constraint:

$$w_{EVCS,i}\text{min} \leq w_{EVCS,i} \leq w_{EVCS,i}\text{max}. \tag{16}$$

3.2 Lower Level Planning Model

The lower level model is a typical optimal power flow (OPF), and the objective is to minimize DG output curtailment, which can be shown as follow:

$$\min \sum_{t \in T} \sum_{i \in N_{DG}} P_{cur,i,t}, \tag{17}$$

where $P_{cur,i,t}$ is the active power curtailment of DG.

The constraints of lower level planning model can be described as follows:

(1) Common network constraint:

$$P_{is} = U_i \sum_{j \in i} U_j(G_{ij} \cos \theta_{ij} + B_{ij} \sin \theta_{ij}), \tag{18}$$

$$Q_{is} = U_i \sum_{j \in i} U_j(G_{ij} \sin \theta_{ij} - B_{ij} \cos \theta_{ij}), \tag{19}$$

$$U_i^{min} \leq U_i \leq U_i^{max}, i \in N_{node}, \tag{20}$$

$$S_{ij} \leq S_{ij}^{max}, ij \in N_{line}, \tag{21}$$

where, P_{is} and Q_{is} is active power and reactive power of node i respectively; U_i is the voltage of node i; $j \in i$ represent all the nodes that directly connected with node i; G_{ij} and B_{ij} are the real and imaginary part of node admittance matrix; θ_{ij} is phase angle difference between the nodes i and j; N_{node} is a set of system nodes; S_{ij} is the power flow of branch ij; N_{line} is a set of system branches.

(2) On-load tap-changer (OLTC) transformer tap adjustment constraint.

$$T_k^{min} \leq T_k \leq T_k^{max}, k \in N_T, \tag{22}$$

where, T_k is the position of transformer tap; N_{node} is a set of OLTC branches.

(3) DG output curtailment constraint.

$$P_{cur,i,t}^{min} \leq P_{cur,i,t} \leq P_{cur,i,t}^{max}, i \in N_{DG}. \tag{23}$$

3.3 Bi-level Planning Model

The upper level planning is the sub-problem of siting and sizing for DG and EVCS, and the lower level planning is the sub-problem of optimizing DG output curtailment. While the upper level model transfers the DG and EVCS planning scheme to the lower level, and the lower level model optimizes DG output curtailment, then, the lower model passes the optimized DG output value to the upper model.

The upper level optimization is solved by the BBO [14, 15], BBO was proposed to solve optimization problems, and it is one of the fast-growing nature-inspired algorithms for solving practical optimization problems. BBO includes migration operator and mutation operator, the structure flow chart of the BBO is shown in Fig. 1, and the details are described in [14].

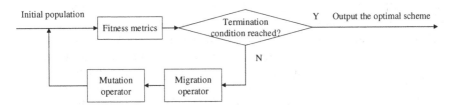

Fig. 1. Structure flowchart of BBO.

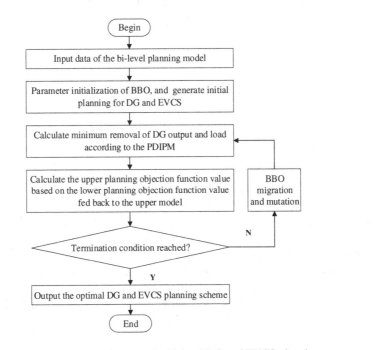

Fig. 2. Flow chart of solving the bi-level DG and EVCS planning

The lower level is solved by the PDIPM [16], Monte Carlo simulation (MCS) [17] is used for the uncertainties sampling of EVCS charging load. Then, WTG, PVG, and load, then, the DG output curtailment can be calculated by PDIPM, which is the lower level objective value.

The BBO and PDIPM are used to solve the upper and lower level planning, respectively, the whole process is shown in Fig. 2.

4   Simulation Results

4.1   Study Introduction

The case used for siting and sizing of DG and EVCS is IEEE-33 nodes system as shown in Fig. 3 [18]. The example is a 12.6 kV system and the planning is fixed to 20 years. The rated wind speed, cut-in and cut-out wind speed are 14 m/s, 3.5 m/s, and 20 m/s respectively; power factor is 0.95; the rated light intensity is 1000 W/m^2; load and EVCS charging load square variance are both 0.1; MCS hits are 500. Installation and investment cost of DG and EVCS are set as 400 \$/kW and 443 \$/kW. Fix and variable investment cost of EVCS are set as 285.71 and 714.29 \$/kW. Operation and maintenance costs of WTG, PVG and EVCS are set as 0.05 \$/kWh, 0.03 \$/kWh, and 0.09 \$/kWh. Electricity purchasing price is 0.08 \$/kWh, AM cost for WTG and PVG are both 0.01 \$/kWh, the environmental subsidies for WTG and PVG are both 0.04 \$/kWh.

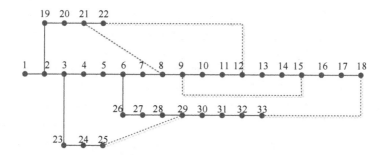

Fig. 3. 33 nodes distribution power system of IEEE

There are three candidate nodes of WTG in the distribution system, which are the nodes 8, 12 and 17. Three candidate nodes of WTG are nodes 5, 25 and 30, and six candidate nodes of EVCS are the nodes 4, 8, 12, 15, 25, and 30. The rated capacity of unit DG is 10 kW, access limit is both 10 of WTG and PVG. DG penetration is less than 10%, and the EVCS charging load requirements is 600 kW.

The typical load curve of EVCS is based on the data in [19], and the 1440 charge load points are normalized and averaged for each hour. The charge load per hour is shown in Fig. 4.

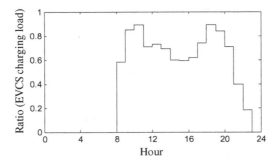

Fig. 4. Typical charging profile of EVCS

4.2 Analysis of the Results

Apply the above mentioned bi-level model to the case as scheme 1. For comparative analysis the effects of the DG and EVCS joint planning, scheme 2 is done under the same parameters, and the DG and EVCS are individual planning in scheme 2.

The DG and EVCS siting and sizing planning results for scheme 1 and scheme 2 are shown in Tables 1 and 2, respectively. It is known from Table 1 that the DG access capacities for schemes 1 and 2 are 370 kW and 310 kW, respectively, compared with scheme 2, the DG access capacity of scheme 1 is increased by 16.35%, so the joint planning of DG and EVCS can improve the access capacity of DG. From Table 2, schemes 1 and 2 access to 5 EVCSs (nodes 4, 8, 15, 25, and 30) and 6 EVCSs (nodes 4, 8, 12, 15, 25, and 30), respectively. However, the total access capacity of both schemes is 600 kW, which meets the EVCS charging load requirements.

Table 1. The DG planning results of two schemes

	Node number (DG capacity/kW)	Total capacity (kW)
Scheme 1	8(80),12(80),17(100),5(60),25(50),30(0)	370
Scheme 2	8(50),12(20),17(30),5(80),25(60),30(70)	310

Table 2. The EVCS planning results of two schemes

	Node number (EVCS capacity/kW)	Total capacity (kW)
Scheme 1	4(118),8(110),12(0),15(73),25(150),30(149)	600
Scheme 2	4(103),8(128),12(56),15(70),25(136),30(107)	600

The relevant expenses of two schemes is shown in Table 3. The annual comprehensive cost of scheme 1 is 95.92 thousand dollars less than scheme 2, and the annual active losses cost of scheme 1 is 3.15 thousand dollars less than scheme 2, which show that joint planning of DG and EVCS can save the total cost of DG and EVCS planning, reducing the active power loss of active distribution network.

Table 3. The relevant expenses of two schemes

Item	Cost (One thousand dollars)	
	Scheme 1	Scheme 2
$F_{inv,DG}$	17.94	15.62
$F_{inv,EVCS}$	218.06	252.46
$F_{OM,DG}$	62.19	45.70
$F_{OM,EVCS}$	177.64	179.07
F_{loss}	147.16	150.31
F_{AM}	16.82	14.81
F_U	48.34	42.58
F_{total}	519.47	615.39

Figure 5 compares the node voltage under two schemes at the same time, the maximum voltage amplitude allowed by each node is 1.1 p.u., and the minimum voltage amplitude allowed is 0.9 p.u. The node voltage of scheme 1 is better than that of scheme 2, so the joint planning of DG and EVCS can improve the node voltage of distribution network.

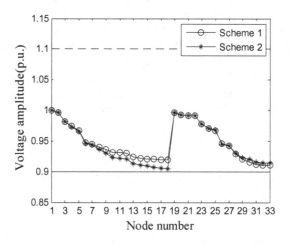

Fig. 5. The node voltage of two schemes

5 Conclusions

In this paper, a bi-level joint planning model of DG and EVCS under AM mode is established. The siting and sizing model of DG and EVCS is proposed by taking lowest annual comprehensive cost as the upper level objective, and the upper level is solved by BBO. Then, based on the upper level planning, the lower level model optimizes DG output curtailment, and is solved by PDIPM. The experimental results of the IEEE-33 nodes distribution network show that the joint planning of DG and EVCS can obtain the better planning scheme.

The energy storage system access distribution network has put forward the new challenge to ADN planning, it is necessary to carry on the comprehensive planning from many aspects such as power grid stability, and the influence on power quality. Therefore, how to evaluate power quality and put forward measures to improve power quality is also a worthy research problem in the future.

Acknowledgments. This work was supported in part by the national Science Foundation of China under Grant No.61773253, and project of Science and technology Commission of Shanghai Municipality under Grants No. 15JC1401900, 14JC1402200, and 17511107002.

References

1. Du, D.J., Chen, R., Fei, M.R., et al.: A novel networked online recursive identification method for multivariable systems with incomplete measurement information. J. IEEE Trans. Sign. Inf. Process. Netw. **3**(4), 744–759 (2017)
2. Du, D.J., Chen, R., Fei, M.R., et al.: Malicious data deception attacks against power systems: a new case and its detection method. J. Trans. Inst. Meas. Control. (2018). DOI: 10.1177/0142331217740622
3. Sedghi, M., Ahmadian, A., Aliakbar-Golkar, M.: Optimal storage planning in active distribution network considering uncertainty of wind power distributed generation. J. IEEE Trans. Power Syst. **31**(1), 304–316 (2016)
4. Jia, H., Qi, W., Liu, Z., et al.: Hierarchical risk assessment of transmission system considering the influence of active distribution network. J. IEEE Trans. Power Syst. **30**(2), 1084–1093 (2015)
5. Liu, Z., Wen, F., Ledwich, G.: Optimal planning of electric-vehicle charging stations in distribution systems. J. IEEE Trans. Power Deliv. **28**(1), 102–110 (2012)
6. Sheppard, C.J.R., Harris, A., Gopal, A.R.: Cost-effective siting of electric vehicle charging infrastructure with agent-based modeling. J. IEEE Trans. Transp. Electrif. **2**(2), 174–189 (2016)
7. Quevedo, P.M.D., Muñoz-Delgado, G., Contreras, J.: Impact of electric vehicles on the expansion planning of distribution systems considering renewable energy, storage and charging stations. J. IEEE Trans. Smart Grid. **PP**(99), 1 (2017)
8. Aien, M., Fotuhi-Firuzabad, M., Rashidinejad, M.: Probabilistic optimal power flow in correlated hybrid wind-photovoltaic power systems. J. IEEE Trans. Smart Grid **5**(1), 130–138 (2014)
9. Cao, Y., Zhang, Y., Zhang, H., et al.: Probabilistic optimal PV capacity planning for wind farm expansion based on NASA data. J. IEEE Trans. Sustain. Energy **8**(3), 1291–1300 (2017)
10. Ran, X., Miao, S.: Three-phase probabilistic load flow for power system with correlated wind, photovoltaic and load. J. IET Gener. Transm. Distrib. **10**(12), 3093–3101 (2016)
11. Gill, S., Kockar, I., Ault, G.W.: Dynamic optimal power flow for active distribution networks. J. IEEE Trans. Power Syst. **29**(1), 121–131 (2013)
12. Salih, S.N., Chen, P.: On coordinated control of OLTC and reactive power compensation for voltage regulation in distribution systems with wind power. J. IEEE Trans. Power Syst. **31**(5), 4026–4035 (2016)
13. Luo, T., Dolan, M.J., Davidson, E.M., et al.: Assessment of a new constraint satisfaction-based hybrid distributed control technique for power flow management in distribution networks with generation and demand response. J. IEEE Trans. Smart Grid **6**(1), 271–278 (2015)

14. Dan, S.: Biogeography-based optimization. J. IEEE Trans. Evol. Comput. **12**(6), 702–713 (2008)
15. Wang, Y., Li, X.: A hybrid chaotic biogeography based optimization for the sequence dependent setup times flowshop scheduling problem with weighted tardiness objective. J. IEEE Access **5**, 26046–26062 (2017)
16. Jiang, Q., Geng, G., Guo, C., et al.: An efficient implementation of automatic differentiation in interior point optimal power flow. J. IEEE Trans. Power Syst. **25**(1), 147–155 (2010)
17. Torquato, R., Shi, Q., Xu, W., et al.: A monte carlo simulation platform for studying low voltage residential networks. J. IEEE Trans. Smart Grid **5**(6), 2766–2776 (2014)
18. Baran, M.E., Wu, F.F.: Network reconfiguration in distribution systems for loss reduction and load balancing. J. IEEE Trans. Power Deliv. **4**(2), 1401–1407 (1989)
19. Ding, H., Hu, Z., Song, Y.: Value of the energy storage system in an electric bus fast charging station. J. Appl. Energy **157**, 630–639 (2015)

Real-Time Adjustment of Load Frequency Control Based on Controllable Energy of Electric Vehicles

Yan Li[1], Qian Zhang[1(✉)], Chen Li[2], and Chunyan Li[1]

[1] The State Key Laboratory of Power Transmission Equipment and System
Security and New Technology,
Chongqing University, Chongqing 400044, China
zhangqian@cqu.edu.cn
[2] EHV Power Transmission Company of China Southern Power Grid,
Guangzhou 510620, China

Abstract. The time-varying characteristics of electric vehicle (EV) controllable energy and the rationality of frequency regulation (FR) task allocation have significant influences on participating in system FR. Considering the various types of EV, the controllable quantities and the real-time controllable energy of EVs are simulated and calculated. On the basis of the real-time changes of EV's controllable energy, the real-time allocating scheme of system FR coefficient is put forward. The simulation results show that the real-time adjustment of load frequency control (LFC) model based on dynamic controllable energy of EV can effectively suppress the system frequency deviation; under the same total battery energy, the electric private car participates in the system FR for the longest time, the real-time controllable energy of which is the largest; the real-time allocating ratio of system FR has a wide range of fluctuation, and the FR effect under real-time allocation mode is better than that under the fixed allocation mode.

Keywords: Electric vehicle · Controllable energy · Load frequency control
Dynamic change · Real-time allocation

1 Introduction

With the implementation of energy saving, emission reduction and low-carbon economic policies, renewable energy sources will occupy a larger proportion in the grid. Due to high climbing rate of traditional regulation unit, power system respond slowly to the frequency fluctuations caused by intermittent fluctuations of renewable energy. Therefore, a number of researches about solar, wind energy and energy storage technology participating in system FR began to arise.

As a branch of energy storage technology, the EV has good prospects for participation in system FR due to large-scale development of EVs. The continuous improvement of V2G technology makes the operability of EVs participating in system FR increases. By adjusting the charging and discharging power, EVs can suppress the frequency fluctuations caused by intermittent energy sources such as wind and solar energy [1]. Efficient frequency support can be provided in smart grid by utilizing fleet

© Springer Nature Singapore Pte Ltd. 2018
K. Li et al. (Eds.): ICSEE 2018/IMIOT 2018, CCIS 925, pp. 105–115, 2018.
https://doi.org/10.1007/978-981-13-2381-2_10

of EVs which act as controllable loads and closely coordinate with aggregators and charging stations [2, 3]. The controllable energy of EV affected by its own traffic attributes varies with the time of day, and the varying controllable energy of EV further affects the system FR at varying times.

Considering the traffic characteristics and state transition characteristics of EVs, this paper presents a real-time controllable energy calculation method. On this basis, the real-time allocating scheme of system FR is proposed to analyze the influence of real-time controllable energy of EVs of different types on participating in the system FR. With constraints of real-time controllable energy and charging/discharging power, EVs can share the pressure of traditional regulation unit. Because EV's participation in FR is a way to make full use of existing energy storage resources, EV energy storage resources should be given priority in the allocation of FR tasks. So according to the real-time changes of EV's controllable energy, the real-time allocation scheme of system FR coefficient is proposed to improve the rationality of FR task allocation. The simulation results show that the proposed methods are correct and effective.

2   Dynamic Model of EV's Controllable Quantity

In-controlled state refers to that the EV changes from idle or charging state into controllable state depending on its SOC, and out-controlled state refers to that the EV changes from controllable state into idle or charging state. In a day, the controllable quantity of EVs in the region changes dynamically with the transition of the EV's state. Combing with the driving rules of EVs [4], the changing characteristics of EV's controllable quantity is analyzed.

t_0 is defined as the starting time, and the initial number of controllable EVs at t_0 is N_0. The number of controllable EVs at t, $N_c(t)$, is defined in (1) below,

$$N_c(t) = N_0 + N_{in}(t) - N_{out}(t) \tag{1}$$

The cumulative number of EVs under in-controlled state and out-controlled state at time t, $N_{in}(t)$ and $N_{out}(t)$, can be calculated by (2) and (3),

$$N_{in}(t) = \sum_{j=t_0}^{t} N'_{in}(j) \tag{2}$$

$$N_{out}(t) = \sum_{j=t_0}^{t} N'_{out}(j) \tag{3}$$

where $N'_{in}(j)$ and $N'_{out}(j)$ is the number of EVs under in-controlled state and out-controlled state at every moment j, respectively, which can be gained through statistical analysis of EV's timetable of transforming into and out of controlled state.

t_1 and T_2 are defined as plug-in time into grid and EV's necessary charging duration to meet the condition for participating in FR, respectively. Therefore, the time when EV transforms into controllable state t_3 is calculated as (4),

$$t_3 = t_1 + T_2 \tag{4}$$

where T_2 is determined by the characteristics of battery and charging power. It is assumed that lithium-ion battery is adopted.

Lithium-ion battery charging power P_{ev} (kW) and battery SOC (100%) change with the increase of charging duration h (hours) as follows [5],

$$P_{ev} = \begin{cases} 29.25h & 0 \leq h \leq 0.222 \\ 6.5 & 0.222 \leq h \leq 4.43 \\ -11.4h + 57 & 4.43 \leq h \leq 5 \end{cases} \tag{5}$$

$$SOC = \begin{cases} 21.43h & 0 \leq h < 4.43 \\ 41.34\sqrt{h} + 0.85 & 4.43 \leq h \leq 5 \end{cases} \tag{6}$$

It can be derived from the Eqs. (5) and (6) that the relation between P_{ev} (kW) and battery SOC (100%) can be expressed by (7),

$$P_{ev} = \begin{cases} 1.36SOC & 0 \leq SOC < 4.76 \\ 6.5 & 4.76 \leq SOC < 95 \\ 66.69 - 6.67 \times 10^{-3}SOC^2 & 95 \leq SOC \leq 100 \end{cases} \tag{7}$$

Then T_2 can be obtained through (8),

$$T_2 = \begin{cases} \frac{(SOC_m - SOC_0) \cdot E_{ev}}{\eta_{ev} \cdot 1.36SOC} & 0 \leq SOC_0 < 4.76 \\ \frac{(SOC_m - SOC_0) \cdot E_{ev}}{\eta_{ev} \cdot 6.5} & 4.76 \leq SOC_0 < SOC_m \\ 0 & SOC_0 \geq SOC_m \end{cases} \tag{8}$$

where E_{ev} (kWh) is the battery capacity of single EV and η_{ev} is the charging efficiency. It is assumed that discharging power is equal to P_{ev} and discharging efficiency is equal to η_{ev}. The discharging power is set to be positive.

The time when EV leaves controllable state t_4 contains two state transition scenarios. One scenario is that the EV breaks away from grid directly, changing into driving state; the other is that when the SOC cannot meet the owner's driving need, the EV will transform into charging state before the travel. Considering the time margin, t_4 equals to EV's planned departure time minus charging duration.

Through simulating each EV's time parameters mentioned above by Monte Carlo method [6], the controllable quantities of EVs can be calculated.

3 Dynamic Model of EV's Real-Time Controllable Energy

The real-time controllable energy dynamic model of EVs is determined on the basis of controllable quantity dynamic model of EVs. At time t, the real-time controllable energy of EVs in the region, $E_c(t)$ (MWh), can be calculated as follows,

$$E_c(t) = E_0 + E_{in}(t) - E_{out}(t) - E_{LFC}(t) \qquad (9)$$

where E_0 (MWh) is EV's initial controllable energy at time t_0 and $E_{in}(t)$ (MWh) is the energy increment brought by EVs under in-controlled state as shown in (10) and (11) respectively, and 1/1000 is the unit conversion coefficient,

$$E_0 = \frac{1}{1000} SOC_m N_0 E_{ev} \qquad (10)$$

$$E_{in}(t) = \frac{1}{1000} SOC_m N_{in}(t) E_{ev} \qquad (11)$$

$E_{out}(t)$ (MWh) is the energy reduction brought by EVs under out-controlled state. As the synchronization control method of SOC in [7] is adopted, the SOC of each EV battery is approximately equal to the average SOC of all controllable EVs. Thus, $E_{out}(t)$ can be calculated by (12),

$$E_{out}(t) = \frac{N_{out}(t)}{N_0 + N_{in}(t)} (E_0 + E_{in}(t) - E_{LFC}(t)) \qquad (12)$$

$E_{LFC}(t)$ (MWh) is the energy change brought by controllable EVs participating in system FR during the period from t_0 to t, as shown in (13),

$$E_{LFC}(t) = \frac{1}{3600} \int_{t_0}^{t} P_a(\tau) d\tau \qquad (13)$$

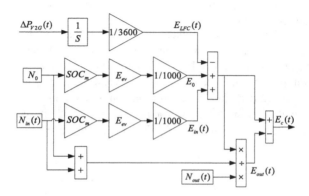

Fig. 1. Real-time controllable energy dynamic model of EVs

where $\Delta P_a(t)$ (MW) is the actual FR power output of all controllable EVs, and the discharging/charging power is set to be positive/negative.

To sum up, the model of the total controllable energy of all controllable EVs in this region is shown in Fig. 1.

4   Real-Time Adjustment Model of FR Coefficient

EV's participation in FR is a way to effectively utilize the existing energy storage resources as well as reduce the waste of resources from traditional units. So the utilizing of EV energy storage is put in priority in the allocation of FR tasks.

In the process of FR, the variation of the EVs' controllable energy affects the power allocation for system FR. $K_{ev}(t)$ is the ratio coefficient of EV's FR power output, which is adjusted in real time with changed in the controllable energy as shown in (14),

$$K_{ev}(t) = \begin{cases} K_{ev}^d(t) & \Delta f < 0 \\ K_{ev}^c(t) & \Delta f > 0 \\ 0 & \Delta f = 0 \end{cases} \quad (14)$$

When $\Delta f(t) < 0 / \Delta f(t) > 0$, EVs discharge to participate in FR, as in (15, 16 and 17),

$$K_{ev}^d(t) = \begin{cases} \frac{E_c(t)}{E_{cmax}(t)} & E_c(t) \le E_{cmax}(t) \\ 1 & E_c(t) > E_{cmax}(t) \end{cases} \quad (15)$$

$$K_{ev}^c(t) = \begin{cases} \frac{E_{cmax}(t) - E_c(t)}{E_{cmax}(t)} & E_c(t) \le E_{cmax}(t) \\ 0 & E_c(t) > E_{cmax}(t) \end{cases} \quad (16)$$

$$\Delta P_{ev}(t) = P_{dev}(t) \times K_{ev}(t) \quad (17)$$

where $K_{ev}^d(t)/K_{ev}^c(t)$ is the ratio coefficient of EV's discharging/charging power output for FR; $P_{dev}(t)$ (MW) is obtained from system frequency deviation signal $\Delta f(t)$ through PI control, representing the power output required for FR; $\Delta P_{ev}(t)$ (MW) is the FR task allocated to EV by the system; $E_{cmax}(t)$ is the upper limit of real-time controllable energy of EVs, as shown in (18),

$$E_{cmax}(t) = \frac{1}{1000} SOC_{max} N_c(t) E_{ev} \quad (18)$$

$\Delta P_{V2G1}(t)$ (MW) is EV's power output for up-regulation, as in (19),

$$\Delta P_{V2G1}(t) = \min\{\Delta P_{ev}(t), P_{lim}^d(t)\} \quad (19)$$

where $P_{\lim}^d(t)$ (MW) is the limit of controllable EVs' discharging power, as in (20),

$$P_{\lim}^d(t) = \frac{1}{1000}N_c(t)P_{ev}/\eta_{ev} \tag{20}$$

$\Delta P_{V2G2}(t)$ (MW) is EV's power output of for down-regulation, as in (21),

$$\Delta P_{V2G2}(t) = \max\{\Delta P_{ev}(t), P_{\lim}^c(t)\} \tag{21}$$

where $P_{\lim}^c(t)$ (MW) is the limit of controllable EVs' charging power, as in (22),

$$P_{\lim}^c(t) = -\frac{1}{1000}N_c(t)P_{ev}\eta_{ev} \tag{22}$$

In summary, EV's power output for FR $\Delta P_{V2G}(t)$ can be expressed by (23),

$$\Delta P_{V2G}(t) = \begin{cases} \Delta P_{V2G1}(t) & \Delta f < 0 \\ \Delta P_{V2G2}(t) & \Delta f > 0 \\ 0 & \Delta f = 0 \end{cases} \tag{23}$$

Traditional units and EVs coordinate to participate in FR. $\Delta P_g(t)$ (MW) is the FR task allocated to traditional units, as shown in (24),

$$\Delta P_g(t) = \begin{cases} P_{dev}(t) \times K_g(t) & K_{ev}(t) \neq 0 \\ 0 & K_{ev}(t) = 0 \end{cases} \tag{24}$$

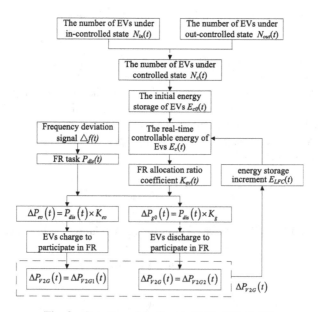

Fig. 2. Output model of controllable EVs in FR

where $K_g(t)$ is the ratio coefficient of traditional unit's FR power output, as in (25),

$$K_g(t) = \begin{cases} 1 - K_{ev}(t) & \Delta f \neq 0 \\ 0 & \Delta f = 0 \end{cases} \qquad (25)$$

The output model of controllable EVs in FR is shown in Fig. 2, which illustrates the process of EV's participation in system FR. The input of this model contains $N_{in}(t)$, $N_{out}(t)$ and $\Delta f(t)$. The output of this model is $\Delta P_{V2G}(t)$, the response power of all controllable EVs in the region. The SOC of EVs is maintained at a high level to ensure the driving need of EVs and avoid excessive discharging/charging.

5 Case Simulation Analysis

5.1 Analysis of Controllable Energy Changes

This paper analyzes the frequency stability of a two-area interconnection system [8–10] containing wind power, which is affected by the dynamic changes of EV's real-time controllable energy. As electric taxi almost stays in driving state in a whole day, it is not suitable for participation in FR, thus only electric private car, electric official vehicle and electric bus are considered. The basic capacity of the entire power system is set to be 1000 MVA and the basic frequency is 50 Hz.

As driving rules are different, EVs of various types participate in system FR in different time periods. In order to compare different FR effects of various EV types, it is assumed that the total energy of various types of EVs is set to be the same: $12000 \cdot 30$ kWh. Scenario 1: The number of electric private cars is 12,000; Scenario 2: The number of electric buses is 2,000; Scenario 3: The number of electric official vehicles is 12,000; Scenario 4: The number of electric private cars, electric buses and electric official vehicles is 4000, 667 and 4000, respectively. And the ratio of various types of EVs in Scenario 4, K_{car}:K_{bus}:K_{off} is 0.0667:0.0667:0.0667. The ratio of capacity of traditional unit and EVs is set to be 0.8:0.2.

The dynamic change of EV's controllable quantity in single area on working day is shown in Fig. 3. As the unified scheduling management is adopted, outside working hours, electric buses and electric official vehicles are connected to grid to participate in system FR. The controllable quantity of electric private cars on working day is maximum thus has the largest potential to participate in FR. The overall trend of controllable energy curve is roughly the same as the controllable number curve in Fig. 3, but the two curves are slightly different since EVs will participate in FR through charging and discharging. Real-time controllable energy in four scenarios are shown in Fig. 4(a–d), where with V2G and without V2G represent that EVs participate in FR or not, respectively. It can be seen that real-time controllable energy of EVs with V2G fluctuates more than without V2G. This is because when frequency increases/decreases, EVs charge/discharge for FR so that the real-time controllable energy increases/decreases, which reflects the active role of EVs in LFC model.

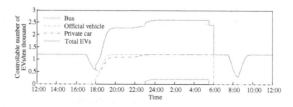

Fig. 3. Controllable number of EVs

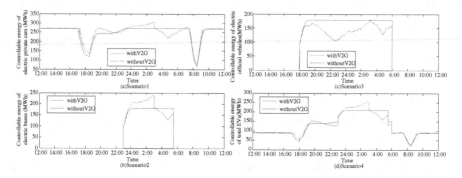

Fig. 4. Controllable energy of EVs

In period 7:30–9:30 and 17:00–23:00 of Scenario 1, with EV owners commute to work, there is a large fluctuation in controllable energy caused by the changes of controllable quantity. In the rest of time in a day, the fluctuation of controllable energy is due to the participation in FR, and real-time controllable energy of electric private cars is maintained at about 300 MWh. In Scenario 2, electric bus's real-time controllable energy starts to increase at 23:00 and jumps to zero at 5:30. In Scenario 3, electric official vehicle's real-time controllable energy starts to increase at 18:00 and jumps to zero at 6:00. Scenario 4 is the sum of real-time controllable energy of three types of EV, which fluctuates greatly.

5.2   Analysis of Frequency Regulation Effect

As private EVs have a relatively large quantity and remain connected to the gird for relatively long time, private EVs are taken as an example to analyze the influence of the dynamic change of EV's controllable energy on system FR. Figure 5 shows the allocation ratio of the real-time system FR power. According to the real-time change of EV controllable energy and frequency deviation, the system FR allocation ratio changes in real time. When $K_e(t) \neq 0$, $K_e(t) + K_g(t) = 1$, as shown in Fig. 5. In the period of 1:30–2:30, $K_e(t)$ equals the minimum value of the allocating ratio of EVs, while $K_g(t)$ equals to the maximum value of allocating ratio of units. Since the frequency deviation fluctuates around the reference value of 50 Hz, $K_e(t)$ varies between $K_e^d(t)$ and $K_e^c(t)$ correspondingly.

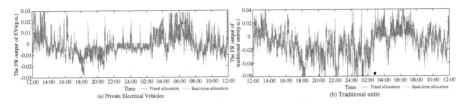

Fig. 5. System power of frequency regulation

System FR power output and system frequency deviation are shown in Figs. 5 and 6, respectively. The fixed allocation in Fig. 6 means that the allocation ratio between the private EV and the traditional unit is fixed and it is set to 3:7. The real-time allocation means adopting the real-time adjustment strategy proposed in this paper. In the period of 22: 00–02: 00 (the next day) in Fig. 6, under the fixed ratio allocation mode, the power output of EVs is much lower than it under the real-time allocation mode, while the power output of traditional units is more than it under the real-time allocation mode. In the corresponding time period of Fig. 5, both $K_e(t)$ and $K_g(t)$ keep around 0.8 in half of the time, respectively. Therefore, private electric cars are able to provide a large amount of power output. However, private electric cars only provide 30% of the FR power output under fixed allocation mode, less than that under real-time allocation mode, which means that the power output of the traditional unit needs to increase correspondingly. In the corresponding time period of Fig. 6(a), the system frequency deviation under the real-time allocation mode is less than under the fixed allocation mode, indicating that the FR effect under the fixed allocation mode is worse than that under the real-time allocation mode. In addition, the root mean square value of the system frequency deviation with and without V2G in Fig. 6(b) are 0.01022 Hz and 0.01263 Hz, respectively, which indicates that the FR effect is obviously better when EVs participate in FR.

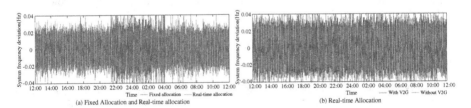

Fig. 6. Frequency deviation

6 Conclusion

The basic function of an EV is as a driving tool used by people, so the utilizing of EVs must take into account the randomness and convenience of EV users. Only EVs in the controllable state are able to respond to the system FR control signal and provide FR service to the grid. In this paper, the dynamic characteristics of EV's real-time controllable energy are discussed, and the system frequency control model considering the dynamic changes of EV's controllable energy is established, and the effect of EVs participating in system FR are analyzed. Through case simulation, the following conclusions can be obtained:

(1) the proposed real-time controllable energy model takes into account the traffic rules and driving needs, which is relatively in accordance with the actual situation and ensures the basic function of EV;

(2) Under the same total battery energy, private electric cars participate in the system FR for the longest time and provide the largest amount of real-time controllable energy among various types of EVs;

(3) In the FR strategy considering real-time allocation based on the real-time controllable energy of EVs, the FR effect is better than the fixed allocation mode, and the fluctuation range of the system FR real-time allocation ratio is relatively large.

Acknowledgment. This work was supported by the National Natural Science Foundation of China (51507022).

References

1. Zhao, J., Xue, L., Fu, Y., Hu, X., Li, F.: Coordinated microgrid frequency regulation based on DIFG variable coefficient using virtual inertia and primary frequency control. IEEE Trans. Energy Conv. **31**(3), 833–845 (2016)

2. Kaur, K., Rana, R., Kumar, N., Singh, M., Mishra, S.: A colored petri net based frequency support scheme using fleet of electric vehicles in smart grid environment. IEEE Trans. Power Syst. **31**(6), 4638–4649 (2016)

3. Rana, R., Singh, M., Mishra, S.: Design of modified droop controller for frequency support in microgrid using fleet of electric vehicles. IEEE Trans. Power Syst. **32**(5), 3627–3636 (2017)

4. Luo, Z., Hu, Z., Song, Y., Xu, Z., Lu, H.: Optimal coordination of plug-in electric vehicles in power grids with cost-benefit analysis-part ii: a case study in china. IEEE Trans. Power Syst. **28**(4), 3556–3565 (2013)

5. Qian, K., Zhou, C., Allan, M.M., Yuan, Y.: Modeling of load demand due to ev battery charging in distribution systems. IEEE Trans. Power Syst. **26**(2), 802–810 (2011)

6. Sarabi, S., Davigny, A., Courtecuisse, V., Riffonneau, Y., Robyns, B.: Potential of vehicle-to-grid ancillary services considering the uncertainties in plug-in electric vehicle availability and service/localization limitations in distribution grids. Appl. Energy **171**, 523–540 (2016)

7. Shimizu K., Masuta T., Ota Y., A. Yokoyama.: A new load frequency control method in power system using vehicle-to-grid system considering users' convenience. In: 17th Power System Computation Conference, pp. 1–7. Technical Program Committee, Stockholm (2011)

8. Shinji, T., Sekine, T., Akisawa, A., Kashiwagi, T., Fujita, G., Matsubara, M.: Reduction of power fluctuation by distributed generation in micro grid. Elect. Eng. Japan **163**(2), 22–29 (2008)

9. Vachirasricirikul, S., Ngamroo, I.: Robust LFC in a smart grid with wind power penetration by coordinated V2G control and frequency controller. IEEE Trans. Smart Grid **5**(1), 371–380 (2014)
10. Takagi M., Yamaji K., Yamamoto H.: Power system stabilization by charging power management of plug-in hybrid electric vehicles with LFC signal. In: IEEE Vehicle Power and Propulsion Conference, pp. 822–826. IEEE Press, Dearborn (2009)

An Orderly Charging and Discharging Scheduling Strategy of Electric Vehicles Considering Demand Responsiveness

Wenrui Xie[1], Qian Zhang[1(✉)], Huazhen Liu[2], and Yi Zhu[1]

[1] State Key Laboratory of Power Transmission Equipment and System Security and New Technology (Chongqing University), Chongqing 400044, China
zhangqian@cqu.edu.cn
[2] Guangdong Power Grid Corporation Foshan Power Supply Bureau, Foshan 528000, China

Abstract. In the research of Vehicle-to-grid (V2G), the large-scale EVs needs to be aggregated to participate in the charging/discharging strategy. Aiming at the problem of electric vehicles (EVs) in aggregator participating in dispatching plan, this paper proposed an orderly scheduling strategy of the EV in the aggregator (Vehicle-to-Aggregator, V2A). Under the condition of real-time price, an index evaluation system of the EVs has been established, which consider the randomness and credit of EV users. This paper first analyzed the impact of the declaration information on the schedule plan. With the consideration of declared scheduling capacity, EV user's credit, battery loss and the degree of participation as the evaluation index, the evaluation index system of the EV aggregator is proposed. Then, the weight of each index is determined, which uses the method of combination weighting based on the Accelerated Genetic Algorithm. Then the scheduling priority of EVs in the aggregator can be obtained. Finally, combining with the dispatching plan of power grid, the actual scheduling capacity of aggregators at different nodes in each period is determined. The simulation results show that the strategy proposed in this paper can consider the influence of various indexes of EVs on schedule, and effectively realize the dispatching plan for aggregators.

Keywords: Electric vehicles · Combination weighting · Real-time price
Charging and discharging dispatching plan · Scheduling strategy

1 Introduction

Under the background of the world's energy crisis, environment and economic crisis, EVs have been highly valued by various countries and social enterprises because of the obvious advantages of low pollution and low carbon emissions [1]. With the increase in the number of EVs, The V2G technology has been introduced. With the rational schedule of EVs, the power grid not only reduces the negative impact of EVs on grid, but also gains economic benefits [2–4].

A lot of researches were about how the EV aggregator played a role in the power grid scheduling. It's unrealistic to dispatch all the vehicles directly by dispatching

© Springer Nature Singapore Pte Ltd. 2018
K. Li et al. (Eds.): ICSEE 2018/IMIOT 2018, CCIS 925, pp. 116–126, 2018.
https://doi.org/10.1007/978-981-13-2381-2_11

center of the power grid. The concept of EV aggregator and the hierarchical control method reduce the number of EVs that the power grid needs to dispatch directly [5]. However, most of the studies remain on the level of the EV aggregator, but the rational and orderly scheduling strategy of the individual behavior of each vehicle needs to be formed. Therefore, it is of great significance to further study the rational and orderly arrangement of all EVs in the aggregator to participate in the power grid scheduling (V2A) [6].

On the other hand, the concept of demand side response can be applied to optimize the interaction between users and the power grid [7]. This paper also analyzes the impact of demand side response on EV charging and discharging schedule.

This paper aims at the problem of orderly schedule of individual EVs participating in the dispatching interaction plan in the EV aggregator, then analyzes the influence of the user's declaration information on the dispatching plan for the vehicle aggregator. At the same time, the impact of demand side response on EV charging and discharging schedule is analyzed. Based on this, considering the real time tariff, the EV evaluation system with multiple indicators is established. Then the weight of the system is solved by the optimal combination weighting method. Finally, an ordered control strategy of EV aggregator considering demand side response is proposed.

2   The Index Evaluation System Model of EV Aggregator

2.1   Factors Affecting the Scheduling Strategy of EV Aggregator

Before the users respond to the dispatching plan, the EV aggregator must collect several information about EVs like declaration information, battery loss and so on. At the same time, the grid will determine real-time scheduling based on history records and information reported by aggregator.

(1) **Declaration Schedulable Capacity**

According to the user's declaration information, schedulable period T_d and schedulable capacity S_d can be obtained, and S_d is calculated by Eq. (1).

$$S_d = S_{B.\max} - S_{B.\min} \tag{1}$$

where $S_{B.\max}$ and $S_{B.\min}$ indicate maximal and minimal energy of an EV during an schedule respectively, which can be calculated based on the state of charge (SOC) limits set by the user and the battery capacity of the EV.

(2) **The Credit of Electric Vehicles Participating in the Dispatching Plan**

In order to take the situation of electric vehicles that violate the dispatching plan into account, the concept of credit membership is introduced into the schedulable capacity calculation. If an EV suddenly connects or leaves the grid outside of the plan, its declaration capacity will be included in the schedulable capacity based on the proportion of the credit degree of the user. The specific expression of the credit degree is as follows:

$$\rho = \frac{\bar{S}_d}{\bar{S}_h} = \begin{cases} 1 & \rho \geq \rho_{up} \\ \frac{\bar{S}_d}{\bar{S}_h} & \rho_{down} \leq \rho \leq \rho_{up} \\ 0 & \rho \leq \rho_{down} \end{cases} \qquad (2)$$

where $\bar{S}_h$ means day-ahead average declaration capacity, and $\bar{S}_d$ means day-ahead average actual scheduled capacity. When the credit degree is large enough, the value is 1, and if it is too small, the value is 0.

(3) **The Demand Response of EV Users**

The charging or discharging behavior of EVs is a kind of demand response. EV users can make their own consumption according to the price signal or incentive mechanism. Therefore, this paper considers the economic benefits of EVs participating in V2G to describe the degree of responsiveness of EV users.

① The Response of EV to Electricity Price Mechanism

The response to the electricity price refers to the user's choice of period, and the transfer of the electric load from the high-price period to the low-price period to reduce the cost of electricity [8].

The change of electricity price will cause the change of the demand of the user, so the electricity price elasticity is adopted to express the response degree of the user to the electricity price mechanism. That is, the ratio of the degree of electricity price change to the degree of electricity change in a certain period, as shown in Eq. (3).

$$\varepsilon = \frac{\Delta S/S}{\Delta p/p} = \frac{(\Delta S/T)/(S/T)}{\Delta p/p} = \frac{\Delta P/P}{\Delta p/p} \qquad (3)$$

where S, ΔS respectively indicates the amount of electricity and its relative increase. p, Δp respectively indicates the amount of price and its relative increase. The higher the price, the lower the electricity.

② The Response of EV Users to The Grid Incentive Mechanism

Sometimes the system cannot satisfy user's charging requirements, or the discharging capacity cannot meet the grid dispatching plan. The grid will compensate and adjust the load through incentives, which means that EVs will charge or discharge out of the dispatching plan.

Users can voluntarily choose whether to respond to the incentive of the system. If EV users are willing to participate in demand side response, the response of EV users to the grid incentive mechanism can be defined:

$$\delta = \frac{C_e(t) - C_p(t)}{C_p(t)} \qquad (4)$$

where $C_p(t)$ means the charging cost of EVs, and $C_e(t)$ means the income of incentive mechanism.

For the charging plan, when the required charging capacity is not reached, the incentive income includes the interruption compensation and the price difference after the transfer to a lower price period. For the discharging plan, the incentive income is consist of battery compensation, extra discharging income and compensation.

Thus, the degree of demand responsiveness that defines the participation of EV users in grid dispatching plans is:

$$\mu = \alpha\varepsilon + (1-\alpha)\delta \tag{5}$$

where α is proportion factor and can be calculated by the entropy weight method.

Equation (5) indicates the degree of response of the EV user to the electricity price signal or the incentive mechanism.

2.2   The Index Evaluation System Model

For a single EV, it can only select one of the charging or discharging state to declare in a single period. Based on the analysis of the factors affecting the EV to participate in scheduling, an index evaluation system is established. In order to make sure that the aggregator's charging and discharging plan is consistent with the grid real-time scheduling as much as possible, the sum of variance of scheduling capacity and planned capacity is further minimized. It also enables a smoother fluctuation caused by large-scale EV. The entire process is shown in Fig. 1.

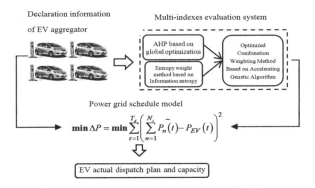

Fig. 1. Flow chart of orderly scheduling strategy for EV aggregator

In order to eliminate the dimension effect of each evaluation index and make the modeling universal, the index should be normalized. Suppose x_{ij} is the evaluation value of the j object for the i index, and r_{ij} is the value after the normalization of x_{ij}. The resulting $R = \left(r_{ij}\right)_{K \times N}$ can be used as a fuzzy evaluation matrix

$$\begin{cases} \text{Cost index:} \quad r_{ij} = \dfrac{x_{ij}^{\max} - x_{ij}}{x_{ij}^{\max} - x_{ij}^{\min}} \\[2mm] \text{Benefit index:} \quad r_{ij} = \dfrac{x_{ij} - x_{ij}^{\min}}{x_{ij}^{\max} - x_{ij}^{\min}} \end{cases} \qquad (6)$$

where $x_{ij}^{\max}/x_{ij}^{\min}$ refers to the maximum/minimum value of the same index.

Each index will be weighted to obtain the basis of EV scheduling. Among them, the larger the schedulable capacity, the higher the user credit, the higher demand responsiveness and the smaller the battery loss will be scheduled first.

3 An Orderly Scheduling Strategy Using Optimal Combination Weighting Method for Electric Vehicle Aggregator Based on Accelerating Genetic Algorithm

3.1 Determining Comprehensive Weight Based on Optimized Combination Weighting of Deviation Function

In the decision analysis theory, because different evaluation methods are difficult to identify the better one, it is necessary to make full use of the information contained in the various methods to obtain a satisfactory weight solution. This paper uses the optimal combination weighting method based on the accelerating genetic algorithm to solve the problem.

$$\begin{cases} W_c = \theta_1 w_1 + \theta_2 w_2 \\ \theta_1 + \theta_2 = 1 \end{cases} \qquad (7)$$

where $W_c = (W_{c1}, W_{c2}, \ldots W_{cK})^T$ is attribute combination weighting coefficient vector, and θ_1, θ_2 are combination coefficient.

The comprehensive evaluation value is:

$$U_j = \sum_{i=1}^{K} W_{ci} r_{ij}, \, j = 1, 2\ldots \qquad (8)$$

In order to determine the attribute combination weight vector W_c, the absolute value of the deviation is introduced:

$$d_{jn} = \left| \left(W_{ci} - w_i^n \right) r_{ij} \right| \qquad (9)$$

where d_{jn} denotes the absolute value of the deviation between the weight of the nth weighting scheme and the weighting of the combined weighting method for the jth evaluation object.

In order to comprehensively utilize the subjective and objective weights of each evaluation index the deviation between the evaluation result under the optimal combination weights and the evaluation result under subjective and objective weights is supposed to as small as possible for all indicators of all evaluation targets. So, by solving the minimization of the absolute sum of the weighted deviations to estimate the optimal combination weights, the following model can be constructed:

$$\min f = \min \sum_{j=1}^{N} \sum_{i=1}^{K} \left[\alpha |w_1(i) - W_{ci}| r_{ij} + (1-\alpha)|w_2(i) - W_{ci}| r_{ij} \right] \tag{10}$$

$$\text{s.t.} \quad \sum_{i=1}^{K} W_{ci} = 1, \ W_{ci} \geq 0 \tag{11}$$

3.2 Electric Vehicle Orderly Scheduling Considering Index Evaluation System

After the index evaluation system is modeled and solved by optimal combination weighting method, the index weight and the comprehensive evaluation value can be obtained. Then the order and schedulable capacity in different period of every single EV in the aggregator can be obtained. However, to avoid the system fluctuation caused by the insufficient or excessive power provided by the aggregator during a certain period, in the orderly scheduling strategy, the schedulable capacity of the EV should also be adjusted to meet the given dispatching plan. So, for a certain EV aggregator:

$$\mathbf{\min \Delta P = \min} \sum_{t=1}^{T_d} \left(\sum_{n=1}^{N_t} \tilde{P_n}(t) - P_{EV}(t) \right)^2 \tag{12}$$

where $\tilde{P_n}(t)$ is the actual power of the nth EV at period t; N_t is the total number of scheduled EVs; $P_{EV}(t)$ is the dispatching plan at period t.

$$\text{s.t.} \begin{cases} N_c(t) \leq N_c^{\max}(t), \quad N_{dc}(t) \leq N_{dc}^{\max}(t) \\ \sum_{n=1}^{N_c(t)} P_{c,n}(t) \leq \sum_{n=1}^{N_c^{\max}(t)} P_{c,n}(t) \\ \sum_{n=1}^{N_{dc}(t)} P_{dc,n}(t) \leq \sum_{n=1}^{N_{dc}^{\max}(t)} P_{dc,n}(t) \\ N_c^{\max}(t) + N_{dc}^{\max}(t) \leq N_t^{\max} \end{cases} \tag{13}$$

where $N_c^{\max}(t)$ and $N_{dc}^{\max}(t)$ are the number of all EVs that declare the charging/discharging plan, respectively; $N_t^{\max}$ is the total amount of EVs at period t; $P_{c,n}(t)$, $P_{dc,n}(t)$ are the charging/discharging power of the n-th EV during the period t, respectively.

4 Case Studies

In order to verify the superiority of the proposed strategy, this strategy is applied to the 6-node system in [9]. The optimal first-level plan of grid-side are obtained using the model in [10].

The node 4 in certain period which requires EVs to discharge 3.98 MW as an auxiliary service is selected as the case with the priority scheduling strategy. Assume the number of EVs participating in the schedule in node 4 is 265. For ease of management, the aggregator organizes the day-ahead information for each EV and divides the EVs participating in the schedule into 30 fleets. EVs in the same fleet have the similar characteristics. The real-time declaration information can be obtained through the declaration information. The Monte Carlo method is used to simulate the SOC information of 30 fleets, and the declaration information is based on a variety of actual situations that may occur.

With the EV fleet's day-ahead participation information under dispatching plan provided by aggregator, users' participation degree can be calculated at time 17 through the entropy weight method, so the participation degree in the period is:

$$\mu = 0.5541\varepsilon + 0.4459\delta$$

According to the parameter information above, the evaluation value of each parameter is obtained, which is standardized by Eq. (6), as shown in Table 1.

Table 1. Normalization results of decision matrix of each EV fleet

Fleet	1	2	3	...	28	29	30
S_d	0.51	0.10	0.65	...	0.71	0.31	0.68
ρ	0.99	0.94	0.90	...	0.93	0.80	0.96
μ	0.65	0.20	0.62	...	0.76	0.80	0.34
B_r	0.21	0.17	0.21	...	0.24	0.16	0.24

The subjective weights and objective weights of each index are obtained according to the weighting methods, then the comprehensive weighting coefficient of each indicator is obtained by the optimized combination weighting method based on accelerated genetic algorithm. The weight of s_d, ρ, μ, B_r is 0.1583, 0.3198, 0.3322, 0.1897, respectively.

Then the result of priority dispatching plan of 30 eV fleets of node can be obtained, as shown in Table 2. Through the Table 2, the value of dispatching priority of each EV fleet can be obtained. Combining the results of Table above, we can see that:

(1) If EVs' declaration capacity is too low, the grid will give them a low priority in the initial stage of the plan (e.g. the fleets numbered 2, 4, 9, 10, 12, etc.).
(2) The comprehensive weight coefficient of the two indicators of user credit and responsiveness is higher, so the fleets whose comprehensive evaluation value in the

Table 2. Priority and schedulable capacity of EV fleets (kW)

Schedule order	1	2	3	4	5	6	7	8	9	10
U_j	0.743	0.737	0.720	0.707	0.696	0.679	0.675	0.660	0.657	0.654
EV fleets	16	25	19	28	20	11	22	21	6	1
Declaration capacity	123.051	170.495	143.706	205.942	125.900	150.72	193.2	130.8	119.82	91.44
Schedulable capacity considering ρ	112.132	170.495	137.471	192.516	115.880	134.416	178.026	107.025	110.691	90.799
Schedule order	11	12	13	14	15	16	17	18	19	20
U_j	0.639	0.637	0.605	0.604	0.603	0.590	0.583	0.580	0.572	0.552
EV fleets	15	3	5	23	29	8	24	7	30	13
Declaration capacity	132.715	99.429	102.413	138.928	205.942	96.297	132.550	97.120	218.634	120.445
Schedulable capacity considering ρ	126.075	89.728	69.556	126.009	192.516	94.869	75.429	89.995	209.600	114.063
Schedule order	21	22	23	24	25	26	27	28	29	30
U_j	0.530	0.489	0.436	0.416	0.403	0.356	0.337	0.276	0.076	0.005
EV fleets	27	14	17	2	4	26	12	18	10	9
Declaration capacity	187.293	104.554	130.176	67.564	86.539	145.779	87.705	111.870	88.096	82.129
Schedulable capacity considering ρ	169.754	31.356	84.665	63.601	45.086	123.863	51.650	80.027	11.371	0.000

above two indexes in declaration information is more than 0.5 will be scheduled in advance (e.g. the fleets numbered 16, 25, 19, 28, 20 and so on).

(3) If EVs actively participate in scheduling, their battery loss will be slightly higher. Although they will get more V2G compensation, the grid and EV users should be aware that in order to protect the EVs, it is not appropriate to participate in scheduled charging and discharging frequently.

When EVs participate in power grid dispatching plan, their declaration information and day-ahead participation record are the key to determining the real-time dispatching order. Then the real-time schedulable capacity in each period can be obtained, and further adjusted according to the dispatching plan of the power grid to reduce the impact of large-scale EVs connecting to grid and finally realize real-time orderly scheduling strategy. The priority and schedulable capacity of EV fleets can be calculated, also shown in Table 2.

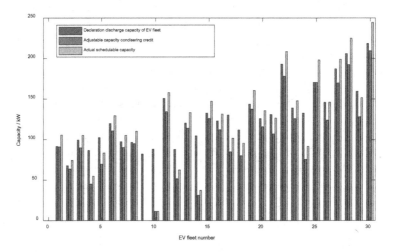

Fig. 2. Comparison of capacity of each fleet in aggregator.

From Table 2, it is known that the total schedulable capacity of the aggregator considering credit is 3.134 MW, which cannot meet the grid dispatching plan capacity (3.98 MW). in this case, the demand response is used to guide high-priority vehicles to continue to provide electricity within their own acceptance margins, so it is necessary to further adjust the schedulable capacity and the actual scheduled situation of EVs to achieve the consistency with the grid dispatching plan as much as possible. The results are shown in Fig. 2.

The actual schedulable capacity after adjustment is 3.681 MW, which is closer to the dispatching plan. The shortage is reduced from 0.846 MW to 0.299 MW.

Combined with Table 2 and Fig. 2, we can get:

(1) Although some EVs have more declaration capacity during the period, if their credits are too low, they will not be invoked basically when considering credit.

(e.g. fleets numbered 9, 10). Some less creditworthy EVs (e.g. fleets numbered 12, 17 and 24) are incompletely scheduled.

(2) At the same time, some fleets (e.g. number 25, 28, 22, 30 and 27) have a slightly higher actual scheduled capacity than their declaration capacity. Users' EV are can voluntarily choose to schedule more capacity than the declared capacity within the accepted range to obtain more profits.

(3) In fact, the EVs located behind schedule have lower priority. When there are large-scale EVs, these EVs will not be considered in the scheduling process. This is consistent with the results shown in Fig. 2.

Due to the large number of vehicles and longer scheduling periods, the present example only selects a node for a certain period as an example to simulate the orderly scheduling strategy proposed in this paper to verify its feasibility. Actually, the aggregator collects EV declaration information for multiple periods and has different scheduling arrangements for each period. Therefore, when there are a lot of mature data of EVs participating in the grid scheduling strategy, continuous real-time dispatching plans can be obtained.

5 Conclusion

This paper aims at the problem that in order scheduling strategy of large-scale EVs, each EV can't be scheduled by grid directly, considers the EV's characters, and proposes an orderly scheduling strategy for EV aggregator under the condition of real-time electricity price. The strategy uses the declaration scheduling capacity, credit degree, battery loss, and users' participation degree as the evaluation indexes to establishes the evaluation index system of EV aggregator. The comprehensive weight of each index is determined by the optimization combination weighting method, which is based on the accelerated genetic algorithm. Then each EV's scheduling priority in the aggregator can be obtained, and the actual scheduling capacity of the aggregator at different periods is determined. Finally, combined with the power grid scheduling plan, adjust each EV schedule in the aggregator to be consistent with power grid dispatching plan as much as possible, and reduce the impact of large-scale EV integration on the stability of power system.

Acknowledgment. This work was supported by the National Natural Science Foundation of China (51507022).

References

1. Wirasingha, S.G., Emadi, A.: Classification and review of control strategies for plug-in hybrid electric vehicles. IEEE Trans. Veh. Technol. **60**(1), 111–122 (2011)
2. Rotering, N., Ilic, M.: Optimal charge control of plug-in hybrid electric vehicles in deregulated electricity markets. IEEE Trans. Power Syst. **26**, 1021–1029 (2011)

3. Han, S., Han, S., Sezaki, K.: Estimation of achievable power capacity from plug-in electric vehicles for V2G frequency regulation: case studies for market participation. IEEE Trans. Smart Grid 2(4), 632–641 (2011)
4. Clement-Nyns, K., Haesen, E., Driesen, J.: The impact of charging plug-in hybrid electric vehicles on a residential distribution grid. IEEE Trans. Power Syst. 25(1), 371–380 (2010)
5. Ma, J., Yang, H.: Distributed parallel coordinated control strategy for provincial regional grid based on subarea division of the power system. In: 2012 China International Conference on Electricity Distribution, vol. 16(2), pp. 130–137 (2012)
6. Zhang, Q., Cai, J., Liu, C., et al.: Optimal control strategy of cluster charging and discharging of electric vehicles based on the priority. Trans. China Electrotech. Soc. 30(17), 117–125 (2015). (in Chinese)
7. Wang, L., Sharkh, S., Chipperfield, A., et al.: Dispatch of vehicle-to-grid battery storage using an analytic hierarchy process. IEEE Trans. Veh. Technol. 66(4), 2952–2965 (2017)
8. Kumar, K.N., Tseng, K.J.: Impact of demand response management on chargeability of electric vehicles. Energy 111, 190–196 (2016)
9. Cai, Q., Wen, F., Xue, Y., et al.: An SCUC-based optimization approach for power system dispatching with plug-in hybrid electric vehicles. Autom. Electr. Power Syst. 36(1), 38–46 (2012)
10. Qian, Z., Chao, L., Lin, Z., et al.: A bi-level economy dispatch model considering temporal and spatial optimal distribution of electric vehicles. Autom. Electr. Power Syst. 38(20), 40–45 (2014). (in Chinese)

Energy Saving

Technological Updating Decision–Making Model for Eco–Factory Through Dynamic Programming

Erheng Chen[1], Huajun Cao[1(✉)], Kun Wang[1], Salman Jafar[1],
and Qinyi He[2]

[1] State Key Laboratory of Mechanical Transmission,
Chongqing University, Chongqing 400044, China
hjcao@cqu.edu.cn
[2] Pittsburgh Institute, Sichuan University, Sichuan 610207, China

Abstract. As the key subject of the green manufacturing system, the construction of eco–factory has become an important content in order to achieve the sustainable development of enterprises. In this paper, a technological updating decision-making model is established based on dynamic programming (DP) for eco–factory. Firstly, the evaluation index system for eco–factory is established. Secondly, the local weight and global weight of each index are calculated based on analytic network process (ANP) and Delphi method. Finally, the decision-making model of eco-factory is established to find the optimal investment plan by using the method of logarithmic fitting and DP. The ANP and Delphi method present a great potential in solving complex and ambiguous problems and the decision-making based on DP can obtain the better ecological benefits through an example of a foundry factory, therefore the feasibility of the proposed method is proved.

Keywords: Eco-factory · Ecological benefits · Analytic network process
Dynamic programming · Decision-making

1 Introduction

A plenty of non–renewable resources are used in the economic construction and it leads to the increasing exhaustion of resources and serious environmental pollution in developing countries. Therefore, the green manufacturing is the inevitable trend of sustainable development. The technologies of green manufacturing is important research areas with significant potential impact on human lives today and even more in the future [1].

The eco-factory is a key part of building the green manufacturing system. According to "Made in China 2025", the eco-factory is defined as "the factory that realizes the intensive use of land, harmless raw materials, cleaner production, waste recycling and low–carbon energy". The eco-factory concept with clean manufacturing solutions for green products represents the present high end in factory design [2]. In the current competitive and regulated landscape, manufacturing enterprises struggle to improve their performances, encompassing environmental as well as economic

© Springer Nature Singapore Pte Ltd. 2018
K. Li et al. (Eds.): ICSEE 2018/IMIOT 2018, CCIS 925, pp. 129–138, 2018.
https://doi.org/10.1007/978-981-13-2381-2_12

objectives, toward sustainable manufacturing and the future eco–factories [3]. Research on eco-factory will help to set the benchmark in the industry, guide and standardize factories to implement green manufacturing, and take the social responsibility for green development. Eco–factories will enable the quantum leap in integrating environmental issues in factory planning and factory operations [4].

Evaluation is the basis of decision-making, and selection of evaluation method is crucial. In the introduction of ecological concept to manufacturing, many evaluation methods are presented. An integrated analytic hierarchy process is used for eco – industrial parks to multi–objective optimization for resource network synthesis [5]. May G pointed that the energy management will become a way toward eco-factory of the future and research should focus more on the opportunities that human participants in a manufacturing system can foster change toward eco–factories [6]. The single simulation model combined discrete event simulation, material flow analysis, and life cycle assessment was presented in eco-factory for sustainable decision-making [7]. There are more evaluation methods for eco–industrial parks and manufacturing systems, and less research on eco-factory.

The decision-making is very important in order to establish the eco-factory. The dynamic programming was applied to calculate optimal decision sequence and maximum total profits in resource allocation of factory production line [8]. Aiming at the reliability allocation problem of series manufacturing system's reliability design, the dynamic programming (DP) method was adopted to solve the reliability allocation problem under the existing constraints [9]. The DP model is adopted by addressing the division of investment allocations of production lines [10]. However, few scholars have studied the investment decision based on DP in the construction of eco-factory.

In this paper, the ecological benefits evaluation and investment decision of eco-factory are combined to find the investment decision plan when the ecological benefits are greatest. The weight of each indicator is determined through the analytic network process (ANP) and Delphi method based on the reasonable evaluation index system. The ecological benefits as the comprehensive index are calculated quantitatively by DP in order to put forward the optimal investment decision scheme to update the factory.

2   Ecological Benefits Evaluation Index System

In order to describe and evaluate the green manufacturing ability and level of the factory scientifically and quantitatively, as well as to strengthen the decision management, it is essential to establish a set of evaluation index system which can be designed reasonably and practically.

The evaluation index system for factory was constructed according to the opinions provided by experts from relevant fields, some standards, and policies of the government, which includes green manufacturing technology (B1), green manufacturing process (B2) and resources and environment effect (B3), along with eight quantitative sub–criteria, and the ecological benefits (A1) is target. The ecological benefits evaluation index system is illustrated in Fig. 1.

B1 reflects the green level of the factory relative to the early production technology, and mainly includes the green technology (C1) and green processes (C2). C1 indicate

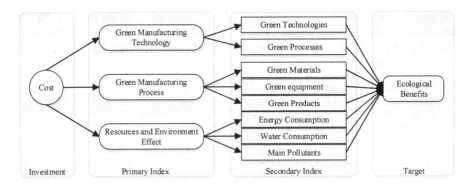

Fig. 1. The ecological benefits evaluation index system

the imported number of energy saving and emissions reduction technology. C2 indicate the number of process transformation during establishing the factory.

B2 reflects the green degree in the process of factory production, mainly including green materials (C3), green equipment (C4) and output of green products (C5). C3 indicate the quantity of green materials used. C4 indicate the quantity of high efficiency and energy saving equipment used. C5 indicate the value of green products.

B3 reflects the comprehensive green level about resources and the ecological environment during factory production process, and the energy consumption (C6), water consumption (C7) and the main pollutants (C8) are used as secondary indicators. C6 indicates energy consumption per unit product, including electricity, natural gas, and compressed air and so on. C7 indicates water consumption per unit product. C8 indicate the environmental pollutants produced by the unit product, mainly including waste solid, waste water and waste gas and so on.

The framework of ecological benefits evaluation index system is constructed in this paper, which can calculate the ecological benefits of the factory after obtaining the global weight of each index.

3 DP Decision-Making Model

Since the ecological benefits evaluation index system has been established for by considering the characteristics of factory, the method of decision-making is employed which consists of two parts. The first part is the weight determination using ANP and Delphi. The second part is the optimal resource allocation through DP method.

3.1 Determine the Weight of Indexes

In ecological benefits evaluation index system, the relationship between the indicators is complex, such as the use of green materials can not only reduce energy consumption, water consumption and environmental pollution but also improve the production value of green products. ANP, which is developed based on analytical hierarchy process (AHP), is more suitable to describe the interaction between elements [11, 12]. Because of dependence and feedback of different indexes, this paper implemented ANP to determine the relative weight coefficient of each evaluation index. In the structure model of ANP, it is not independent between groups and elements, but can be inter-related and influenced [13].

(1) Dimensionless treatment

The each index is processed under dimensionless treatment in ecological benefits evaluation index system in order to compare the different casting plants.

$$x_{pq} = \frac{x'_{pq}}{x^{sum}_{pq}}. \tag{1}$$

In Eq. (1), x_{pq} represents the dimensionless value of the index q relative to the sample p. x'_{pq} represents the original value and x^{sum}_{pq} represents the total value.

There are positive and negative indicators in the ecological benefits evaluation index system of the factory. For instance, the ecological benefits will be improved when C2 becomes big and C6 becomes small, so C2 is a positive index and C6 is a negative indicator. Therefore, in order to make the later data processing easy and convenient, a unified index is needed through the Eq. (2).

$$x''_{pq} = \begin{cases} x_{pq} & \text{positive index} \\ \frac{1}{x_{pq}} & \text{negetive index} \end{cases}. \tag{2}$$

(2) Calculation of weighted supermatrix

In the structure model of ANP, the elements of control layer contain $A_1, A_2, \cdots, A_N$. The supermatrix W will be obtained under the criteria of A_N, as shown in expression (3).

$$W = \begin{bmatrix} W_{11} & W_{12} & \cdots & W_{1N} \\ W_{21} & W_{22} & \cdots & W_{2N} \\ \cdots & \cdots & \cdots & \cdots \\ W_{N1} & W_{N2} & \cdots & W_{NN} \end{bmatrix}. \tag{3}$$

A_N as a criteria and the importance of each element set is compared to other element sets, also then a weighted matrix is formed, as shown in expression (4).

$$A = \begin{bmatrix} a_{11} & \cdots & a_{1N} \\ \cdots & \cdots & \cdots \\ a_{N1} & \cdots & a_{NN} \end{bmatrix}. \tag{4}$$

Building a matrix $\bar{W} = (\bar{W}_{ij})$, whose elements are denoted by $\bar{W} = a_{ij}(W_{ij})$. $\bar{W}$ is the weighted supermatrix.

Super Decision (SD) is used to input the judgment matrix and output the weighted supermatrix and the limit supermatrix [14]. The weights of ecological benefits evaluation indexes under the respective criteria are obtained from the limit supermatrix.

3.2   DP of Resource Allocation

Suppose the total investment is a, considering the construction of the project, there are m investment allocation schemes marked as d_t. The total investment effect is evaluated by n casting plants, and when the investment x_w is assigned to the casting plant w, the corresponding investment effect is $g_w(x_w)$. The question now is how to allocate investment to make the total ecological benefits best, and it is the resource allocation problem. The DP is good at solving resource allocation [15].

(1) Phase and state

The problem is transformed into a multi–stage investment decision-making process. The variables in the description phase are called phase variables and are expressed in k. With each casting plant as a stage, in other word, $k = w$. The investment is considered to assign to n casting plants, that is, there are n stages, $k = 1, 2, \cdots, n$. In this paper, the k presents three casting plants.

The state is described by a variable s_k, which represents the number of investment allocated to the casting plant from the k_{th} to the n_{th}. The evolution of the system from one stage to the next is completely determined by the state and decision of the system at this stage, regardless of the system's previous state and decisions.

(2) Decision and state transfer equation

When the state of each stage is determined, decisions are made to determine status of the next stage, described by the decision variable x_k, indicating the number of investment allocated to build the k_{th} casting plant. The values are often within a certain range, which is called a set of permitting decisions, used $D_k(s_k)$ as representation, and it is defined as follows:

$$D_k(s_k) = \{x_k | 0 \leq x_k \leq s_k, x_k \in \{d_t\}\}. \tag{5}$$

The state variables of $k + 1$ are written according to the state variables and decision variables in the k_{th} phase, namely:

$$s_{k+1} = s_k - x_k. \tag{6}$$

(3) Optimal index function

The decision is $D_k(s_k)$ when the state is s_k, $v_k(s_k, D_k)$ reflects the k_{th} casting plant, it is the index function of phase k and described as follows:

$$V_k(s_k, x_k) = v_k(s_k, x_k) + V_{k+1}(s_{k+1}, x_{k+1}). \tag{7}$$

The optimal index function $f_k(s_k)$ represents the maximum ecological benefits obtained by allocating investment of s_k to casting plant from the k_{th} one to the n_{th} one. The basic equations of DP are listed below:

$$\begin{cases} f_k(s_k) = \max_{0 \le x_k \le s_k} [v_k(s_k, x_k) + f_{k+1}(s_{k+1})] \\ f_{n+1}(s_{n+1}) = 0 \end{cases}. \tag{8}$$

Calculations are based on the reverse algorithm, the maximum ecological benefits of the factory is expressed in the equation $f_1(s_1)$.

4 Case Study

In this paper, an example of a casting factory is analyzed. The green upgrade of the casting factory is expected to cost 50 million. The investment decisions are made for eco–factory according to the ten–year capital investment and the ecological benefits of three casting plant.

ANP is used to establish the network structure model of the ecological benefits indicator system with SD software, and its detail specifications as shown in Table 1.

Table 1. Indicators explanation and correlations between indicators

Index	Index explanation	Correlativity
C1	Energy saving and emissions reduction technology in melting, die–casting and machining, etc.	C1→C2,C4,C5, C6,C7,C8
C2	Total process: melting, transport and heat preservation, high–pressure casting, remove waste scrap, shot blasting, machining, cleaning	C2→C5,C6,C7, C8
C3	Water recycling, aluminum recycling, waste heat recovery	C3→C1,C2,C4, C5,C6,C7,C8
C4	Special equipment, general equipment, electromechanical equipment, industrial control equipment, etc.	C4→C1,C2,C5, C6,C7,C8
C5	The value of green products	C5→C1,C2,C3, C4,C6,C7,C8
C6	Power consumption, gas consumption	C6→C1,C2,C3, C4
C7	Water consumption	C7→C1,C2,C3, C4
C8	Waste gas and waste water, etc.	C8→C1,C2,C3, C4,C6,C7

5   Result and Discussion

(1)   Determine the weight of indicators at all levels

Due to the different degree of influence of each index to ecological benefits, the experts rated the relationship between the indicators on a 1–9 scale. Input the judgment matrix between the element groups and the judgment matrix between the indexes in the SD software, the global weight of the secondary indexes is shown in Fig. 2.

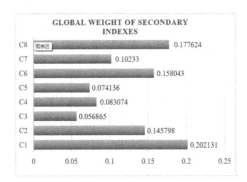

Fig. 2.   Global weight of the secondary indexes in evaluation index system

(2)   Determine the relationship between investment and ecological benefits

The ecological benefits of the three casting plants can be obtained by combining global weights of the secondary indexes after the ten–year historical data are processed with dimensionless processing, as shown in Table 2.

Table 2.   The former ten years of investment and ecological benefits for casting plant

	Casting plant (D1)		Casting plant (D2)		Casting plant (D3)	
	Investment ($\times 10^4$ RMB)	A1	Investment ($\times 10^4$ RMB)	A1	Investment ($\times 10^4$ RMB)	A1
2007	364.13	5.1053	224.04	3.2027	458.39	6.5528
2008	455.57	5.528	276.78	3.3776	535.41	6.746
2009	617.83	6.1495	380.14	3.7219	588.74	7.1655
2010	756.45	6.7062	467.53	4.1971	777.77	7.8151
2011	823.12	6.9156	556.27	4.3839	827.28	8.1087
2012	904.08	7.2113	627.96	4.6369	1138.12	8.9863
2013	1023.83	7.5472	741.19	4.8983	1256.45	9.3798
2014	1204.63	7.961	856.91	5.2706	1290.32	9.5702
2015	1392.71	8.5662	920.42	5.2283	1516.47	9.9219
2016	1592.62	8.9535	1039.42	5.4082	1753.24	10.6837

The growth rate of ecological benefits is gradually slowing down through comparing the data in Table 3, so the relationship between investment and ecological benefits is obtained based on logarithmic fitting by MATLAB, and the corresponding ecological benefits can be obtained, as shown in Table 3.

Table 3. The relationship between investment and three casting plants

Investment/million RMB	D1	D2	D3
10	7.55	5.37	8.73
20	9.37	6.43	10.85
30	10.43	7.05	12.08
40	11.19	7.49	12.96
50	11.78	7.83	13.64

(3) DP of investment allocations

Based on the relationship between the investment and the ecological benefits of three casting plants, the problem is divided into three stages ($k = 1, 2, 3$) based on the DP. The optimal investment allocation scheme is obtained, as shown in Fig. 3.

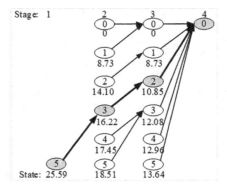

Fig. 3. The optimal investment scheme for ecological benefits

It can be seen from Fig. 6 that the optimal solution is obtained when $x_1^* = 2$, $x_2^* = 1$, $x_3^* = 2$. In other words, the investment of D1 is 20 million RMB, the investment of D2 is 10 million RMB, and the investment of D3 is 20 million RMB. Its optimal value of ecological benefits is 25.59.

6 Conclusion

In this paper, the investment allocations decision-making of a factory have been modelled through ANP and DP under the ecological benefits evaluation index system. The following conclusions may be drawn:

(1) The local weight and global weight of each index in ecological benefits evaluation index system are calculated based on ANP and Delphi method. The method can effectively deal with the complex relationship between each element group and indexes, and improve the accuracy and reliability of evaluation for eco-factory.

(2) The decision-making model of eco-factory is established to find the optimal investment plan by logarithmic fitting and DP. The optimization of ecological benefits problem is divided into three stages, and the global optimal allocation plan is obtained through finding the optimal solution for each stage, respectively. This method presents the higher theoretical value and practical significance.

(3) An example analysis shows that 50 million funds are divided into 20 million, 10 million and 20 million to D1, D2, and D3 respectively. Its optimal value of ecological benefits for the factory is 25.59. This distribution scheme can improve the ecological benefits of the factory, so the feasibility of this method is verified.

References

1. Ahn, S.H.: An evaluation of green manufacturing technologies based on research databases. Int. J. Precis. Eng. Manuf.-Green Technol. **1**(1), 5–9 (2014)

2. Kai, S., Leino, T., Joutsiniemi, A.: Sustainable manufacturing and eco-factories within sustainable industrial areas within fast growing eco-cities sustainable manufacturing and eco-factories within sustainable industrial areas within fast growing eco-cities. In: Flexible Automation and Intelligent Manufacturing, FAIM (2011)

3. Fantini, P., Palasciano, C., Taisch, M.: Back to intuition: proposal for a performance indicators framework to facilitate eco-factories management and benchmarking. Procedia CIRP **26**, 1–6 (2015)

4. Taisch, M., Stahl, B.: Requirements analysis and definition for eco-factories: the case of EMC2. In: Emmanouilidis, C., Taisch, M., Kiritsis, D. (eds.) APMS 2012. IAICT, vol. 397, pp. 111–118. Springer, Heidelberg (2013). https://doi.org/10.1007/978-3-642-40352-1_15

5. Leong, Y.T., Lee, J.Y., Tan, R.R., et al.: Multi-objective optimization for resource network synthesis in eco-industrial parks using an integrated analytic hierarchy process. J. Clean. Prod. **143**, 1268–1283 (2017)

6. May, G., Stahl, B., Taisch, M.: Energy management in manufacturing: toward eco-factories of the future–a focus group study. Appl. Energy **164**, 628–638 (2016)

7. Reinhard, J., Zah, R., Wohlgemuth, V., et al.: Applying life cycle assessment within discrete event simulation: practical application of the Milan/EcoFactory material flow simulator (2013)

8. Wen, J.H., Jiang, H.L., Zhang, M., et al.: Application of dynamic programming in resources optimization allocation of factory production line. Key Eng. Mater. **474–476**(1), 1632–1637 (2011)

9. Jia, J., Yang, Y., Yang, T., et al.: Research on dynamic programming of the series manufacturing system reliability allocation. J. Converg. Inf. Technol. **7**(7), 17–25 (2012)

10. Abdul-Zahra, In, Abbas, I.T., Kalaf, B.A., et al.: The role of dynamic programming in the distribution of investment allocations between production lines with an application in the (men's clothing factory in Najaf holy). Int. J. Pure Appl. Math. **106**(2), 365–380 (2016)

11. Kabak, M., Dağdeviren, M.: A hybrid approach based on ANP and grey relational analysis for machine selection. Tehnicki Vjesnik **24**, 109–118 (2017)

12. Ayağ, Z., Özdemir, R.G.: Evaluating machine tool alternatives through modified TOPSIS and alpha-cut based fuzzy ANP. Int. J. Prod. Econ. **140**(2), 630–636 (2012)
13. Saaty, T.L., Vargas, L.G.: Decision Making with the Analytic Network Process. Springer, Berlin (2013). https://doi.org/10.1007/978-1-4614-7279-7
14. Li, H., Tao, M., Sun, Z.: Research on the process evaluation of green university based on concordance analysis. In: International Conference on Chinese Control and Decision Conference, pp. 3642–3646. IEEE Press (2009)
15. Ullah, S.M.S., Muhammad, I., Ko, T.J.: Optimal strategy to deal with decision making problems in machine tools remanufacturing. Int. J. Precis. Eng. Manuf.-Green Technol. **3**(1), 19–26 (2016)

A Configurable On-Line Monitoring System Towards Energy Consumption of Machine Tools

Pengcheng Wu[1], Yan He[1(✉)], Ming K. Lim[1], Yan Wang[2], Yulin Wang[3], and Linming Hu[1]

[1] The State Key Laboratory of Mechanical Transmission, Chongqing University, Shazheng Street 174, Shapingba, Chongqing 400044, China
heyan@cqu.edu.cn
[2] Department of Computing, Engineering and Mathematics, University of Brighton, Brighton BN2 4GJ, UK
[3] School of Mechanical Engineering, Nanjing University of Science and Technology, Nanjing 210094, China

Abstract. The environmental impacts of manufacturing systems can be improved by reducing the energy consumption of machine tools. To meet the requirements for reducing energy consumption of machine tools, it is critical to monitor and analyze energy usage of machine tools. However, machine tools are composed of multiple energy consumers and the requirements towards monitoring energy of machine tools are different. This paper proposes a configurable on-line monitoring system to obtain energy data for the specific energy consumption components of machine tools, which can be used to analyze energy characteristics considering different energy monitoring requirements and different machine tools. The case study of the system implemented in lathe and machining center shows that the system can be used to monitor energy consumption of different types of machine tools and satisfy different monitoring requirements of energy consumption. The results can provide a better understanding of energy and support refined energy management in the manufacturing system.

Keywords: Machine tools · Energy consumers · Configurable on-line monitoring system

1 Introduction

The global environment is getting worse. Manufacturing consumes substantial amounts of energy and has measurable impact on environment [1]. Over one third of global energy consumption are related with manufacturing industry [2, 3]. Machine tools plays an important role in manufacturing industry, nearly one third of energy is consumed by industry, besides, far more than half of energy in industry is consumed in machining processes [4, 5]. Reducing energy consumption of machine tools can significantly improve environmental impacts of manufacturing systems.

© Springer Nature Singapore Pte Ltd. 2018
K. Li et al. (Eds.): ICSEE 2018/IMIOT 2018, CCIS 925, pp. 139–150, 2018.
https://doi.org/10.1007/978-981-13-2381-2_13

To meet the requirements of reducing energy consumption, it is vital to quantify energy usage of machine tools. Many researches have been done by using theoretical modeling method to quantify the energy usage of machine tools. Kara et al. presents an empirical model to characterize the relationship between energy consumption and process variables for material removal processes [6]. Herrmann et al. presents an innovative energy oriented simulation model for planning of manufacturing systems [7]. He et al. proposes a modeling method of task-oriented energy consumption for machining manufacturing system [8]. However, due to the complexity of machine tools, many unknown parameters such as mechanical friction, plastic and elastic deformations, and the resulting heat losses in the theoretical models are difficult to obtain [9].

In the context, energy monitoring systems often have been used to quantify energy consumption of machine tools. Delgado-Gomes et al. presents a real-time data acquisition and monitoring system to acquire the total energy consumption of machine tools [10]. Mourtzis et al. presents an energy consumption estimation method based on real-time shop floor monitoring via wireless sensor networks to get the energy consumption of machine tools [11]. Chiotellv et al. presents a concept for real-time analysis of electrical power based on data stream analysis, and event-driven system approaches has been developed and implemented as a software application [12].

Machine tools, especially modern CNC machines are always composed of multiple motors and auxiliary components, energy consumption can vary strongly during production activities [13]. During machining process, different energy-consumed components of machine tools works cooperatively to guarantee the constant machining processes. However, the previous study mainly focused on the total energy consumption or the energy consumed by the specific components. Few study focuses on the monitoring of different energy consumed components while considering the different requirements towards monitoring the machine tools.

This study presents a configurable on-line monitoring system towards energy characteristics of machine tools. The system can be used to obtain energy data of multiple energy consumers while taking into account different requirements about monitoring energy consumption of machine tools. The system is conducted on the CJK6136C lathe machine tool and HAAS VF5/50 X milling machine tool, the energy consumption of different components of the machine tools under different state have been analyzed, the energy efficiency of machine tools is also discussed.

2 The Problem Description for the Configurable Energy Monitoring of the Machine Tools

The machine tools are composed of energy consumers, and different energy consumer has different energy characteristic in different state of machining processes. The requirements towards monitoring machine tools are decided by the types of machine tools and the demands of the users.

In this paper, the state of machine tools during machining is divided into three parts, the air-cutting state, basic state, cutting state. The basic state is state of readiness, which is that the machine tool is turned on, the control system, spindle system is in a state of readiness. The air cutting state is the state that includes spindle rotation and feeding, cutting without load. The cutting state is the state of cutting with material remove [14]. This division is to better understand the energy composition of machine tools.

Different machine tools have different energy consumers. Table 1 shows an example for the energy-consumed components of a typical of three-axis CNC machine tools [13]. As shown in Tables 2 and 3, the energy consumers of CK6136C and YD31125CNC6 are very different. For CNC machine tools, the cutting energy for material removing is only 15%–25% of the total energy, most of energy are consumed by spindle motor, tool change systems, cooling systems, servo systems, fan systems, etc. [15, 16]. According to the ISO14955-1, the total energy consumption of the machine tools is obtained by the sum of the energy consumed by all of the energy consumed components.

Table 1. Energy-consumed components of a typical of three-axis CNC machine tools

No.	Energy-consumed components	Function
1	Computer and monitor	Process and display computer numerical control information
2	Fan	Generate air flow for cooling off the electrical components
3	Lubricant pump motor	Drive pump to supply lubricant for slide ways, gears, etc.
4	Hydraulic pump motor	Convert hydraulic power to mechanical power
5	Machine light	Light the working area
6	Turret motor	Rotate tool turret for tool change
7	Coolant pump motor	Drive pump to spray coolant
8	Spindle inverter	Convert the input grid power to required voltage and frequency
9	Spindle motor	Rotate the spindle at a certain rotational speed
10	Servo unit	Convert the input grid power to required voltage and frequency for feed speed control of feed motor
11	Feed motor-X axis	Drive the working table to move along X-axis
12	Feed motor-Y axis	Drive the working table to move along Y-axis
13	Feed motor-Z axis	Drive the working table to move along Z-axis

Additionally, different users have different requirements on energy monitoring of machine tools. For designers, they always focus on the detail energy consumption information of the specific component of machine tools to optimize parameters and realize the high energy-efficient design. The operator prefers to the total energy consumption, and then to make optimized machining processes in the workshop. Production managers pay attention to the energy consumption of each machine in order to optimize schedule in the production.

Table 2. Energy consumers of CJK6136C

Energy consumers	Power (kW)
Main spindle motor Y132S-4	5.5
Feed motor X axis 110SJT-M060D(A)	4.6
Feed motor Z axis110SJT-M060D(A)	4.6
Cooling motor AB-25	0.09
Fan motor	0.1

Table 3. Energy consumers of YD31125CNC6

Energy consumers	Power (kW)
Spindle motor 1PH4163-4NF26-Z	37.00
Feed motor X axis 1FT6084-1AF71-3AG0	4.60
Feed motor Z axis 1FT6086-8AF71-3AH1	5.80
Feed motor Y axis 1FT6044-4AF71-3EH0	1.40
Workbench rotation motor1FT6134-6AC71-1EK3	13.60
Rotation feed motor 1FT6064-6AF71-3EB0	2.20
Hydraulic pump motor Y2-132 M-4	7.50
Hydrostatic pump motor Y2-132 M-4	7.50
Cooling motor STA404/350	2.20
Lathe bed flushing scraps motor STA402/250	1.30
Groove flushing scraps motor STA404/350	2.20
Hydrostatic cooling motor HBO-3RPSB	7.90
Cooling oil-cooled machine controllerAKZJ568-H	4.00
Oil mist separation motor GMA 30-02D-R/U/1.8/h	1.05

According to the description about energy monitoring of machine tools, the configurable monitoring system are required to be developed, which can be used to acquire energy data from different energy consumers in different states and satisfy different requirements by different users.

3   Structure of the Configurable On-Line Monitoring System

The framework of the configurable on-line monitoring system is constructed as shown in Fig. 1. The realization of this system includes three steps. In the first step, the energy consumers of machine tools are analyzed. The second steps are data collecting and processing. The last step is power data analyzing.

(1) Analyzing the energy consumers of the machine tools

As shown in the Fig. 1, different machine tools have different types and numbers of energy consumers. In the first step, the structure of the machine tools is analyzed to identify energy consumers of machine tools. And the number and type of power

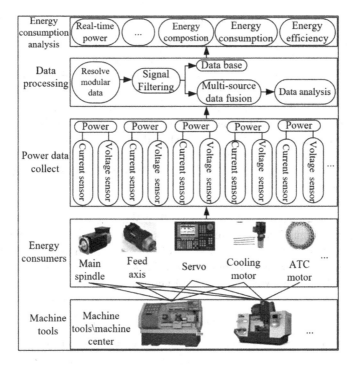

Fig. 1. Framework of the configurable on-line monitoring system

sensors are determined according to the type and number of the energy consumer as well as the requirements of the users.

(2) Data collecting and processing

The voltage and current data are collected by the power sensor, which mount on the energy consumers. The protocol of the data transmission is modularized according to transmission protocol of the sensors, and the current data and voltage data are resolved according to corresponding rules of the modular, in order to make sure the other types sensors could be used. The real time power is obtained by filtered data and kept in the database. The state of machine tools is obtained through multi-sensor data fusion, including the state of power off, basic state, cutting state, the results can support the analysis of energy consumption in different state during machining process.

(3) Power data analyzing

The power data from multiple energy consumers are analyzed, in order to obtain energy consumption information of machine tools, such as total energy consumption and energy consumed by specific energy consumers, the results can support different users to make energy reduction strategies.

3.1   Identification of the Running States

The power data could fluctuate with the change of the running-state of the machine tools and contains complex energy characteristics during machining. The power information of energy consumers could be changed during machining. According to the ISO14955-1, the state of the machine tools is identified by the state (on/off) of the energy consumers. At first, the state of the energy consumers is obtained by the filtered power data. The zero drift of the power sensor are identified as the valve. The states of the energy consumers are identified as off when the power sensor collects a continuously five power data, which under the valve. The states of the energy consumers are identified as on when the power sensor collects a continuously five power data, which higher than the valve.

Take the machine tool CJK6136C as an example. The state of the machine tools is obtained by the collected data as shown in Table 4. When all the energy consumers are off, the state of the machine tools are off. If only the state of the servo system and fan system are on, the machine tools are in a state of air-cutting. If all the energy consumers of the machine tools are on, but the motor of the X axis and Y axis is in a state of on/off, the machine tools would in a state of cutting.

Table 4. Identification the state of the CJK6136C

No	Fan and servo system	Spindle motor	Feed X axis	Feed Y axis motor	States
1	Off	Off	Off	Off	Off
2	On	Off	Off	Off	Air cutting
3	On	On	On/Off	On/Off	Cutting

3.2   Analysis of the Energy Data

The energy consumption information is analyzed based on the obtained power data, which comes from the energy consumers. The strategies made by the users are supported by the different energy consumption information including the energy consumed by the specific energy consumers, total energy consumption of the machine tools, the energy consumed in the different state and the energy efficiency. The designers can optimize their design towards machine tools according to the energy consumption data of the specific energy consumers. The operators would choose the best energy reduction strategy according to the energy efficiency and energy consumed in the cutting state, and the management would prefer to obtain the total energy consumption information of the machine tools to optimize schedule plan of the machining process.

(1) Energy consumption of the specific energy-consumed component

The energy consumption of the energy consumers means the energy consumed by the energy components during the machining process, it can be calculated as follows:

$$E_i = \int P_i dt \tag{1}$$

Where E_i is energy consumption; P_i is the power; i is the specific energy-consumed component.

(2) The total energy consumption of the machining processes

The total energy consumption of the machining process is obtained by the sum of the energy consumption of all the energy consumers, as shown in Eq. 2.

$$E_{all} = \sum_i E_i = \sum_i P_i dt \tag{2}$$

Where E_{all} is the total energy consumption.

(3) The energy consumption under different state

The energy consumption under different state, including the off, basic state, cutting state. The energy consumption of different state is obtained by Eq. 3.

$$E_k^s = \int_{t_k^s} P_k dt \tag{3}$$

Where E_k^s is the energy consumption; t_k^s is the running time of the specific state; s is specific state;

(4) Energy consumption of material removing

Energy consumption of material removing means the energy consumed during material remove process. The energy, which consumed in the cutting state, is supplied by the spindle motor. However, the energy consumed by the main spindle mainly have two parts, the first part is maintaining the rotate speed of the main spindle, the second part is consumed in the material remove process. So the energy consumed in the cutting state is obtained by Eq. 4.

$$E_c = E_s - E_s^0 = \int P_s dt - \int P_s^0 dt \tag{4}$$

Where E_c is energy consumed by the material remove process; E_s is the energy consumption of the main spindle motor; E_s^0 is air cutting energy consumption of the main spindle; P_s is the real time power of the main spindle motor; P_s^0 is the power of air cutting.

(5) Energy efficiency

Energy efficiency is obtained by the power consumed in material remove process to divide the total energy consumption, the potential of saving the energy and the use of the energy are obtained by the energy efficiency, as shown in Eq. 5.

$$Ef = \frac{E_c}{E_{all}} \times 100\% \tag{5}$$

Where Ef is the energy efficiency of the machining process.

4 Case Study

The configurable on-line monitoring system is developed under the structure as is shown in Fig. 2. The C# was used to the development of the system which implemented in the Windows. At first, the power sensor is mounted on the machine tools according to the structure and energy consumers of the machine tools. Then, the setting of the prototype system is set according to the matching information between energy consumers and power sensor. Later, the power data of the different energy consumers are collected according to the requirement and present it on-line in a real time. After that, the energy consumption information is analyzed according to the collected power data, and the analyzed results are shown in the system's GUI, the results can provide an energy information of the machine tools.

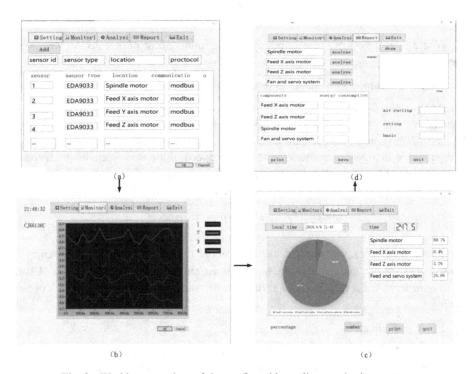

Fig. 2. Working procedure of the configurable on-line monitoring system

The system is conducted on the lathe tools CJK6136C, the power sensor is EDA9033, the machining process is machining the workpiece of intake shaft. At first, the structure and energy consumers of the machine tools are analyzed, the spindle motor, feed X axis motor, feed Z axis motor and the total input are the place that are chosen to mount the power sensor. The real time power of the machine tools and energy consumption information of the energy consumers are obtained by the system, and the results are shown in the system's GUI.

The energy consumption information of machining the intake shaft is obtained by the analyzed power data, which collected from the multiple energy consumers based on the developed system. The results are shown in Table 5. The total energy consumption is 68.3 W . h, 15.9 W . h is used for turning process, and the energy efficiency of the machine tool is 23.3%.

Table 5. Energy consumption information during machining process

Objects	Number
Total energy consumption	68.3 W . h
Energy consumption of material remove	15.9 W . h
Energy efficiency	23.3%

The energy consumption information of the specific energy consumers is obtained based on the developed system. The analyzed results of the energy consumers are shown in Fig. 3. The energy consumed by the main spindle, feed X axis, feed Z axis are respectively 47.6 W . h, 0.3 W . h, 2.2 W . h. The energy used in the basic state is 18.2 W . h.

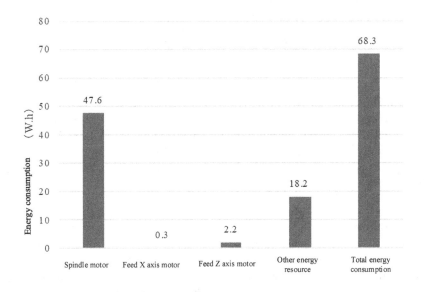

Fig. 3. Energy consumption information of different energy consumer.

The energy consumption percentage of different components is shown in Fig. 4. The energy consumed by the main spindle is 47.6%, which is the largest energy consumer in the machine tools. However, the energy consumed by the feed X axis motor and feed Z axis motor only take little parts of all the energy consumption.

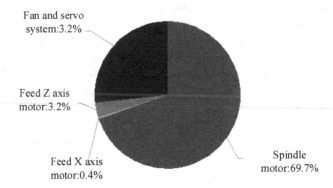

Fig. 4. Energy consumption percentage of different components

The energy consumed in the different state is obtained by further analyzing the energy consumption of the energy consumers. The results are shown in Table 6. The energy consumed in the air-cutting state is 8.1 W . h, and the energy consumed in the cutting state is 60.2 W . h.

Table 6. Energy consumption information during different states

States	Power
Air-cutting	8.1 W . h
Cutting	60.2 W . h

In order to identify the adaptability of the developed system, the system is applied to the machining center HAAS VF5/50, the energy consumption of the pallet during the milling process have been monitored, as shown in Fig. 5. The analyzed results are shown in Table 7, the energy consumed by the spindle motor is 281.1 W . h, which is the largest energy consumption during the process. The second largest energy consumption is the energy consumed by the fan and servo system, the energy consumed by the fan and servo is 124.2 W . h.

5   Conclusions

This paper presents a configurable on-line monitoring system which is configured according to the users' requirements and the multiple energy consumers of the machine tools. The system is conducted on two machine tools. The case shows that the system

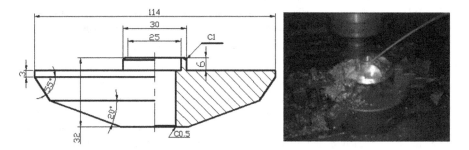

Fig. 5. The pallet during milling process.

Table 7. Energy consumption information of different energy resources during machining process

Objects	Power
Servo and fan system	124.2 W . h
Main spindle	281.8 W . h
Tool change	10 W . h
Cooling system	8.25 W . h
Feed motor X axis	10 W . h
Feed motor Y axis	10 W . h
Feed motor Z axis	13 W . h

could not only obtain the total energy during machining process, but also it can make the energy consumed by the specific energy consumer transparent. The results can provide a refined energy management to the users.

The main energy consumers are identified by analyzing energy consumption of the energy consumers, this analyzed results can help the designers to optimize the design of machine tools. For example, the designer could choose the high energy-efficiency motor for the main energy consumer.

The obtained energy efficiency and the energy consumed by the specific energy consumer can support the operators to make an energy reducing plan. The obtained total energy consumption and the energy consumed in the different state can support the management to make schedule in the factory.

Acknowledgements. The authors would like to thank the support from the National Natural Science Foundation of China (Grant No. 51575072), Chongqing Research Program of Basic Research and Frontier Technology (No. cstc2015jcyjBX0088).

References

1. Park, C.W., Kwon, K.S., Kim, W.B., Min, B.K., Park, S.J.: Energy consumption reduction technology in manufacturing—a selective review of policies. Int. J. Precis. Eng. Manuf. **10**, 151–173 (2009)

2. ISO WD 14955-1: Environmental evaluation of machine Tools-Part 1: energy-saving design methodology for machine tools. International Organization for Standardization (2010)
3. Seow, Y., Goffin, N., Rahimifard, S., Woolley, E.: A 'Design for Energy Minimization' approach to reduce energy consumption during the manufacturing phase. Energy **109**, 894–905 (2016)
4. Liu, S., Liu, F., Hu, S., Yin, Z.: Energy survey of machine tools: separating power information of the main transmission system during machining process. J. Adv. Mech. Des. Syst. Manuf. **6**(4), 445–455 (2012)
5. Zhao, G.Y., Liu, Z.Y., He, Y., Cao, H.J., Guo, Y.B.: Energy consumption in machining: classification, prediction, and reduction strategy. Energy **133**, 142–157 (2017)
6. Kara, S., Li, W.: Unit process energy consumption models for material removal processes. CIRP Ann. Manuf. Technol. **60**(1), 37–40 (2011)
7. Herrmann, C., Thiede, S., Kara, S., Hesselbach, J.: Energy oriented simulation of manufacturing systems – concept and application. CIRP Ann. Manuf. Technol. **60**(1), 45–58 (2011)
8. He, Y., Liu, B., Zhang, X., Gao, H., Liu, X.: A modeling method of task-oriented energy consumption for machining manufacturing system. J. Clean. Prod. **23**(1), 167–174 (2012)
9. Zhou, Z., Yao, B., Xu, W., Wang, L.: Condition monitoring towards energy-efficient manufacturing: a review. Int. J. Adv. Manuf. Technol. 1–21 (2017)
10. Delgado-Gomes, V., Oliveira-Lima, J.A., Martins, J.F.: Energy consumption awareness in manufacturing and production systems. Int. J. Comput. Integr. Manuf. **30**(1), 84–95 (2017)
11. Mourtzis, D., Vlachou, E., Milas, N., Dimitrakopoulos, G.: Energy consumption estimation for machining processes based on real-time shop floor monitoring via wireless sensor networks. In: CIRP Conference on Manufacturing Systems – CIPR CMS (2016)
12. Chiotellis, S., Grismajer, M.: Analysis of electrical power data streams in manufacturing. In: Dornfeld, D., Linke, B. (eds.) Leveraging Technology for a Sustainable World, pp. 533–538. Springer, Heidelberg (2012). https://doi.org/10.1007/978-3-642-29069-5_90
13. Peng, T., Xu, X.: An interoperable energy consumption analysis system for CNC machining. J. Clean. Prod. **140**, 1828–1841 (2016)
14. Lv, J., Tang, R., Jia, S., Liu, Y.: Experimental study on energy consumption of computer numerical control machine tools. J. Clean. Prod. **112**, 3864–3874 (2015)
15. Behrendt, T., Zein, A., Min, S.: Development of an energy consumption monitoring procedure for machine tools. CIRP Ann. Manuf. Technol. **61**(1), 43–46 (2012)
16. Dahmus, J.B., Gutowski, T.G.: An environmental analysis of machining. In: Proceedings of International Mechanical Engineering Congress and RD&D Expo, Anaheim, pp. 643–652 (2004)

Research on a Multi-scenario Energy Efficiency Evaluation Method for an Industrial Park Multi-energy System

Chao Shi[1(✉)], Wenzhong Gao[1,2], Liting Tian[2], and Lin Cheng[2]

[1] School of Electrical Engineering, Beijing Jiaotong University, Haidian District
Beijing 100044, China
16121511@bjtu.edu.cn
[2] China State Key Laboratory of Power System, Department of Electrical
Engineering, Tsinghua University, Beijing, China

Abstract. Based on the consideration of the system primary energy utilization and renewable energy consumption, the energy efficiency evaluation indices of multi-energy system of an industrial park is proposed. The weight of each index is determined by the information entropy principle, and the comprehensive energy efficiency evaluation index and evaluation method of the multi-energy system of industrial park are also established. Considering the change of energy demand in typical days of summer, winter and transition season, the two operating strategies of "Electric Load Following" and "Thermal Load Following" are used to simulate multiple system operating scenarios. Based on the established index system, the comprehensive energy efficiency of each scenario is calculated and its comprehensive energy efficiency is evaluated for an industrial park in Beijing. The case study shows that the comprehensive evaluation model and evaluation method of energy efficiency can fully reflect the characteristics of multi-energy complementary operation and cascading energy utilization in the park, which has practical significance for the design and operation of multi-energy system.

Keywords: Multi-energy systems · Comprehensive energy efficiency
Entropy weight method · Cooling Heating and Power · Multi-scenario

1 Introduction

To address energy crisis and environment issues, the integration of multiple energy sources has become a hot topic in academia and industries in recent years, which is expected to improve the comprehensive energy utilization efficiency and help solve major concern of sustainability in many countries around the world [1]. The

The paper is supported in part by National Key R&D Program of China (2017YFB0903300); National Natural Science Foundation of China (NSFC) (51777105); Science and Technology Program of State Grid Corporation of China (Research and Application of Micro-grid Planning and Operation); and project SKLD17KM03 of China State Key Lab. of Power System.

© Springer Nature Singapore Pte Ltd. 2018
K. Li et al. (Eds.): ICSEE 2018/IMIOT 2018, CCIS 925, pp. 151–162, 2018.
https://doi.org/10.1007/978-981-13-2381-2_14

construction of the multi-energy system of industrial park has recently been considered as a feasible approach scholars and enterprises. For example, in June 2017, the National Energy Administration of China announced the first batch of "Internet+" smart energy demonstration projects, out of which twelve projects are for park-level multi-energy systems [2]. At present, constructing high energy efficiency multi-energy system for industrial parks is considered to be one of the effective ways to solve the energy demand problem in China at this stage [3–5].

Many scholars have studied the energy efficiency of the distributed energy CCHP (Combined Cooling Heating and Power) system. There are many studies based on the first law of thermodynamics; e.g., some studies [6, 7] evaluate the performance of the CCHP system based on the energy analysis method using the first law of thermodynamics. The research based on the second law of thermodynamics generally uses exergy efficiency as an evaluation index. Some studies [8, 9] reveal the energy utilization status of the CCHP system from the perspective of the second law of thermodynamics. Some other studies [10, 11] analyze in detail the exergy efficiency and primary energy efficiency, and point out that the efficiency of the gas turbine has a great influence on the optimization of the operation of the CCHP system.

In this paper, based on the first and second law of thermodynamics analysis and utilization rate of renewable energy, the specific evaluation indices of energy efficiency for multi-energy system of industrial park is constructed. Secondly, the information entropy principle is used to determine the weight of each index, and to form an energy efficiency assessment method of the multi-energy system. Finally, through the operation process simulation of the multi-energy system in an industrial park, the comprehensive energy efficiency of the park is evaluated to verify the proposed method.

2 Energy Efficiency Evaluation Index

2.1 Multi-energy System of an Industrial Park

The multi-energy system of an industrial park may include renewable energy power generation (such as photovoltaic power generation, wind power generation, biomass power generation, etc.), distributed cogeneration units (CHP), heat pumps, gas boilers, and electric refrigeration units and so on. The input and output energy flow of a typical multi-energy system is shown in Fig. 1 [12].

Among these devices, wind power generation, photovoltaic power generation and cogeneration units are used for the electric energy production. The electrical energy storage devices are used to smooth the fluctuation of power output and load demand of the park. The electricity load demand is partly supplemented by purchasing power from external grid; the residual heat generated by the power generation process of the cogeneration unit is used to drive the residual heat unit for cold and hot water to meet the cold and heat load requirements, the insufficient part of which are supplemented by a heat pump.

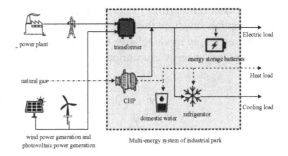

Fig. 1. Input and output energy flow diagram of multi-energy system for an industrial park

2.2   Energy Efficiency Evaluation Index

In order to reflect the energy utilization level of the park from multiple viewpoints, this paper combines the first and second laws of thermodynamics analysis to establish energy efficiency evaluation indices.

Primary Energy Consumption. The multi-energy system of an industrial park operates under a combined cooling, heating, and electricity power supply mode. And the primary energy consumption (Q_{in}^1) is the sum of the consumed amount of gas heat (Q_{gas}) and the purchased electricity (E_{ep}) which is converted to the corresponding primary energy consumption; On the other hand, Q_{in}^0 refers to the energy consumption of system operating under the separated supply mode in which cooling, heating, and electricity power will be supplied separately.

$$Q_{in}^1 = Q_{gas} + \frac{E_{ep}}{\eta} \tag{1}$$

$$Q_{in}^0 = \frac{Q_e}{\eta} + \frac{Q_c}{COP \bullet \eta} + \frac{Q_h}{\eta_h} \tag{2}$$

where η means the total efficiency of the traditional coal-fired power plant delivering electric energy; COP means the refrigeration coefficient of an electric refrigerator; η_h means heating efficiency; Q_e, Q_c and Q_h are the electricity, cooling, and heat load energy consumption quantity in the industrial park. For example, $\eta = 0.3348$, COP = 3.6 in this paper.

Primary Energy Ratio. PER refers to the ratio of system output energy to primary energy consumption under the combined cooling, heating, and electricity power supply mode [13].

$$PER = \frac{Q_e + Q_c + Q_h}{Q_{in}^1} \tag{3}$$

Primary Energy Saving Rate. The primary energy saving rate refers to the ratio of the primary energy consumption saved by the park operating in the combined cooling, heating, and electricity power supply mode relative to the operation under the separated supply mode to the total primary energy consumption.

$$\Delta q = \frac{Q_{in}^0 - Q_{in}^1}{Q_{in}^0} \tag{4}$$

Renewable Energy Consumption Rate. The consumption rate of renewable energy refers to the ratio of the amount of renewable energy generated that is used by the load in the park to the actual amount of renewable energy generated in the park.

$$R_{re} = \frac{Q_{re}^1}{Q_{re}^0} \tag{5}$$

Exergy Efficiency. Exergy efficiency refers to the ratio of the total exergy output by the entire system to the total exergy input by the system. Exergy efficiency reflects the degree of energy conversion in the system [14].

$$\varphi = \frac{E_{out}}{E_{in}} = \frac{Q_e + \varepsilon_{Qh} \cdot Q_h - \varepsilon_{Qc} \cdot Q_c}{\varepsilon_0 \cdot E_{gas} + Q_{re}^1} = \frac{Q_e + (1 - T_o/T_{Qh}) \cdot Q_h - (1 - T_o/T_{Qc}) \cdot Q_c}{\varepsilon_0 \cdot E_{gas} + Q_{re}^1} \tag{6}$$

where ε_0, ε_{Qh} and ε_{Qc} respectively means the natural gas energy quality coefficient, the thermal energy quality coefficient, and the cold energy quality coefficient; E_{gas} means the natural gas consumption; T_o, T_{Qh} and T_{Qc} respectively means the environment temperature, heat source temperature, and cold source temperature.

3   Multi-scenario Energy Efficiency Evaluation Method Based on Information Entropy

3.1   The Operation Scenarios of Multi-energy System in an Industrial Park

The energy efficiency of an industrial park depends on the input-output conversion relationship and the operation strategies of the multi-energy system [15]. During the operation of multi-energy system, the comprehensive energy efficiency will vary from seasons and operating strategies.

There is a coupling relationship between the park's electric energy and thermal energy output, and the two operation strategies of "Thermal Load Following" and "Electric Load Following" are considered. According to season and operation strategy, this paper summarizes five scenarios of the multi-energy system of a typical industrial park as shown in Table 1.

Table 1. The scenarios of energy efficiency criteria

Number	Evaluation scenario
S1	"Electric Load Following" operating strategy on a typical winter day
S2	"Thermal Load Following" operating strategy on a typical winter day
S3	"Electric Load Following" operating strategy on a typical summer day
S4	"Thermal Load Following" operating strategy on a typical summer day
S5	"Electric Load Following" operating strategy on a typical transition season day

3.2 Comprehensive Energy Efficiency Evaluation Method

(1) Normalization of indicators [16]

Participate in the assessment scenario, denoted as $M = (m_1, m_2, \cdots, m_m)$; the evaluation index is marked as $D = (d_1, d_2, \cdots, d_n)$, and the value of the j-th index of the evaluated i-th scene is denoted as $x_{ij}(i = 1, 2, \cdots, m, j = 1, 2, \cdots, n)$, then an index matrix $X = [x_{ij}]_{m \times n}$ composed of evaluation indices is formed.

The larger the index value, the better the characterization result, according to the normalization formula (7); the smaller the index value, the better the characterization result, according to the normalization formula (8):

$$v_{ij} = \frac{x_{ij} - \min(x_j)}{\max(x_j) - \min(x_j)} \tag{7}$$

$$v_{ij} = \frac{\max(x_j) - x_{ij}}{\max(x_j) - \min(x_j)} \tag{8}$$

After standardization and dimensionless treatment, and the evaluation index matrix X is specified as a matrix V. The characteristic proportion p_{ij} of the i-th evaluation scenario is calculated under the j-th index, and form the normalized matrix P.

$$P_{ij} = \frac{V_{ij}}{\sum_{i=1}^{m} V_{ij}} \tag{9}$$

(2) Calculation of index information entropy

Therefore, we can judge the weight of the indicator in the comprehensive evaluation by judging the information entropy value of the index. The calculation formula of the information entropy value of the j-th index:

$$e_j = -\frac{1}{\ln(m)} \sum_{i=1}^{m} p_{ij} \bullet \ln p_{ij} \qquad (10)$$

(3) Determination of the weight of the index

First, the entropy weight w_j of the j-th index is determined by formula (11):

$$w_j = \frac{d_j}{\sum\limits_{j=1}^{n} d_j} = \frac{1 - e_j}{\sum\limits_{j=1}^{n} 1 - e_j} \qquad (11)$$

(4) Calculation of the comprehensive evaluation result

The comprehensive evaluation value of i-th scene is:

$$v_i = \sum_{j=1}^{n} w_j P_{ij} \qquad (12)$$

4   Case Studies

4.1   Load Demand

This paper takes the multi-energy system of an industrial park in Beijing as an example. The park serves commercial centers, industrial manufactures, and residential buildings. Each kind of user has demand for cold, heat, and electricity loads. There are a wind turbine and photovoltaic generation in the park. The distributed renewable energy and natural gas generation in the park is grid-connected but no back-feed is allowed to the grid. The main equipment capacity in the park energy system is shown in Table 2.

Table 2. Equipment capacity

Equipment	Wind turbine	PV	CHP	BESS	HP
Total capacity	2 MW	1.5 MW	3 MW	0.3 MW	2.5 MW

Through DeST software simulation, the typical daily cooling, heating and electrical load curves of the park in summer, winter and transition seasons are obtained, as is shown in Figs. 2, 3 and 4.

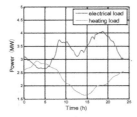

Fig. 2. Typical daily load demand during the winter

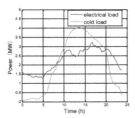

Fig. 3. Typical daily load demand during the summer

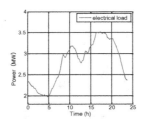

Fig. 4. Typical daily load demand during the transition season

4.2 Simulation of Each Scene in the System

The hourly power of each equipment can be obtained by using the two operating strategies of "Thermal Load Following" and "Electric Load Following" for multi scenario simulation in the typical days. The electricity power and thermal power curves of each device of the system under each scenario are shown in Figs. 5, 6, 7, 8, 9, 10, 11, 12 and 13.

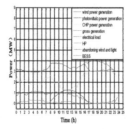

Fig. 5. Typical electricity consumption under the "Electric Load Following" strategy during the winter season

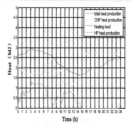

Fig. 6. Typical calorific figure under the "Electric Load Following" strategy during the winter season

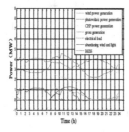

Fig. 7. Typical electricity consumption under the "Thermal Load Following" strategy during the winter season

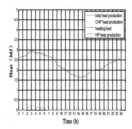

Fig. 8. Typical calorific figure under the "Thermal Load Following" strategy during the winter season

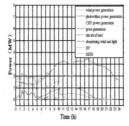

Fig. 9. Typical electricity consumption under the "Electric Load Following" strategy during the summer season

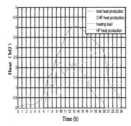

Fig. 10. Typical calorific figure under the "Electric Load Following" strategy during the summer season

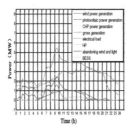

Fig. 11. Typical electricity consumption under the "Thermal Load Following" strategy during the summer season

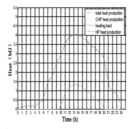

Fig. 12. Typical calorific figure under the "Thermal Load Following" strategy during the summer season

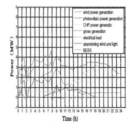

Fig. 13. Typical electricity consumption under the "Electric Load Following" strategy during the transition season

4.3 Calculation Results of Evaluation Indicators in Each Scenario

Based on the actual operation of each scenario, and according to the calculation formula of the indices, the specific values of energy efficiency indices are calculated, as shown in Table 3. Because S1 adopts the "Electric Load Following" operation strategy, renewable energy is completely accommodated; and because part of energy comes from the solar and wind, the primary energy ratio of S1 exceeds 1.0. CHP cannot meet the demand of electrical load at the maximum power operation after 16 o'clock, the electricity is purchased from the grid. Because waste of the heat makes the primary energy ratio of S1 to be lower than that of S3.

Table 3. The result of energy efficiency criteria

Number	Energy efficiency evaluation index	S1	S2	S3	S4	S5
A1	Primary energy ratio	1.153	0.954	1.352	1.030	0.947
A2	Primary energy saving rate	0.587	0.501	0.627	0.510	0.620
A3	Renewable energy consumption rate	1	0.500	0.881	0.325	0.722
A4	Exergy efficiency	0.800	0.822	0.761	0.763	0.715

S2 adopts the "Thermal Load Following" operation strategy. The heat of the CHP is fully utilized, so the exergy efficiency is high. S2 produces more electricity while meeting the higher heat load demand, which results in obvious curtailment of wind and PV power, and lower renewable energy consumption rate than S1.

When S3 adopts the operation strategy of the "Electric Load Following", in order to avoid the frequent start and stop of CHP, CHP still runs at the minimum power though CHP does not need to generate electricity, during the period from 0 to 10 o'clock, which causes wind curtailment. So the rate of renewable energy consumption is lower than S1.

S4 adopts the "Thermal Load Following" operation strategy. As the cooling load demand increases rapidly between 6 and 9 o'clock, the amount of electricity generated by CHP is redundant, so that the wind and PV power abandoning is obvious, and the rate of renewable energy consumption is very low.

For S5, the wind power in the transitional season is relatively large. Between 0 to 8 o'clock, the amount of wind power generated even exceeds the electric load demand, resulting in the wind power curtailment. Due to the lack of cooling and heating load requirements in the transition season of S5, the heat of CHP is wasted, making the energy efficiency not high.

4.4   Evaluation Results of Entropy Weight Method

The entropy value and weight of each indices are calculated as shown in Table 4. The result shows that under the 5 scenarios the largest difference exists in primary energy ratio and primary energy saving rate, and the corresponding information entropy value is the smallest. Therefore, in the final evaluation calculation, these two indices have the largest weight [17].

Table 4. Evaluation results

Indicators	A1	A2	A3	A4
Information entropy	0.606	0.735	0.801	0.822
Weight	0.380	0.256	0.192	0.172

According to the index information entropy and index weights, the comprehensive evaluation value of each system scheme can be calculated, as shown in Table 5.

Table 5. Evaluation results

Scenarios	S1	S2	S3	S4	S5
Evaluation value	0.918	0.728	0.974	0.716	0.780

According to the evaluation results, CHP chooses the operation strategy of "Electric Load Following" in the heating season, cooling season and transition season.

5   Conclusion

On the basis of full consideration of the utilization efficiency of non-renewable energy and the rate of renewable energy consumption, this paper establishes a comprehensive evaluation index model of energy efficiency of the multi-energy system of an industrial park. Entropy weight method is used to calculate the weight of each index, thus the specific value of the comprehensive energy efficiency can be evaluated under various operating scenarios. Finally, a case analysis is carried out using the evaluation indices and method established in this paper. Through the simulation of multi scenario operation in the park, the operation strategy of the park has a great influence on the comprehensive energy efficiency of the system. This paper provides an effective and practical method for the evaluation of the multi-energy system of an industrial park, which is significant for the construction of multi-energy system.

References

1. Ma, Z., Zhou, X., Shang, Y.: Exploring the concept, key technologies and development model of energy internet. Power Syst. Technol. **39**(11), 3018–3022 (2015). (in Chinese)
2. Announcement of the National Energy Administration on Announcement of the First "Internet+" Smart Energy (Energy Internet) Demonstration Project. http://zfxxgk.nea.gov.cn/auto83/201707/t20170706_2825.htm
3. Cheng, L., Liu, C., Zhu, S., et al.: Study of micro energy internet based on multi-energy interconnected strategy. Power Syst. Technol. **40**(1), 132–138 (2016). (in Chinese)
4. Cheng, L., Zhang, J., Huang, R., et al.: Multi-energy complementary based on multi-scenario planning case analysis of integrated energy system. Electr. Power Autom. Equip. **37**(6), 282–287 (2017). (in Chinese)
5. Wang, W., Wang, D., Jia, H., et al.: Review of steady-state analysis of typical regional integrated energy system under the background of the energy internet. Proc. CSEE **36**(12), 3292–3305 (2016)
6. Kong, X.Q., Wang, R., Huang, X.H.: Energy efficiency and economic feasibility of CCHP driven by Stirling engine. Energy Convers. Manag. **45**(9–10), 1433–1442 (2004)
7. Li, H., Fu, L., Geng, K., et al.: Energy utilization evaluation of CCHP systems. Energy Build. **38**(3), 253–257 (2006)
8. Cai, R.: Heating supply criteria and basic analysis of heat supply for gas turbine. Eng. Thermophys. **8**(3), 201–205 (1987). (in Chinese)
9. Lin, F., Yi, J.: Energy analysis of a combined heating, cooling and electricity system from the viewpoint of the second law. Energy Technol. **9**(3), 142–147 (2000). (in Chinese)
10. Jia, M., Ling, C.: An analysis of several main evaluation models of combined heating cooling and power production. Refrigeration Air Cond. **4**(4), 34–38 (2004). (in Chinese)
11. Huangfu, Y., Wu, J.Y., Wang, R.Z., et al.: Evaluation and analysis of novel Micro-scale Combined Cooling, Heating and Power (MCCHP) system. Energy Convers. Manag. **48**(5), 1703–1709 (2007)
12. Xue, Y., Guo, Q., Sui, H.: Energy comprehensive utilization index for multi-energy collaborative parks. Electric Power Autom. Equip. **37**(6), 117–122 (2017). (in Chinese)
13. Wang, Q., Fang, F.: Optimal configuration of CCHP system based on energy, economical, and environmental considerations. In: Proceedings of the 2nd International Conference on Intelligent Control and Information Processing, ICICIP 2011, pp. 489–494 (2011)
14. Guo, Y., Cheng, L.: Efficiency-based energy efficiency analysis model for integrated energy system. Renew. Energy Resour. **35**(9), 1387–1393 (2017). (in Chinese)
15. Zhang, X., Chen, Z.: Energy consumption performance of combined heat cooling and power system. Proc. CSEE **27**(5), 93–98 (2007). (in Chinese)
16. Sun, S.N., Nie, X.T.: Assessment of agent system project risk based on entropy method. In: International Conference on Management and Service Science, Piscataway, pp. 1–4. IEEE (2010)
17. Zhang, T., Zhu, T.: Optimization design and multi-criteria comprehensive evaluation method of combined cooling heating and power system. Proc. CSEE **35**(14), 3706–3713 (2015). (in Chinese)

Green Supply Chain Management Information Integration Framework and Operation Mode Analysis

Zhou Zhou[✉], Kaihu Hou, and Hui Zhang

Kunming University of Science and Technology, Chenggong, Kunming 650000, China
372398896@qq.com

Abstract. So far, the connotation and system of Green supply chain Management (GSCM) have already had quite a lot of content, and its theoretical research has also achieved fruitful results. However, at present, the connotation and system of Green supply chain Management still lack the support of information foundation, so it is difficult to monitor, analyze and evaluate the implementation of Green supply chain Management. Based on the connotation and system of green supply chain management, this thesis discusses how to build the information base of Green supply chain Management, and puts forward a new information integration framework and operation mode of green supply chain. It lays a foundation for realizing the connotation and system of Green supply chain Management and the integration of enterprise management information system, and provides a way to solve the problem that the Green supply chain Management system is difficult to monitor, analyze and evaluate.

Keywords: Green supply chain Management (GSCM) · Integration framework Operation pattern

1 Introduction

"Green supply chain Management (GSCM)", as a feasible way to solve the problem of not only economic benefit but also saving environmental protection in manufacturing industry, has been paid more and more attention and research by many scholars. For the GSCM, domestic and foreign scholars have carried out a lot of research: Anne Touboulic and Helen Walker have studied the theoretical development and present situation of sustainable supply chain, and put forward that integration and comprehensive understanding of the concept of "sustainable" will be the main challenge facing the development of sustainable supply chain in the future. Based on the analysis of a large number of literatures with high recognition at present, it is pointed out that more microscopic and multi-level methods should be used to study the sustainable supply chain in the future [1]. Stephan Vachon conducted a survey of North American packaging and printing plants (USA and Canada) using statistical probabilistic models to analyze the data, indicating that there is a link between environmental management in supply chains and the quality management norms used by factories. It is speculated that the

© Springer Nature Singapore Pte Ltd. 2018
K. Li et al. (Eds.): ICSEE 2018/IMIOT 2018, CCIS 925, pp. 163–172, 2018.
https://doi.org/10.1007/978-981-13-2381-2_15

environmental cooperation in the supply chain is more to prevent the production of unqualified products than to solve the disputes or evaluate the enterprises in the supply chain [2]. Green Jr and others collected data from 159 managers of manufacturing enterprises, analyzed and evaluated the practical application and performance model of supply chain management by using structural equation modeling method, analyzed suppliers and manufacturers. The impact of different cooperation links between customers on environmental performance and enterprise economic performance. Only by grasping the balance point between environmental performance and economic performance can we maximize the economic benefits of enterprises [3]. Marco Formentini and Paolo Taticchi have studied how to implement sustainability method and management mechanism in enterprises. Through the perspective of contingency theory, strategic adjustment and enterprise resource-based perspective, seven cases are analyzed. A sustainable supply chain management mechanism was developed and validated in the surveyed company [4].

In China, the research of Green supply chain Management has also made a lot of achievements. Sun Tingting and others analyzed and summarized the process, environment and technical support of green supply chain management, and put forward the establishment and management methods of green supply chain in our manufacturing industry [5]. Zhang Jinhua proposed the "three-level information integration model" by modeling the operational framework of green supply chain management and analyzing its information integration mode [6]. By studying the integration of three dimensions of enterprise environment management, innovation management and supply chain management, Yang Jiehui and others put forward the sustainable innovation system of supply chain and its model, and analyzed the key points of applying this model to different levels [7]. Yisheng and Xue draw up the following three conclusions by using multiple linear regression model: the internal environment management in the enterprise green supply chain management has the positive effect on the enterprise green innovation; The ecological design of enterprise green supply chain management is positively related to green innovation, and the cooperation between enterprises and consumers is beneficial to the green innovation of enterprises [8].

At present, most of the researches mainly focus on two aspects: on the one hand, how to establish and implement the theory of green supply chain management in enterprises, and on the other hand, the research on how to integrate new ideas and technologies into green supply chain. But in the environment and background of industry 4.0, the above research generally lacks the support of manufacturing informatization. And for the green supply chain management information research is less. Although the operational framework and integration mode of green supply chain are studied in reference [6], the main concern is the integration of the whole information from the outside of the enterprise and the inside of the enterprise, but the green supply chain within the enterprise is seldom discussed. This thesis starts with the information integration framework and operation mode of GSCM, takes the internal supply chain of enterprise as the object, and combines the idea of product life cycle management and discussed how to realize the informatization of GSCM in manufacturing enterprises.

2   The Connotation of GSCM Informatization

By supplementing and integrating the management systems of each link in the internal supply chain, a complete green supply chain management system within the enterprise can be constructed completely. A complete green supply chain management system oriented to the internal enterprise should be the different management information systems involved in the production and operation of the enterprise. The functions of each department are integrated and planned rationally and effectively, and the indicators, processes, standards and systems of the green supply chain management are integrated into it, thus a new, more complete and completely new green supply chain management system which combines the functions of each part of the system is built.

The GSCM system has the basic information of the whole enterprise and the business data generated in the operation of the enterprise, and these quantitative data can be extracted by technical means. And these data are stored in the enterprise database. Therefore, the GSCM system can solve the problem that the green supply chain management lacks the information support and the green supply chain management is difficult to quantify. Following is an analysis of the GSCM integration framework to illustrate how to address these two issues in detail.

3   GSCM Information Integration Framework

In order to solve the problem that green supply chain management lacks information support and is difficult to quantify, three key points must be grasped: (1) GSCM should be integrated according to what technical route, the business data involved in the operation of the enterprise should be preserved to the maximum extent, to ensure the integrity of the data, and make it become the information support of the enterprise. (2) which management systems should be integrated in GSCM to ensure the overall coverage of the main business of manufacturing enterprises; (3) In view of the problem that the evaluation of green supply chain management is difficult to quantify, what evaluation indexes should be set up in the GSCM system to evaluate the degree of green supply chain management? The following three problems are discussed in detail.

3.1   Technical Integration Framework for GSCM

From the technical level, GSCM system should be based on business system, through database integration planning, business logic integration planning and business process redesign to ensure data integrity. Realize the goal of unified access and unified business collaboration.

Therefore, the technology integration framework of green supply chain management system is divided into four levels: application system layer, data layer, logical abstraction layer, business process layer and access layer. As shown in Fig. 1:

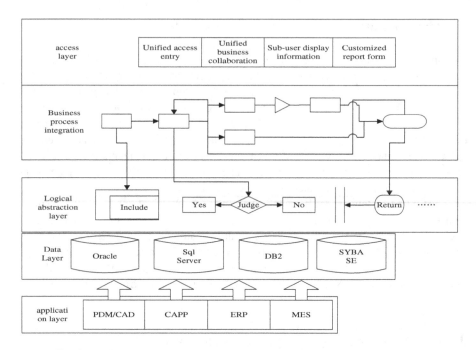

Fig. 1. Technology integration framework of Green supply chain Management

Technology Integration Framework of GSCM explains how to realize the integration of GSCM system from the technical level.

The application layer includes the basic business system involved in the production and operation of the enterprise, which reflects the basic information needed for the production and operation of the enterprise. The data layer includes all the business and production data of the enterprise and these data may be independent and dispersed before integration, so it is necessary to integrate the new business process planning in the business process layer, according to the actual situation of the enterprise. The lowest integration mode, the data-based integration mode and the function-based integration mode are selected to share and transfer information in the data layer through the processing of logical abstraction layer. Eventually, the user realizes the unified access to the new system through the unified access portal of the access layer, the cooperation of the business, the display of system information by role and the display of different reports according to the user's role.

3.2   Application Layer Integration Framework for GSCM

Application layer Integration Framework for GSCM explains what the GSCM system should contain from the concept level, the relationship between each module and how they work to form a complete system.

Different from the technology integration framework of GSCM, the technology integration framework of GSCM provides the technical route and integration strategy for the implementation of the application layer integration framework of GSCM. The application layer integration framework of GSCM indicates which aspects of enterprise operation and which management information system should be involved in GSCM system. The technology integration framework of GSCM is the theoretical foundation of GSCM application layer integration framework. The application layer integration framework of GSCM is the concrete content of GSCM system. Both of them constitute the whole integration framework of GSCM system, which is indispensable.

The application layer integration framework of GSCM is an important foundation. What is different from the common enterprise information integration system is that the application system integration framework of GSCM must be combined with the connotation and system of green supply chain management. By controlling several important stages in the product life cycle, the design is carried out.

(1) Product design stage

In the design phase, through the secondary development of the PDM system, we can identify and identify the materials that need to be under key control, including hazardous substances, controlled substances and recycled materials, etc. At present, the country has clearly defined the environmental pollution materials and recyclable materials. The concrete classification may refer to the national standard "green production enterprise green supply chain management guideline" appendix C. Do not allow or restrict designers to use environmentally hazardous materials, in the system for controlled materials for clear color or marking. For recyclable materials, it should be arranged in advance in the system to make it the first choice for product designers.

(2) Acquisition phase

In the procurement process, the purchasing and warehousing module of the ERP system needs to be developed in a second time, and the material audit and warehousing workflow in the system is modified. In the supplier management of purchasing module, the supplier should be given green supplier rating according to the environmental protection degree of the material provided in a supplier evaluation cycle, which can be used in the future business of the enterprise to select the supplier with higher rating. In the process of material audit, in addition to the quality and quantity of materials, it is also necessary to audit their environmental protection to ensure that the materials purchased by enterprises meet the requirements of the green supply chain management system. In addition, in the storage module, It is also necessary to identify and mark all kinds of materials to facilitate managers to check and count all kinds of materials that need to be controlled.

(3) Process planning stage

In the process planning, we need to improve and expand the CAPP system, add the green characteristic evaluation module into the hybrid CAPP system, and evaluate the green performance of the processing process from the aspects of resource consumption and environmental pollution and so on. The results of process planning and evaluation are fed back to PDM system or PLM system, so that the designer can get enough information to improve and optimize the product design.

(4) Production phase

In the process of production, MES system must be introduced, based on the real-time data in the production process, and the configuration technology of the MES system is used to realize the material consumption in the production workshop, machining workshop, assembly workshop and other production areas. The waste generated, pollutant discharge and energy consumption can be monitored in real time, and alarm warnings can be set for some production links that need to be monitored in accordance with the pre-set pollution targets. Help enterprises to improve the green production execution, monitoring ability and the ability to respond to the alarm in the actual production process.

Through the above analysis, the integrated framework of GSCM and the management system involved in it have been described and analyzed in detail. The following is a diagram of the application layer integration framework for GSCM, as shown in Fig. 2:

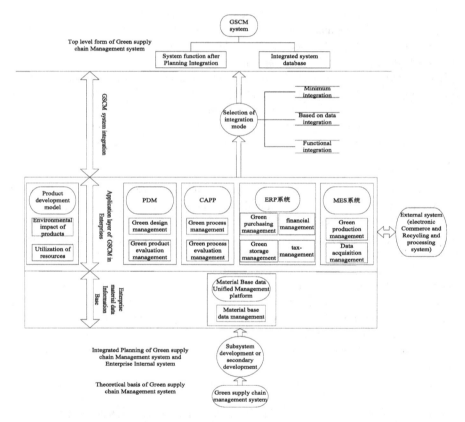

Fig. 2. Application layer integration framework diagram of GSCM

3.3   Evaluation Indexes in Each Stage of GSCM

In order to quantitatively evaluate the GSCM, different indicators need to be set at different stages of business operations:

(1)   Product design stage

In this stage, the proportion of green or recyclable materials to the whole product (PGWP) and the proportion of heavy polluted or controlled materials to the whole product (PPWP) should be taken as the evaluation index.

(2)   Acquisition phase

In this stage, the proportion of green or recyclable materials in the purchased materials (PGMP) should be used as an evaluation index. For suppliers of green materials required by the government, the proportion of green or recyclable materials provided by suppliers can be used as an indicator to evaluate the green grade of suppliers.

(3)   Process planning stage

In this stage, the waste ratio of the process output used (WRPO) and the ratio of pollutants produced (RPP) should be used as an evaluation indicator.

(4)   Production phase

In this stage, the utilization ratio of actual materials (URAM), the consumption of energy (CE) and the quantity of pollutant emission (QPE) should be taken as the evaluation index.

4   Analyses on the Operation Mode of GSCM

Practice shows that the economic benefit and management height of the same system are completely different under different operating modes. Therefore, how to reasonably design and plan the operation mode of GSCM to achieve the system requirements of high cohesion and low coupling, It is crucial and important problem to realize the efficient operation of the whole supply chain management system and to embody the green supply chain management system in the operation of the system. Next part will carry on the discussion and the analysis to the GSCM operation pattern.

The essence of the GSCM system is firstly the existence of the production and operation management system of the enterprise. Therefore, the first consideration of the operation mode of green supply chain management system is to design according to the operation mode of enterprises. From product research and development to product design, raw material procurement, production, accumulation of enterprise material information database to product sales. After that, the third party system manages the transportation and recycling of the products. Figure 3 is the operation mode of the green supply chain management system designed according to the production and operation mode of the enterprise:

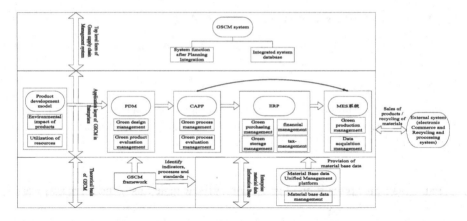

Fig. 3. Operation Mode of GSCM system

The product design system according to the green design standard design product style, build a product BOM list. Determine the required materials, transfer the relevant documents and materials to the process management system, the process management system according to the green production process standards to arrange the appropriate processing process and process, Then the raw material information needed to be purchased can be transferred to the ERP system according to the demand of the enterprise, and the information can be selectively transferred to the ERP system in order to support the function of quota material collection and so on. At the same time, the product drawings, processing technology, BOM list and so on are passed to the MES system. The raw material inventory status information in the warehouse is passed to the MES system by the ERP system. If the stock is sufficient, it is ready to produce, if the stock is insufficient, then the raw material is waited to complete the production after the raw material purchase. In the production process, the MES system carries on the production management and the each production process monitor according to the green production standard, guarantees the production smoothly, finally hands the product to the third party system to carry on the management.

The operation mode of GSCM system designed according to the above model accords with the production operation of the enterprise and can support the normal production operation management of the enterprise. However, this mode belongs to the "propulsive" mode of operation. Although it can normally carry out various business blocks, it lacks feedback to form a closed-loop information flow, and it is difficult to improve the management level of an enterprise. Secondly, there is a lack of quantitative indicators to evaluate and improve the operation model, which will limit the flexibility of the GSCM system, once the implementation is completed, it is difficult to improve and improve. Therefore, in order to make up the shortcomings and shortcomings of the "advanced " operation mode, this paper puts forward the operation mode of the improved operation green supply chain management system, as shown in Fig. 4:

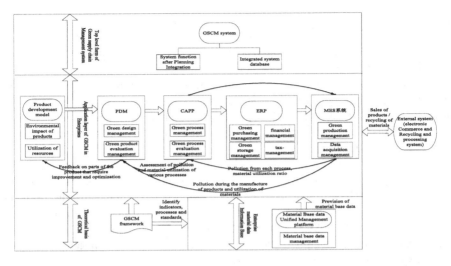

Fig. 4. Improved operation mode of GSCM system

In view of the problems in the "propulsive" operation mode, the improved GSCM system adds the data feedback flow monitored and collected from the production process to the improved GSCM system, thus realizing the closed-loop flow of information. Through the quantitative data such as pollution situation and material utilization rate collected in the process of product manufacture and each process, the system of product design and process management is fed back to the product design system and the process management system. Facilitate designers and process managers to better analyze the causes of pollution, pollution and raw materials are fully utilized. Thus, the pollution treatment methods or product and process solutions are given, and the new generation of products and corresponding process processes are designed. At the same time, the designers feed back to the R & D department the parts of the next generation products that need to be improved and optimized. So that R&D department has targeted R&D. This process is repeated in the process of production and manufacture of the new generation of products, and a continuous improvement and innovation of the enterprise operation mode is formed.

The two operational models are compared here in one year using the evaluation indicators mentioned above, thus illustrating the improved operational model being more refined and mature, as shown in Table 1:

Table 1. Promotion comparison table

	Product design stage		Acquisition phase	Process planning stage		Production phase		
Promotion	PGWP	PPWP	PGMP	WRPO	RPP	URAM	CE	QPE
Unused system	–	–	–	–	–	–	–	–
"Propulsive" operation mode	24%	56%	70%	10%	40%	85%	90%	–
Improved model	32%	50%	82%	8%	38%	88%	90%	–

5 Conclusion

Green supply chain is a new mode and inevitable trend of the development of our manufacturing industry in the future. Based on the connotation and system of green supply chain management, this paper further expounds the integrated framework and two operation modes of green supply chain management system. The two operation modes are analyzed and compared. The GSCM system after planning and integration has solved the problem that traditional supply chain management system lacks systematic support and is difficult to quantify.

The GSCM system after planning and integration has solved the problem that traditional supply chain management system lacks systematic support and is difficult to quantify. Through the practical application in a certain equipment manufacturing enterprise, this model provides a supporting platform for the system realization and quantitative evaluation of the GSCM system of the enterprise. The logistics and information flow of the enterprise are unified effectively, which improves the management level of the enterprise and the ability of the GSCM.

References

1. Touboulic, A., Walker, H.: Theories in sustainable supply chain management: a structured literature review. Int. J. Phys. Distrib. Logist. Manag. **1**(2), 16–42 (2015)
2. Vachon, S., Klassen, R.D.: Environmental management and manufacturing performance: the role of collaboration in the supply chain. Int. J. Prod. Econ. **2**, 299–315 (2008)
3. Green Jr., K.W., Zelbst, P.J., Meacham, J., et al.: Green supply chain management practices: impact on performance. Chain. Manag. **3**, 290–305 (2012)
4. Formentini, M., Taticchi, P.: Corporate sustainability approaches and governance mechanisms in sustainable supply chain management. J. Clean. Prod. **112**, 1920–1933 (2014)
5. Sun, T., Xi, D., Wang, Y.: Suggestions on the implementation of green supply chain management in manufacturing enterprises. Stand. China **03**, 77–81 (2017)
6. Zhang, J.: Analysis of operation framework and information integration model of green supply chain management. Inf. Sci. **32**(12), 105–108+114 (2014)
7. Yang, J., Han, Q., Shui, H.: Three-dimensional Integration of enterprise environment management, innovation management and supply chain management-construction and application of supply chain sustainable innovation system. Sci. Technol. Prog. Count. Measures **32**(08), 18–23 (2015)
8. Yi, S., Xue, Q.: Green supply chain management and green innovation-an empirical study based on Chinese manufacturing enterprises. Manag. Res. Dev. **37**(06), 103–110 (2016)
9. Sauvé, S., Bernard, S., Sloan, P.: Environmental sciences, sustainable development and circular economy: alternative concepts for trans-disciplinary research. Environ. Dev. **17**, 48–56 (2016)
10. Bai, C., Tang, J.: The game analysis of green supply chain cooperation in manufacturing-sales enterprises. J. Syst. Eng. **32**(06), 818–828 (2017)
11. Liu, Y., Wang, T.: Green supply chain management: development process, foreign experience and enlightenment. Ecol. Econ. 32(06), 138–141+204 (2016)
12. Dubey, R., Gunasekaran, A., Papadopoulos, T., Childe, S.J., Shibin, K.T., Wamba, S.F.: Sustainable supply chain management: framework and further research directions. J. Clean. Prod. **142**, 1119–1130 (2016)

Design of Temperature Monitoring System with Low Power Consumption for High Voltage Electrical Equipment

Hongqing Wang, Minjie Zhu$^{(\boxtimes)}$, Yining Bi, Xiaohui Liu,
and Haiping Ma

Department of Electrical Engineering, Shaoxing University, Shaoxing 312000,
Zhejiang, China
zhuminjiesx@gmail.com

Abstract. In order to ensure the high voltage electrical equipment working efficiently and safely, a wireless temperature monitoring system with low power consumption was designed based on C8051F930 and Si4438. The system includes the host and the slave,both of which are composed of main control module, wireless communication module, power module and so on. The slave is installed in electric equipment, and it sends temperature data to the host through wireless communication. When the temperature exceeds the preset value, the system sends warning information. The system has the advantages of low power consumption, high precision, long distance and low cost, which enables users to remote temperature monitoring of high-voltage electrical equipment in time.

Keywords: Wireless communication · Low power consumption
C8051F930 · Si4438

1 Introduction

Nowadays fire or explosion caused by high voltage electrical equipment or their poor installation quality is common, which results in hidden danger for major public projects and infrastructures. Therefore, the temperature monitoring system for high voltage electrical equipment is an important measure to ensure the power networks safely operating [1].

There are three ways about the temperature monitoring of high voltage electrical equipment: surface temperature induction strips, infrared temperature measurement, and optical fiber grating temperature measurement [2, 3]. Surface temperature induction strips used widely in electric power industry have low cost, easy installation and maintenance, but its disadvantage is artificial observation. So it could not achieve temperature alarm in time or constitute a monitoring network. The infrared equipment is complicated, and it has high power consumption. In particular, infrared signals can't penetrate obstacles [4]. The optical fiber is not used widely because of its disadvantage of insulation performance, which would be greatly reduced in rainy season or humid climate, and be easy to snap and no-resistant to high temperature.

© Springer Nature Singapore Pte Ltd. 2018
K. Li et al. (Eds.): ICSEE 2018/IMIOT 2018, CCIS 925, pp. 173–180, 2018.
https://doi.org/10.1007/978-981-13-2381-2_16

This paper develops a temperature monitoring and warning system with low power consumption based on wireless communication, which is designed to provide a solution for temperature monitoring for high voltage electrical equipment.

2 System Constitution

Figure 1 shows the system structure. Slave machine (signal transmitter) uses high-temperature lithium battery for power supply, which is installed on the electrical equipment for testing. The slave machine collects temperature data and sends it to the host machine (wireless signal acquisition unit) through wireless communication. The host machine receives and stores the temperature data, and communicates with the data processing system through the RS485 bus. Data processing system sends host machine instructions and delivers the alarm information to the operator for electric power networks in time by SMS, and synchronizes data to the central server through internet. The management for power networks masters each testing point's situation by the data center server. This paper will mainly discuss the design of the slave and host machine.

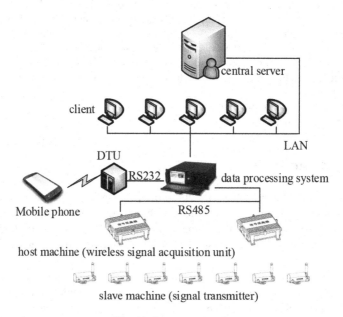

Fig. 1. System structure

3 System Hardware Design

The host and slave machine are all composed of main control unit, wireless communication unit and power unit. Since the host machine communicates with the data processing system and collects information to display timely, the hardware is more complicated than that of slave machine. The slave machine's PCB board is the same as one in host machine, and some electronic components didn't require welding.

3.1 Control Unit

Figure 2 shows the main control unit. C8051F930 is selected as the main MCU, which has low power consumption and convenient programming or debugging [5]. Since the host and slave machines need to store system parameters such as device address, the parameters are stored in non-volatile memory by key setting, and 24C01 is chosen as storage device. The OLED display is chosen for the host machine working and slave machine debugging [6, 7]. Considering the interface flexibility, the RS485 interface and the USB interface are designed in host machine, which are easily used through the J1 and J2 jumpers.

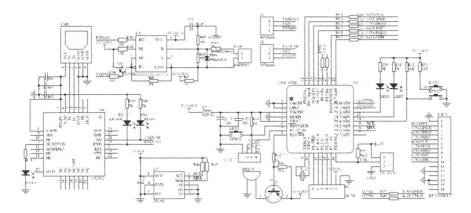

Fig. 2. Main control unit

The RS485 interface has anti-jamming processing to ensure reliable performance. CP2102 is used as the USB interface chip, because its excellent performance can realize serial communication between host machine and data processing system, and realize program serial download.

DS18B20 is chosen as the slave machine's temperature sensor. The slave machine is placed in particular metal EMI shield which is installed in temperature measurement point by thermal conductive silica gel to ensure reliable performance [8]. J-rf1 is an interface between the main control unit and the wireless communication unit. In practice, slave machine's serial communication circuit (including RS485 and USB) does not need welding, and the OLED display does also not need welding after mass production. The temperature sensor in host machine does not need welding either.

3.2 Wireless Communication Unit

Silicon Labs' Si4438 is used as the communication unit, which is a low-power, high-performance wireless transceiver chip. The chip communicates with the MCU by SPI interface, and its communication frequency band can cover 425–525 MHz with duplex sending and receiving mechanism. In addition, the shutdown current is only 30 nA, the standby current is only 50 nA, and the receiving sensitivity is −124 db (@500 bps), which extends the transmission distance for wireless transmission and provides reliable communication link [9]. Figure 3 shows the si4438's schematic.

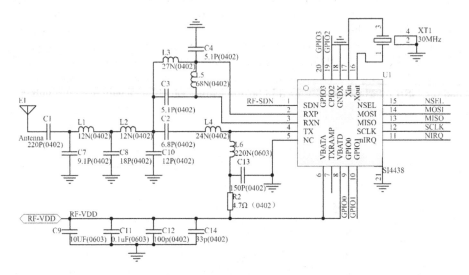

Fig. 3. Communication unit

3.3   Power Unit

The salve machine is installed in isolating switch contacts, all kinds of wire clips, cable junctions, and transformer contacted separately. It uses 4.2 V high-temperature lithium batteries for power supply, and uses a LDO chip AMS1117-3.3 to provide 3.3 V voltage. The circuit is shown in Fig. 4.

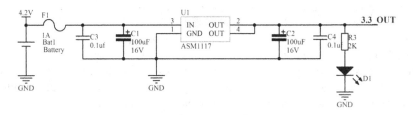

Fig. 4. Power unit

Since the working environment is various, the power supply for host machine has four modes: battery power supply; USB power supply; debugging interface C2 power supply and AC adapter thought USB. The mode of power supply works conveniently through the switch.

4   System Software Design

The key of software design is low-power consumption and reliable to communicate. The low-power consumption is important to slave machine design, and there are two keys to solve it: using the MCU's suspend mode reasonably and planning the temperature data launch time intervals. C8051F930 has a 32-bit real-time clock with dedicated 32 kHz oscillator, and it works normally in 0.9–3.6 V voltage without any external resistance or load capacitance in the MCU's lowest-power consumption mode [10–13]. Considering the reduction of power consumption, slave machine acquires temperature data every 10 min and then judges that whether the temperature value exceeds its limit or not. The salve machine uploads temperature data every 4 h without exception, and uploads temperature data's time interval according to the different situation with exception. The MCU of slave machine suspends when acquiring or uploading temperature data. The software procedure of slave machine is shown in Fig. 5.

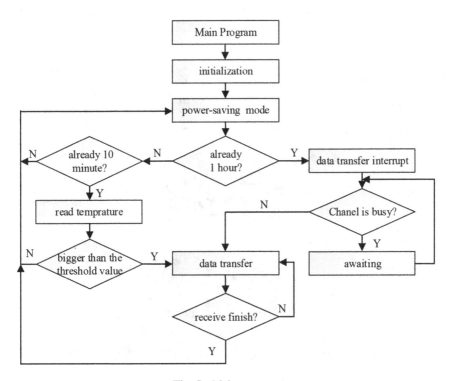

Fig. 5. Main program

Wireless communication employs DLT645 protocol, which is used widely in power industry and mainly based on the main-slave and semi-duplex communication structure [14, 15]. The establishment and termination of communication link are controlled by the information frame from the host machine. Each frame is composed of seven domains, including start frame, slave machine address frame, control code frame, data length frame, data frame, verification frame and terminator frame. Each element is consisted of a number of bytes. When the host machine detects the data frame, the length of the packet is checked firstly, and then the frame head, the frame tail and the frame length are checked.

The frame information is preserved when all information is right. If temperature exceeds its limit, the host machine uploads alarm information for displaying or storing in PC via a serial port. In addition, the users can modify temperature limit.

5 Performance Testing

The experimental test is performed, as shown in Fig. 6. The test environment is divided into normal temperature, high temperature and low temperature. The communication frequency is set to 433 MHz and the communication distance is set to 100 m. The data is transmitted every 10 min. The system is powered by 4.2 V and 1200 mA in a single lithium battery. Table 1 shows the reliability of test data, and Table 2 shows test data about the power consumption of system.

Fig. 6. System Testing

Based on the testing results, the system works well in all the test conditions, and can meet the actual requirements. Furthermore, we find that each data time is short, which is tested within 100 ms. The average current is very small, and transmit interval is far longer than 10 min in practice. By theoretical calculation, the system can continue to work more than five years with a single lithium battery.

Table 1. Test data for system reliability

	Work 24 h at 25 °C	Work 6 h at 80 °C	Work 2 h at 0 °C
Actual reception number	8639	2156	719
Theoretical reception number	8640	2160	720
Reliable rate (%)	99.98	99.81	99.86

Table 2. Test data for the power consumption of slave machine

Dormant operating current	<30 uA
Maximum transmitting current (100 m)	10 mA

This paper show that the proposed system can be applied to the wireless temperature measurement for high voltage equipment in power industry, and it can effectively solve the problem of untimely manual inspection.

References

1. Sun, Y.H., Li, Y.F., Liu, Z.Y., Dou, W.J.: Research on diagnosis technology of insulation performance of high voltage electrical equipment. In: 2017 Chinese Automation Congress, pp. 5398–5403. IEEE Press, New York (2017)
2. Liu, T., Zhang, Q., Li, G.L., Ma, Z.L., Zhang, M.S.: Design and implementation of the temperature monitoring system of infrared rotary kiln shell. In: 12th IEEE Conference on Industrial Electronics and Applications, pp. 253–257. IEEE Press, New York (2017)
3. Roy, A., Das, P., Das, R.: Temperature and humidity monitoring system for storage rooms of industries. In: 2017 International Conference on Computing and Communication Technologies for Smart Nation, pp. 99–103. IEEE Press, New York (2017)
4. Zhang, Y., Tian, J., Ye, F.: Development of temperature real-time monitoring network for high voltage switch cabinet on IR sensor. High Volt. Apparatus **41**(2), 91–94 (2005)
5. Zhang, Y., Liu, R.: Remote pipeline temperature and pressure monitoring system based on C8051F930. Electron. Des. Eng. **18**(10), 83–85 (2010)
6. Barth, N.D., Bender, V.C., Marchesan, T.B.: An analysis of frequency response on OLED for lighting applications. In: Industry Applications Society Annual Meeting, pp. 1–5. IEEE Press, New York (2017)
7. Kundrata, J., Baric, A.: Application of ferrite layers in low-profile OLED drivers. IET Power Electron. **11**(2), 92–99 (2018)
8. Shu, Y.F., Wei, X.C., Yu, X.Q., Liu, C.J.: Effects of grounded-lid apertures for package-level electromagnetic interference (EMI) shielding. In: 2017 IEEE International Symposium on Electromagnetic Compatibility and Signal/Power Integrity, pp. 345–348. IEEE Press, New York (2017)
9. Si4438 datasheet. https://www.silabs.com/documents/public/data-sheets/Si4438.pdf
10. C8051F92X-C8051F93X. https://www.silabs.com/products/mcu/8-bit/c8051f92x-f93x
11. C8051F2xx Small Form Factor Microcontrollers. https://www.silabs.com/products/mcu/8-bit/c8051f2xx

12. Wang, P.: Design of temperature and humidity intelligent control system based on C8051F. In: Proceedings of 2011 International Conference on Electronics and Optoelectronics, pp. 63–66. IEEE Press, New York (2011)

13. Sui, T., Teng, J.Z., Li, B., Du, Z.T.: The application of multi-serial-interface system in small-scale monitoring device based on C8051f020. In: 2009 WASE International Conference on Information Engineering, pp. 389–390. IEEE Press, New York (2009)

14. The multi-function watt-hour meter communication protocol. https://wenku.baidu.com/view/b25c61eff80f76c66137ee06eff9aef8941e48f4.html

15. Li, L., Hu, X., Huang, J., He, K.: Design of new architecture of AMR system in smart grid. In: 6th IEEE Industrial Electronics and Application Conference, pp. 21–23. IEEE Press, New York (2011)

Energy Storages

FRA and EKF Based State of Charge Estimation of Zinc-Nickel Single Flow Batteries

Yihuan Li[1(✉)], Kang Li[1], Shawn Li[1], and Yanxue Li[2]

[1] School of Electronic and Electric Engineering, University of Leeds,
Leeds LS2 9JT, UK
{elyli2,K.Li1,elxli}@leeds.ac.uk
[2] State Grid Energy Conservation Service Co., LTD, Beijing, China
liyanxue1215@126.com

Abstract. The reliable state of charge (SOC) estimation is indispensable for flow batteries to maintain the safe and reliable operation. The widely adopted Extended Kalman filter (EKF) algorithm is a model-based method, however, the uncertainties in battery model will cause large errors in SOC estimation. An accurate battery model is the essence to capture the behaviors of batteries. In this paper, a novel framework for the SOC estimation of Zinc-nickel flow batteries is proposed based on the fast recursive algorithm (FRA) and extended Kalman filter (EKF). The FRA is firstly used to determine the model structure and identify the model parameters. Due to merits of FRA, a compact and accurate model of flow battery is built. Then, the SOC is estimated using the EKF based on the proposed linear-in-the-parameter model. Experimental studies and resultant simulations manifest the modelling accuracy of the proposed SOC estimation framework.

Keywords: Flow battery · State of charge (SOC)
Fast recursive algorithm (FRA) · Extended Kalman filter (EKF)

1 Introduction

Batteries have become increasingly popular in smart grid and electric vehicles (EV) applications for energy storage. The redox flow battery (RFB) is characterized by the long life cycles and high charging/discharging efficiency, and has undergone rapid development in recent years [1]. Cheng and Zhang et al. [2] have proposed a novel RFB system, namely the single flow zinc-nickel battery system. Zinc-nickel single flow batteries (ZNBs), known as electrochemical energy storage sources, have attracted a lot of attention due to their advantages of high energy density, safety, and low cost [3]. The advantages of ZNBs include moderate cost, modularity, transportability and flexible operation [4]. Similar to solid batteries and other type of flow batteries, the battery management system (BMS) is vital for zinc-nickel flow batteries to ensure the optimal, reliable and

© Springer Nature Singapore Pte Ltd. 2018
K. Li et al. (Eds.): ICSEE 2018/IMIOT 2018, CCIS 925, pp. 183–191, 2018.
https://doi.org/10.1007/978-981-13-2381-2_17

efficient operation, and to provide accurate battery internal state information for the energy management modules is an important issue to address in the BMS [5]. In particular, the battery state of charge (SOC) estimation is an essential part of a BMS, it provides fundamental knowledge about the real-time remaining capacity and energy of the battery.

During the last decade, a large number of real-time SOC estimation methods have been developed. The methods can be classified into four groups, including the looking-up table based methods, ampere-hour integral method, model-based estimation methods, and data-driven estimation methods [6]. Among these groups of methods, the looking-up table based approach is more suitable for laboratory environment. While the reliability of the ampere-hour method is affected by measurement errors and available capacity. The data-driven methods are very sensitive to their identified parameters extracted from the training data, though they may achieve high prediction accuracy. Contrary to model-free methods, the model-based estimation methods require accurate battery models. Electrochemical model (EM), equivalent circuit model (ECM) and black-box model are among the most commonly used models. These models often require to incorporate state estimation algorithms and adaptive filters to estimate and infer the internal states of batteries, such as open circuit voltage (OCV), the state of charge (SOC), and the state of health (SOH), etc. Among these methods, the extended Kalman filter (EKF) and other Kalman filter variants are widely adopted for SOC estimation.

In this work, the fast recursive algorithm (FRA) [7] is applied for battery model identification. The relationship between battery terminal signals and SOC is first interpreted by a linear-in-the-parameters model, then EKF based SOC estimation is presented.

This paper is organized as follows. A brief review of the FRA is presented in Sect. 2. Then the battery state equations deduced by FRA is introduced in Sect. 3, and the EKF based battery SOC estimation method is also described in details. Section 4 validates the efficacy of the SOC estimation and the proposed batteries models. Finally, Sect. 5 concludes the paper.

2   Preliminaries

The accuracy of battery SOC estimation heavily depends on the accuracy of the battery model. This section first gives a brief introduction to the state of charge (SOC) of batteries, followed by the fast recursive algorithm used for the model identification.

2.1   Battery State of Charge (SOC)

SOC is an important internal state that describes the ratio of the remaining capacity to the present capacity of a battery. The relationship between the SOC at time instant k and SOC at time instant $k + 1$ can be calculated below [8].

$$SOC_{k+1} = SOC_k + \frac{\eta \Delta t}{Q} I_k \tag{1}$$

where Q is the nominal capacity, η is the coulombic efficiency, Δt is the sampling interval, and I_k is the current at time instant t. When the battery is charging, the current value is assumed positive, vice versa. Since SOC calculation based on Eq. (1) is subject to a number of uncertainties associated to the initial value estimation of SOC, and noises and inaccuracies introduced into the terminal current measurements. Therefore, both a good model to capture the relationship of SOC with a set of readily available measurements and the EKF for SOC estimation subject to measurement noises and other inaccuracies are employed.

2.2 Fast Recursive Algorithm for Model Identification

The fast recursive algorithm (FRA) is an efficient method for nonlinear dynamic system identification and modeling developed by Kang and his co-workers [7]. FRA is able to select and determine both the model structure and the model parameters simultaneously. In this work, the FRA is used to correlate the non-linear relationship between the battery terminal voltage and SOC, which is described by a linear-in-parameter equation.

A normal nonlinear discrete-time dynamic system can be represented in a matrix form as follows:

$$\mathbf{y} = \mathbf{\Phi\Theta} + \mathbf{\Xi} \tag{2}$$

where $\mathbf{y} = [y(1), ..., y(m)]^T$ are the system outputs, $\mathbf{\Phi} = [\varphi_1, ..., \varphi_n]$ is the regression matrix and each $\varphi_i = [\varphi_i(1), ..., \varphi_i(m)]^T, (i = 1, ..., n)$ contains all candidate model terms, $\mathbf{\Theta} = [\theta_1, ..., \theta_n]^T$ and $\theta_i(i = 1, ..., n)$ is the unknown parameters to be identified, and $\mathbf{\Xi} = [\xi_1, ..., \xi_m]^T$ is the model residual matrix.

Two recursive matrixes M_k and R_k, are predefined in FRA to fulfill the forward model selection procedure as:

$$\mathbf{M}_k = \mathbf{\Phi}_k^T \mathbf{\Phi}_k \tag{3}$$

$$\mathbf{R}_k = \mathbf{I} - \mathbf{\Phi}_k \mathbf{M}_k^{-1} \mathbf{\Phi}_k^T \tag{4}$$

where $\mathbf{\Phi_k}$ contains the first k columns of the full regression matrix $\mathbf{\Phi}$, additionally, $k = 1, ..., n$, and $\mathbf{R}_0 = \mathbf{I}$. When $\{\varphi_i, i = 1, 2, ..., n\}$ in $\mathbf{\Phi}$ are mutually linearly independent, the recursive matrix $\mathbf{R}_k$ will has the following distinguished properties [9]:

$$\mathbf{R}_{k+1} = \mathbf{R}_k - \frac{\mathbf{R}_k \varphi_{k+1} \varphi_{k+1}^T \mathbf{R}_k^T}{\varphi_{k+1}^T \mathbf{R}_k \varphi_{k+1}}, \quad k = 0, 1, ..., (n-1) \tag{5}$$

$$\mathbf{R}_k^T = \mathbf{R}_k, \quad \mathbf{R}_k \mathbf{R}_k = \mathbf{R}_k, \quad k = 0, 1, ..., n \tag{6}$$

$$\mathbf{R}_k \mathbf{R}_j = \mathbf{R}_j \mathbf{R}_k = \mathbf{R}_k, \quad k \geq j; \ k, j = 0, 1, ..., n \tag{7}$$

$$\mathbf{R}_k \varphi_i = 0, \quad \forall i \in \{1, ..., k\} \tag{8}$$

Assuming E_k denotes the cost function. When the first k columns in $\mathbf{\Phi}$ are selected, and E_k can be expressed as

$$E_k = \mathbf{y}^T \mathbf{R}_k \mathbf{y} \tag{9}$$

To simplify the formulas and decrease the computational complexity, three quantities are consequently defined as

$$
\begin{cases}
\varphi_i^{(k)} \triangleq \mathbf{R}_k \varphi_i, \quad \varphi_i^{(0)} \triangleq \mathbf{R}_0 \varphi_i = \varphi_i \\
a_{k,i} \triangleq \left(\varphi_k^{(k-1)} \right)^T \varphi_i^{(k-1)}, \quad a_{1,i} \triangleq \varphi_1^T \varphi_i \\
a_{k,y} \triangleq \left(\varphi_k^{(k-1)} \right)^T \mathbf{y}, \quad a_{1,y} \triangleq \left(\varphi_1^{(0)} \right)^T \mathbf{y} = \varphi_1^T \mathbf{y}
\end{cases}
\tag{10}
$$

where $i = 1, ..., n$, and $k = 0, 1, ..., n$. According to the properties of $\mathbf{R}_k$ and the new quantities definition, the net contribution of the selected model term φ_{k+1} to the cost function can be calculated as

$$
\Delta E_{k+1} = \frac{\left(\mathbf{y}^T \varphi_{k+1}^{(k)} \right)^2}{\left(\left(\varphi_{k+1}^{(k)} \right)^T \varphi_{k+1}^{(k)} \right)} = \frac{\left(a_{k+1,y}^T \right)^2}{a_{k+1,k+1}}, \quad k = 0, 1, ..., n-1
\tag{11}
$$

By calculating the net contribution of each term, the model terms with maximum contributions will be selected. Then an effective formula will be given for model parameters identification procedure as follows:

$$
\hat{\theta}_j = \frac{a_{j,y} - \sum_{i=j+1}^{k} \hat{\theta}_i a_{j,i}}{a_{j,j}}, \quad j = k, k-1, ..., 1
\tag{12}
$$

Equations (11) and (12) constitute the FRA, which solves the least-squares problem recursively.

3   Battery SOC Estimation

This section introduces the SOC estimation based on the EKF algorithm. The main idea is to use the model built by FRA to predict the terminal voltage in real-time which is then compared with the actual measured voltage signals. The estimated error is used to update the SOC estimation using the Extended Kalman Filter (EKF).

3.1   Battery State Space Model

The detailed EKF algorithm for battery SOC estimation can be found in [10]. As discussed before, to have an accurate estimation of the SOC, a good battery model is essential. As described in Sect. 1, EM, ECM and data-driven black-box models are three popular types of battery models. The EMs are the most accurate, but they are hard to establish because they require detailed first principle knowledge and the computational complexity restricts its real-time applications. The ECMs are expressed by a combination of voltage and current source, capacitance, and resistance, where the resistance of the single flow Zinc-Nickle battery model changes with the battery SOC, this varying parameter may introduce error in SOC estimation [11]. The black-box models describe the relationship between the voltage and SOC using nonlinear functions, and do not require detailed first principle knowledge of the battery. FRA is an effective method to build a mathematical model. In this paper, the state space model of the battery is deduced using the coulomb counting equation for the SOC and FRA, where the SOC is an model state and its relationship with readily measurable terminal voltages and terminal currents are established. The state equation is expressed as follows:

$$\begin{cases} SOC_{k+1} = SOC_k + \frac{\eta \Delta t}{Q} I_k + w_k \\ Z_{k+1} = h(SOC_{k+1}, I_{k+1}) + v_k \end{cases} \tag{13}$$

where Z_k is the terminal voltage at time instant k, w_k and v_k are the process noise and measurement noise respectively, I_k denotes the terminal current signals. To capture the relationship of Z_k with SOC and terminal voltage, some linear or nonlinear functions associated to the SOC_k are selected from a predefined model candidate pool using the FRA method. The candidate pool consists of current, terminal voltage, SOC, their nonlinear forms, and nonlinear combinations of these two or three terms. Then, using the FRA approach, the system parameter identification and the selection of nonlinear terms associated to the model are conducted simultaneously.

3.2   EKF Based SOC Estimation

To produce an accurate estimation of the SOC based on the real-time measurements of terminal currents and voltages, the EKF algorithm is applied to the battery SOC model Eq. (13), and the EKF is briefly introduced below.

The nonlinear battery state-space model of the EKF are shown in Eq. (14),

$$\begin{cases} SOC_{k+1} = f(SOC_k, I_k) + w_k \\ Z_{k+1} = h(SOC_{k+1}, I_{k+1}) + v_k \end{cases} \tag{14}$$

where function $f(SOC_k, I_k)$ is the nonlinear state transition function and function $h(SOC_k, I_k)$ is the nonlinear measurement function. Vector w_k and v_k are uncorrelated zero-mean white Gaussian noise with covariance matrixes Q and R respectively.

At each time step, the function $f(SOC_k, I_k)$ and $h(SOC_k, I_k)$ are linearized using Taylor-series expansion, assuming that they are differentiable at all operating points, the elements of the state vector matrix are defined as:

$$\mathbf{A}_k = \frac{\partial f(SOC_k, I_k)}{\partial SOC_k}\Big|_{SOC_k = S\hat{O}C_k^-} \tag{15}$$

$$\mathbf{C}_k = \frac{\partial h(SOC_k, I_k)}{\partial SOC_k}\Big|_{SOC_k = S\hat{O}C_k^-} \tag{16}$$

To start filtering, the first step is to set initial values, the initialization of the state and error covariance at $k = 0$ are made as follows:

$$\begin{cases} S\hat{O}C_0 = E[SOC_0] \\ \mathbf{P}_0 = E[(SOC_0 - S\hat{O}C_0)(SOC_0 - S\hat{O}C_0)^T] \end{cases} \tag{17}$$

Then using Eqs. (18) and (19) we can predict the state and error covariance at time instant k:

$$S\hat{O}C_k^- = f(S\hat{O}C_{k-1}, I_{k-1}) \tag{18}$$

$$\mathbf{P}_k^- = \mathbf{A}_k \mathbf{P}_{k-1} \mathbf{A}_K^T + \mathbf{Q} \tag{19}$$

According to the predictions and the measurements, the Kalman gain can be calculated, and the state and error covariance are corrected:

$$\mathbf{K}_k = \mathbf{P}_k^- \mathbf{C}_k^T \left(\mathbf{C}_k \mathbf{P}_k^- \mathbf{C}_k^T + \mathbf{R} \right)^{-1} \tag{20}$$

$$S\hat{O}C_k = S\hat{O}C_k^- + \mathbf{K}_k \left(Z_k - h(S\hat{O}C_k^-, I_k) \right) \tag{21}$$

$$\mathbf{P}_k = (\mathbf{I} - \mathbf{K}_k \mathbf{C}_k) \mathbf{P}_k^- \tag{22}$$

4   Experiment and Results

4.1   Data Acquisition

In order to verify the proposed model determined by FRA and the EKF-based SOC estimation method, experiments were conducted. The data was obtained from a handmade ZNBs. During the tests, the rating capacity of the battery is around 3.7Ah. Additionally, 1 mol ZnO and 20 g/L LiOH are dissolved by the 10 mol/L KOH support solution as the prepared electrolyte. The operating flow rate remains constantly at 19 cm/s. The testing current signals are generated by the NEWARE CT-3008 which are fed into the ZNBs. The measurement ranges of voltage and current are 15 V and 3 A, respectively, and nominal measurement error bounds are within 0.1%.

4.2   Experiment Results

The battery charging data are used to build a model by FRA to correlate the terminal voltage with SOC and terminal current, and the candidate model terms for selection are V_k, SOC_k, I_k as well as their nonlinear variants. The terms which have the maximum contributions are selected as the optimal model inputs. Besides, the weights of each terms are calculated to complete the model. As shown in Eq. (23), the selected model terms are V_{k-1}, $ln\sqrt{V_{k-1}}$, $sin(SOC_k)$ and $sin(\sqrt{SOC_k})$.

$$V_k - 1.0053V_{k-1} + 0.0282ln\sqrt{V_{k-1}} = 0.0031sin(SOC_k) - 0.0041sin(\sqrt{SOC_k}) \tag{23}$$

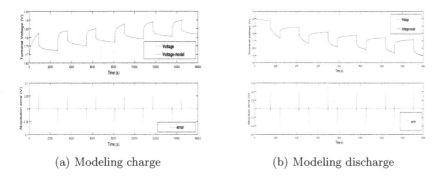

(a) Modeling charge   (b) Modeling discharge

Fig. 1. Results of modeling using FRA

The results are shown in Fig. 1(a), the model output fits well to the measured terminal voltage, and the error is acceptable. Use the same model in the discharging procedure, it also fits well, as shown in Fig. 1(b).

This model is compared with the model established by orthogonal matching pursuit (OMP) algorithm, which selects model terms from an over-complete dictionary. We use 'wmpdictionary' function in Matlab to generate a dictionary for OMP, this dictionary contains the shifted Kronecker delta subdictionary, polynomial subdictionary, cosine and sine subdictionary, and discrete cosine transform-ii orthonormal basis, etc. The 'wmpalg' function is then used to directly return the approximation of terminal voltage in the dictionary. The comparison of these two models is shown in Fig. 2 with absolute error on the horizontal and time on the vertical. The mean square error (MSE) for this model is 6.4378e-05, while for the FRA-based model is 9.2432e-06. It is clear that the error of the model identified by FRA is less than that of the model identified by OMP. Considering the accuracy of the FRA method and its ability to describe the relationship between terminal voltage and SOC, FRA is a good choice for battery model identification.

In Eq. (23), we use Z_k to represent the left side of this equation, the battery state-space model are:

$$\begin{cases} SOC_{k+1} = SOC_k + \frac{\eta \Delta t}{Q} I_k + w_k \\ Z_{k+1} = 0.0031 sin(SOC_{k+1}) - 0.0041 sin(\sqrt{SOC_{k+1}}) \end{cases} \tag{24}$$

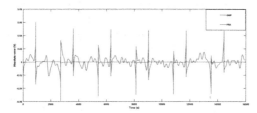

Fig. 2. Model error

The EKF algorithm is then used for SOC estimation. Figure 3 depicts the performance of the proposed method. It can be found that the SOC value estimated by the EKF method is very close to the reference values. The absolute error between these two values is less than 2%, even when the estimation tend to steady, the error is less than 0.7%. By setting the initial value to 20% while the actual initial value is 0, the robustness of this algorithm is verified, as Fig. 3 shows, the estimated SOC converge to the actual value quickly.

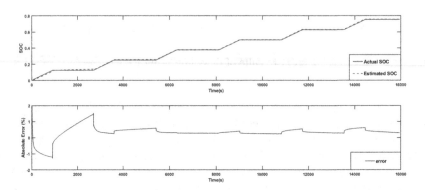

Fig. 3. SOC estimation results using EKF

5   Conclusion

In this paper, an accurate terminal voltage model of flow battery has been built for EKF-based SOC estimation by applying the fast recursive algorithm (FRA), which is a computationally efficient and stable model identification method. The model performs well and is used as a measurement equation in EKF-based SOC estimation. Future works will both focus on improving model accuracy and improving the estimation method. Some advanced algorithms, such as neural networks and support vector machines, will be studied for further improvement of model accuracy, while dual estimation methods and other methods will be studied to decrease the SOC estimation error.

Acknowledgments. YH. LI would like to thank the China Scholarship Council (CSC) for sponsoring her research. S. LI, YX. LI and K. LI would like to thank the Macao Science and Technology Development Fund (FDCT) s support with the project (111/2013/A3)-Flow Battery Storage System Study and Its Application in Power System and Dr. CK Wong to provide the data and experimental resource.

References

1. Li, Y.X., et al.: Modeling of novel single flow zinc-nickel battery for energy storage system. In: 2014 IEEE 9th Conference on Industrial Electronics and Applications (ICIEA), pp. 1621–1626. IEEE (2014)

2. Cheng, J., Zhang, L., Yang, Y.S., Wen, Y.H., Cao, G.P., Wang, X.D.: Preliminary study of single flow zinc-nickel battery. Electrochem. Commun. **9**(11), 2639–2642 (2007)
3. Zhang, H., Li, X., Zhang, J.: Redox Flow Batteries: Fundamentals and Applications. CRC Press (2017)
4. De Leon, C.P., Frías-Ferrer, A., González-García, J., Szánto, D., Walsh, F.C.: Redox flow cells for energy conversion. J. Power Sources **160**(1), 716–732 (2006)
5. Rahimi-Eichi, H., Ojha, U., Baronti, F., Chow, M.Y.: Battery management system: an overview of its application in the smart grid and electric vehicles. IEEE Ind. Electron. Mag. **7**(2), 4–16 (2013)
6. Xiong, R., Cao, J., Yu, Q., He, H., Sun, F.: Critical review on the battery state of charge estimation methods for electric vehicles. IEEE Access **6**, 1832–1843 (2018)
7. Li, K., Peng, J.X., Irwin, G.W.: A fast nonlinear model identification method. IEEE Trans. Autom. Control **50**(8), 1211–1216 (2005)
8. Gregory, L.P.: Extended kalman filtering for battery management systems of lipb-based hev battery packs, part 2: modeling and identification. J. Power Sources **134**(2), 262–276 (2004)
9. Li, K., Peng, J.X., Bai, E.W.: A two-stage algorithm for identification of nonlinear dynamic systems. Automatica **42**(7), 1189–1197 (2006)
10. Gregory, L.P.: Extended kalman filtering for battery management systems of lipb-based hev battery packs: part 1. background. J. Power Sources **134**(2), 252–261 (2004)
11. Lin, X., Qin, J.: Joint estimation of single flow zinc-nickle battery state and parameter using unscented kalman filter. IEEE Power Energy Soc. General Meet. (2015)

An Approach to Propose Optimal Energy Storage System in Real-Time Electricity Pricing Environments

Shiqian Ma[1,2], Tianchun Xiang[2], Yue Wang[1(✉)], Xudong Wang[2], Yue Guo[2], Kai Hou[1], Yunfei Mu[1], and Hongjie Jia[1]

[1] Key Laboratory of Smart Grid of Ministry of Education, Tianjin University, Tianjin 300072, China
Msql12358@126.com, yue.wang03@hotmail.com, {khou,yunfeimu,hjjia}@tju.edu.cn
[2] State Grid Tianjin Electric Power Research Institute, Tianjin 300384, China
goodxtc@sohu.com, tjwangxudong@sina.com, 137425099@qq.com

Abstract. Based on the fact that the penetration of renewable energies is increasing dramatically, almost all the energy markets have changed and taken action to present the strategy of real-time pricing over the last decade. However, the research on how these renewables, which is going to become the vital part in the integrated energy system, coordinate with other energy sources under the real-time pricing. Moreover, with the development of energy storage system, issues about how to evaluate the participation of them in the integrated energy system and how to provide an optimal capability for them in a given settings should be given more consideration. This paper will focus on introducing an approach to coordinate the participation of all the energy resources in the integrated energy systems within and without energy storage system.

Keywords: Optimal energy flow · Real-time pricing · Energy storage system Integrated energy system

1 Introduction

In recent years, the role of clean energy and optimized allocation of all kinds of energy is presented in our view to address the issue of resource constraints, environment pollution and climate change. Although the growth of the renewables penetration is increasing rapidly, large scale clean energy cannot be applied unless it is transformed into electricity directly. Regions rich in renewables are usually located far from energy

This work was supported by the State Grid Technology Project: Research and Application on Flexibility Improvement of Power Distribution System Based on Distributed/Mobile Energy Storage (SGTJDK00DWJS1800008), the National Natural Science Foundation of China (51707129) and the National Key Research and Development Foundation of China (2017YFB0903300).

K. Li et al. (Eds.): ICSEE 2018/IMIOT 2018, CCIS 925, pp. 192–200, 2018.
https://doi.org/10.1007/978-981-13-2381-2_18

consumption users. The energy storage systems (ESS) could be a feasible solution dealing with these issues. Furthermore, the utility of energy storage, like batteries, as an energy power buffer, on the other hand, could be able to smooth the power demand flections. Thus, it is important to conduct research on how to utilize different kinds of energy storage to sustainable develop the environment.

Integrated energy system has received a wild of attention these years and has been studied on components, structure, regulation even operation and other aspects. In the paper [1], the concept of integrated energy system was proposed, which coupled and interacted with different energy systems at all kinds of level. Combined heat and power (CHP) plants play a vital role in the integrated energy system, which simultaneously produce electrical and thermal energy from a single input fuel. Integrated energy systems directly connect to various energy consumers and couple different forms of energy carriers with flexible topological structure [2]. This concept not only makes these subsystems interdependence, but also effectively improves energy efficiency. Ref. [3–7] constructed an optimal energy flow model for integrated energy system including both inequalities and equalities constraints. However, the participation of energy storage system should get more attention, which could be a significant part in the integrated energy system. In addition, there should be a kind of research that focus on the planning of energy storage system based on real-time pricing under different seasons. This work could provide strategies to engineers for choosing the most appropriate facilities for an integrated energy system.

Main contributions of this paper state as follows: an energy storage system model has been applied in an integrated energy system; a varying pricing participation model has been proposed to help calculate the optimal power flow in an integrated energy system. Case studies are simulated to demonstrate the application of varying pricing participation model, the approach of calculating the optimal power flow with an energy storage system and the proposed strategies for an integrated energy system.

2 Model Description

The integrated energy system could be able to contain a lot of sub-units. This paper will focus on the model of photovoltaic power generation, combined heat and power plant and energy storage.

2.1 Photovoltaic Power Generation System

Based on huge amount of experiment, the value of solar radiation and ambient temperature are the most important factor that influence the output power of photovoltaic cells. The temperature of the solar cells can be described as

$$T_{cells} = T_a + \frac{30R}{1000} \tag{1}$$

0 is the temperature of the solar cells, T_a is the temperature of the environment, R is the solar radiation absorbed by solar cells.

The output of photovoltaic cells P_{PV} can be described as

$$P_{PV} = P_{STC}I\frac{1+k(T_C - T_R)}{I_{STC}} \tag{2}$$

Where P_{STC} represents the maximum test power based on standard test conditions; I represents the intensity of light; k represents the power temperature coefficient; T_C represents the temperature of working solar cells; T_R represents the reference temperature; I_{STC} is the intensity of light under standard test conditions.

2.2   Combined Heat and Power Plant

Combined Heat and Power (CHP) Plant is an established technology in many countries, which provide the heat power and electricity demands in several building applications and industrial. A traditional CHP plan consists of five basic components: the engine, electrical power compatible with national grid, heat system recovered from the engine cooling system, the oil and the exhaust system, which can be used for space heating, for domestic cooling or hot water.

The mathematical model of a CHP plant can be illustrated as follows:

$$\begin{cases} Q_{MT} = \frac{P_e(1-\eta_e-\eta_1)}{\eta_e} \\ Q_{he} = Q_{MT}K_{he} \\ Q_{CO} = Q_{MT}K_{co} \\ V_{MT} = \frac{\sum P_e \Delta t}{\eta_e L} \end{cases} \tag{3}$$

Where Q_{MT} is the remaining amount of the exhaust excess heat in gas turbine; η_e is the efficiency of electricity generation; η_1 is the coefficient of the heat loss for gas turbine; Q_{he} and Q_{CO} are the amount of heat and cooling provided by the exhaust excess heat in gas turbine, respectively; K_{he} and K_{CO} are the heating efficiency and the cooling efficiency of the Li-Br Absorption Chiller; V_{MT} is the total amount of natural gas that consumed by gas turbine during its operation; Δt represents the operation time; L is the gross heat value(GHV) of natural gas.

2.3   Energy Storage System

There are a lot of energy storage technologies and some of them are already implemented in the industrial production and operation. Different energy storage has different characteristics. This is the reason why researchers need to conduct experiments on different applications to find out the most appropriate energy storage material in a given scenario.

The state of charge (SOC) of the energy storage in a given moment is related to the before SOC and the self-decreasing of the energy storage.

In the duration t of charging, the SOC can be illustrated as

$$S_{oc}(t) = S_{oc}(t-1)(1-\sigma) + \eta_c \frac{P_{ch,t}\Delta t}{E_{bat}} \qquad (4)$$

In the duration t of discharging, the SOC can be illustrated as

$$S_{oc}(t) = S_{oc}(t-1)(1-\sigma) - \frac{P_{dis,t}\Delta t}{E_{bat}\eta_d} \qquad (5)$$

Where $S_{oc}(t)$ is the state of charge of the energy storage at the moment of t, σ is the rate of discharge of the energy storage itself; η_c and η_d are the charging efficiency and discharging efficiency, respectively; $P_{ch,t}$ is the power of charging of the energy storage; $P_{dis,t}$ is the power of discharging of the energy storage; E_{bat} is the capacity of the energy storage.

3 System Operation Cost Calculation

3.1 Varying Pricing Model

In our studies, we purposed varying pricing model that will give a curve to describe the participation of power system to meet the demand in a micro-integrated energy system. This curve, based on the real-time pricing of the power system, can help the whole system foresee the variation of the price. Based on this varying pricing participating curve, the whole system is going to relocate the output of its energy resources during the operation to realize the maximum benefit for both the energy department and our environment.

In this varying pricing participation model, we use [0, 1] to describe the level of the participation of power system. This curve will provide a kind of parameter to help the whole system to find a relatively low-cost operation point.

3.2 Optimization Model

To describe the output of each energy resource and minimize the total cost of the micro-integrated energy system, the optimization problems can be described as follow:

$$\min f_{DG} = \sum_{t=1}^{N_t} \sum_{i=1}^{N_{DG}} \left[C_f\left(P_{Gi,t}\right) + C_{OM}\left(P_{Gi,t}\right) + C_{dp}\left(P_{Gi,t}\right) + C_{eav}\left(P_{Gi,t}\right) \right] \qquad (6)$$

$$\min f_{Gas} = \sum_{t=1}^{N_t} \sum_{i=1}^{N_{CHP}} C_{gas} \qquad (7)$$

$$\min f_{grid} = \sum_{t=1}^{N_t} C_{pp}(P_{grid,t}) \qquad (8)$$

s.t.

$$\sum_{i=1}^{N_{DG}} P_{Gi,t} + P_{CHPe,t} + P_{grid,t} + P_{ES,t} = P_{Le,t} \tag{9}$$

$$\sum_{i=1}^{N_{MT}} H_{i,t} = P_{Lh,t} \tag{10}$$

$$P_{Gi,t,\min} \leq P_{Gi,t} \leq P_{Gi,t,\max} \tag{11}$$

$$S_{oc,\min} \leq S_{oc} \leq S_{oc,\max} \tag{12}$$

3.3   Framework of Operation Cost Calculation

The framework of the purposed method of operation cost calculation is described in Fig. 1. The varying pricing participating curve will provide the participating point for integrated energy system to calculate the optimal power flow.

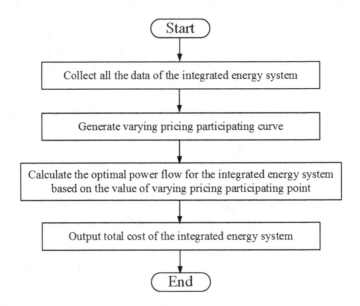

Fig. 1. The framework of operation cost calculation

4   Case Studies

Case studies are performed on a real integrated energy system, which involve photovoltaic power generation system, combined heat and power plant, electrical load and heat load. Parameters of this system are obtained from [6].

4.1   Varying Pricing Participation of the Integrated Energy System

Based on the methodology proposed in Sect. 3.1 and data of real-price for this IES, we generate the curve of varying pricing participation. This curve, illustrate expectation of the input ability of the grid, is going to be input to the process of optimal power flow. The Fig. 2 clearly shows that the level of participation will be decreasing as the real-time price is increasing.

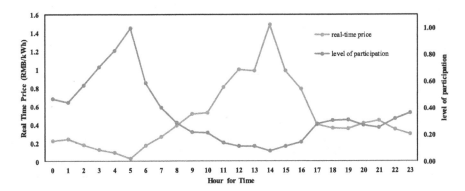

Fig. 2. Varying pricing participation of the integrated energy system

4.2   Output Variation Under the Real Pricing in 24 h

This case study is going to verify the availability of the varying pricing participation method. Firstly, Fig. 3 demonstrates the output variation of each energy source of the IES without any energy storage system under real pricing.

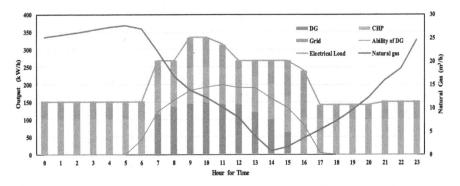

Fig. 3. Output variation under the real pricing in 24 h without ESS

Under this circumstance, the distributed generation, CHP plants and energy grid devote to meet the load demand in the IES.

Figures 4 and 5 show the output variation of each energy source of the IES within energy storage system under real pricing within and without the varying pricing participation method, respectively.

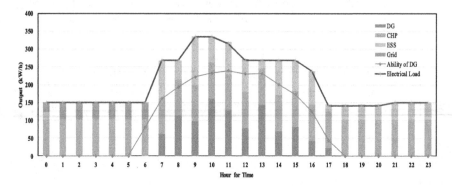

Fig. 4. Output variation within the varying pricing participation method

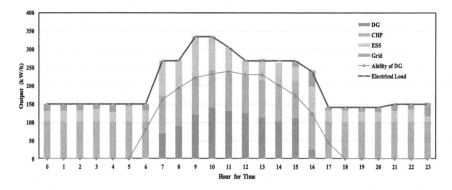

Fig. 5. Output variation without the varying pricing participation method

Through those figures and the data of real-time pricing, it is clear that the varying pricing participation method will provide a better strategy for electricity grid to participate the energy generation process during the lower price, which will benefit the whole system to some extent.

4.3 Total Cost for the IES Under Different Energy Storage System

The origin IES in this case is going to install the energy storage system actually. Therefore, this study investigates the total cost for one-year and ten-year separately, under different capability of the energy storage system in order to obtain the most beneficial investment point.

Figures 6 and 7 illustrate the total cost for the IES under different capability of the energy storage system in the season of winter and summer, respectively.

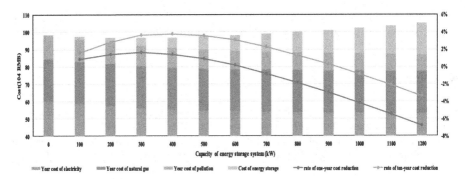

Fig. 6. Total cost in winter for the IES under different energy storage system

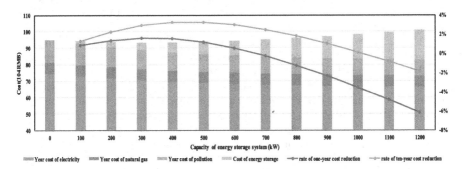

Fig. 7. Total cost in summer for the IES under different energy storage system

From the prospective of load, the amount of electrical load in summer is far more than electrical load in winter due to the utility of air conditioner in the IES. This is the reason that the one-year cost of electricity is higher in summer. Besides, it is clear that the amount of heat load will be in a higher level during winter. Natural gas, the energy source of CHP plant, is going to be consumed more in winter because of meeting the demand of heat load.

Although the investment of the energy storage system is seemly like a burden to the whole system, it will reduce the total cost in the long run and benefit to the environment dramatically. This is because the amount of pollution will decrease under the utility of energy storage system.

Combining the simulation results of Figs. 6 and 7, we proposed that the capacity of energy storage system for the IES could be from 300 kW to 600 kW.

5   Conclusions

This paper proposed a varying pricing model strategy to calculate a more meaningful operation point for the whole system under real-time pricing. Through the calculation of optimal energy flow in the integrated energy system, this paper analyzes the benefits of energy storage system and give a range of an optimal capability of the energy storage system for the given integrated energy system.

References

1. Moein, M.A., Ali, A., Mahmud, F.F., Ehasn, H.: A decomposed solution to multiple-energy carriers optimal power flow. IEEE Trans. Power Syst. **29**(2), 707–716 (2014)
2. Xu, X., Hou, K., Jia, H., et al.: A reliability assessment approach for the urban energy system and its application in energy hub planning. In: IEEE Pes General Meeting, Denver, CO, USA (2015)
3. An, S., Li, Q., Gedra, T.W.: Natural gas and electricity optimal power flow. In: Transmission and Distribution Conference and Exposition Conference, Dallas, TX, USA (2003)
4. Wang, Y., Kai, H., Jia, H., et al.: Decoupled optimization of integrated energy system considering CHP plant based on energy hub model. In: International Conference on Applied Energy (2017)
5. Lei, Y., Hou, K., Wang, Y., et al.: A new reliability assessment approach for integrated energy systems: using hierarchical decoupling optimization framework and impact-incensement based state enumeration method. Appl. Energ. **201**, 1237–1250 (2018)
6. Wang, Y., Hou, K., Jia, H.: A computational approach for modeling, evaluating and optimizing the reliability of integrated community energy systems. In: 1st IEEE Conference on Energy Internet and Energy System Integration, Beijing, China (2017)
7. Wang, J., Gu, W., Lu, S., et al.: Coordinated planning of multi-district integrated energy system combining heat network mode. Autom. Electri. Power Syst. **40**, 17–24 (2016)

The Electrochemical Performance and Applications of Several Popular Lithium-ion Batteries for Electric Vehicles - A Review

Xuan Liu$^{(\boxtimes)}$, Kang Li, and Xiang Li

School of Electronic and Electrical Engineering, University of Leeds,
Leeds LS2 9JT, UK
{elxl,k.li1,elxli}@leeds.ac.uk

Abstract. The Lithium-ion battery is one of the most common batteries used in Electric Vehicles (EVs) due to the specific features of high energy density, power density, long life span and environment friendly. With the development of lithium-ion battery technology, different materials have been adopted in the design of the cathodes and anodes in order to gain a better performance. $LiMn_2O_4$, $LiNiMnCoO_2$, $LiNiCoAlO_2$, $LiFePO_4$ and $Li_4Ti_5O_{12}$ are five common lithium-ion batteries adopted in commercial EVs nowadays. The characteristics of these five lithium-ion batteries are reviewed and compared in the aspects of electrochemical performance and their practical applications.

Keywords: LMO · NMC · NCA · LFP · LTO · Lithium-ion battery
Electrochemical performance

1 Introduction

Due to the concerns on the pollutant emissions and the climate change due to large consumption of fossil fuels to support a variety of anthropogenic activities, electrification of the transport sector has been included as one of the national strategies by many countries. As an alternative to the internal combustion engine (ICE) vehicle, Electric Vehicle (EV) has become increasingly popular in recent years due to the improvement of performance in acceleration and endurance. Comparing to the ICE vehicles, the advantages of EVs can be summarised as following aspects:

(1) Higher efficiency: Generally, the average Tank-to-wheel efficiency of ICE cars are around 30% and even lower than 15% if stop-and-start behaviour occurs frequently [1,2]. However, ICEs do not work in high-efficiency region in most cases, especially when the vehicles are running at a low speed in urban areas. In contrast, the average battery-to-wheel efficiency of EVs can be up to 87% which is much higher than ICE based vehicles [1].

© Springer Nature Singapore Pte Ltd. 2018
K. Li et al. (Eds.): ICSEE 2018/IMIOT 2018, CCIS 925, pp. 201–213, 2018.
https://doi.org/10.1007/978-981-13-2381-2_19

(2) Environmentally friendly: A Battery Electric Vehicle (BEV) is fully powered by the batteries, thus there is no emission produced when an EV is running on the road. Moreover, the emissions of a gasoline Hybrid Electric Vehicle (HEV) is around 30% less than an gasoline ICE based vehicle due to the high efficiency benefit [2].

(3) Less noise pollution: EVs produce less noise pollution (especially at low speed driving mode) due to the result of using electric motors to replace ICEs [3]. An EV eliminates at least 25% and 10% of noise compared to an ICE vehicle at operation speed of 10 km/h and 5 km/h respectively [3,4].

(4) Government support: The promotion of EVs has become a national strategy for many countries today, sales of new petrol and diesel vehicles will be banned for the coming decades in many countries. Many government policies have been proposed in order to increase the competitiveness of EVs in the automotive market, such as lower taxes, free charging facilities and free parking, etc.

As the power source of the electric motor and other electric systems, battery plays an very important role to ensure the EVs can operate effectively and reliably. Several popular types of batteries are used in EVs, such as lead acid, nickel-cadmium, nickel-metal hybrid and Lithium-ion battery. Table 1 presents the key characteristics of these batteries [5–9].

Table 1. Comparison of different types of EV batteries

Characteristic	Lead-acid	Ni-Cd	NiMH	Li-ion
Nominal voltage (V)	2	1.2	1.2	3.2–3.7
Energy density (Wh/kg)	30–50	45–80	60–120	100–265
Power density (W/kg)	180	150	250–1000	250–676
Charging efficiency	50–95%	70–90%	66%	80–90%
Self-discharge rate (per month)	5–20%	20–30%	30–35%	3–10%
Charging temperature (°C)	−20–50	0–45	0–45	0–45
Discharging temperature (°C)	−20–50	−20–65	−20–65	−20–60
Cycle life	200–400	500–1000	300–500	600–3000
Memory effect	No	Yes	Yes	No
Green product	No	No	Yes	Yes

Lithium-ion battery is one of the most popular rechargeable batteries which is widely adopted in EVs and HEVs nowadays due to its noticeable advantages, such as high energy and power density, low self discharge rate, no memory effect, low self-discharge rate and longer life span, etc. [10,11].

Due to the different materials used in the design of the cathodes and anodes, lithium-ion batteries can be subdivided into different categories. Some lithium-ion batteries have been applied in EVs successfully, such as $LiMn_2O_4$ (LMO) battery, $LiNiMnCoO_2$ (NMC) battery, $LiNiCoAlO_2$ (NCA) battery, $LiFePO_4$ (LFP) battery and $Li_4Ti_5O_{12}$ (LTO) battery. These five types of lithium-ion battery have their unique advantages. As the power source of EVs, the battery must meet the specific safety and performance requirements with an appropriate cost. This paper presents a review and comparisons of these five lithium ion batteries over two aspects, namely the electrochemical performance and their applications in EVs.

2   Electrochemical Performance

These five types of lithium-ion battery have various electrochemical performances due to the adoption of different chemical materials. In this section, the comparisons of their structure, nominal voltage, energy density, high current rate capability, thermal stability, cyclabilty and safety performance are presented.

2.1   Structure

LMO has a three dimensional spinel structure which improves the diffusion of lithium ions [12–14]. The electrochemical reactions are associated with the insertion and extraction of lithium ions between the cathode ($LiMn_2O_4$) and the anode (lithium) [15–17]. NMC battery is one of the most successful lithium-ion batteries which balances the specific features of Lithium Cobalt Oxide (LCO) battery and LMO battery. NMC contains a layered structure and the battery cathode is compounded by three chemical elements (Nickel, Manganese and Cobalt) with a certain ratio. The difference ratios of these three chemical elements lead to variant battery performances [18–21]. In order to balance the electrochemical performance, stability and cost, NMC-111 (the ratio of Nickel:Manganese:Cobalt equals to 1:1:1) battery has been developed and widely adopted in EVs. NCA battery has similarities with NMC battery, which replaces manganese with aluminium in order to improve specific energy and life span [22,23]. LFP battery has an ordered olivine structure, the FeO_6 octahedras share the common corners [24]. Unlike the lithium-ion batteries with graphite anode, LTO battery adopts Li-titanate as the anode to offer a zero-strain spinel structure [25].

2.2   Specific Energy and Capability at High Current Rate

In order to increase the mileage of EVs after one charge, the battery of the EVs should offer high energy at a safety level. Increasing the operational voltage is one of the methods that can be applied to enhance battery specific energy. A typical $LiMn_2O_4$ battery offers an average working voltage of 3.7 V, the theoretical gravimetric capacity and energy density are 148 mAh/g [12,26,27]. Unfortunately, the highest gravimetric capacity of $LiMn_2O_4$ battery has been attained is around 130 mAh/g (at the small current rate) [27,28]. A LMO battery has no reversible capacity change when operates at 1 C charge or discharge current rate;

when the charge current remains 1 C and discharge current increases to 50 C, the reversible capacity decreases to 78% of its initial capacity; when the charge and discharge current both change to 20 C, the reversible capacity still remains 58% of its initial capacity [29]. These experimental results strongly suggest that LMO battery has low cell resistance and excellent capability at high current rate.

In order to improve the energy density, some researchers doped other chemical materials, such as Ni in LMO battery cathode to form a doped spinel, and the doped spinel battery can provide a higher theoretical gravimetric capacity of 150–160 mAh/g [30–34]. However, some high energy derivatives of $LiMn_2O_4$ have not been adopted in large-scale in EVs yet due to the limitation of thermal stability and cyclability.

As a possible alternative of $LiCoO_2$ battery, NMC battery offers an average working voltage of 3.6 V and a theoretical gravimetric capacity of 280 mAh/g [35]. However, the actual commercial gravimetric capacity in commercial cells is around 170 mAh/g [35]. The reversible capacity of a NMC-111 battery decreases to 78–80% of initial capacity at 4 C discharge current rate [36,37] and the capacity decreases to 73–74% of initial capacity at 8 C discharge current rate [38,39]. This indicates that NMC battery contains high specific energy and good capability at high current rate.

NCA battery and NMC battery have relatively similar electrochemical performance. A typical NCA ($LiNi_{0.8}Co_{0.15}Al_{0.05}O_2$) battery offers an average operation voltage of 3.7 V, and theoretical gravimetric capacity of 279 mAh/g [35]. The actual gravimetric capacity in commercial cells is around 200 mAh/g [35]. The capacity of a NCA battery decreases to 93.3% of the initial capacity at the discharge current rate at 0.5 C, and there is no extra capacity loss when the discharge current rate increases to 3 C [40]. It obviously can be found that both NCA and MNC batteries have high specific energy and can provide satisfactory performance at high current rate.

LFP has low electrical conductivity (10^{-9} to 10^{-10} S/cm) due to its ordered olivine structure [24,41–44]. A typical LFP battery offers an average operational voltage of 3.3 V [9] and a theoretical gravimetric capacity of 170 mAh/g [24]. The capacity of a LFP battery decreases to 96% of its initial capacity at a discharge current rate of 1 C; the capacity decreases to 82% and 76% at discharge current rate of 3 C and 5 C respectively [45]. The specific energy of LFP battery is lower than the above three lithium-ion batteries. The capacity fades significantly at high current rate.

Unlike the four types of lithium-ion batteries above, LTO battery replaces the graphite in the anode with $Li_4Ti_5O_{12}$ to form a zero-strain spinel structure [25]. As an anode, the operation voltage is 1.5 V for Li/$Li_4Ti_5O_{12}$ battery cell [46]. When the $Li_4Ti_5O_{12}$ anode couples with cathodes like LMO, NMC, NCA, the operating voltage is 2.1–2.5 V [47]. The theoretical gravimetric capacity of $Li_4Ti_5O_{12}$ anode battery is 175 mAh/g [25]. Although the specific energy of LTO battery is low, it has an excellent capability when operates at high current rate, the capacity decreases to 87% of the initial capacity at 11.4 C charge/discharge current rate [48].

However, it should be noted that in the production process of commercial batteries, the theoretical energy densities are very difficult to achieve due to safety, cost and technology limitation reasons. Table 2 shows the average energy densities for commercial products of these five types of lithium-ion battery [49].

Table 2. Nominal voltage and energy density of commercial products

Cathode	Nominal voltage	Energy density in commercial products
LMO	3.7–3.75	100–240 Wh/kg
NMC	3.6–3.7	150–220 Wh/kg
NCA	3.65	200–260 Wh/kg
LFP	3.2	100–140 Wh/kg
LTO	2.2–2.4	50–80 Wh/kg

Comparing the operational voltage and energy density of these five lithium ion batteries, it can be found that LMO, NMC and NCA batteries enable the EVs to gain a longer mileage on single charge due to the higher energy density. LFP and LTO batteries have low energy density which means the EVs need to bring more battery cells to achieve the energy requirement. However, this results the increasing of vehicle weight, the mileage one a single charge still cannot be improved in essence. On the other hand, more batteries are adopted in EVs leads the Battery Management System (BMS) to face greater challenges.

2.3 Thermal Stability and Safety

Apart to the energy and power requirements, safety is another important issue in EV management. Many factors may cause battery failures, such as over voltage, under voltage, short circuit, over charge/discharge, overheat and collision, etc., and a few accidents due to battery failures have been reported in the public media. However, the most common factor is the generation of heat and gas [5,10,50]. Thus, to have desirable thermal stability is another important aspect in assessing the battery quality. Good thermal stability of a battery enables an EV to operate in a wider temperature range, and reduces the difficulty of the thermal management in an EV.

Thermal stability is a key that directly determines the safety of the battery operation. A typical LMO battery can operate safely at 55 °C, but the capacity decreases to 75% of its initial capacity [26]. The main reason of the capacity fading of a LMO battery during cycling is the Mn dissolution into the electrolyte [51]. The Solid Electrolyte Interphase (SEI) breaks at 90.5 °C and the thermal runaway occurs at 250 °C, then O_2 is released due to the decomposition of $LiMn_2O_4$ [52].

A typical NMC battery loses 7.5% capacity at 85 °C after 26 cycles (0.29% capacity loss per cycle) and loses 22% capacity at 120 °C after 29 cycles [53]. At

80 °C, the SEI has no obvious change but it becomes thicker and forms spherical particles at 120 °C [53]. Flammable and toxic gas (H_2 and CO) are released when the temperature reaches 170 °C and the thermal runaway occurs at 220 °C [54].

For a typical NCA battery, the anodic reactions occur at 90 °C and the SEI film breaks at 120 °C; the cathodic reactions occur at 140 °C and the thermal runaway occurs when the temperature reaches 180 °C [55]. Moreover, thermal runaway could occur at 65 °C if the NCA battery is overcharged. [56]. NCA battery has a drastic behaviour when the temperature reaches thermal runaway, a large amount of gas (317mmol) are released [56]. Oxygen gas is released when Ni^{4+} is reduced to Ni^{2+}, and the thermal runaway may be caused by the reaction of oxygen and flammable electrolyte [57,58]. As a Ni-rich cathode, NCA battery has higher specific energy than NMC-111 battery but lower thermal stability [59].

A typical LFP battery reaches its maximum capacity in a temperature range of 20 °C–30 °C and the capacity decreases to 95% when the temperature reduces from 20 °C to 10 °C [60]. The discharge capacity measured at −10 °C shows that 25.8% loss after 600 cycles but 1.9% gain after 300 cycles from the initial capacity [61]. When the temperature reaches 45 °C, the capacity decreases to 92.7% after 300 cycles and decreases to 85.7% after 600 cycles [61]. When the temperature reaches to 60 °C, 37% of the initial capacity loss after 100 cycles and 45% of initial capacity loss after 110 cycles [62]. The thermal runaway occurs at 260 °C [63] and the thermal runaway occurs at 140 °C for an overcharged LFP battery [56]. The amount of gas is released of a LFP battery at thermal runaway temperature is 61mmol, which is much less than NCA battery [56].

The capacity of a typical LTO battery decreases to 91.3% after 280 cycles (0.25% capacity loss per cycle) at 60 °C, the thermal runaway occurs when the temperature exceeds 260 °C [64]. The research [47] shows that graphite anode produces large amount of C_2H_6 and C_2H_4 at 100 °C, but there is no generation of gaseous decomposition products of LTO anode.

Therefore, the thermal stability and safety level of these five types lithium-ion batteries can be summarised in Table 3.

Table 3. Comparisons of thermal stability and safety level

Type of Lithium-ion battery	Thermal stability	Safety level
$LiMn_2O_4$	Low	Moderate
$LiNiMnCoO_2$	Moderate	Moderate
$LiNiCoAlO_2$	Low	Low
$LiFePO_4$	High	High
$Li_4Ti_5O_{12}$	Very high	Very high

3   Applications

All of these five types of lithium-ion battery have been widely adopted in EVs due to their own specific advantages. The application examples of these five types of lithium-ion battery in EVs are provided in Table 4 based on the information available in the public domain.

Table 4. The applications of various lithium-ion batteries in EVs.

Product model	Battery type	Battery weight (kg)	Nominal driving distance (km)	Top speed (km/h)	Charge time (h)	Release year
Nissan leaf	LMO (with LiNiO2)	294	117–200	150	0.5–20	2010
BMW i3	NMC	230	130–160	150	0.5–9	2013
Tesla model S	NCA	535–556	370–426	193–214	0.5–1.25	2012
BYD e6	LFP	500	330	140	2–10	2010
citron C-zero	LTO	165	127	130	0.25–6	2010

Apart from the electrochemical performance of the batteries, cost and market trend are another two important factors which determine the battery application capability in EVs. In this section, the application capability of these five types of lithium-ion battery are reviewed and compared from the aspects of cost and market trend.

3.1   Cost

The cost of a lithium-ion battery contains the following components: materials of cathode and anode, electrolyte, separator, assembly of cell and module, labour, etc. [65]. Due to the different raw materials adopted and the manufacturing processes, the cost of the mentioned five types of Li-ion battery are also different. Table 5 compares the key properties and cost of the several popular types of lithium-ion used in EVs. [65–68].

Due to the high cost of Co and Ti raw materials and the complex process of manufacturing, the cost of NMC, NCA and LTO batteries are much higher than LMO and LFP batteries. It also should be noted that when LTO is selected as the anode material, the cathode material may be chosen from NMC or NCA, the cost of NMC/LTO or NCA/LTO battery will be much higher. Even though the cost of LTO battery is high, the battery replacement frequency can be reduced for the EVs which require to be recharged often. In contrast, although LMO

Table 5. The key properties and cost comparison of the lithium-ion batteries

Battery type	Energy density	Life span	Cost
LMO	Medium	Low	Low
NMC	High	High	High
NCA	High	Medium	High
LFP	Low	High	Low
LTO	Very low	Very high	Very high

battery has a lower cost, the drawback of poor cyclability and thermal stability, the total operation cost may increase for the EVs to be recharged frequently. Sometimes LMO battery and NMC battery are combined to power an EV in order to enhance the performance and also decreases the battery cost. LMO can be used to improve the acceleration performance with the benefit of high current boost, and the NMC brings good cyclability and thermal stability to the entire power system. LTO battery is generally applied to the price-insensitive and low energy requirement vehicles. Due to the properties of high safety, long life and fast-charge, LTO batteries are favoured by electric buses.

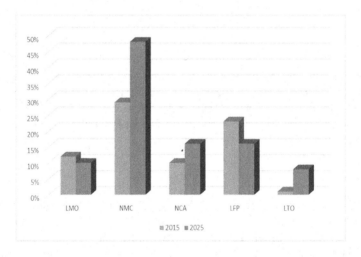

Fig. 1. The market share of different lithium-ion batteries in 2015 and 2025

3.2   Market Trend

According to the estimation results in [69], the market share of NMC, NCA and LTO batteries in 2025 will increase substantially, the expected market growth (from 2015 to 2025) are 4.8 times, 2.9 times and 26.7 times respectively [70].

Figure 1 summarises the market share of lithium-ion battery in 2015 and 2025 respectively [70]. It indicates that NMC, NCA and LTO batteries have a huge potential market in the next few years. Moreover, although the market share of LFP and LMO may decrease, the total market volume is showing a climbing trend [70].

4 Conclusion

$LiMn_2O_4$, $LiNiMnCoO_2$, $LiNiCoAlO_2$, $LiFePO_4$ and $Li_4Ti_5O_{12}$ batteries have been adopted in EVs successfully with their specific features. $LiMn_2O_4$ battery has low resistance due to the spinel structure, this allows $LiMn_2O_4$ battery to offer an excellent performance at high current rate in applications. The extremely low cost makes it highly favoured by the market. Poor performance at high temperature and limited cyclability are the downsides. $LiNiMnCoO_2$ battery has a satisfactory overall performance especially for the high specific energy. A variety of derivatives of $LiNiMnCoO_2$ enable this type lithium-ion battery to face different applications. The extremely high specific energy and moderate life span allows $LiNiCoAlO_2$ to be a good candidate for EVs. High cost and low level of safety are the negatives. The key benefits of $LiFePO_4$ battery are the long life span and low cost. It has good thermal stability when it operates at high temperature but the capacity is greatly attenuated at low temperature. Low specific energy and elevated self-discharge are the main disadvantages. $Li_4Ti_5O_{12}$ battery has the best thermal stability, cyclability and safety performance among these five lithium-ion batteries. No lithium plating at high current rate supports $Li_4Ti_5O_{12}$ battery for fast charging. However, the low specific energy and extremely high cost are the major disadvantages.

Acknowledgements. Xuan Liu would like to thank The Department for the Economy Northern Ireland and W-Tec Centre, Queen's University Belfast for sponsoring his research.

References

1. Campanari, S., Manzolini, G., Garcia De la Iglesia, F.: Energy analysis of electric vehicles using batteries or fuel cells through well-to-wheel driving cycle simulations. J. Power Sour. **186**(2), 464–477 (2009)
2. Williamson, S.S., Emadi, A.: Comparative assessment of hybrid electric and fuel cell vehicles based on comprehensive well-to-wheels efficiency analysis. IEEE Trans. Veh. Technol. **54**(3), 856–862 (2005)
3. Sandberg, U., Goubert, L., Mioduszewski, P.: Are vehicles driven in electric mode so quiet that they need acoustic warning signals. In 20th International Congress on Acoustics (2010)
4. Japan JASIC. A study on approach warning systems for hybrid vehicle in motor mode. Informal document No. GRB-49-10, 49th GRB (2009)
5. Wang, Q., Jiang, B., Li, B., Yan, Y.: A critical review of thermal management models and solutions of lithium-ion batteries for the development of pure electric vehicles. Renew. Sustain. Energy Rev. **64**, 106–128 (2016)

6. Hua, A.C.C., Syue, B.Z.W.: Charge and discharge characteristics of lead-acid battery and LiFePO4 battery. In: 2010 International Power Electronics Conference (IPEC), pp. 1478–1483. IEEE (2010)
7. Ruetschi, P.: Review on the lead-acid battery science and technology. J. Power Sources $2(1)$, 3–120 (1977)
8. Hadjipaschalis, I., Poullikkas, A., Efthimiou, V.: Overview of current and future energy storage technologies for electric power applications. Renew. Sustain. Energy Rev. 13(6–7), 1513–1522 (2009)
9. Hannan, M.A., Lipu, M.S.H., Hussain, A., Mohamed, A.: A review of lithium-ion battery state of charge estimation and management system in electric vehicle applications: challenges and recommendations. Renew. Sustain. Energy Rev. 78, 834–854 (2017)
10. Languang, L., Han, X., Li, J., Hua, J., Ouyang, M.: A review on the key issues for lithium-ion battery management in electric vehicles. J. Power Sources 226, 272–288 (2013)
11. Etacheri, V., Marom, R., Elazari, R., Salitra, G., Aurbach, D.: Challenges in the development of advanced Li-ion batteries: a review. Energy Environ. Sci. 4(9), 3243–3262 (2011)
12. Thackeray, M.M., Johnson, P.J., De Picciotto, L.A., Bruce, P.G., Goodenough, J.B.: Electrochemical extraction of lithium from LiMn2O4. Mater. Res. Bull. 19(2), 179–187 (1984)
13. Thackeray, M.M., David, W.I.F., Bruce, P.G., Goodenough, J.B.: Lithium insertion into manganese spinels. Mater. Res. Bull. 18(4), 461–472 (1983)
14. Choa, J., Thackeray, M.M.: Structural changes of LiMn2O4 spinel electrodes during electrochemical cycling. J. Electrochem. Soc. 146(10), 3577–3581 (1999)
15. Lazzari, M., Scrosati, B.: A cyclable lithium organic electrolyte cell based on two intercalation electrodes. J. Electrochem. Soc. 127(3), 773–774 (1980)
16. Guo, D., et al.: Synthesis and electrochemical properties of high performance polyhedron sphere like lithium manganese oxide for lithium ion batteries. J. Alloys Compd. 632, 222–228 (2015)
17. Ouyang, C.Y., Shi, S.Q., Wang, Z.X., Li, H., Huang, X.J., Chen, L.Q.: Ab initio molecular-dynamics studies on LixMn2O4 as cathode material for lithium secondary batteries. EPL (Europhysics Letters) 67(1), 28 (2004)
18. Li, D.-C., Muta, T., Zhang, L.-Q., Yoshio, M., Noguchi, H.: Effect of synthesis method on the electrochemical performance of LiNi1/3Mn1/3Co1/3O2. J. Power Sources 132(1–2), 150–155 (2004)
19. Dolotko, O., Senyshyn, A., Mühlbauer, M.J., Nikolowski, K., Ehrenberg, H.: Understanding structural changes in NMC Li-ion cells by in situ neutron diffraction. J. Power Sources 255, 197–203 (2014)
20. Choi, J., Manthiram, A.: Role of chemical and structural stabilities on the electrochemical properties of layered LiNi1/ 3Mn1/ 3Co1/ 3O2 cathodes. J. Electrochem. Soc. 152(9), A1714–A1718 (2005)
21. Ohzuku, T., Makimura, Y.: Layered lithium insertion material of LiNi1/2Mn1/2O2: a possible alternative to LiCoO2 for advanced lithium-ion batteries. Chem. Lett. 30(8), 744–745 (2001)
22. Tran, H.Y., Greco, G., Täubert, C., Wohlfahrt-Mehrens, M., Haselrieder, W., Kwade, A.: Influence of electrode preparation on the electrochemical performance of LiNi0. 8Co0. 15Al0. 05O2 composite electrodes for lithium-ion batteries. J. Power Sources 210, 276–285 (2012)
23. Kim, G.-Y., Dahn, J.R.: Effects of electrode density on the safety of NCA positive electrode for Li-ion batteries. J. Electrochem. Soc. 160(8), A1108–A1111 (2013)

24. Padhi, A.K., Nanjundaswamy, K.S., Goodenough, J.B.: Phospho-olivines as positive-electrode materials for rechargeable lithium batteries. J. Electrochem. Soc. **144**(4), 1188–1194 (1997)
25. Ohzuku, T., Ueda, A., Yamamoto, N.: Zero-strain insertion material of Li [Li1/3Ti5/3] o 4 for rechargeable lithium cells. J. Electrochem. Soc. **142**(5), 1431–1435 (1995)
26. Guyomard, D., Tarascon, J.M.: Li metal-free rechargeable LiMn2O4/carbon cells: their understanding and optimization. J. Electrochem. Soc. **139**(4), 937–948 (1992)
27. Potapenko, A.V., Kirillov, S.A.: Lithium manganese spinel materials for high-rate electrochemical applications. J. Energy Chem. **23**(5), 543–558 (2014)
28. Tu, J., Zhao, X.B., Zhuang, D.G., Cao, G.S., Zhu, T.J., Tu, J.P.: Studies of cycleability of LiMn2O4 and LiLa0. 01Mn1. 99O4 as cathode materials for Li-ion battery. Physica B: Condens. Matter **382**(1–2), 129–134 (2006)
29. Tang, W., et al.: Nano LiMn2O4 as cathode material of high rate capability for lithium ion batteries. J. Power Sources **198**, 308–311 (2012)
30. Amine, K., Tukamoto, H., Yasuda, H., Fujita, Y.: A new three-volt spinel Li1+ x Mn1. 5Ni0. 5 O 4 for secondary lithium batteries. J. Electrochem. Soc. **143**(5), 1607–1613 (1996)
31. Strobel, P., Palos, A.I., Anne, M., Le Cras, F.: Structural, magnetic and lithium insertion properties of spinel-type Li2Mn3MO8 oxides (m= Mg, Co, Ni, Cu). J. Mater. Chem. **10**(2), 429–436 (2000)
32. Morales, J., Sánchez, L., Tirado, J.L.: New doped Li-M-Mn-O (M= Al, Fe, Ni) spinels as cathodes for rechargeable 3 V lithium batteries. J. Solid State Electrochem. **2**(6), 420–426 (1998)
33. Wagemaker, M., Ooms, F.G.B., Kelder, E.M., Schoonman, J., Mulder, F.M.: Extensive migration of Ni and Mn by lithiation of ordered LiMg0. 1Ni0. 4Mn1. 5O4 spinel. J. Am. Chem. Soc. **126**(41), 13526–13533 (2004)
34. Liu, G.Q., Wen, L., Liu, Y.M.: Spinel LiNi$_{0.5}$Mn$_{1.5}$O$_4$ and its derivatives as cathodes for high-voltage Li-ion batteries. J. Solid State Electrochem. **14**(12), 2191–2202 (2010)
35. Nitta, N., Wu, F., Lee, J.T., Yushin, G.: Li-ion battery materials: present and future. Mater. Today **18**(5), 252–264 (2015)
36. Park, S.H., Yoon, C.S., Kang, S.G., Kim, H.-S., Moon, S.-I., Sun, Y.-K.: Synthesis and structural characterization of layered Li [Ni1/3Co1/3Mn1/3] O2 cathode materials by ultrasonic spray pyrolysis method. Electrochimica Acta **49**(4), 557–563 (2004)
37. Sun, Y., Ouyang, C., Wang, Z., Huang, X., Chen, L.: Effect of co content on rate performance of limn0. 5- x Co2x Ni0. 5- x O 2 cathode materials for lithium-ion batteries. J. Electrochem. Soc. **151**(4), A504–A508 (2004)
38. Santhanam, R., Rambabu, B.: Improved high rate cycling of Li-rich Li1. 10Ni1/3Co1/3Mn1/3O2 cathode for lithium batteries. Int. J. Electrochem. Sci. **4**(12), 1770–1778 (2009)
39. Yabuuchi, N., Ohzuku, T.: Novel lithium insertion material of LiCo1/3Ni1/3Mn1/3O2 for advanced lithium-ion batteries. J. Power Sources **119**, 171–174 (2003)
40. Myung, S.T., Cho, M.H., Hong, H.T., Kang, T.H., Kim, C.S.: Electrochemical evaluation of mixed oxide electrode for Li-ion secondary batteries: Li1. 1Mn1. 9O4 and Lini0. 8Co0. 15Al0. 05O2. J. Power Sources **146**(1–2), 222–225 (2005)
41. Takahashi, M., Tobishima, S., Takei, K., Sakurai, Y.: Characterization of LiFePO4 as the cathode material for rechargeable lithium batteries. J. Power Sources **97**, 508–511 (2001)

42. Andersson, A.S., Kalska, B., Häggström, L., Thomas, J.O.: Lithium extraction/insertion in LiFePO4: an x-ray diffraction and mössbauer spectroscopy study. Solid State Ionics 130(1–2), 41–52 (2000)

43. Barker, J., Saidi, M.Y., Swoyer, J.L.: Lithium iron (ii) phospho-olivines prepared by a novel carbothermal reduction method. Electrochem. Solid-State Lett. 6(3), A53–A55 (2003)

44. Shin, H.C., Cho, W.I., Jang, H.: Electrochemical properties of the carbon-coated LiFePO4 as a cathode material for lithium-ion secondary batteries. J. Power Sources 159(2), 1383–1388 (2006)

45. Huang, Y., Ren, H., Yin, S., Wang, Y., Peng, Z., Zhou, Y.: Synthesis of LiFePO4/C composite with high-rate performance by starch sol assisted rheological phase method. J. Power Sources 195(2), 610–613 (2010)

46. Ferg, E., Gummow, R.J., De Kock, A., Thackeray, M.M.: Spinel anodes for lithium-ion batteries. J. Electrochem. Soc. 141(11), L147–L150 (1994)

47. Belharouak, I., Koenig Jr., G.M., Amine, K.: Electrochemistry and safety of Li4Ti5O12 and graphite anodes paired with LiMn2O4 for hybrid electric vehicle Li-ion battery applications. J. Power Sources 196(23), 10344–10350 (2011)

48. Lai, C., Dou, Y.Y., Li, X., Gao, X.P.: Improvement of the high rate capability of hierarchical structured Li4Ti5O12 induced by the pseudocapacitive effect. J. Power Sources 195(11), 3676–3679 (2010)

49. Battery Universtiy. Bu-205: Types of lithium-ion. http://batteryuniversity.com/learn/article/types_of_lithium_ion. Accessed 01 Apr 2018

50. Levy, S.C., Bro, P.: Battery hazards and accident prevention of cell components with the thermal behavior of a complete cell (1994)

51. Xia, Y., Zhou, Y., Yoshio, M.: Capacity fading on cycling of 4 V Li/LiMn2 O 4 cells. J. Electrochem. Soc. 144(8), 2593–2600 (1997)

52. Wang, Q., Sun, J., Chen, C.: Thermal stability of delithiated LiMn2O4 with electrolyte for lithium-ion batteries. J. Electrochem. Soc. 154(4), A263–A267 (2007)

53. Bodenes, L., et al.: Lithium secondary batteries working at very high temperature: capacity fade and understanding of aging mechanisms. J. Power Sources 236, 265–275 (2013)

54. Golubkov, A.W., et al.: Thermal-runaway experiments on consumer li-ion batteries with metal-oxide and olivin-type cathodes. RSC. Adv. 4(7), 3633–3642 (2014)

55. Wen, J., Yan, Y., Chen, C.: A review on lithium-ion batteries safety issues: existing problems and possible solutions. Mater. Express 2(3), 197–212 (2012)

56. Andrey, W., et al.: Thermal runaway of commercial 18650 Li-ion batteries with LFP and NCA cathodes-impact of state of charge and overcharge. RSC. Adv. 5(70), 57171–57186 (2015)

57. Belharouak, I., Wenquan, L., Vissers, D., Amine, K.: Safety characteristics of Li (Ni0. 8Co0. 15Al0. 05) O2 and Li (Ni1/3Co1/3Mn1/3) O2. Electrochem. Commun. 8(2), 329–335 (2006)

58. Yoon, W.S., Chung, K.Y., McBreen, J., Yang, X.Q.: A comparative study on structural changes of LiCo1/3Ni1/3Mn1/3O2 and LiNi0. 8Co0. 15Al0. 05O2 during first charge using in situ XRD. Electrochem. Commun. 8(8), 1257–1262 (2006)

59. Bak, S.M., et al.: Structural changes and thermal stability of charged lini x Mn y Co z O2 cathode materials studied by combined in situ time-resolved XRD and mass spectroscopy. ACS Appl. Mater. Interfaces 6(24), 22594–22601 (2014)

60. Chen, K., Li, X.: Accurate determination of battery discharge characteristics-a comparison between two battery temperature control methods. J. Power Sources 247, 961–966 (2014)

61. Zhang, Y., Wang, C.-Y., Tang, X.: Cycling degradation of an automotive LiFePO4 lithium-ion battery. J. Power Sources **196**(3), 1513–1520 (2011)
62. Dubarry, M., et al.: Identifying battery aging mechanisms in large format Li ion cells. J. Power Sources **196**(7), 3420–3425 (2011)
63. Mayza, A.B., et al.: Thermal characterization of LiFepO4 cathode in lithium ion cells. ECS Trans. **35**(34), 177–183 (2011)
64. Huang, P., et al.: Experimental and modeling analysis of thermal runaway propagation over the large format energy storage battery module with Li4Ti5O12 anode. Appl. Energy **183**, 659–673 (2016)
65. Berckmans, G., Messagie, M., Smekens, J., Omar, N., Vanhaverbeke, L., Van Mierlo, J.: Cost projection of state of the art lithium-ion batteries for electric vehicles up to 2030. Energies **10**(9), 1314 (2017)
66. Deng, D.: Li-ion batteries: basics, progress, and challenges. Energy Sci. Eng. **3**(5), 385–418 (2015)
67. Mekonnen, Y., Sundararajan, A., Sarwat, A.I.: A review of cathode and anode materials for lithium-ion batteries. In: SoutheastCon, 2016, pp. 1–6. IEEE (2016)
68. Smekens, J., et al.: Influence of electrode density on the performance of Li-ion batteries: experimental and simulation results. Energies **9**(2), 104 (2016)
69. Pillot, C.: The rechargeable battery market and main trends 2014–2025. In: 31st International Battery Seminar & Exhibit (2015)
70. Lebedeva, N., De Periso, F., Boon-Brett, L.: Lithium ion battery value chain and related opportunities for europe. European Commission, Petten (2016)

A Large-Scale Manufacturing Method to Produce Form Stable Composite Phase Change Materials (PCMs) for Thermal Energy Storage at Low and High Temperatures

Zhu Jiang, Guanghui Leng, and Yulong Ding[✉]

BCES Birmingham Centre of Energy Storage,
University of Birmingham, Birmingham B15 2TT, UK
y.ding@bham.ac.uk

Abstract. High performance Phase Change Materials (PCMs) play a vital role in Thermal Energy Storage (TES) technologies. A cost-effective and easy-controllable fabrication process by mix-sintering method is an effective approach to produce composite PCMs at a large scale. In this work, a series of form stable composite PCMs with different phase change temperatures were prepared by mix-sintering method. These composite PCMs could be applied in a cascading manner in thermal storage system. DSC measurements and analyses show that the cascading system has an energy storage density of 1068.96 J/g within a working temperature range from 50 °C to 550 °C. Besides, an SEM study shows homogenous microstructure of the prepared composite PCMs.

Keywords: Thermal energy storage · Phase Change Materials
Mix-sintering method · Large-scale fabrication
Cascading thermal storage system

1 Introduction

Renewables have been intensively studied in recent years as they play a vital role in a less carbon-intensive and more sustainable energy system [1]. However, the intermittency nature of renewable has become the main bottleneck for obtaining continuous and stabilized energy. Therefore, thermal energy storage (TES) technology which could store and release thermal energy according to requirements could be regarded as an effective method to address the intermittency issue of the renewable [2]. High performance TES material is the key challenge for TES technology. Phase change material (PCM) which presents a relatively high energy density and an easy-controllable heat charging and discharging property has attracted growing attention in decades. Nowadays, PCM has been applied in heat recovery, solar power generation system, electricity peak load shifting [3], intensive cascading energy storage system [4], etc. Encapsulation of phase change materials (PCMs) is an effective way of preventing leakage during phase change process and solving possible chemical incompatibility with the surroundings. Different encapsulation methods have been studied to obtain a structural stabilized composite PCM, for instance, physical, physic-chemical,

© Springer Nature Singapore Pte Ltd. 2018
K. Li et al. (Eds.): ICSEE 2018/IMIOT 2018, CCIS 925, pp. 214–221, 2018.
https://doi.org/10.1007/978-981-13-2381-2_20

and chemical methods. When the fabrication method is verified in lab scale and needs to be scaled up for pilot or industrial application, the costs of encapsulation method and the controllability of the fabricating process are the most important issues need to be considered.

Mix-sintering method is a mature process which has been used in sintering metallic and ceramics powders a long time ago. In the late 1980s, it has been firstly used to prepare form-stable composite PCMs, when Randy and Terry [5–7] used 80 wt% $NaCO_3$-$BaCO_3$ as phase change material and 20 wt% MgO as supporting material to prepare a composite PCM. This composite PCM had been thermal cycled 22 times and showed good stability with only 1% mass loss and 1% decrease in density. In the 1990s, Gluck [8] and Hame [9] compressed Na_2SO_4 and silica mixtures at 70 MPa and sintered for 2 h at 1000 °C to fabricate PCM bricks for high temperature heat storage. Their work showed that heat storage capacity of the ceramic brick compromising 20 wt % inorganic salts increased by 2.5 times than that of the pure ceramic in the same volume. In the 21st century, mix-sintering process has been widely used to prepare form-stable PCMs. Gokon [10] used mix sintering method to fabricate the composite materials of molten alkali-carbonate/MgO ceramics. They had tested the composite PCM in a catalyst bed which revealed a good thermal storage property of the composite PCM. Ye [11] mixed multi-walled carbon nanotubes (MWCNTs) into Na_2CO_3/MgO form-stable composite and found that the thermal conductivity of the composite had increased significantly with increasing addition of MWCNTs. Zhu [12] mix-sintered porous calcium silicate with quaternary nitrates $LiNO_3$–$NaNO_3$–KNO_3–$Ca(NO_3)_2$ to get a mid-low temperature composite PCM. This composite shows high thermal conductivity and thermal stability than the other organic PCMs.

Although mix-sintering method has been applied in preparing composite PCM a long time ago, most of the previous work is based on lab scale. A large-scale fabrication process by mix-sintering differs from lab scale preparation. In this work, a large-scale fabrication process was introduced to prepare composite PCMs with different working temperature range. These composite PCMs can be used in a cascading manner in thermal storage system with a relatively high energy storage capacity.

2 Material and Methodology

2.1 Materials

KNO_3 (98%), MgO (99%), Li_2CO_3 (99%), Na_2CO_3 (99%), Graphite powders (99%) were purchased from Sigma-Aldrich company. The diatomite is a kind of mineral with natural porous structure, which was bought from JJS Minerals company. Vermiculite is a porous phyllosilicate mineral purchased from Dupreminerals company. The Erythritol is a kind of surgar which was purchased from Naturtotal company. Three different form stable composite PCMs were prepared by the following formulation shown in Table 1.

Table 1. Composition of the prepared composite PCMs

cPCMs	PCM	Skeleton material	Thermal conductivity enhancer
1	Erythritol	Vermiculite	Graphite
2	KNO_3	Diatomite	–
3	Na_2CO_3-K_2CO_3	MgO	Graphite

2.2   Manufacturing Process for CPCMs

The procedure to produce composite PCMs in large scale is by mix-sintering method, which is shown in Fig. 1. Firstly, the raw materials are ground and sieved separately to an expected size. The powder size which can affect the density of the composite should be controlled in the manufacturing process. Then, the ground powders are mixed uniformly in their adequate amount and pelletized into larger particles to increase the fluidity when being compressed. Afterwards, the pelletized particles were compressed in a mould at 40 MPa to green tablets. During the compression process, the void space between particles has been reduced significantly. Then the green tablets were dried at 100 °C to get rid of the water. Finally, the green tablets were sintered above the melting point of each PCM, in which process the grains of skeleton material were rearranged and pulled together by the melting PCM due to good wettability between the PCM and skeleton materials. This process has resulted in a densified composite with a relatively high rigidity.

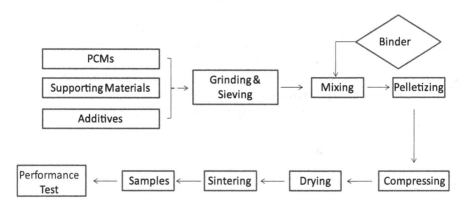

Fig. 1. Schematic diagram of fabrication process by mix-sintering

2.3   Characterization of cPCMs

A differential scanning calorimeter (DSC 2, Mettler Toledo, Germany) was used to measure the phase change parameters and specific heat capacity of Erythritol/Vermiculite/Graphite and KNO_3/Diatomite cPCMs. The temperature range is 25 °C to 180 °C for Erythritol/Vermiculite/Graphite cPCM and 25 °C to 400 °C for

KNO$_3$/Diatomite cPCM with a heating rate of 5 °C/min and a purge of 100 ml/min N$_2$ gas. Meanwhile, a simultaneous thermal analyzer (STA 449F3 Jupiter®, Netzsch, Germany) was used to characterize the phase change process of Na$_2$CO$_3$-K$_2$CO$_3$/ MgO/Graphite cPCM with a heating rate of 10 °C/min and a purge of 50 ml/min N$_2$ gas. A scanning electron microscopy coupled with an energy-dispersive X-ray spectroscopy (SEM&EDS, Hitachi TM-3030) was used to study the microscopic morphology and element distribution of the material.

3   Results and Discussion

3.1   Sample Observation

The aforementioned composite PCMs prepared by mix-sintering method in lab scale are shown in Fig. 2. These composite PCMs show good shape stability without any leakage after sintering. A batch of composite PCMs prepared in pilot scale following mix-sintering process is shown in Fig. 3. The shape of the composite PCMs can be designed according to the needs. These prepared cPCMs show good shape stability as the ones prepared in lab. No deformation and leakage are observed after being sintered above the melting point.

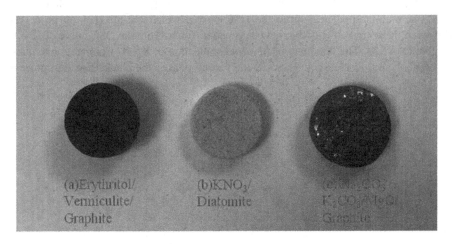

Fig. 2. Composite PCMs prepared by mix-sintering method in lab scale

Fig. 3. Composite PCMs prepared by mix-sintering method in pilot scale: Na$_2$CO$_3$-K$_2$CO$_3$/MgO/Graphite

3.2   Energy Storage Properties

3.2.1   Melting Point and Melting Enthalpy

Phase Change Materials (PCMs) which stores heat mainly in form of latent heat are commonly used at a temperature range around phase transition point. The phase change parameters of the cPCMs are measured and shown in Fig. 4. One can see that both the Erythritol/Vermiculite/Graphite cPCM and the Na$_2$CO$_3$-K$_2$CO$_3$/MgO/Graphite cPCM have one endothermal peak from the DSC curves which are the melting processes. However, there are two endothermal peaks can be found from the DSC curve of KNO$_3$/Diatomite cPCM. The first peak is the crystal transition of KNO$_3$ from aragonite phase to rhombohedral formation [13], while the second peak is the phase transition process.

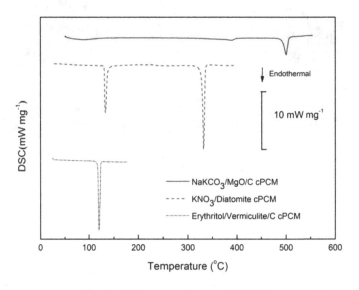

Fig. 4. DSC curves of composite PCMs

Table 2. Melting point and latent heat of composite PCMs

cPCMs	T_m (°C)	ΔH (J/g)
Erythritol/Vermiculite/Graphite	119.8	164.8
KNO$_3$/Diatomite	335.3	51.8
Na$_2$CO$_3$-K$_2$CO$_3$/MgO/Graphite	500.2	170.8

The phase transition temperature and enthalpy for each composite PCM are shown in Table 2. As can be seen that the composite PCMs have melting points of 119.8 °C, 335.3 °C, and 500.2 °C respectively, which can be used in a cascading manner in intensive energy storage system [4] within temperature range from 50 °C to 550 °C.

Therefore, the thermal storage energy density of each composite PCM can be calculated. The energy density of composite PCM should consider both sensible heat and latent heat. From T_0 to T_1, the energy density can be calculated as the following:

$$Q = \int_{T_0}^{T_m} C_{p,s} dT + \Delta H + \int_{T_m}^{T_1} C_{p,l} dT$$

where Q is the total thermal energy stored in a unit mass of the composite PCM, $C_{p,s}$, $C_{p,l}$ are heat capacities of composite PCM in solid state and liquid state respectively. T_0, T_1 and T_m denote the lower bound temperature, upper bound temperature and the melting temperature of the PCM, respectively. ΔH represents the latent heat of PCM.

The heat capacity and the calculated energy density of each cPCM at a certain application temperature range are shown in Table 3. Therefore, integrating the prepared composite PCMs in a cascading manner in thermal storage system, a total energy storage density of the system can reach 1068.96 J/g from 50 °C to 550 °C.

Table 3. Heat capacities and energy density of the composite PCMs

cPCMs	Temperature range (°C)	$C_{p,s}$ (J·K^{-1} g^{-1})	$C_{p,l}$ (J·K^{-1} g^{-1})	Q (J·g^{-1})
Erythritol/Vermiculite/Graphite	50–200	1.25	1.21	349.09
KNO$_3$/Diatomite	200–400	1.10	1.12	273.09
Na$_2$CO$_3$-K$_2$CO$_3$/ MgO/Graphite	400–550	1.80	1.92	446.78

3.3   SEM

The microstructure of the fabricated composite PCMs has been studied by SEM. Besides, EDS mapping shows the elements distribution of the composite PCM has been investigated and displayed in Fig. 5. One can see that each composite PCM presents a different microstructure. The Erythritol/Vermiculite/GraphitecPCM has a flat structure and some localized macro-pores. From the EDS mapping, particles of graphite and vermiculite are distributed uniformly. In terms of the KNO$_3$/Diatomite cPCM,

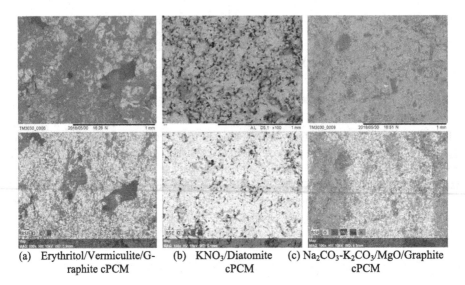

(a) Erythritol/Vermiculite/G-   (b) KNO₃/Diatomite   (c) Na₂CO₃-K₂CO₃/MgO/Graphite
        raphite cPCM   cPCM   cPCM

Fig. 5. SEM and EDS images of the fabricated composite PCMs

it shows a densified microstructure with some micro-voids between particles. EDS mapping shows that each component is mixed homogeneously. The Na₂CO₃-K₂CO₃/MgO/Graphite cPCM show a similar microstructure as the KNO₃/Diatomite cPCM, except for some graphite particles embedded inside the composite can be observed.

4 Conclusions

A series of composite PCMs have low and high melting temperature was manufactured by a large-scale preparation method in this work, which is aiming for cascading thermal energy storage. These composite PCM normally contains a phase change material and a skeleton material. Graphite could also be used as an additive to enhance the overall thermal conductivity of the composite material. The composite PCMs prepared by mix-sintering method are characterized preliminarily in this work and could be summarized as follow:

- Mix-sintering method is a fabrication method which can be applied both in lab scale and pilot scale. Composite PCMs prepared by this method in lab or pilot scale both display a great shape stabilization property without any deformation and leakage after sintering over its melting point.
- The prepared composite PCMs show melting points of 119.8 °C, 335.3 °C, and 500.2 °C respectively, which could be used in a cascading manner in thermal energy storage system.
- The stored energy density of the cascading thermal storage system can reach as high as 1068.96 J/g within a temperature range from 50 °C to 550 °C.
- The microstructure of each composite PCM has been studied by SEM and EDS, which shows a homogeneous distribution of all the components.

Acknowledgments. The authors gratefully acknowledge the financial supports from SGRI of China State Grid under Project: Establishment of research capability in thermal energy storage SGRI-DL-71-16-017.

References

1. Hasan, R., Mekhilef, S., Seyedmahmoudian, M., Horan, B.: Grid-connected isolated PV microinverters: a review. Renew. Sustain. Energy Rev. **67**, 1065–1080 (2017)
2. Li, Y., Jin, Y., Huang, Y., Ye, F., Wang, X., Li, D., et al.: Principles and new development of thermal storage technology. Energy Storage Sci. Technol. **2**, 69–72 (2013)
3. Farid, M.M., Khudhair, A.M., Razack, S.A.K., Al-Hallaj, S.: A review on phase change energy storage: materials and applications. Energy Convers. Manag. **45**, 1597–1615 (2004)
4. Michels, H., Pitz-Paal, R.: Cascaded latent heat storage for parabolic trough solar power plants. Sol. Energy **81**, 829–837 (2007)
5. Claar, T.D., Ong, E.T., Petri, R.J.: Composite salt/ceramic media for thermal energy storage applications. In: Proceedings of the Intersociety. Energy Conversion Engineering. Conference (United States), vol. 4, pp. 2043–2048 (1982)
6. Petri, R.J., Claar, T.D., Ong, E.T.: High-temperature salt/ceramic thermal storage phase-change media. In: Proceedings of the Intersociety. Energy Conversion Engineering. Conference (United States) (1983)
7. Petri, R.J., Ong, E.T., Marianowski, L.G.: High-temperature composite thermal energy storage for industrial applications (1985). https://www.osti.gov/scitech/biblio/6071974
8. Glück, A., Tamme, R., Kalfa, H., Streuber, C., Weichert, T.: Development and testing of advanced TES materials for solar central receiver plants (1991)
9. Hame, E., Taut, U., Grob, Y.: Salt ceramic thermal energy storage for solar thermal central receiver plants. In: Proceedings of the Solar World Congress (1991)
10. Gokon, N., Nakano, D., Inuta, S., Kodama, T.: High-temperature carbonate/MgO composite materials as thermal storage media for double-walled solar reformer tubes. Sol. Energy **82**, 1145–1153 (2008)
11. Ye, F., Ge, Z.: Multi-walled carbon nanotubes added to Na_2CO_3/MgO composites for thermal energy storage. Particuology **15**, 56–60 (2014)
12. Jiang, Z., et al.: Form-stable $LiNO_3$–$NaNO_3$–KNO_3–$Ca(NO_3)_2$/calcium silicate composite phase change material (PCM) for mid-low temperature thermal energy storage. Energy Convers. Manag. **106**, 165–172 (2015)
13. Jurado-Lasso, F., Jurado-Lasso, N., Ortiz, J., Jurado, J.F.: Thermal dielectric and Raman studies on the KNO_3 compound high-temperature region. DYNA **83**, 244 (2016)

Power System Analysis

Research on Smart Grid Comprehensive Development Level Based on the Improved Cloud Matter Element Analysis Method

Chengze Song[1(⊠)], Junyong Wu[1], Meiyang Shao[1], Liangliang Hao[1], and Lin Liu[2]

[1] Electrical Engineering School of Beijing Jiaotong University, Haidian District, Beijing, China
16121514@bjtu.edu.cn
[2] State Grid Energy Research Institute, Future Science and Technology City, Changping District, Beijing, China

Abstract. According to the characteristics of the smart grid, in order to solve the problem of subjective hierarchical boundary cloud model and the problem of real-time data collection, this paper proposes an objective cloud matter element analysis based on cluster analysis. According to the development and planning, this paper puts forward an index system of the smart grid comprehensive development level. Because of non-national-standard data, this paper classifies the data into several levels according to cluster analysis, and then gets each hierarchical boundary cloud model of each index by calculating, then the correlation degree between the sample data and the hierarchical boundary cloud model is calculated; By combining ANP and principal component analysis method, the integrated weight vector is obtained and the weighted evaluation result is obtained. By multiple operations, the evaluation is ordered by using the standard deviation. The model illustrates the validity and superiority of the method.

Keywords: Cloud matter element theory · Objective · Smart grid
Comprehensive development level · Evaluation

1 Introduction

The shortage of traditional energy and the problem of environmental pollution are the greatest challenges faced by the continuous development of human society. In order to solve the energy crisis and environmental issues, various low-carbon technologies are rapidly developing and will be applied on a large scale [1–3].

To achieve communication and cooperation, learn the advantages of smart grids in different countries, it is essential to conduct a comprehensive assessment of the current state of smart grid development in various countries. For example, the EU Joint

Project Supported by STATE GRID CORPORATION OF CHINA "Analysis model and application of global energy Interconnection development index" (SGHAJY00RZJS1700026).

© Springer Nature Singapore Pte Ltd. 2018
K. Li et al. (Eds.): ICSEE 2018/IMIOT 2018, CCIS 925, pp. 225–235, 2018.
https://doi.org/10.1007/978-981-13-2381-2_21

Research Center and the U.S. Department of Energy cooperated in 2012 to conduct a comparative study of the European and American smart grids [4].

For comparative study, this article uses the cloud element analysis which can reflect the randomness and fuzziness to establish evaluation model [5], because the real-time of the data in the index system cannot be fully guaranteed. The advantage of this method is that, based on the trend of the development of the index data, it can minimize time disunity problem of the data by giving index data of a certain interval. However, there are only two ways to divide the grade interval in traditional cloud element analysis: artificial division or national standard. In view of the fact that the indicators of the smart grid have no national standard level for reference, in order to avoid the subjective impact of artificial division, this paper proposes an objective cloud matter element method based on cluster analysis. It can divide the grade interval objectively which theoretically reduce the subjective influence to improve the objectivity and accuracy; At the same time, the weight is determined by combining subjective method and objective method to avoid subjective influence.

2 The Cloud Model

The cloud model has three important parameters: Expectation, represents the center of cloud distribution; Entropy, represents the fuzziness of the concept value, the greater the entropy, the greater the randomness and fuzziness; Hyper-entropy, represents the dispersion degree of the reaction cloud droplets.

The object element is usually denoted as $R = (N, c, v)$, which N represents things, c represents the characteristics of things, and v represents the magnitude of the characteristics.

As usual, the cloud model is substituted into the matter-element theory [6], and v is replaced with (E_x, E_n, H_e). In this paper, the steps of the calculation of correlation degree are as follows:

(1) Consider the eigenvalues of the cloud model (E_x, E_n, H_e) as a hierarchical boundary cloud model;
(2) Randomly generate a normal random number E_x' with the expectation E_n and the standard deviation H_e;
(3) Consider the sample value of this indicator x as a cloud drop, and calculate the association of the index value with the hierarchical boundary cloud model [7]:

$$y = \exp\frac{-(x - E_x)^2}{2(E_n')^2} \tag{1}$$

3 The Improved Cloud Model

3.1 The Hierarchical Classification of Hierarchical Boundary Cloud Model

This paper proposes a hierarchical interval classification method based on cluster analysis. Applying the characteristics of cluster analysis makes the level limit cloud model more objective, so that the evaluation results of cloud matter element analysis method are also more objective.

This paper uses cluster analysis to cluster all the sample values of the smart grid comprehensive development level. The steps are as follows:

(1) Determine the number of levels of the level limit cloud model $c_1, \ldots, c_i$;
(2) Randomly select data from the sample dataset as the initial clustering center [8];
(3) Calculate the distance between each data and the initial clustering center, and determine the level of the data according to the distance. The principle is to minimize the square sum of the data in each level to the clustering center as much as possible.
(4) After all the data have been determined, the cluster center is recalculated to determine whether the clustering criterion function has changed.

3.2 The Determination of the Hierarchical Boundary Cloud Model

After clustering the sample data, the cluster center of each level $a_1, a_2, \ldots, a_i$ is obtained. The value of each index grade interval is regarded as a double-constraint interval $[c_{min}, c_{max}]$, and the calculation formula of the upper and lower limits of the interval is [9]:

$$c_{min(i)} = \frac{a_{i-1} + a_i}{2} \quad (1 < i \leq n) \tag{2}$$

$$c_{max(i)} = \frac{a_i + a_{i+1}}{2} \quad (1 < i \leq n) \tag{3}$$

The upper limit of the highest level and the lower limit of the lowest level are determined by the nature of the index. If the index has obvious upper and lower limit values, then the scale interval does not exceed [1,100]. If the index is purely a quantitative indicator and there are no clear upper and lower limits, the formula is:

$$c_{min(1)} = a_1 - (c_{max(1)} - a_1) = 2a_1 - c_{max(1)} \tag{4}$$

$$c_{max(max)} = a_{max} + (a_{max} - c_{min(max)}) = 2a_{max} - c_{min(max)} \tag{5}$$

Among them, $c_{min(1)}$ represents the lower limit of the lowest level; $c_{max(1)}$ represents the upper limit of the lowest level; $c_{min(max)}$ represents the lower limit of the highest level; $c_{max(max)}$ represents the upper limit of the highest level.

The interval median point represents the expectation of the entire interval E_x, and the entropy value E_n is calculated according to the principle of "$3E_n$", and the hyper-entropy value is determined by considering the randomness and fuzziness of the boundary of the constraint:

$$E_x = \frac{c_{min} + c_{max}}{2} \tag{6}$$

$$E_n = \frac{c_{max} - c_{min}}{6} \tag{7}$$

$$H_e = s \tag{8}$$

After the expectations, entropy, and hyper-entropy values are determined, they are considered as a hierarchical boundary cloud model, and then the relevance of the sample data points to each level of hierarchical boundary cloud model is calculated.

4 Evaluation of Comprehensive Development Level of the Smart Grid Based on Improved Cloud Matter Element Analysis

4.1 The Smart Grid Comprehensive Development Level Index System

The establishment of an evaluation index system for the smart grid comprehensive development level is the basis for the assessment [10]. According to the basic characteristics of the smart grid, taking the possibility of the index data collection into consideration, this paper establishes an index system as shown in Table 1.

4.2 Hierarchical Boundary Cloud Model of Each Index for the Smart Grid Comprehensive Development Level

By the literature review, sample data from 16 major countries were collected [11, 12]. According to Eqs. (2)–(5), the level limits are obtained.

According to the Eqs. (6)–(8), this paper calculates the expectation, the entropy to obtain the hierarchical limit cloud model, as shown in Table 2.

4.3 Determination of Weight Coefficient

In this paper, a combination of ANP and principal component analysis [13] is used to determine the weight coefficients. This method not only satisfies the subjective experience of experts, but also is loyal to the objectivity of the index data.

Assume that the subjective weight coefficient is ω_s and the objective weight coefficient is ω_o. First, calculate the relative importance factor coefficient α of the subjective weight and the relative importance factor coefficient β of the objective weight:

Table 1. The index system of the smart grid comprehensive development level

First-level index	Second-level index	No.
Energy Use Scale	Thermal power installed capacity	1
	Hydropower Installed capacity	2
	Nuclear Power Installed Capacity	3
	Wind power installed capacity	4
	Photovoltaic power installed capacity	5
	Pumped storage installed capacity	6
Smart Facility Scale	UHV AC/DC Transmission Scale (km)	7
	Flexible HVDC transmission scale (km)	8
	Intelligent distribution network capacity ratio	9
	Terminal plug-and-play charging station scale	10
	Smart meter application scale (million)	11
Strong and Self-healing	Strong grid structure	12
Economic and Efficiency	Line loss intelligent optimization capability	13
	User power usage	14
	Wind Power Access Capability	15
	Photovoltaic Access Capability	16
Integration and Compatibility	User-side demand response capability	17
Environmentally Friendly	Greenhouse gas emission intensity	18
	Electrical energy substitution ratio	19
Policies and Regulations	Cooperation and mechanism	20
	Smart Grid Planning and Support Policy	21
	Related special policies and incentives	22

$$\alpha_i = \frac{\omega_{si}}{\omega_{oi} + \omega_{si}}, \quad 1 \leq i \leq n \tag{9}$$

$$\beta_i = \frac{\omega_{oi}}{\omega_{oi} + \omega_{si}}, \quad 1 \leq i \leq n \tag{10}$$

Finally, calculate the subjective and objective composite weights [15]:

$$\omega_i = \frac{\alpha_i \omega_{si} + \beta_i \omega_{oi}}{\sum\limits_{i=1}^{n} (\alpha_i \omega_{si} + \beta_i \omega_{oi})}, \quad 1 \leq i \leq n \tag{11}$$

4.4 Determination of the Smart Grid Comprehensive Development Level

The correlation between each sample index component and the hierarchical boundary cloud model of each evaluation level is calculated by formula (1). The comprehensive evaluation matrix is obtained, and the comprehensive evaluation result is weighted with

Table 2. The hierarchical limit cloud model of smart grid comprehensive development level

	The hierarchical boundary cloud model (E_x, E_n)				
	Excellent	Good	Medium	Qualified	Failed
1	(0.15,0.05)	(0.41,0.03)	(0.572,0.022)	(0.71,0.03)	(0.89,0.04)
2	(0.81,0.06)	(0.55,0.03)	(0.371,0.032)	(0.20,0.02)	(0.07,0.02)
3	(0.67,0.10)	(0.27,0.03)	(0.151,0.011)	(0.328,0.07)	(0.27,0.09)
4	(0.58,0.13)	(0.14,0.01)	(0.086,0.007)	(0.05,0.01)	(0.02,0.01)
5	(0.58,0.13)	(0.14,0.01)	(0.077,0.01)	(0.03,0.02)	(0.01,0.003)
6	(0.53,0.15)	(0.07,0.004)	(0.041,0.004)	(0.02,0.003)	(0.01,0.002)
7	(23325,3539)	(7321,1795.98)	(1508,141.53)	(642,147.15)	(100.3,33.4)
8	(1227,85)	(694.5,92)	(311.43,35.69)	(143.5,20.3)	(41.3,13.77)
9	(0.92,0.02)	(0.73,0.041)	(0.047,0.047)	(0.22,0.04)	(0.051,0.02)
10	(18000,1667)	(10106,964.58)	(4404.2,936.1)	(1567.4,9.5)	(769.45,256)
11	(18500,2500)	(7138.85,1287)	(2519.55,253)	(1215,181)	(334.9,111)
12	(15.17,5.05)	(55.80,8.49)	(120.875,13)	(498.5,112)	(1460,207)
13	(0.03,0.01)	(0.07,0.01)	(0.105,0.007)	(0.15,0.008)	(0.59,0.14)
14	(12975,466)	(10095.9,492.7)	(7162,4862)	(4365,446)	(1514,504.7)
15	(0.95,0.02)	(0.86,0.013)	(0.782,0.013)	(0.55,1.17)	(0.18,0.06)
16	(0.92,0.03)	(0.80,0.01)	(0.72,0.017)	(0.49,0.06)	(0.15,0.05)
17	(0.52,0.16)	(0.03,0.003)	(0.022,0.0002)	(0.02,0.001)	(0.01,0.002)
18	(1.6,0.53)	(6.1,0.97)	(11.728,0.923)	(15.42,0.32)	(17.46,0.36)
19	(0.28,0.01)	(0.24,0.01)	(0.214,0.005)	(0.18,0.01)	(0.08,0.03)
20	(95.83,1.39)	(89.5,0.72)	(85.08,0.75)	(80.62,0.74)	(39.2,13.07)
21	(95.83,1.39)	(89.5,0.72)	(85.08,0.75)	(80.62,0.74)	(39.2,13.07)
22	(95.25,1.58)	(85.33,1.72)	(74.42,1.92)	(63.08,1.86)	(28.75,9.58)

Note: In this paper, $H_e = 0.002$

the composite weights [14]. At the end of the rating process, the level with the highest degree of association is the final level of assessment [5]:

$$K_j = \max_{j \in (1,2,\ldots,m)} B_j(q) \tag{12}$$

Among them, $B_j(q)$ represents the q level of the sample j, and K_j represents the evaluation level of the sample j.

When calculating the associated of cloud droplets with the hierarchical cloud model, we need to generate a normal random number, so the calculation process has a large randomness, and its conclusion is always uncertain. In order to avoid the randomness, this article needs to perform multiple calculations.

Because the standard deviation is a measure of the result dispersion, this paper uses the standard deviation to judge the reliability of the assessment results. After multiple calculations, the expected and the standard deviation of the final evaluation result can be calculated [4]:

$$E_k = \frac{k_1 + k_2 + \ldots + k_h}{h} \tag{13}$$

$$\sigma = \sqrt{\frac{1}{h}\sum_{i=1}^{h}[k_i - E_k]^2} \tag{14}$$

Among them, h indicates the number of operations, in this article $h = 20000$. The smaller the standard deviation, the smaller the dispersion of assessment results and the more reliable the assessment results.

5   Analysis of the Examples

This paper assesses the level of the smart grid comprehensive development in 16 major economies. Sample data for 16 countries are shown in Schedule 1 in Appendix.

Through the ANP method, the subjective weights of various indicators are obtained. Based on the sample data of each country, the objective weights are obtained using principal component analysis. The final comprehensive weights are calculated according to Eqs. (9)–(11). The results are shown in Table 3.

After calculating the weights, firstly a normal random number table of 22×5 is generated. Because there are data from 16 countries, the original sample data to be evaluated is a matrix of 16×22. According to Eq. (1), the correlation between each country's index and each level of the index in the above-mentioned normal random number table is calculated. Therefore, a three-dimensional matrix of $16 \times 22 \times 5$ is formed to store the relevance. Secondly, weighting the association degree table and weights to obtain a comprehensive evaluation matrix and calculate to obtain the assessment level of each country according to Formula (12). Finally, the calculation process is repeated 20,000 times, and the standard deviation is calculated at the same time. The assessment result is shown in Table 4:

Based on the above, it can be clearly concluded:

The United States, China, Japan, and Germany are countries with excellent levels. Italy, South Korea, the United Kingdom, Canada, and France are countries with a good level. Brazil, India and Australia are countries with a comprehensive level. Argentina and South Africa are countries with a qualified level, while Russia and Egypt are countries with unsatisfactory level.

Although China is in second place, but from the data point of view, we can see that China currently has a lot of work in terms of the intelligence of power transmission and distribution, and the gap with Europe and the United States is relatively small. China vigorously develops renewable energy, and the gap with Europe is decreasing. But compared with Europe and the United States, the theoretical research on improving the flexibility of power grids is not enough and is limited by various factors, and the demand response is weak. Therefore, China needs to establish relevant policies and invest heavily in these areas in order to shorten the gap as soon as possible.

Table 3. The index weight of smart grid comprehensive development level

No.	Subjective weights	Objective weights	Comprehensive weights	No.	Subjective weights	Objective weights	Comprehensive weights
1	0.0126	0.0489	0.0362	12	0.0996	0.0462	0.0721
2	0.0222	0.0341	0.0257	13	0.0711	0.0491	0.0542
3	0.0176	0.0157	0.0146	14	0.0819	0.0514	0.0612
4	0.0624	0.0167	0.0460	15	0.0506	0.0567	0.0470
5	0.0577	0.0072	0.0455	16	0.0508	0.0487	0.0434
6	0.0377	0.0211	0.0277	17	0.0215	0.0559	0.0404
7	0.0524	0.0390	0.0407	18	0.0565	0.0433	0.0443
8	0.0564	0.0042	0.0461	19	0.0170	0.0550	0.0402
9	0.0275	0.0686	0.0469	20	0.0382	0.0409	0.0346
10	0.0190	0.0680	0.0500	21	0.0666	0.0770	0.0630
11	0.0178	0.0816	0.0612	22	0.0570	0.0708	0.0564

Table 4. The evaluation result of the smart grid comprehensive development level

Country	Level					Level	$\alpha \times 10^{-3}$
	Excellent	Good	Medium	Qualified	Failed		
USA	20000	0	0	0	0	Excellent	0.01
China	20000	0	0	0	0	Excellent	0.06
Japan	20000	0	0	0	0	Excellent	0.20
Germany	20000	0	0	0	0	Excellent	0.49
Italy	0	20000	0	0	0	Good	0.06
Korea	0	20000	0	0	0	Good	0.13
Britain	0	20000	0	0	0	Good	0.19
Canada	0	20000	0	0	0	Good	0.31
France	526	15304	4170	0	0	Good	0.52
Brazil	0	0	20000	0	0	Medium	0.02
India	0	0	20000	0	0	Medium	0.03
Australia	0	0	20000	0	0	Medium	0.76
Argentina	0	0	0	20000	0	Qualified	0.11
South Africa	0	0	0	19843	157	Qualified	0.59
Russia	0	0	607	0	19393	Failed	0.23
Egypt	0	0	0	0	20000	Failed	0.74

6 Conclusion

This paper proposes an objective cloud matter element analysis method based on cluster analysis. The improved objective cloud matter element method achieves objectively dividing the hierarchical range of the hierarchical boundary cloud model, which can significantly improve the objectivity and accuracy of the comprehensive development level assessment. At the same time, this paper combines the ANP and the principal component analysis method to determine the weight of the smart grid comprehensive development level index, which can make the weight determination more objective. In order to simplify the analysis of the assessment results, this article cites the concept of standard deviation to judge the reliability of the assessment results. Therefore, this paper can not only use the improved objectified cloud matter element method to evaluate the sample level, but also can use the standard deviation to judge the sample ranking of the same level. This article uses the smart grid comprehensive development level assessment case to prove that this method significantly improves the objectivity and accuracy of the assessment results.

Appendix

Schedule 1. The raw data of the smart grid system comprehensive development level

No.	America	China	Japan	Germany	Britain	France	India	Italy
1	68.50%	65.30%	57.10%	42.80%	61.10%	17.00%	68.90%	56.90%
2	8.70%	20.20%	14.30%	5.70%	4.30%	17.70%	14.00%	14.00%
3	8.70%	1.50%	10.50%	6.40%	10.40%	47.00%	2.20%	0.00%
4	5.67%	8.36%	0.93%	18.42%	13.77%	7.08%	8.68%	6.84%
5	1.73%	2.06%	7.61%	17.21%	5.63%	4.39%	0.34%	14.78%
6	2.14%	2.02%	8.80%	10.20%	5.60%	9.00%	2.70%	7.52%
7	300	23325	487.2	0	0	64.5	1800	2.8
8	238	159.7	0	1227	260	60	0	0
9	96.60%	50.00%	100%	96%	90%	90%	21%	71%
10	2.7	19.0599	10.97	2.4667	1.1	1	0.35	0.27
11	6500	18000	8000	162	275	2500	200	3300
12	1.5	15.2	0.3	0.25	1.17	5	63	1.78
13	6.32%	6.64%	4.73%	4.34%	7.64%	7.29%	22.70%	6.38%
14	10408	4078	7701	6815	5156	7125	1100	5050
15	93.70%	83%	85%	87%	88.60%	86.00%	69%	85.60%
16	80.00%	82.00%	78.00%	88.00%	82.00%	85.00%	60.00%	76.00%
17	4.53%	0.45%	1.23%	3.24%	3.10%	2.85%	0.14%	1.68%
18	3.63	16.98	2.64	2.28	1.57	1.3	12.91	1.78
19	21.90%	21.50%	28.00%	19.70%	20.70%	23.70%	14.30%	21.00%
20	95	93	90	94	89	87	88	82
21	97	93	93	95	91	92	85	88
22	92	87	93	89	90	88	75	90

No.	Brazil	Canada	Korea	Russia	Australia	Argentina	S.A.	Egypt
1	18.90%	23.20%	66.70%	67.80%	74.60%	60.00%	89.90%	88.00%
2	66.50%	57.60%	7.00%	21.90%	11.10%	32.49%	1.50%	8.70%
3	1.40%	10.20%	18.00%	10.20%	0.00%	3.30%	4.10%	0%
4	4.48%	7.28%	0.60%	0.05%	6.25%	0.97%	1.27%	2.16%
5	0.00%	1.29%	2.59%	0.25%	6.38%	3.24%	2.16%	1.25%
6	0%	0.14%	4.93%	0.57%	2.64%	0%	1.07%	0%
7	2092	0	0	1853	0	0	1667	0
8	0	0	0	0	714	0	0	0
9	55%	75%	85%	40%	46%	35%	20%	0%
10	0.55	1.02	2	0.6	1	0.42	0.5	0
11	6350	2500	850	200	150	100	20	5
12	57	48	11.5	18.9	50	108	213	1460

(continued)

Schedule 1. (*continued*)

No.	Brazil	Canada	Korea	Russia	Australia	Argentina	S.A.	Egypt
13	15.73%	9.54%	3.55%	10.94%	5.99%	13.79%	9.53%	10.66%
14	2602	12975	10380	6608	9750	3186	4241	1733
15	88.20%	80%	89.30%	0	86%	78%	72.60%	75%
16	0.00%	74.00%	75.00%	0.00%	70.00%	0.00%	81.00%	0.00%
17	2.90%	2.77%	1%	0	0.32%	0	0	0
18	4.25	3.82	5.52	17.59	4.11	5.61	14.06	15.44
19	18%	20.50%	24.60%	15.20%	21.90%	17.70%	22.40%	21.50%
20	78	84	79	89	76	78	79	74
21	86	89	89	83	84	80	83	78
22	72	76	70	55	75	65	55	55

References

1. Wang, M.J.: Smart grid and smart energy resource grid. Power Syst. Technol. **34**, 1–5 (2010). (in Chinese)
2. Xu, X.H.: Smart Grid Introduction. China Electric Power Press, Beijing (2009). (in Chinese)
3. Chen, S.Y., Song, S.F., Li, L.X., et al.: Survey on smart grid technology. Power Syst. Technol. **33**, 1–7 (2009). (in Chinese)
4. Zhang, D.X., Yao, L.Z., Ma, W.Y.: Development strategies of smart grid in China and abroad. Proc. CSEE. **33**, 1–14 (2013). (in Chinese)
5. Xia, F., Fan, L., et al.: A comprehensive evaluation model of power quality based on the theory of cloud element analysis. Power Syst. Prot. Control **40**, 6–10 (2012). (in Chinese)
6. Dai, Z.Y., Zhang, W.L., et al.: The application of cloud matter-element in information security risk assessment. In: 3rd International Conference on Information Management, pp. 218–222 (2017)
7. Li, P., et al.: Study on fault diagnosis for power transformer based on cloud matter element analysis principle and DGA. In: Proceedings of the 9th International Conference on Properties and Applications of Dielectric Materials, Harbin, pp. 244–248 (2009)
8. Liu, W.: Principle and Application of K-harmonic Mean Clustering Analysis. Shanxi Medical University (2014). (in Chinese)
9. Wu, Y.H.: Cluster algorithm overview. Comput. Sci. **42**, 491–542 (2015). (in Chinese)
10. Wang, Z.H., Li, H., et al.: Smart grid evaluation index system. Power Syst. Technol. **33**, 14–18 (2009). (in Chinese)
11. Liu, Z.Y.: Global Energy Internet. China Electric Power Press, Beijing (2015). (in Chinese)
12. State Grid Energy Research Institute: Global Energy Analysis and Outlook, State Grid Corporation (2016). (in Chinese)
13. Xu, Q.H.: A Comprehensive Evaluation Study on Intelligent Transmission and Distribution Network Based on Grey Association and Combination. North China Electric Power University (2015). (in Chinese)
14. Jiang, H., Zhang, Q.L., Peng, J.C.: Evaluation of wind power quality based on improved cloud matter model. Power Syst. Technol. **38**, 205–210 (2014). (in Chinese)

Distributed Accommodation for Distributed Generation – From the View of Power System Blackouts

Boyu Liu[1], Bowen Zhou[1(✉)], Dianke Jiang[2], Ziheng Yu[1],
Xiao Yang[1], and Xiangjin Ma[1]

[1] College of Information Science and Engineering, Northeastern University,
Shengyang 110819, Liaoning, China
{1223118445, 291969861, 490078420, 44706602}@qq.com,
zhoubowen@ise.neu.edu.cn
[2] State Grid Dalian Electric Power Supply Company, Dalian 116001, Liaoning,
China
jdkdhr@126.com

Abstract. With the rapid increase of the installed capacity and generation capacity of renewable generation, the topology and structure of modern power systems get more complicated, which promotes higher requirements for power system secure and stable operation. However, power system large-scale blackouts often occur. This paper firstly reviewed 51 major blackouts in history worldwide. The main causes of blackouts were summarized afterwards. Finally, distributed accommodation for distributed energy in energy internet was proposed as a key research direction to avoid large-scale blackouts.

Keywords: Power systems · Large-scale blackout · Cascading failure
Energy internet · Review

1 Introduction

At 15:48 on March 21, 2018, another major blackout occurred in Brazil, causing northern and northeastern Brazilian power grids disconnected from the main grid. Hence 2049 cities in 14 states were severely influenced, accounting for 93% of all cities in the region. Besides, 9 states from southern, southeastern and middle-western Brazil were affected at certain extent [1]. Among all 26 states and 1 federal district in Brazil, there were 85% of states or federal district that were affected by the blackout. 19 760 MW in total was shed in the blackout, which takes up to 25% of the total load of the Brazilian national power grid. The accident caused the northern and northeastern grid disconnected from the southern, southeastern and middle-western grid, both grids went collapsed, and the rest of the grids received minor disturbance.

Preliminary investigation revealed that the accident was caused by the 500 kV AC bus breaker in the Xingu converter station, which was the sending end of the Belo Monte ±800 kV DC transmission project Phase I. Because the setting values were preset at factory, during the day the load increased and the line load current exceeded

© Springer Nature Singapore Pte Ltd. 2018
K. Li et al. (Eds.): ICSEE 2018/IMIOT 2018, CCIS 925, pp. 236–246, 2018.
https://doi.org/10.1007/978-981-13-2381-2_22

the preset value, resulting in overload tripping, and thus made the Xingu converter station to lose the only 500 kV AC bus power supply while in its trial operating stage, which triggered bipolar locking. At the same time, since the stability control device in the trial operating stage did not take the situation that single bus loses its voltage into account, instead of issuing shutdown command, it judged the signal of the removal of 6 units as an error signal, resulting in the continuance operation of 7 units of the Belo Monte Hydropower Station. Eventually all units were shut down by its own protection, and the failure was exacerbated. It is initially judged that the inappropriate structure of the Brazilian power grid and the inconsistency in the protecting controlling device are the main causes for this major blackout. Detailed reasons are still under investigation.

Throughout history of power blackouts, the inappropriate grid structure and its operating method as well as protection control system malfunctioning which leads to large-scale power flow transfer have always been the main factors that causing a blackout. The paper firstly reviews major blackouts in global history and describes the main processes of them. Secondly, main reasons of the blackouts are analyzed and corresponding countermeasures are put forward. Finally, combined with current hot-spots of power grid development and research, distributed accommodation for distributed energy in energy internet was proposed as one of the research directions.

2   A Review on the Global Major Blackouts

There have been 51 relatively serious blackouts that took place in history, and 20 of them occurred between 1965 to 2009. The date, location and the cause of the accidents are shown in Table 1. On the other hand, there have been 22 major blackouts in foreign countries since 2010, as shown in Table 2. It can be concluded that the frequency of blackouts is much higher than before. Table 3 lists blackouts happened in China.

Global blackouts have been concentrated in two periods. The first period was from 2003 to 2006, when the electricity market is gradually developing, power trading, equipment overhaul and several other factors have aggravated the burden of the power flow of the grid. At this time, relay protection or automatic safety device malfunction or operating due to overload may trigger large-scale power flow transfer, resulting in further overloading of lines and transformers that are already overloaded, eventually leading to chain accidents and major blackouts.

The second period was from 2010 to the present. Although the blackout caused by chain actions from protection control device malfunctioning has also occurred several times, more initial failures were caused by natural disasters such as thunderstorms, strong winds, earthquakes, tsunamis, freezing rain and snow, etc. With the continuous increase in the level of grid informatization and access to renewable energy, new types of failure began to emerge. As of Ukrainian power grids suffered blackouts caused by "BlackEnergy" malware attack on December 23, 2015. This was the first large-scale blackout accident caused by human deliberately using malicious software or computer viruses to attack the protection control device of a power grid. On September 28, 2016, extreme weather such as typhoons and heavy rains hit southern Australia, where owns very high penetration of renewable energy installation. Weathers triggered a mass disconnection of renewable energy, and this was the first case of blackout caused by massive off-grid of renewable energy.

Table 1. Major blackouts from 1965 to 2009 in the world

Date	Country/Region	Blackout cause
Nov. 9, 1965	Northeastern USA Canada [2, 3]	Two 275 kV lines tripped due to protection malfunction. Generators are overloaded and shut down due to the power flow transfer
July 13, 1977	New York, USA [4]	Lightning tripped off a line and protection malfunction caused cascading failure
Dec. 27, 1983	Sweden [5]	A major substation fault triggered multiple cascading tripping
Mar. 13, 1989	Quebec, Canada [6]	Sunspot activity resulted in strong magnetic interference caused multiple substations outages
June 8, 1995	Israel [7]	A fire caused two lines tripped and triggered power flow transfer. Overexciting shutdown aggravated the transfer, and tie lines held too much flow and triggered distance protection actions hence caused disconnection
July 2, 1996	Western USA [8]	A 345 kV and a 230 kV line protection device malfunctioned, causing multiple line tripped
Aug. 10, 1996	Western USA [8]	Three 500 kV AC lines and 2 DC lines were heavy loaded and short-circuited with trees, causing a series of tripping. Power plant shutdown caused system oscillations
Mar. 11, 1999	Brazil [9]	Lightning trips off a line, and power flow transfer caused multiple lines tripped and system oscillations
Aug. 14, 2003	Northeast USA Canada [10, 11]	Multiple system line trips caused system oscillations. The EMS status was miscalculated and the dispatch lost relevant grid intelligence
Aug. 23, 2003	London, UK [9]	Transformer failed. Meanwhile, the protection settings were manually wrong
Sept. 23, 2003	Sweden Denmark [10]	Failure of the generator unit led to outage. The transformer station disconnector failure caused 4 lines tripping. After power flow transfer, lines were overloaded. Eventually the generators were oscillated and disconnected in accompany with voltage collapse in the power shortage regions
Sept. 28, 2003	Italy [10]	A line was overloaded and tripped. The power angle was too large and the reclosing failed. The power flow transfer caused multiple lines tripped, and thus led to the generators oscillated and disconnected
Nov. 8, 2003	Libya [9]	Substation failed and lack of adequate protection preparation
July 12, 2004	Athens, Greece [12]	Substation fault triggered low voltage load shedding
May 25, 2005	Moscow, Russia [13]	A current transformer in a 500 kV substation caught a fire and exploded. The bus differential protection activated, and the bus exited operation. The two-phase grounding of another bus in the station resulted in a

(*continued*)

Table 1. (*continued*)

Date	Country/Region	Blackout cause
		complete stop of the substation, which caused another 220 kV substation to stop completely. Power flow transfer caused multiple lines tripping and multiple power plants shutdown
Aug. 14, 2006	Tokyo, Japan [14]	The crane boom of a construction company crane ship collided with six 275 kV transmission lines across a river during operation
Sept. 24, 2006	Pakistan [14]	Transmission system failure led to the blackout
Nov. 4, 2006	Western Europe [15]	Two heavy-duty high-voltage transmission lines tripping caused cascading tripping of multiple lines, resulted in disconnection from grids
Apr. 26, 2007	Colombia [16]	General power plant technical failure led to the blackout
Nov. 10, 2009	Brazil [17]	Strong cold air caused hurricanes, heavy rainfall, and intensive lightning, resulted in short-circuits in three different phases of different lines. The Itaipu Hydropower station was shut down, and the system oscillated and caused a large-scale tripping of the load center. The high-frequency protection system in the nuclear power plant malfunctioned further deteriorates the fault, caused load side low frequency and low voltage load shedding and power supply side high frequency shutdown

Table 2. Major blackouts since 2010 in the world

Date	Country/Region	Blackout cause
Jan. 16, 2011	Melbourne, Australia [16]	Forest fires burned down the generator and the power flow transfer caused overloading and tripping
Feb. 4, 2011	Brazil [16, 18]	The bus-bar protection in the substation failed and malfunctioned. The bus was completely stopped, and the low-voltage protection setting of the hydropower station was inappropriate, causing cascading failure
Mar. 11, 2011	Japan [16]	A 9.0 earthquake and tsunami caused nuclear power units shut down
Apr. 19, 2011	Costa Rica [16]	Technical failure of the largest domestic substation caused blackouts
June 26, 2011	Manila, Philippine [16]	Lightning hit a transmission line caused a trip, led the other two lines to trip
June 27, 2011	New York, USA [16]	Lightning hit lines near the substation caused multiple lines to trip
July 4, 2011	Georgia [16]	A major line from west to east failed

(*continued*)

Table 2. (*continued*)

Date	Country/Region	Blackout cause
July 23, 2011	Barcelona, Spain [16]	A substation cable failed, resulting in cascading failure in other 6 substations
Sept. 8, 2011	San Diego, USA USA-Mexico Border [16, 19, 20]	Manual malfunction resulted in a 500 kV line tripped, and the low-frequency load shedding device mis-tripped, leading to the shutdown of the power plant units
Sept. 15, 2011	South Korea [16]	Negative deviations in load prediction and lack of backup generation caused regional blackouts in shift to avoid nationwide overall blackout
Sept. 24, 2011	Central Chile [16]	The transmission line vibrated and caused line pressed. A substation failure occurred at the same time
Oct. 31, 2011	Northeastern USA [16]	Due to sudden blizzard, multiple lines tripped
July 30, 2012	India [21, 22]	A 220 kV line fault caused the power flow transfer. Then the 400 kV line III sections protection device malfunctioned, and the system oscillated and disconnected
July 31, 2012	India [21, 22]	After the generator tripped and power flow transferred, a 220 kV line overload tripping aggravated the flow transfer, and the 400 kV line III protection device malfunctioned
May 22, 2013	Southern Vietnam [23]	A 500 kV line permanently grounded short-circuited caused cascading failure of multiple lines and generators
Nov. 1, 2014	Bangladesh [24]	DC blocking resulted in low-frequency load shedding
Aug. 31, 2014	Tunisia [25]	Critical line short-circuited and tripped
Mar. 27, 2015	Holland [26]	Substation technical failure caused blackouts
Mar. 31, 2015	Turkey [27, 28]	A heavy-duty 400 kV line tripping caused a long-distance parallel line to trip successively and caused disconnection from the grid
Dec. 23, 2015	Ukraine [29, 30]	Computer virus attack caused blackout (first time in history)
Sept. 28, 2016	Southern Australia [31]	Extreme weather such as typhoon and rainstorm caused large-scale renewable energy sources disconnection (first time in history)
Mar. 21, 2018	Brazil [1]	Voltage lost in AC bus bar in the converter station. The Belo Monte Hydropower station mis-tripped. DC line bipolar locked

Table 3. Major blackouts in China

Date	Province/Region	Blackout Cause
July 29, 1999	Taiwan, China [32]	Heavy rains have caused transmission line towers to lean, causing power plants in middle-north Taiwan to trip due to protection mechanisms
Sept. 26, 2005	Hainan Prov. [33]	Severe damage to power equipment caused by typhoon made multiple lines permanently failed
July 1, 2006	Henan Prov., Central China [34]	Two 500 kV lines faulted to trip. Some units in Henan power grid and 220 kV lines tripped. The stability control device mis-tripped and the central China power grid oscillated
Mar. 4, 2007	Liaoning Prov. [35]	Extratropical storm surge caused cascading trips on multiple transmission and distribution lines, and multiple substations stopped
Jan.– Feb. 2008	Middle-southern China [36, 37]	Severe rain, snow and freezing weather caused the collapse of multiple transmission lines
Apr. 10, 2012	Shenzhen [38]	A one-phase switcher in the 220 kV side line of Shenzhen 500 kV substation exploded. Dring isolation, the switch-support insulator of another phase broke, causing a 220 kV substation and seven 110 kV substations lost voltage
June 5, 2013	Shanghai [38]	A 500 kV cable broke down led to a power outage of a 500 kV and a 220 kV main substation, resulting in power outage in three 110 kV substations in the downstream
Nov. 7, 2015	Liaoning Prov. [35]	Heavy wind, rain, snow and freezing weather have caused several chain trips on multiple transmission and distribution lines. Almost All substations have been completely stopped
Aug. 15, 2017	Taiwan, China [39]	Due to the interruption of gas supply without warning, all 6 units in the Taoyuan Dayan Gas Power Plants tripped

3   Main Causes of Blackouts and Their Countermeasures

3.1   Natural Factor

Thunderstorms, strong winds, earthquakes, tsunamis, forest fires, rain, snow, ice, and other natural disasters are very common and can easily cause tripping of transmission and distribution lines in a short period of time, producing load shedding, which can lead to major blackouts. Throughout history of blackout, the proportion of blackouts caused by such accidents was as high as 1/3. Blackouts caused by natural factors generally have a rapid rate of development, a wide range of impacts, slower speed of failure recovery, and frequent repeated failures. Physical damage to equipment caused by natural factors is generally difficult to recover in a short time, and extreme weather conditions generally also cause sharp increase of load to further reduce the safety and stability margin of the faulty power grid.

The power grid should actively use meteorological big data and weather forecast information to combine weather forecasting with load prediction and power generation planning. At the same time, in response to extreme weather conditions, the system operator should further improve early warning and preventive measures, and improve the stability control strategy, and ensure that the power grid has sufficient available spare capacity are effective methods to improve present countermeasures against blackouts.

3.2   Equipment Failure

Transmission line and substation equipment failure is also another important factor in causing blackouts, resulting in more than 60% of blackouts. Among them, blackouts caused by transmission line failure is slightly higher than the substation failure. Because the transient process is rapid, blackouts caused by equipment failure has a rapid speed of development and evolution, and it also has a wider range of impact. Besides the natural factors, the causes of general accidents are mostly equipment aging, quality problems, and malfunction of the protection control. The several well-known major blackouts in history are almost inextricably linked with protection control systems. There are many aspects of the causes of such accidents. The first is that the power grid is relatively weak, and many important lines or standby power supply are under overhaul or long-term outage. The system lacks the necessary regulatory potential. The second aspect is heavy loading. Almost all blackouts occur in the period of typical daily heavy load season or the peak of the daily load curve. The power flow overload causes the line to droop, causing a short circuit to the ground and leading to accidents. The third is protection malfunction. The power flow transfer aggravates the burden of other lines and triggers cascading accidents. The fourth is the lack of the capability of perception and the capability of online computing, and inadequate emergency plans. When the power grid is operating in an emergency status, or when a second failure occurs in a chain accident, it often follows the stability control strategy under normal conditions, and lacks a fast and reliable power grid perceiving and online stability computing capabilities.

For blackouts caused by equipment failures, the power grid should be mainly improved from technical means. Such as construct AC and DC UHV grids to improve strength of the grid; Ensure the spare capacity of the system, using FACTS or HVDC, etc. to flexibly regulate the power flow of the grid; Introduce the "source-grid-load-storage" modes to reduce the heavy loading in transmission grids; Improve the reliability of relay protection and safety automatic devices, and strengthen various security corrections such as N-1, N-2, N-1-1, and N-m; Based on EMS/SCADA/WAMS, establish an on-line security and stability control system in the power company's dispatching to improve the dispatcher's power grid perception and decision support for handling chain accidents.

3.3   Strategic Failure

Strategic failures generally refer to the situation when confronting a certain accident or a certain series of cascading failures, the grid lacks a corresponding security and stability control strategy. This situation often occurred before 2010, but with the gradual improvement of security corrections such as the N-1 security correction, these accidents have occurred only twice in recent years and the situations were rather special. The first was the South Korea blackout in 2011. The grid load prediction had serious negative deviations. In order to avoid the nationwide blackout, the administration took a 30-min regional temporary blackout in shift in the order of minimum load loss. Although this strategy avoided the total blackout, approximately 1.62 million households across the country experienced blackouts in high temperatures. The second was Brazil blackout in 2018. The first phase of the Belo Monte DC project was in its phase of trial operation. The stability control strategy during the trial operation stage did not take into account the voltage loss situation of the temporary operation of the single bus. The safety strategy was designed incompletely, resulted in DC bipolar blocking and loss of major power supply. It can be foreseen that major blackouts caused by strategic mistakes can basically be avoided under the conditions of accurate load prediction, reasonable arrangement of power generation plans and security corrections.

3.4   Manual Malfunction

Operating the power grid is a high-risk profession. Although the operation of the power system has strict operational procedures and safety regulations, manual malfunctions still play a role in the blackout. In response to such accidents, it is necessary to strengthen the sense of safety production responsibilities for maintenance management and operation personnel, to increase their professional training, and to ensure that relevant personnel are familiar with operation risks and related countermeasures.

4   Distributed Accommodation for Distributed Generation

From the above discussions, several countermeasures to avoid power system blackouts are introduced. This section discusses distributed accommodation for distributed generation in energy internet to avoid large-scale blackouts.

Distributed accommodation for distributed generation means to enhance the controllability and regulation potentiality of controllable load or flexible load from the load side, to achieve the "source-grid-load-storage" collaborative optimization control and to accommodate renewable energy. This makes local consumption for local production, which reduces the power flow in high-voltage transmission grids and promotes the transmission capacity to accept power flow transfer during faults.

With the development of new-generation communication technologies, especially the rapid development of wireless communication technologies, at present cyber physical power system as well as energy internet formed by integration of power grids with information technologies, network technologies and communication technologies etc. have gradually become research hotspots. The economic benefits and environmental benefits of a multi-energy interconnected system such as cold, heat, electricity, gas, and oil that are realized through energy hubs are even more impressive. At the same time, system security under multi-energy interconnection conditions should also attract attention. The security of traditional grids only affects the grid itself, which means causing blackouts. In the case of multiple energy interconnections, security requirements vary among forms of energy. Such as natural gas and gasoline, once the electrical equipment fails and forms arcs, sparks or leakage, then the safety threats are very critical and difficult to measure with the loss of power outages. The refrigerants commonly used in refrigeration and heating systems, such as liquid ammonia, also present a risk of detonation, and Freon has an environmental threat after it has leaked. At the same time, due to the convenience and high efficiency of electrical energy, other forms of energy systems are generally connected to the power system. Once the other energy demand is excessive, the burden of the power flow on the grid will be heavy and it is easy to cause blackouts. At present, there are still few studies on the security of multi-energy interconnected systems or energy Internet. Therefore, the research on energy Internet security needs to be carried out urgently.

The current controllable load or flexible load of the power grid is generally electric heat load (electric boiler, heat storage electric boiler, electric heat dryer, etc.), electric cooling load (air conditioning, cold storage, etc.), electric vehicle, energy storage, and the like. The participation of such loads in the distribution accommodation for distributed generation is not only the development of the energy Internet, but also the development of the "source-network-load-storage" smart energy use and renewable energy accommodation [40].

5   Conclusion

1. Blackouts may happen again. Judging from the causes and results of the 51 major blackouts in global history, we have not fully grasped the possibility of blackouts. The major causes of blackouts are natural factors, equipment failures, manual malfunctions, and strategic failures.
2. Combining the history of power grids and accidents and the current development of power grids, the strategies and measures to prevent blackouts can be discussed from distributed accommodation for distributed generation in energy internet.

Acknowledgement. This paper was supported by the National Natural Science Foundation of China (61703081), and Natural Science Foundation of Liaoning Province (20170520113).

References

1. Brazil "Mar. 21" Blackout Report. http://www.sohu.com/a/226390340_793972
2. Friedlander, G.D.: The great blackout of '65. IEEE Spectr. **13**, 83–88 (1976)
3. Loehr, G.C.: The "Good" blackout: the northeast power failure of 9 November 1965. IEEE Power Energ. Mag. **15**, 84–96 (2017)
4. Sugarman, R.: Power/energy: New York City's blackout: A \$350 million drain: ripple effects off the July 13, 1977, lightning stroke cost the public dearly in lost property, services, end income. IEEE Spectr. **15**, 44–46 (1978)
5. Kearsley, R.: Restoration in Sweden and experience gained from the blackout of 1983. IEEE Power Eng. Rev. **PER-7**, 48 (1987)
6. Guillon, S., Toner, P., Gibson, L., et al.: A colorful blackout: the Havoc caused by auroral electrojet generated magnetic field variations in 1989. IEEE Power Energ. Mag. **14**, 59–71 (2016)
7. Hain, Y., Schweitzer, I.: Analysis of the power blackout of June 8, 1995 in the Israel electric corporation. IEEE Trans. Power Syst. **12**, 1752–1758 (1997)
8. Lei, X.: Analysis of the two systemwide disturbances in WSCC system in North American in 1996. Electr. Power Issue **12**, 62–67 (1996)
9. El-Werfelli, M., Dunn, R., Redfern, M., et al.: Analysis of the national 8th November 2003 Libyan blackout. In: 2008 43rd International Universities Power Engineering Conference, pp. 1–5. IEEE Press, New York (2008)
10. Gan, D., Hu, J., Han, Z.: A pondering over several major blackouts in 2003. Autom. Electr. Power Syst. **28**, 1–4,9 (2004)
11. Xue, Y.: The way from a simple contingency to system-wide disaster: lessons from the eastern interconnection blackout in 2003. Autom. Electr. Power Syst. **27**, 1–5,37 (2003)
12. Vournas, C.D., Nikolaidis, V.C., Tassoulis, A.: Experience from the athens blackout of July 12, 2004. In: 2005 IEEE Russia Power Tech, pp. 1–7. IEEE Press, New York (2005)
13. Lu, S., Gao, L., Wang, K., et al.: Analysis and inspiration on blackout of Moscow. Relay **34**, 27–31,67 (2006)
14. Ren, Y.: Analysis on the major blackouts in foreign countries in 2006. Guangxi Electr. Power. Issue **2**, 11–12 (2007)
15. Li, C., Sun, Y., Chen, X., et al.: Preliminary analysis of large scale blackout in Western Europe power grid on November 4 and measures to prevent large scale blackouts in China. Power Syst. Technol. **30**, 16–21 (2006)
16. Lin, W., Sun, H., Tang, Y., et al.: Analysis and lessons of the blackout in Brazil power grid on November 10, 2009. Automat. Electr. Power Syst. **34**, 1–5 (2010)
17. Jian, W., Yifeng, D., Fangfang, S.: The enlightenment of foreign large scale blackouts in 2011 to power grid in China. Mod. Electr. Power **29**, 1–5 (2012)
18. Lin, W., Tang, Y., Sun, H., et al.: Blackout in Brazil power grid on February 4, 2011 and inspirations for stable operation of power grid. Autom. Electric. Power Syst. **35**, 1–5 (2011)
19. Fang, Y.: Lessons from September 8, 2011 Southwest America blackout for prevention and control of cascading outages. Autom. Electr. Power Syst. **36**, 1–7 (2012)
20. Portante, E.C., Folga, S.F., Kavicky, J.A., et al.: Simulation of the September 8, 2011, San Diego blackout. In: 2014 Winter Simulation Conference (WSC), pp. 1527–1538. IEEE Press, New York (2014)
21. Liang, Z., Ge, R., Dong, Y., et al.: Analysis of large-scale blackout occurred on July 30 and July 31, 2012 in India and its lessons to China's power grid dispatch and operation. Power Syst. Technol. **37**, 1831–1848 (2013)

22. Tang, Y., Bu, G., Yi, J.: Analysis and lessons of the blackout in Indian power grid on July 30 and 31, 2012. Proc. CSEE **32**, 167–174 (2012)

23. Huy, N.-D., Huy, C.-D., Chien, N.-D., et al.: Simulation of a power grid blackout event in Vietnam. In: 2015 IEEE Power & Energy Society General Meeting, pp. 1–5. IEEE Press, New York (2015)

24. Kabir, M.A., Sajeeb, M.M.H., Islam, M.N., et al.: Frequency transient analysis of countrywide blackout of Bangladesh power system on 1st November, 2014. In: 2015 International Conference on Advances in Electrical Engineering (ICAEE), pp. 267–270. IEEE Press, New York (2015)

25. Hasni, A., Khadraoui, H., Bacha, F.: Dynamic stability assessment of a medium size power system towards large disturbances case study of the blackout of August 2014 of the Tunisian power system. In: 2017 International Conference on Advanced Systems and Electric Technologies (IC_ASET), pp. 279–284. IEEE Press, New York (2017)

26. Xiang, M., Zuo, J., Xie, X., et al.: Analysis of Holland blackout on March 27th, 2015 and revelations to security for Hunan grid. Hunan Electr. Power **36**, 31–35 (2016)

27. Shao, Y., Tang, Y., Yi, J., et al.: Analysis and lessons of blackout in Turkey power grid on March 31, 2015. Autom. Electr. Power Syst. **40**, 9–14 (2016)

28. Li, B., Li, J., Li, H., et al.: Analysis of Turkish blackout on March 31, 2015 and lessons on China power grid. Proc. CSEE **36**, 5788–5795 (2016)

29. Guo, Q., Xin, S., Wang, J., et al.: Comprehensive security assessment for a cyber energy system: a lesson form Ukraine's blackout. Autom. Electr. Power Syst. **40**, 145–147 (2016)

30. Liang, G., Weller, S.R., Zhao, J., et al.: The 2015 Ukraine blackout: implications for false data injection attacks. IEEE Trans. Power Syst. **32**, 3317–3318 (2017)

31. Zeng, H., Sun, F., Li, T., et al.: Analysis of "9. 28" blackout in South Australia and its enlightenment to China. Autom. Electr. Power Syst. **41**, 1–6 (2017)

32. Blackout over Taiwan: the most serious one after 1999. http://taiwan.huanqiu.com/roll/2017-08/11131306.html

33. Tang, S., Zhang, M., Li, J., et al.: Review of blackout in Hainan on September 26th: causes and recommendations. Autom. Electr. Power Syst. **30**, 1–7 (2006)

34. Zhou, Y., Chen, Z.: A pondering on the accident of central China (Henan province) grid in July 1st. Hunan Electr. Power **28**, 28–30,47 (2008)

35. Wang, Z.: The treatment process and analysis of liaoning power grid November 7th blackout. In: 2016 China International Conference on Electricity Distribution (CICED), pp. 1–5. IEEE Press, New York (2016)

36. Chen, Q., Yin, X., You, H., et al: Review on blackout process in China Southern area main power grid in 2008 snow disaster. In: 2009 IEEE Power & Energy Society General Meeting, pp. 1–8. IEEE Press, New York (2009)

37. Pan, L., Zhang, W., Tang, J., et al.: Overview of the extraordinarily serious ice calamity to hunan power grid in 2008. Power Syst. Technol. **32**, 20–25 (2008)

38. Wu, H.: Study on Risk Analysis and Emergency Mechanism of Large Area Blackout in Taizhou Power Grid. North China Electric Power University, Beijing (2017)

39. Taiwan blackout triggered political storm. http://www.zaobao.com/realtime/china/story20170816-787664

40. Cui, M., Ke, D., Sun, Y., et al.: Wind power ramp event forecasting using a stochastic scenario generation method. IEEE Trans. Sustain. Energ. **6**(2), 422–433 (2015)

A New Out-of-Step Splitting Strategy Based on Compound Information

Youqiang Xiao[1], Hangpeng Ni[2], Wen Qian[1], Tao Lin[2(✉)],
and Ruyu Bi[2]

[1] Yunnan Power Grid Co., Ltd., Kunming, China
[2] School of Electrical Engineering, Wuhan University, Wuhan, China
tlin@whu.edu.cn

Abstract. The existing out-of-step splitting device may be worse in adaptability under multi-frequency out-step oscillation scenario. Aiming at this problem, this paper presents an out-of-step splitting strategy based on compound information to adapt to the migration of oscillating center. In detail, the proposed strategy can obtain bus voltage amplitude/phase information provided by WAMS and local $U\cos\varphi$ criterion to determine position of out-of-step oscillation center and out-of-step period. The proposed strategy can greatly simplify the configuration and parameter setting of out-of-step splitting devices. Simulation results show that the correctness of the proposed strategy under multi-frequency out-step oscillation scenario.

Keywords: Criterion based on $U\cos\varphi$ · WAMS · Compound information
Out-of-step splitting strategy

1 Introduction

The operating modes and failure modes of AC-DC interconnected power grids are becoming more and more complex and diverse, and the possibility of out-of-step oscillation between multiple clusters in the system is increasing [1]. The law of oscillation center migration based on the two-machine model is no longer applicable in multi-frequency out-step oscillation scenario [2]. Thus the existing out-of-step splitting device based on the equivalent two-machine model has the risk of misjudgment. Although the out-of-step splitting device can locate the out-of-step center position through offline simulation and parameters setting in a fixed operation mode, once the operation mode is changed, the out-of-step splitting device parameters cannot continue to be applied, and the adaptability is greatly reduced. Literature [3] analyzed the influence of different tunings on oscillation center deviation and the problem of migration of oscillation center caused by the change of dominant instability mode Literature [4] proposed three basic factors leading to the oscillation center migration: the dominant oscillation mode changes, the equivalent potential and the system impedance ratio changes. Literature [5] shows that the three out-of-step solution criteria based on the $U\cos\varphi$ trajectory has the risk of misjudgment under multi-frequency out-step oscillation. Literature [6] proposed a out-of-step splitting criteria based on wide-area information, but this criterion only considers wide-area frequency information, and

© Springer Nature Singapore Pte Ltd. 2018
K. Li et al. (Eds.): ICSEE 2018/IMIOT 2018, CCIS 925, pp. 247–252, 2018.
https://doi.org/10.1007/978-981-13-2381-2_23

it cannot coordinate with existing out-of-step splitting devices based on in-place information, and it also faces information, security and communication delay issues.

Therefore, this paper proposes an out-of-step splitting strategy based on compound information considering the migration of oscillation center under multi-frequency out-step oscillation scenario, and simulation is made to verify its adaptability.

2 Multi-frequency Out-of-Step Oscillation Center

Three machine system model is showed as Fig. 1 to do detailed analysis. X_1, X_2, X_3 are selected as impedances of three lines, w_1, w_2, w_3 are selected as angular velocity of three machine power potential, δ_1, δ_2, δ_3 are selected as three machine power potential initial phase angle, and $k_{21} = E_2/E_1$ $k_{31} = E_3/E_1$ are selected as power potential amplitude ratio of unit 2 and 3 to unit 1.

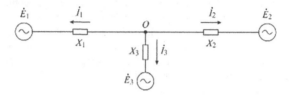

Fig. 1. Model of multi-frequency out-of-step oscillation three machine system

Suppose: $k_1 = \dfrac{X_2 X_3}{X_1 X_2 + X_2 X_3 + X_3 X_1}$ $k_2 = \dfrac{k_{21} X_3 X_1}{X_1 X_2 + X_2 X_3 + X_3 X_1}$ $k_3 = \dfrac{k_{31} X_1 X_2}{X_1 X_2 + X_2 X_3 + X_3 X_1}$

And:

$$\begin{cases} p = k_1 + k_2 \cos((w_2 - w_1)t + (\delta_2 - \delta_1)) + k_3 \cos((w_3 - w_1)t + (\delta_3 - \delta_1)) \\ q = k_2 \sin((w_2 - w_1)t + (\delta_2 - \delta_1)) + k_3 \sin((w_3 - w_1)t + (\delta_3 - \delta_1)) \end{cases} \tag{1}$$

Position of the oscillation center is derived as follows [7]:

$$m = \begin{cases} \frac{1-p}{1-2p+p^2+q^2} & p < p^2 + q^2 \\ 1 & p \geq p^2 + q^2 \end{cases} \tag{2}$$

The voltage of oscillation center is derived as follows:

$$U_m = \frac{|q|}{\sqrt{1 - 2p + p^2 + q^2}} E_1 \tag{3}$$

3 A New Out-of-Step Splitting Strategy Based on Compound Information

Based on the wide-area measurement system (WAMS) to provide bus line voltage amplitude/phase information at both ends of the line and the Ucosφ criteria of the line out-of-step splitting device, this paper proposes a new out-of-step splitting strategy. The idea is to determine the system out-of-step condition by using the Wide Area Measurement System (WAMS) to provide bus line voltage amplitude/phase information at both ends of the line and the local out-of-step splitting device Ucosφ criterion to determine the line oscillation center voltage amplitude and position. And out the specific steps are showed as follows.

(1) Substation side: Line out-of-step splitting device uses the Ucosφ criterion to find the line where the out-of-step oscillation center may be located

(2) Dispatching center side: To calculate the oscillation center position $m = \frac{1-k\cos\delta}{1-2k\cos\delta+k^2}$ [8] by measuring the amplitude ratio and phase angle difference at each end of each line through WAMS. Check whether the out-of-step oscillation center is located on the line

(3) The substation side cooperates with the dispatching center side: If the oscillation center position satisfies $0 < m < 1$ the out-of-step oscillation center falls on the line, and then WAMS sends a starting signal to the related out-of-step splitting devices based on the Ucosφ criterion on the line. After the devices receive the starting signal, the out-of-step splitting devices start. The out-of-step splitting devices perform the splitting action after detecting the setted out-of-step period; if the position of the oscillation center does not satisfy $0 < m < 1$, the oscillation center migrates out of the line, and the WAMS sends the blocking signal to the out-of-step splitting devices on the line, and after receiving the blocking signal, the out-of-step splitting device is locked. The out-of-step splitting strategy flow is shown in Fig. 2.

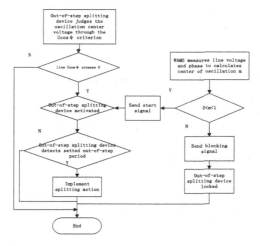

Fig. 2. Flow diagram of the proposed out-of-step splitting strategy

The out-of-step splitting device based on the Ucosφ criterion has been added a signal based on the position information of the oscillation center. Only when the oscillation center falls on the line where the device is located, the device can perform the splitting action. Therefore, the proposed out-of-step splitting strategy can avoid the misoperation of the out-of-step splitting device based on the traditional local information criterion and accurately determine the out-of-step center position.

4 Simulation

The following verification of the proposed out-of-step splitting strategy is performed. $X1 = X2 = X3 = 1$, $\omega21 = 3°/s$, $\omega31 = 5°/s$, $\delta_1 = 0°$, $\delta_2 = 20°$, $\delta_3 = 40°$, the phase difference between the voltages of the two ends is shown in Fig. 3.

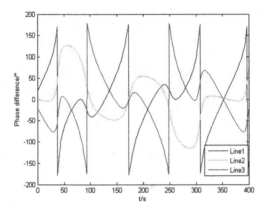

Fig. 3. The voltage phase difference between the two ends of three lines

When T = 37.5 s, 172.5 s, 307.5 s, and 397.5 s, the out-of-step center falls on line 1. When T = 94.3 s and 248.6 s, the out-of-step center migrates to line 3.

The simulation results in the Ucosφ and the location of the oscillation center of the three lines, as shown in Fig. 4.

It can be seen from Fig. 4 that Ucosφ measured on line 1 at T = 0–57 s, 138–206 s, 290 s–350 s passes through at least 4 areas step by step, and it satisfies the zero-sum condition of Ucosφ and $0 < m < 1$, so there are four out-of-step cycles; Line 2 does not satisfy the condition and out-of-step center does not fall on the line; Line 3 satisfies the condition at t = 80–110 s, 230–262 s, and there are two out-of-step cycles. The results obtained by this strategy matches the actual out-of-step center distribution on each line and splitting action can be correctly made after the out-of-step splitting device detects the setted out-of-step cycles.

From the above, we can see that because the proposed strategy contains Ucosφ zero-crossing and oscillation center position conditions, the proposed strategy can reflect oscillation center migration under multi-frequency out-of-step scenario. It can

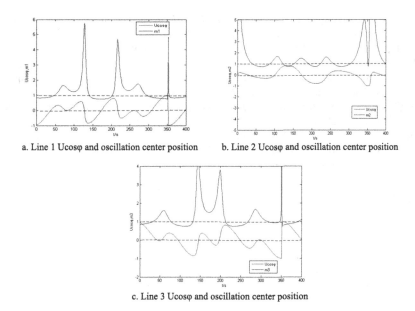

a. Line 1 Ucosφ and oscillation center position   b. Line 2 Ucosφ and oscillation center position

c. Line 3 Ucosφ and oscillation center position

Fig. 4. Ucosφ and location of oscillation center of the three lines in mode 1

accurately locate out-of-step oscillation center position and out-of-step period, which is not affected by the migration of oscillation center.

5 Conclusion

In this paper, based on the equivalent three-machine system model, a new strategy based on compound information for out-of-step splitting strategy is proposed and simulated. The results show that the out-of-step splitting strategy based on compound information in multi-frequency out-step oscillation scenario can accurately capture the out-of-step oscillation center and detect the out-of-step oscillating cycle, which has a good adaptability to migration of oscillation center under multi-frequency out-step oscillation scenario.

Acknowledgement. The authors would like to gratefully acknowledge the support of project of Multi-frequency Out-of-step Oscillation in Yunnan Power Grid.

References

1. Xue, Y.: Space-time cooperative framework for defending blackouts part I: from isolated defense lines to coordinated defending. Autom. Electr. Power Syst. **30**(1), 8–16 (2006)
2. Liu, F., et al.: Out-of-step oscillation center change rules and its location under multi-frequency oscillation. Autom. Electr. Power Syst. **38**(20), 68–73 (2014)

3. Liu, F., et al.: Multi-frequency oscillation under the out-of-step oscillation center change law and positioning. Power Syst. Autom. **38**(20), 68–73 (2014)
4. Liu, F., et al.: Basic factors and sensitivity analysis of oscillation center migration. Proc. CSEE **37**(06), 1695–1702 (2017)
5. Xia, C., et al.: Applicability analysis of out-of-step solution criterion under multi-frequency oscillation. Autom. Electr. Power Syst. **40**(04), 26–31 (2016)
6. Tang, F., et al.: Research on the oscillation center of interconnected area power grids based on voltage frequency characteristics. High Volt. Eng. **41**(03), 754–761 (2015)
7. Gao, P., et al.: Study on oscillation center. In: Proceedings of the CSU-EPSA (2005)
8. Hou, J., et al.: An oscillation center identification method and application in electro-mechanic transient simulation. Proc. CSEE **33**(25), 61–67 (2013)

Risk Assessment of Voltage Limit Violation Based on Probabilistic Load Flow in Active Distribution Network

Jing Dong[✉], Xue Li[✉], and Dajun Du

Shanghai Key Laboratory of Power Station Automation Technology, Shanghai University,
Shanghai 200072, China
dongjing3526@163.com, lixue@i.shu.edu.cn

Abstract. This paper mainly investigates risk assessment of voltage limit violation in active distribution network with integration of wind generation (WG),
photovoltaic generation (PVG) and electric vehicles (EVs). Firstly, to avoid additional peak load caused by random EV charging, a controlled EV charging and
discharging strategy is designed. Then, for the correlations of spatially near WGs
and PVGs, Nataf transformation and orthogonal transformation (OT) are integrated to solve the problem, and this provides a path for point estimate method
(PEM) based probabilistic load flow (PLF) to obtain steady-state voltage of active
distribution network. Furthermore, based on the voltage results, a model for
quantifying the risk of voltage limit violation is developed by considering loss of
load caused by voltage limit violation, which is different from the previous risk
indices calculated by possibility and severity of voltage limit violation. Finally,
the proposed model is tested on the modified IEEE 33-bus system. Simulation
results confirm that the effective EV charging/discharging strategies and penetration increment of WG and PVG help to decrease operation risk of active distribution network.

Keywords: Risk assessment · Voltage limit violation
Active distribution network · EV charging/discharging strategy · Correlation
Loss of load

1 Introduction

To solve energy shortage and environmental degradation problems, renewable energy
especially wind generation (WG) and photovoltaic generation (PVG) has been rapidly
employed, which makes active distribution network revolutionize electrical generation
and consumption. By the end of 2017, the cumulative installed capacity of WG and PVG
in China were 164 GW and 130 GW, respectively, accounting for 16.5% of the country's
generation capacity in total. Meanwhile, electric vehicles (EVs) are favored by advantages of environmental protection, and the governments around the world provide
forceful support to the promotion of EVs. However, with promotion of renewable energy
and EVs, the intermittent power output of WG/PVG and additional EV charging load

© Springer Nature Singapore Pte Ltd. 2018
K. Li et al. (Eds.): ICSEE 2018/IMIOT 2018, CCIS 925, pp. 253–263, 2018.
https://doi.org/10.1007/978-981-13-2381-2_24

would likely have negative impacts on distribution network and potentially increase risks [1].

To explore the impacts of WG, PVG, and EVs on the power system security and quantify the risk, risk assessment has been used widely [2, 3]. For example, based on risk calculation, voltage security assessment is accomplished by accounting for uncertainties in power system and consequences associated with voltage collapse and violation of limits [4]. For a PV integrated power system [5], risk is quantified by computing over-limit probabilities and severities. Moreover, the temporal and annual indices of voltage profile and line flow related attributes are introduced to measure the risks of installing DGs [6]. Considering the correlations of wind generations and loads, a model for transmission overload risk assessment is proposed [7], while risk associated with frequency response inadequacy is assessed simultaneously with steady-state voltage and overload evaluations [8]. Specially, when the voltage at any bus exceeds the allowable range, the load located at or near the bus is disconnected in small blocks until the violation is cleared [8]. However, the above researches did not consider the impact of voltage limit violation on loss of load. Therefore, how to develop a model for risk assessment of voltage limit violation in active distribution network considering loss of load is main motivation of this paper.

To quantify the risk of voltage limit violation, point estimate method (PEM) based probabilistic load flow (PLF) is employed to obtain the operational state of active distribution network owing to the uncertainties of WG, PVG, and EVs. Moreover, spatial correlations of WGs and PVGs should be considered [12]. But PEM requires that input random variables are independent. Therefore, the correlations should be properly handled to solve PLF problems using PEM.

To address these problems, this paper aims at evaluating risk of voltage limit violation in active distribution network with the integration of EVs while considering spatial correlations of WGs and PVGs. The main contributions of this paper include: (1) With Nataf transformation and orthogonal transformation (OT) integrated to deal with spatial correlations of WGs and PVGs, the PLF problem is solved by the 2 m + 1 scheme of PEM. (2) Based on voltage results of PLF calculation, a model for quantitative risk indices is developed accounting for the possibility of voltage limit violation and the consequent loss of load.

The rest of the paper is outlined as follows. Section 2 presents the problem formulation. Section 3 provides PLF analysis. The model for risk assessment of voltage limit violation is presented in Sect. 4. Simulation results are detailed in Sect. 5, followed by the conclusions in the Sect. 6.

2 Problem Formulation

Quantitative risk can be defined as the product of the occurrence probability of the undesired event (i.e. voltage limit violation) and the related consequence (i.e. loss of load). For example, for voltage V, the risk index $R(V)$ can be expressed as

$$R(V) = P(V)P_{load}(V), \tag{1}$$

where $P(V)$ is the probability of voltage limit violation, and $P_{load}(V)$ is the consequent loss of load. To calculate the risk index $R(V)$, the stochastic characteristics of V are obtained by employing PEM based PLF while Nataf and orthogonal transformation (OT) are integrated to handle correlations of WGs and PVGs. The outline structure of risk assessment of voltage limit violation is shown in Fig. 1.

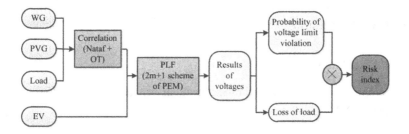

Fig. 1.   Outline structure of risk assessment of voltage limit violation

3   PLF Analysis

Risk assessment of voltage limit violation is based on PLF calculation. A probabilistic modeling and method of PLF calculation are introduced hereinafter.

3.1   Probabilistic Models for EV, WG, PVG and Load

A controlled EV charging and discharging strategy is proposed to achieve peak load shifting. According to the statistics on behaviors of drivers [11], those EVs with short daily distance are controlled to discharge during the peak load period (11:00–14:00 and 19:00–22:00) considering the responsiveness of the users (i.e., ratio of EVs that discharge to all EVs). Meanwhile, the state of charge (SOC) should be reserved more than 20% to extend the battery lifetime.

Then, EVs are controlled to charge during the off-peak load period (0:00–7:00). If the duration of EV charging exceeds the off-peak load period, it starts charging at the beginning of the off-peak load period; otherwise, it starts charging randomly as long as it can be fully charged during the off-peak load period. Therefore, the start-time t_s of charging can be expressed as

$$t_s = \begin{cases} t_{os}, & T_c > (t_{oe} - t_{os}), \\ t_{os} + r \times (t_{oe} - t_{os} - T_c), & 0 \leq T_c \leq (t_{oe} - t_{os}), \end{cases} \tag{2}$$

where T_c is duration of EV charging, t_{os} is start-time of the off-peak load period, t_{oe} is end-time of the off-peak load period, r is a random number and ranges from 0 to 1. Considering start-time and duration of EV charging, the charging power P_c^t at t can be calculated by

$$P'_c = \begin{cases} 0, t_s > t \& t_s + T_c \le t + 24, t_s + T_c \le t, \\ P_c, \text{otherwise}, \end{cases} \tag{3}$$

where P_c is charging power.

Finally, EV charging power demand can be obtained. Considering the intermittent power output of renewable energy, wind speed is probabilistically described by Weibull distribution [9], and light intensity tends to follow Beta distribution [10]. Load is modelled by normal distribution.

3.2 PLF Calculation

The PLF problem can be formulated by the relations between output random variables and input random variables, i.e.,

$$V = G(X) \tag{4}$$

where V is output variables related to voltages, and X is input variables.

To solve the PLF problem in (4) using PEM, Nataf transformation [13] and OT [14] are combined to deal with the correlations of input random variables. For the sample matrix X, it is divided into three parts: the correlated non-normal vectors X_W of wind speed and X_S of light intensity, the correlated normal vector X_L of load, and the independent vector X_{EV} of EV. The specific procedures of the proposed method are as follows:

(1) X_W and X_S are transformed to the correlated standard normal random vector Z_W and Z_S with Nataf transformation, respectively. X_L is normalized to the standard normal vector Z_L.
(2) Z_W, Z_S, and Z_L are transformed to the independent standard normal random vector Y_W, Y_S, and Y_L by OT, respectively.
(3) X_{EV} is normalized to the standard normal vector Y_{EV}.
(4) Based on Y composed of Y_W, Y_S, Y_L, and Y_{EV}, compute the locations and corresponding weights to construct the $2\,m + 1$ vectors Y'.
(5) Y' is divided to four parts: wind speed Y'_W, light intensity Y'_S, load Y'_L, and EV Y'_{EV}. Y'_W, Y'_S, and Y'_L are remapped to the correlated standard normal vectors Z'_W, Z'_S, and Z'_L by employing inverse OT, respectively.
(6) Y'_W and Y'_S are transformed to X'_W and X'_S by inverse Nataf transformation, respectively. Y'_L is transformed to the correlated normal vector X'_L.
(7) Z'_{EV} is transformed to X'_{EV} in original space.
(8) X'_W, X'_S, X'_L, and X'_{EV} are combined as X'. Based on X', the PLF problem in (4) is solved by the $2\,m + 1$ scheme of PEM.

Following the above procedures, the voltages can be obtained for risk assessment.

4 Risk Assessment of Voltage Limit Violation

Based on the voltages obtained by PLF calculation, the probability and consequent loss of load are determined. Then, the model for risk assessment of voltage limit violation can be established.

4.1 Probability of Voltage Limit Violation

With the assumption that voltages follow normal distribution, for the ith bus, the probability of voltage limit violation $P(V_i)$ can be calculated by

$$P(V_i) = F_I(V_i \notin [V_{i\min}, V_{i\max}]), I = |V_i - E(V_i)| < 3\sqrt{D(V_i)}, \qquad (5)$$

where V_i is voltage of the ith bus, $V_{i\min}$ is the lower limit, $V_{i\max}$ is the upper limit, $E(V_i)$ and $D(V_i)$ is mean and standard deviation of V_i, I is the confidence level when the voltage samples comply with the "3σ principles", F is the cumulative distribution function (CDF) of V_i [6].

4.2 Loss of Load

Based on the voltage results, the worst voltage state is employed to quantify the severity of voltage limit violation, which can be expressed as

$$Sev(V_i) = \begin{cases} Sev(\overline{V}_i) = \left| \dfrac{V_{mi} - V_{i\max}}{V_{i\max}} \right|, V_{mi} > V_{i\max}, \\ Sev(\underline{V}_i) = \left| \dfrac{V_{mi} - V_{i\min}}{V_{i\min}} \right|, V_{mi} < V_{i\min}, \end{cases} \qquad (6)$$

where V_{mi} is the most severe deviation value of the limits, $Sev(\overline{V}_i)$ and $Sev(\underline{V}_i)$ represent the severity index of the voltage over limits and below limits, respectively.

When voltage is out of allowable range, load shedding schemes will automatically trip the load to maintain systemic stability. The load will be totally cut off once the voltage exceeds the over-voltage protection limit, which is set as 1.2 p.u.. Similarly, the under-voltage protection limit is set as 0.8 p.u..

The relationship between loss of load $P_{load}(V_i)$ and severity $Sev(V_i)$ can be described as Fig. 2.

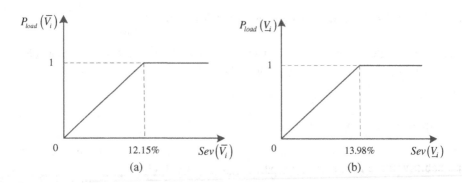

Fig. 2. Loss of the load when voltage exceeds security limits

Remark 1 As shown in Fig. 2(a), when the voltage V_i exceeds the over-voltage protection limit, the severity is $|(1.2 - 1.07)/1.07| = 12.15\%$, and the load is totally cut off, i.e., $P_{load}(V_i) = P_{load}(\overline{V_i}) = 1$. Similarly, as shown in Fig. 2(b), the severity corresponding to the under-voltage protection limit is $|(0.8 - 0.93)/0.93| = 13.98\%$, and the loss of load is $P_{load}(V_i) = P_{load}(\underline{V_i}) = 1$.

4.3 Risk Index of Voltage Limit Violation

Combing the above probability of voltage limit violation $P(V_i)$ and loss of load $P_{load}(V_i)$, the risk index of voltage limit violation $R(V_i)$ can be calculated by

$$R(V_i) = P(V_i)P_{load}(V_i). \tag{7}$$

The risk index of the entire system R_E can be calculated by

$$R_E = \sum_{i=1}^{N} R(V_i) \tag{8}$$

where N is the number of buses in the power system.

5 Simulation Results,

The proposed method for risk assessment was tested on the modified IEEE 33-bus system shown in Fig. 3. The parameters of the system are listed as follows.

(1) EV. It is assumed that there are 150 EVs in the distribution network and one EV charging station is located at bus 7. The responsiveness of EV users is set as 50%. Daily charging/discharging power by one EV is shown in Fig. 4.

(2) WG. Three wind farms are connected to buses 15, 25, and 30, respectively. Each wind farm consists of two doubly fed induction generators with rated power of

100 kW. Daily wind speed profile is shown in Fig. 5. The correlation coefficient matrix of the three wind farms [6] is

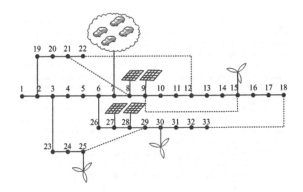

Fig. 3. IEEE-33 bus distribution network

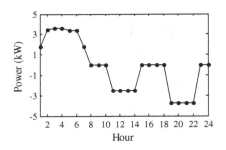

Fig. 4. Daily EV charging/discharging power

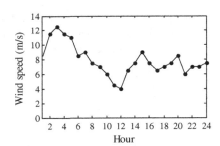

Fig. 5. Daily wind speed profile

$$\rho = \begin{bmatrix} 1 & 0.88 & 0.87 \\ 0.88 & 1 & 0.85 \\ 0.87 & 0.85 & 1 \end{bmatrix} \tag{9}$$

(3) PVG. Four photovoltaic systems are connected to buses 8, 9, 27, and 28, respectively. Each system consists of one photovoltaic generator with rated power of 100 kW. Figure 6 shows daily light intensity profile. The correlation coefficient matrix of four photovoltaic systems is

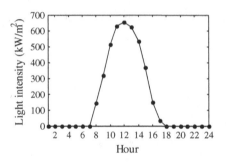

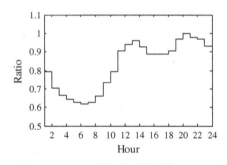

Fig. 6. Daily light intensity profile

Fig. 7. Daily load curve

$$\rho_{PV} = \begin{bmatrix} 1 & 0.4729 & 0.3700 & 0.3838 \\ 0.4729 & 1 & 0.3705 & 0.3701 \\ 0.3700 & 0.3705 & 1 & 0.4655 \\ 0.3838 & 0.3701 & 0.4655 & 1 \end{bmatrix} \tag{10}$$

(4) Load. The ratio of mean to maximum in different periods is defined to describe daily load. The correlation coefficient of loads between two buses is set as 0.9. Figure 7 illustrates daily load curve.

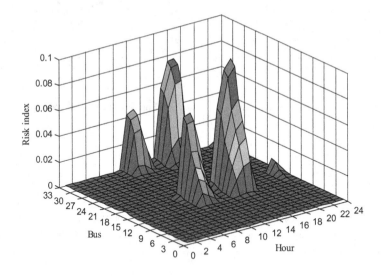

Fig. 8. Risk indices of all buses in different periods

5.1 Risk Assessment with Different EV Charging/Discharging Strategies

Different EV charging and discharging strategies have a significant influence on voltages and further on risk indices of voltage limit violation in active distribution network. With the proposed EV charging and discharging strategy, the risk indices of all buses in different time periods are shown in Fig. 8.

As shown in Fig. 8, risk of voltage limit violation is relatively severe for the end load points during the period (11:00–18:00). To verify the effectiveness of the proposed controlled EV charging and discharging strategy (case 3), its impacts on risk index are compared with those of disordered charging (case 1) and controlled charging (case 2). The risk indices of voltage limit violation of the entire system and bus 18 are shown in Table 1.

Table 1. Risk indices of the entire system and bus 18

Hour	Risk indices of the entire system			Risk indices of bus 18		
	Case 1	Case 2	Case 3	Case 1	Case 2	Case 3
11	1.2397	1.2064	0.3276	0.1573	0.1549	0.0630
12	0.9913	0.9334	0.1699	0.1375	0.1327	0.0388
13	0.1223	0.0925	0.0016	0.0274	0.0217	0.0006
14	0.4200	0.3196	0.0226	0.0698	0.0560	0.0058
15	0.5609	0.3993	0.3825	0.0838	0.0635	0.0613
16	0.8488	0.5886	0.5728	0.1201	0.0916	0.0897
17	0.9422	0.6228	0.6102	0.1307	0.0985	0.0971
18	0.1800	0.0605	0.0584	0.0385	0.0159	0.0154

Table 1 shows that, compared with case 1, the risk of voltage limit violation decreases notably especially from 15:00 to 18:00 in cases 2 and 3, because EV charging load is shifted to 0:00–7:00 to avoid increasing risk of voltage limit violation in peak load periods. From 11:00 to 14:00, the risk index in case 3 is obviously lower than that in case 2, because EVs are controlled to discharge to raise voltage level in the active distribution network. It can be concluded that the proposed EV charging and discharging strategy is effective to decrease risk of voltage limit violation in active distribution network.

5.2   Risk Assessment with Different Penetration Rates of WG and PVG

In active distribution network, the operation condition is also closely related to penetration level of renewable energy. In this section, risk assessment with different penetration rates of WG and PVG is accomplished. Figure 9 illustrates the risk index of voltage limit violation of the entire system with different penetration rates of WG and PVG.

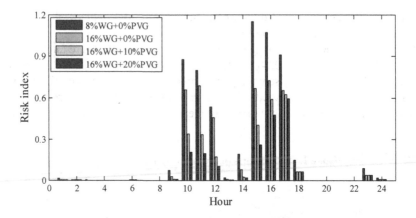

Fig. 9. Risk index of the entire system

Figure 9 shows that the risk index decreases as the penetration rates of WG and PVG increase. Specially, with the integration of PVG, the risk of voltage limit violation declines dramatically from 10:00 to 12:00, because output power of PVG is high during the period. Moreover, WG has a larger impact on risk indices than PVG especially from 15:00 to 17:00 due to low light intensity and large wind speed. Therefore, the penetration increment of renewable energy in a certain range is helpful for decreasing operation risk of distribution network, and WG and PVG forms a mutual complementary relationship in a way.

6   Conclusions

This paper has proposed a method for assessing the risk of voltage limit violation in active distribution network with the integration of EVs. Firstly, a controlled EV charging and discharging model is developed to achieve peak load shifting. Then, with Nataf transformation and OT combined to deal with spatial correlations of WGs, PVGs, and loads, the PLF problem is solved by the 2 m + 1 scheme of PEM. Furthermore, based on the voltage results obtained by PLF calculation, the quantitative risk indices can be calculated by combining possibility of voltage limit violation and loss of load. The proposed method has been verified on the modified IEEE 33-bus system. The results show that the EV charging and discharging strategy can effectively decrease risk of voltage limit violation in peak load periods. Moreover, WG and PVG are mutually complementary in time scale, and the increasing penetration rates of WG and PVG within a certain range contributes to operation risk decrement in active distribution network.

Acknowledgments. This work was supported in part by the national Science Foundation of China under Grant No. 61773253, and project of Science and technology Commission of Shanghai Municipality under Grants No. 15JC1401900, 14JC1402200, and 17511107002.

References

1. Procopiou, A., Quiros-Tortos, J., Ochoa, L.: HPC-based probabilistic analysis of LV networks with EVs: impacts and control. IEEE Trans. Smart Grid **8**(3), 1479–1487 (2017)
2. Liu, X., Shahidehpour, M., Li, Z., Liu, X., Cao, Y., Li, Z.: Power system risk assessment in cyber attacks considering the role of protection systems. IEEE Trans. Smart Grid **8**(2), 572–580 (2017)
3. Yu, S., Hou, H., Wang, C., Hao, G., Hao, F.: Review on risk assessment of power system. Procedia Comput. Sci. **109**, 1200–1205 (2017)
4. Wan, H., Mccalley, J.D., Vittal, V.: Risk based voltage security assessment. IEEE Trans. Power Syst. **15**(4), 1247–1254 (2015)
5. Prusty, B.R., Jena, D.: An over-limit risk assessment of PV integrated power system using probabilistic load flow based on multi-time instant uncertainty modeling. Renew. Energy **116**, 367–383 (2017)
6. Akbari, M.A., et al.: New metrics for evaluating technical benefits and risks of DGs increasing penetration. IEEE Trans. Smart Grid **8**(6), 2890–2902 (2017)
7. Li, X., Zhang, X., Wu, L., Lu, P., Zhang, S.: Transmission line overload risk assessment for power systems with wind and load-power generation correlation. IEEE Trans. Smart Grid **6**(3), 1233–1242 (2015)
8. Negnevitsky, M., Nguyen, D.H., Piekutowski, M.: Risk assessment for power system planning with high wind power penetration. IEEE Trans. Power Syst. **30**(3), 1359–1368 (2015)
9. Cao, Y., Zhang, Y., Zhang, H., Shi, X., Terzija, V.: Probabilistic optimal PV capacity planning for wind farm expansion based on NASA data. IEEE Trans. Sustain. Energy **8**(3), 1291–1300 (2017)
10. Liu, Z., Wen, F., Ledwich, G.: Optimal siting and sizing of distributed generators in distribution systems considering uncertainties. IEEE Trans. Power Deliv. **26**(4), 2541–2551 (2011)
11. Pouladi, J., Sharifian, M.B.B., Soleymani, S.: Determining charging load of PHEVs considering HVAC system and analyzing its probabilistic impacts on residential distribution network. Electr. Power Syst. Res. **141**, 300–312 (2016)
12. Saunders, C.S.: Point estimate method addressing correlated wind power for probabilistic optimal power flow. IEEE Trans. Power Syst. **29**(3), 1045–1054 (2014)
13. Zhou, Y., Li, Y., Liu, W., Yu, D., Li, Z., Liu, J.: The stochastic response surface method for small-signal stability study of power system with probabilistic uncertainties in correlated photovoltaic and load. IEEE Trans. Power Syst. **32**(6), 4551–4559 (2017)
14. Li, X., Chen, H., Lu, P., Du, D.: Space transformation-based interdependency modelling for probabilistic load flow analysis of power systems. J. Donghua Univ. **33**(5), 734–739 (2016)

Power Consumption Strategy in Smart Residential District with PV Power Based on Non-cooperative Game

Chunyan Li$^{(\boxtimes)}$, Wenyue Cai, and Hongfei Luo

State Key Laboratory of Power Transmission Equipment and System Security
and New Technology, Chongqing University, Chongqing 400044, China
lcycqu@cqu.edu.cn

Abstract. With the popularization of intelligent household appliances, the interactions between electric market and customers have become more frequent. Because of Photovoltaic(PV) power intermittency, the customers are encouraged to participate in PV consumption. This paper proposes an optimal smart power utilization model using a non-cooperative game for residential community with distributed PV energy. Firstly, a benefit maximization model for distributed PV energy is established to determine an optimal PV output. Secondly, according to the consumption habits and load curves of residential customers, a power utilization model of community customers is built by clustering analysis. Finally, a non-cooperative game model between PV power supplier and customers in the community is built, and a Nash Equilibrium point is obtained based on the balance between maximum benefit of PV power and minimum electricity bills for customers, which is useful to encourage the consumers to consume PV energy in local areas. The proposed model can not only achieve the maximum benefit of PV power, but also reduce customers' electricity payments, which is indicated in case studies.

Keywords: Photovoltaic power consumption · Clustering analysis
Customer behavior analysis · Game theory

1 Introduction

It is essential to coordinate the construction of PV power and the consumption of solar energy to solve the problem of abandoning solar energy and improve the low-carbon energy development. Therefore, how to involve residential customers to make full use of PV power has become a hot research field recently.

In smart grids, the studies on the electricity consumption patterns of residential customers mainly focus on establishing demand response scheduling models by adjusting and optimizing the scheduling strategy [1–3]. However, most of the models fail to consider the reduction of customer satisfactions when the start-up and shutdown state of electrical appliances changes quickly during scheduling [4]. For satisfaction of appliance usage, customer preferred indoor temperature is evaluated by adding the penalty of thermal discomfort of customer [5]. In addition, user convenience rate is considered to reach a balance between energy saving and a comfortable lifestyle [6].

© Springer Nature Singapore Pte Ltd. 2018
K. Li et al. (Eds.): ICSEE 2018/IMIOT 2018, CCIS 925, pp. 264–273, 2018.
https://doi.org/10.1007/978-981-13-2381-2_25

Nevertheless, the current studies neither have a comprehensive explanation of electrical appliances usage preference, nor carefully calculate different satisfaction stages for different consumption levels. In other words, there lacks a uniform definition for "satisfaction" considering these state changes for different customers.

For multi-user smart power utilization, approaches have been described aiming at optimizing the household energy costs in Smart Residential Districts (SRDs) [7, 8]. For the reduction of costs, game theory has been used to analyze the characteristics of interactions among users, customer benefits and effective energy scheduling strategies [9, 10]. However, to the best of our knowledge, there is no study consider to set up a flexible PV incentive price to encourage different customers to participate in PV consumption, which is one of the main scope of this paper.

To consume PV power from where it generates, a strategy that both brings benefits and meets satisfactions of customers is required. Based on the study of [11], a multi-user smart power utilization strategy based on non-cooperative game in SRD integrated with distributed PV power is proposed in this paper. The customers are clustered on the basis of their consumption habits and load curves. Hence, the power utilization model considering the satisfaction of electricity utilization is built. Then, from two perspectives of PV power supply and the customers, the non-cooperative game is played considering the interactions among residential customers.

The rest of this paper is organized as follows: benefit analysis of PV power supply is introduced in Sect. 2. Smart power utilization model of customers considering satisfaction is established in Sect. 3. In Sect. 4, the non-cooperative game is proposed. Simulation results are provided in Sect. 5 and the conclusions are drawn in Sect. 6.

2 SRD with Distributed PV Power Supply

A typical SRD is intergraded with distributed PV energy in general. PV energy can be directly connected to the distribution terminals or SRD customers, or sold to the grid. The loads in the SRD can obtain power not only from the grid, but also from PV power. Therefore, it is important to achieve a balance of maximum benefit of PV power and minimum customer payments.

2.1 Benefits of PV Supply

The benefit maximization model for PV power supply is:

$$Max \quad Benefit = \sum_{t \in T^{PV}} q_t^{PV} p_t^{PV} + \sum_{t \in T^{PV}} q_{F,t}^{PV} p_{ft} + q^{PV} p_{st} \tag{1}$$

$$q^{PV} = \sum_{t \in T^{pV}} \left(q_t^{PV} + q_{F,t}^{PV} \right) \tag{2}$$

where q_t^{PV} is the portion of PV power that supplies directly to the customers; $q_{F,t}^{PV}$ is the portion of PV power that supplies directly to grid; q^{PV} is the total amount of PV power;

p_t^{PV} is the incentive price that customers pay for PV power; p_{ft} is the on-grid price of PV power; and p_{st} is the subsidy for PV supply financed by government.

In low temperature or solar radiation states, PV generation outputs are small. To ensure that the customers loads have a high-quality and stable power supply, the amount of PV power supply directly to the customer should be zero, which indicates that the load extracts all electricity from the grid, as shown in (3)–(5):

$$q_t^{PV} = 0 \tag{3}$$

$$q_t^{PV} + q_{F,t}^{PV} < \sum_{n \in N} q_{must,t}^n \tag{4}$$

$$\sum_{n \in N} q_t^n = \sum_{n \in N} \left(q_{must,t}^n + q_{control,t}^n \right) = q_t^{GRID} \tag{5}$$

where $q_{must,t}^n$, $q_{control,t}^n$ and q_t^n are the electricity of uncontrollable electrical appliances, controllable electrical appliances, and total demand of customer n at moment t respectively; q_t^{GRID} is the electricity purchased from the grid, and N is the set of customers in SRD.

On the contrary, in high temperature or solar radiation states, PV outputs are large. In these cases, the customers can select either the PV power or the grid to supply the loads, as shown in (6) and (7):

$$\sum_{n \in N} q_t^n = q_t^{PV} + q_t^{GRID} \tag{6}$$

$$q_t^{PV} + q_{F,t}^{PV} \geq \sum_{n \in N} q_{must,t}^n \tag{7}$$

2.2   Analysis of PV Incentive Price

For PV suppliers, the PV incentive price should be greater than the PV on-grid price in order to get greater benefit; for the customers, on the other hand, the PV incentive price should be less than the price directly buying from the grid, i.e., the retail price, as shown in (8).

$$p_{ft} < p_t^{PV} < p_t^{GRID} \tag{8}$$

where p_t^{GRID} is the price that customers purchase electricity from the grid, known as retail price. It should be noted that the prices above are all real-time prices.

3   Smart Power Utilization Model of SRD Customers

3.1   Clustering Analysis of SRD Customers

In general, researchers usually classify the customers into several types using clustering analysis first. The customers in the SRD are divided into five categories by collecting the consumption information from smart meters and combing it with customer behaviors [12], as shown in Fig. 1.

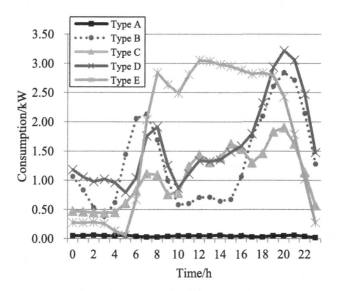

Fig. 1. Load curves of different clusters

3.2   Satisfaction of Power Consumption

In this paper, the customer satisfaction with electricity plan consists of two parts, i.e., electricity payments satisfaction and electricity usage satisfaction, as shown in (9) and (10) respectively.

$$S_1 = \left(1 - \frac{\sum_{t \in T} (p_t^{PV} q_t^{PV} + p_t^{GRID} q_t^{GRID})}{\sum_{t \in T} (p_t^{GRID} (q_{must,t} + q_{control,t}))}\right) \times 100\% \tag{9}$$

$$S_2 = \left(1 - \frac{\sum_{i \in I} w_i \left|x_{i,t}^0 - x_{i,t}\right| + \sum_{j \in J} w_j \left|x_{j,t}^0 - x_{j,t}\right|}{\sum_{i \in I} w_i x_{i,t}^0 + \sum_{j \in J} w_j x_{j,t}^0}\right) \times 100\% \tag{10}$$

where $x_{i,t}^0$ and $x_{j,t}^0$ are the original operation state of electrical appliances i and j at time t respectively; $x_{i,t}$ and $x_{j,t}$ are the optimized operation state of electrical appliance i and j.

3.3   Smart Power Utilization Model of SRD Customers

When the customers use electricity, they prefer less electricity payments and higher electricity consumption satisfaction at the same time. According to the clustering analysis of customers in Sect. 3.1, the smart power utilization models for each type of customers are established, as shown in Table 1.

Table 1. The objective functions of different types of customers.

Customers	Objective functions
Type A	max S_1
Type B	max S_1 & max S_2
Type C	max S_1 & max S_2
Type D	max S_1 & max S_2
Type E	max S_1

4   Power Utilization Model Based on Non-cooperative Game

Due to the mismatch between PV output and customers loads in SRD, it is necessary to develop an incentive PV price in order to consume as much PV as possible, as well as encouraging customers to transfer their loads.

A non-cooperative game of smart power utilization for customers in SRD with distributed PV power is expressed as $G = \{Q^1, \ldots, Q^N; u^1, \ldots, u^N\}$, which the details are described as follows:

Player. All customers who participate in the scheduling in the SRD, regarded as $n \in \Gamma = \{1, 2, \ldots, N\}$.

Strategy. Every customer selects the electricity plan $Q^n = \{q_t^n | t \in T^{PV}\}$ in accordance with their requirements, where q_t^n represents the electricity demand of the electrical appliances which is obtained from the corresponding smart power utilization model in Sect. 3.

Payoff. Pay off function is expressed in (11)–(12).

$$u^n(q^n, q^{-n}) = -F = -\sum_{t \in T^{PV}} p_t^{PV} \cdot q_t^n \tag{11}$$

$$p_t^{PV} = c - k\left(q_t^{PV} + q_{F,t}^{PV} - \sum_{n \in N} q_t^n\right) \tag{12}$$

5 Case Studies

We simulate a 300-household SRD with 150 kW distributed PV power generation system. In SRD, 30 are willing to transform the line to access to PV power. Among them, there are 3 customers for Type A, 7 customers for Type B, 10 customers for Type C, 9 customers for Type D, and 1 customer for Type E. The electrical appliances include the uncontrollable electrical appliances, such as lights, TV, computer, refrigerator, cooker, etc., as well as other controllable appliances like dishwasher, disinfection cabinet, air conditioning, water heater, washing machine, electric vehicle, etc.

The multi-user power consumption system with distributed PV power supply consists of the PV power supply and 30 customers. The PV output is shown as the red dotted line in Fig. 2, of which the effective output time is from 8:00 to 18:00. In addition, the customer demands for 24 h are expressed as black solid line on the same figure. The load fluctuates obviously during the day, and there is more demand at evening than in the other times. Assume PV on-grid price is 0.41 \$/kWh, while the subsidy price is 0.42 \$/kWh.

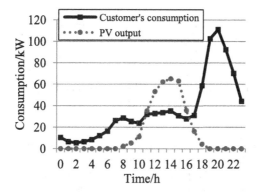

Fig. 2. PV output and load curve (Color figure online)

The 3 customers of Type A have low power consumption that can be ignored. For simplicity, only customers of Type B, C, D and E are considered in the following section.

5.1 Smart Power Utilization Model of SRD Customers

Two cases are discussed as follows: In Case I, the proposed algorithm based on game theory is not adopted, that is, the user chooses the electricity plan adaptively. In Case II, the smart power utilization algorithm based on game theory is adopted.

Supply and Demand Matching. For Case I, no optimal strategy is taken, the customers will choose the electricity consumption plans that they are the most satisfied with based on their own habits. Under this circumstance, the PV output and customers' demands are shown in Fig. 3(a). For Case II, by applying the smart power utilization algorithm based on game theory, the results of PV output and SRD load demands are shown in Fig. 3(b).

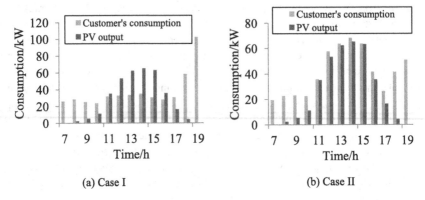

(a) Case I   (b) Case II

Fig. 3. Supply and demand for case I and case II respectively

Figure 3(a) shows that customers arrange the operation periods of the electrical appliances arbitrarily without optimal scheduling. So the degree of matching between load demand and the PV output is very low. For instance, during the period from 11:00 to 16:00, PV output is much greater than the customer's load demand, and during other time period PV output is much lower than the load demand. While in Fig. 3(b), most of PV output can be consumed by the customers.

PV Incentive Price. The PV incentive price is the same as the grid price for Case I without optimal scheduling, which indicates that customers do not have additional benefits. In order to maximize their own interests, they prefer to purchase electricity from the grid. Thus, all the PV power goes on grid through the inverter.

For case II, an incentive price, which is between the PV on-grid price and the retail price, is obtained using the non-cooperative game model, and is provided to customers to stimulate the consumption of PV power. Through the game between customers and PV power, the Nash Equilibrium is reached. The final PV incentive price is shown in Fig. 4. When the PV output is high, such as the period from 11:00 to 16:00, PV incentive price is significantly lower than the retail price, so that the customer will choose to use PV electricity in order to minimize the electricity payment. Meanwhile, solar energy has been absorbed perfectly.

Comprehensive Income Analysis. The comprehensive incomes for both cases are shown in Table 2. The PV income comes from the generation in Case I. There is no PV incentive price, so all the customers in the SRD absorb electricity from the grid.

In Case II, the PV power supplier can achieve higher benefits after optimization. PV power is consumed by customers in SRD, meanwhile, customers can also cut down their electricity payments by consuming PV power at a lower price. Compare with Case I, the income of PV supply increase 7.8% and the payments of customers for Type B, C, D and E decrease 9.6%, 13.1%, 12.8% and 14.0% respectively.

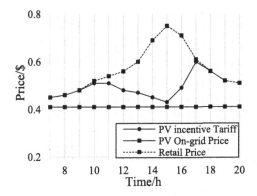

Fig. 4. Optimized PV incentive price

Table 2. Comparison of comprehensive income.

Cases	PV Income/$	Electricity payment of customers/$			
		B	C	D	E
Case I	294.38	11.42	10.63	14.40	18.29
Case II	317.47	10.32	9.24	12.55	15.73

Comparisons of Power Consumption Satisfactions. The power consumption satisfactions of different types of customers are shown in Table 3, where the original consumption in Fig. 1 is considered as the benchmark in comparison of satisfactions.

If we intend to evaluate a comprehensive results of satisfactions, a parameter λ can be set, as shown in (13).

$$S' = \lambda S_1 + \lambda S_2 \tag{13}$$

where $0 \leq \lambda \leq 1$. Further, the customer overall satisfactions can be expressed in Table 4, here we have $\lambda = 0.5$.

Table 3. The power consumption satisfactions of different types of customers.

Customers	Case I		Case II	
	S_1	S_2	S_1	S_2
Type B	−0.095	0.686	0.01	0.896
Type C	0.019	0.253	0.14	0.344
Type D	−0.058	0.261	0.077	0.414
Type E	0.174	0.216	0.28	0.216

Table 4. The overall satisfactions of different types of customers.

Customers	Case I	Case II
Type B	0.2955	0.453
Type C	0.136	0.242
Type D	0.1015	0.2455
Type E	0.195	0.248

In Case I, electricity payments satisfaction of Type B and Type E decreased because of the growth of electricity bills, while their electricity usage satisfaction increased much more than electricity payments satisfaction. Consequently, the reason that Type B and Type E customers change the way they use electricity mainly because it meets the needs of their power consumption. The other types of customers reduce electricity charges while meeting their needs.

By contrast, all types of customer overall satisfactions in Case II are increased after PV incentive pricing. However, Type E's electricity usage satisfaction remains the same for they have high satisfaction for power consumption, their increased satisfaction comes from additional benefits from consuming PV power.

To sum up, it can be found that the customer electricity consumption plans are guided by a non-cooperative game model through an incentive price that is closely related with the PV output and load demands. The game is implemented from two aspects: the customers and PV power, one customer and other customers. At the Nash Equilibrium point, the benefits of PV power supply are increased, while the customers can reduce the electricity payments under the condition of satisfying their own demands. The effectiveness of the model is verified by the case studies.

6   Conclusion

In this paper, the power consumption optimization is conducted from two levels. Firstly, the PV incentive price, which is closely related to PV output and customer demand, is established to optimize smart power utilization. Secondly, by seeking the Nash Equilibrium point, the minimum balance is achieved between the maximum benefit of PV power and the customer electricity payments. The customer selfishness is considered when making the electricity plans. In addition, the PV incentive price guides the customer to optimize the distribution of power consumption, motivating customers to participate in the PV power consumption.

Acknowledgments. This work is supported by National Natural Science Foundation of China (NSFC) (51247006, 51507022). The authors would like to thank all the reviewers for their valuable comments on improving the paper.

References

1. Paterakis, N.G., Tascikaraoglu, A., Erdinc, O., et al.: Assessment of demand-response-driven load pattern elasticity using a combined approach for smart households. J. IEEE Trans. Ind. Inf. **12**(4), 1529–1539 (2006)
2. Shakeri, M., Shayestegan, M., Abunima, H., et al.: An intelligent system architecture in home energy management systems (HEMS) for efficient demand response in smart grid. Energy Build. **138**(1), 154–164 (2017)
3. Killian, M., Andrew, K.: Residential load modeling of price-based demand response for network impact studies. IEEE Trans. Smart Grid **7**(5), 2285–2294 (2016)
4. Li, H., Zang, C., Peng, Z., et al.: Optimal home energy management integrating random PV and appliances based on stochastic programming. In: Control and Decision Conference, Yinchuan, pp. 429–434. IEEE Press (2016)
5. Joo, I.Y., Choi, D.H.: Optimal household appliance scheduling considering consumer's electricity bill target. IEEE Trans. Consum. Electr. **63**(1), 19–27 (2017)
6. Anvari-Moghaddam, A., Monsef, H., Rahimi-Kian, A.: Optimal smart home energy management considering energy saving and a comfortable lifestyle. J. IEEE Trans. Smart Grid **6**(1), 324–332 (2017)
7. Abushnaf, J., Rassau, A., Górnisiewicz, W.: Impact on electricity use of introducing time-of-use pricing to a multi-user home energy management system. Int. Trans. Electr. Energy Syst. **26**(5), 993–1005 (2016)
8. Kaveh, P., Alessandra, P., Henrik, S., et al.: Demand response for aggregated residential consumers with energy storage sharing. In: 2015 54th IEEE Conference Decision and Control, Osaka, pp. 2024–2030. IEEE Press (2015)
9. Mu, L., Yu, N., Huang, H., et al.: Distributed real-time pricing scheme for local power supplier in smart community. In: 2016 IEEE 22nd International Conference on Parallel and Distributed Systems (ICPADS), Wuhan, pp. 40–47. IEEE Press (2016)
10. Fadlullah, Z.M., Quan, D.M., Kato, N., et al.: GTES: an optimized game-theoretic demand-side management scheme for smart grid. IEEE Syst. J. **8**(2), 588–597 (2014)
11. Li, C., Luo, H., Yang, Q.: Smart power consumption strategy considering satisfaction of residential users in the process of utilizing electricity. J. South China Univ. Technol.(Nat. Sci. Ed.) **44**(8), 60–66 (2016)
12. Zhang, S., Liu, J., Zhao, B., et al.: Cloud computing-based analysis on residential electricity consumption behavior. Power Syst. Technol. **37**(6), 1542–1546 (2013)

Design of Low-Resonance Fast Response DC Filter for Enhancing Voltage Quality of DC Distribution Network

Jianquan Liao, Yuhao Wen, Qianggang Wang,
and Nianchen Zhou[✉]

Electrical Engineering, Chongqing University,
174 Shazheng Street, Shapingba District, Chongqing 400044, China
{jquanliao,yuhaowen,qianggangwang,
nianchenzhou}@cqu.edu.cn

Abstract. A bidirectional filter with low ripple and fast response is designed to solve the problem of low frequency fluctuating in DC distribution network of DC side. Firstly, the matched filter design method is used to optimize the filter order and passband frequency. After that, the voltage transfer function of DC side filter network is derived and its voltage transfer characteristic is analyzed. For the resonance problem of the filter network, the parameter selection method of suppressing the peak value of the resonance point is given, and the effect of actual parameter deviation is further analyzed. The simulation model of double-ended and single-ended radiation DC distribution network was built in MATLAB/Simulink, and the experimental platform of single-ended DC distribution network was established.

Keywords: DC distribution network · DC filter design
Low frequency fluctuation · Voltage quality · Resonance suppression
Fast response filter

1 Introduction

With the development of new technologies such as new energy power generation, power electronics and flexible distribution, the distribution network is also transforming from AC grid to AC-DC hybrid grid [1, 2]. With high power quality, power supply and electricity efficiency and other advantages, DC distribution network is becoming a hot research spot around the world [2]. In the background of continuous maturity of power electronics, the scope of DC power distribution network application is constantly expanding, whereas DC power distribution network becomes the reason of increasingly prominent power quality issues [3–5]. Compared with the power quality issues of AC power grid, the power quality issues of DC power distribution network have their unique characteristics such as their different causes and propagation range. The DC voltage is used to power the sensitive load on the DC side through the DC power distribution network, but the DC voltage deviation, low frequency ripple, etc. will affect the normal operation of the DC equipment [5, 6]. Therefore, the DC voltage

© Springer Nature Singapore Pte Ltd. 2018
K. Li et al. (Eds.): ICSEE 2018/IMIOT 2018, CCIS 925, pp. 274–283, 2018.
https://doi.org/10.1007/978-981-13-2381-2_26

quality is crucial. Power electronic converter in the process of generating a large number of modulation harmonics may cause DC voltage quality problems, especially the AC side of the three-phase imbalance (caused by motor start or asymmetric failure) will lead to sharply low-frequency pulsations of the DC voltage [5–7]. This will not only affect the normal operation of the DC outlet device, causing additional line losses, but also easily cause electromagnetic interference or affect the work of communication equipment [6]. In order to reduce the DC voltage modulation harmonics of the DC distribution network and restrain the possible occurrence of low frequency ripple, it is necessary to propose a design of low-resonance fast response DC filter for enhancing voltage quality of DC distribution network.

At present, the DC filter for DC distribution network is divided into active filter [8–11] and passive filter [12–15]. Between them, the active filter combining the DC side of the parallel voltage converter can dynamically eliminate DC voltage fluctuations, the literature [16] studied DC link filter and control strategy of the HVDC active side, the results showed that the active filter had a good suppression effect on harmonics above 24 times. If low frequency sub-harmonics need to be filtered at the same time, the capacity of the filter should increase; the design and control of the DC active filter are complex and costly. DC passive filter design is simple, which does not require additional controller, so it become the main DC voltage filtering of DC power distribution network [14]. DC passive filter is mainly divided into two types: tuned filter and low-pass filter. The former has the problems of requesting large area, affecting severely by power supply, load capacity and parameter offset [17], while the latter can filter out the cut-off frequency although, the design of the cut-off frequency is too narrow to make the parameters of the inductor and capacitor larger, which not only affects the dynamic response characteristics of the system but also limits the power transmission capacity [13, 17]. For this reason, literature [18] designed a bilateral low-pass low-ripple fast response filter using Chebyshev algorithm to reduce the value of DC-side smoothing reactor and increase the transmission capacity. However, the design of the five-order Chebyshev filter element request high parameter precision, the actual component parameters often can not meet this requirement. In order to solve this problem, in literature [19], the fourth-order Butterworth filter is designed by using the standard component values and the evolutionary algorithm is used to optimize the parameters of the filter, which reduces the deviation between the design parameters of the filter and the actual parameters. However, the parameter selection process is complicated and the response time of the DC voltage is increased.

In this paper, according to the DC voltage fluctuation characteristics of DC distribution network, the bilateral DC filter of DC distribution network is designed by using the flattest response algorithm, integrated filter order, passband and component parameters. The filter dynamic response and frequency characteristics are related to the order of the filter. So the order of the filter should be determined firstly. Then based on the equivalent impedance of the both-side system connected through the filter, using the matching design algorithm to select the parameter reference of the filter. At the same time, proposing a method to suppress the resonance peak of the filtering network; Finally, the designed filter is simulated and experimented.

2   Design of Bidirectional Low Pass Filter for DC Distribution Network

2.1   DC Filter Parameters Design

Referring to the π-type Butterworth filter structure, this paper designs a low-pass filter as shown in Fig. 1, where L_1 is a smoothing reactor, L_2, C_1 and C_2 form the π-type Butterworth filter, R_m, R_n are damping resistance.

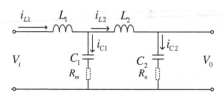

Fig. 1. Bidirectional low-pass DC filter structure

The selection of component parameters adopts the most matching response algorithm. The essence of matching algorithm is that the equivalent impedances of two coupled systems are equal. And the difference between matching algorithm and non-matching algorithm is only a fixed flat decay value. According to the flattest response algorithm, the normalized filter parameters km can be calculated as follows,

$$k_m = \frac{1}{C}[2\sin(2m-1)\frac{\pi}{2n}] \tag{1}$$

Where: m is a natural number, when m is odd, km for the capacitance value; when m is even, km for the inductance value. From (4) shows, the need to take filter auxiliary parameters C. According to Eq. (5) find $C = 1$, where $\alpha_p = 3$ dB.

$$C^2 = 10^{\frac{\alpha_p}{10}} - 1 \tag{2}$$

The voltage and the connection impedance of load side of DC filter determines the filter parameters directly, set the grid side of the equivalent impedance R_1, the load side of the equivalent impedance R_2, the filter reference resistance R_0, the reference inductance L_0, the reference capacitance C_0. Select the system's reference voltage as 10 kV, the reference capacity as 100 MVA, the system's equivalent impedance as 1Ω. In the matching algorithm to meet $R_1 = R_2 = R_0$, the actual inductance and capacitance values meet $L_m = L_0\bar{L}_m$, $C_m = C_0\bar{C}_m$. The actual filter parameters are as follows:

$$L_0 = \frac{R_0}{2\pi f_c} = \frac{1}{2\pi 50} = 3.183 \text{ mH} \tag{3}$$

$$C_0 = \frac{1}{R_0 \cdot 2\pi f_c} = 3.183 \text{ mF} \tag{4}$$

2.2 Resonance Analysis of Filter Network and Parameters Optimization

For the DC filter network, the voltage transfer function directly reflects the voltage changing characteristics with frequency changing. According to the structure of the filter network in Fig. 1, its differential equation is listed as shown in Eq. (5); then, the voltage transfer function (6) of the filter network is deduced.

$$\begin{cases} V_i = L_1 \frac{di_{L1}}{dt} + \frac{1}{C_1} \int i_{C1} dt \\ i_{L1} = i_{L2} + i_{C1} \\ V_0 = \frac{1}{C_1} \int i_{C1} dt - L_2 \frac{di_{L2}}{dt} \end{cases} \tag{5}$$

$$G(s) = \frac{U_0}{U_1} = \frac{1}{L_1 L_2 C_1 C_2 S^4 + (L_1 C_1 + L_2 C_2 + L_1 C_2)S^2 + 1} \tag{6}$$

Using MATLAB to draw the DC side of the filter network voltage transmission characteristics, as shown in the red line in Fig. 2. As can be seen from the voltage transfer characteristics, the network has two resonance points. In the first-order filter resonance frequency, there is $s^2 = -1/L_1 C_1$, at this time the size is:

$$P_1 = |G(j2\Pi f_1)| = \frac{C_1}{C_2} \tag{7}$$

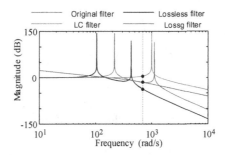

Fig. 2. Voltage transmission characteristics of DC filter network (Color figure online)

In the second-order filter resonance frequency f_2, there are $s^2 = -1/L_2 C_2$, then the size of $G(s)$ is:

$$P_2 = |G(j2\Pi f_2)| = \frac{L_2}{L_1} \tag{8}$$

Since the harmonic content at the resonant frequency is generally very small (taking the parameters of Table 1 as an example, the two resonant frequencies are about 173 Hz and 35 Hz, respectively), which has less impact on the safety of the power grid. The resonance characteristics of DC filter network mainly affect the response speed of the filter itself [18], if you can suppress the resonance peak can speed up the filter response speed. This paper considers both lossless and lossy methods. It can be seen from Eqs. (7) and (8) that limiting the resonance peak at both resonance points to a negative value (attenuation) can satisfy $C_1/C_2 < 1$, $L_2/L_1 < 1$ when selecting the filter parameters, and the voltage transfer characteristic curve of the resulting filter shown in Fig. 2 (black line). It can be seen that this method down-shifts the filter stop-band characteristics, but has less effect on the resonance peak.

Table 1. Filter element parameter value

Component	k_m	Value
C_1	1	3.183 mF
L_1	2	6.366 uH
C_2	1	3.183 mF

Consider increasing the damping component of the filter capacitor branch in Fig. 1. Suppose the added resistance is R_m, R_n respectively. Derive the voltage transfer function of the network as shown in Eq. (9). The voltage transfer characteristics curve shown in Fig. 2 (blue line), which shows that the increase of damping can eliminate the resonance.

$$\frac{U_0(s)}{U_i(s)} = \frac{(1 + sR_2C_2)}{1 + L_1L_2C_1C_2s^4 + (L_1C_1C_2R_2 + L_1C_1C_2R_1)s^3} \cdot$$
$$\frac{(1 + sR_1C_1)}{(L_1C_1 + L_2C_2 + L_1C_2 + R_1R_2C_1C_2)s^2 + (R_1C_1 + R_2C_2)} \tag{9}$$

The following analysis of damping resistance on the zero-pole impact and parameter selection method. Set d be the dissipation factor of the capacitor at the reference frequency, and the normalized admittance of the capacitor branch is:

$$Y(j\Omega) = \overline{C}(j\Omega' + d) \tag{10}$$

Because of $\Omega^2 d \geq 0$, $\Omega' > \Omega$. The poles of n order Butterworth filter are $2N$, distributed over a circle of radius Ω.

$$\sigma_x^2 + \Omega_x^2 = \Omega^2 \tag{11}$$

Therefore, the damping resistor makes the original filter pole shift left. However, the method of suppressing the resonance without damping makes the original matching filter become a non-matching filter, which is characterized by moving the pole downward. The two kinds of changes are shown in Fig. 3. The physical meaning of a pole shift to the left is attenuating the passband frequency of the filter while the dominant resonant frequency generally falls outside of the passband frequency and the attenuation at the resonant frequency increases. When the damping resistor and capacitor inductance parameters are configured, the offset poles $P'((x+\Omega^2 d)/(1+\Omega^2 d^2), y/(1+\Omega^2 d^2))$ are shifted to the position under meeting the formula (11), so as to achieve the effect of suppressing the resonance peak resonance point of the filter. As can be seen from Fig. 2, increasing the damping resistance deteriorates the high-frequency characteristics of the filter, but the stop-band attenuation characteristic is still superior to the LC filter (violet line).

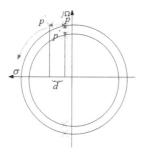

Fig. 3. Analysis of zero pole

3 Simulation Verification

On the rectifier side, the single-terminal radial DC distribution model established in this paper is 6 pulse rectifiers and PWM inverters on the inverter side (Fig. 4). The model parameters are shown in Table 2. The characteristic harmonics on the DC side are $6k$ times ($k = 1,2,3...n$), and non-characteristic harmonics are three times harmonic, even orders harmonic, and the modulating harmonics of switching times which frequencies are $N + 1$ ($N = 0, 1, 2, ... n$) switching times.

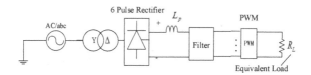

Fig. 4. Simulation model of single-end radiation DC distribution network

The designed filter is compared with the LC filter. The parameters of the LC are 200 uH inductor and 5 mF capacitor (the passband cut-off frequency is 160 Hz). The simulation condition is to set the 3-phase unbalance to 2%. The results are shown in Figs. 5 and 6. The results show that the designed filter has a better effect on suppressing low-frequency ripple caused by three-phase unbalance than the LC filter.

Table 2. Parameters of single-ended distribution model

Parameter	Value	Parameter	Value
Voltage at primary winding/kV	10	Output voltage on inverter side./kV	0.22
DC voltage/kV	0.55	Load rating/kW	2
Smoothing reactor/ mH	0.26	Switching frequency/Hz	1000
Line resistance/Ω	0.1	MOD	0.85

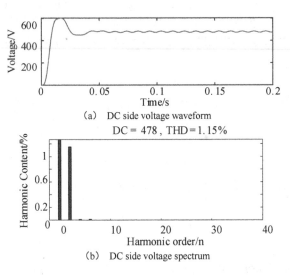

(a)   DC side voltage waveform

DC = 478 , THD = 1.15%

(b)   DC side voltage spectrum

Fig. 5. Test results of LC filter

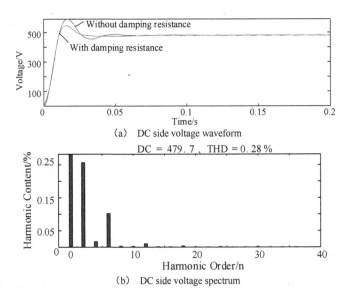

(a)   DC side voltage waveform

DC = 479. 7 ,   THD = 0. 28 %

(b)   DC side voltage spectrum

Fig. 6. Test results of the Butterworth filter

4 Experiment Verification

In order to verify the advantage of the Butterworth filter in improving DC voltage quality of DC distribution network, a single-terminal radial DC distribution network test platform was set up. Experimental platform parameters: adjustable power AC power supply, AC line voltage RMS of 20 V, 6 pulse rectifier bridge to supply the two parallel slide rheostat. Set 6 pulse rectifier bridge trigger angle to 0°, the DC side of the rated voltage to 44.5 V, rated current to 4A, smoothing reactor value as 5.49 mH, tuned filter for the 6 and 12 single tuned filter in parallel. Take 2500 points before filtering of tuned filter and the Butterworth filter output waveform. Through MATLAB programming, getting the Fourier analysis results of these three sets of data. The experimentally obtained waveforms are shown in Figs. 7, 8 and 9. The experimental results show that the total harmonic distortion before filtering is 5.63%, the tuned filter is 2.6% and the Butterworth filter is 0.59%.

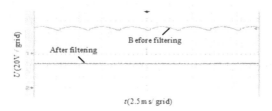

Fig. 7. DC side voltage spectrum without filtering

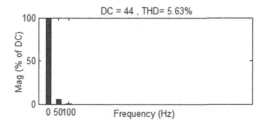

(a) voltage waveform of the Butterworth filter

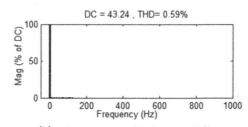

(b) voltage spectrum of the Butterworth filter

Fig. 8. Butterworth filter filtering results

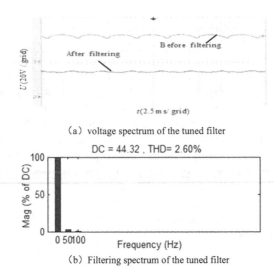

(a) voltage spectrum of the tuned filter

(b) Filtering spectrum of the tuned filter

Fig. 9. Tuned filter filtering test results

5 Conclusion

In this paper, the structure of the filter network proposed aims at improving the quality of the DC voltage of the DC distribution network. In additional, a bidirectional filter with low ripple and fast response is proposed. Through simulation and physical model experiments, the following conclusions are drawn:

(1) The parameter optimization method based on the pole round can reduce the resonant peak of resonance point and speed up the response speed of the filter;
(2) Considering investment cost, floor space, filtering effect and response speed, the filter designed in this paper has advantages in improving the voltage quality of DC distribution network compared with other filters, which is suitable for the DC side filtering of DC distribution network.

Acknowledgements. This work was supported by the National Natural Science Foundation of China (51577018) and Chongqing Science & Technology Commission (cstc2015jcyjBX0033).

References

1. Jung, T.H., et al.: Voltage regulation method for voltage drop compensation and unbalance reduction in bipolar low-voltage DC distribution system. IEEE Trans. Power Deliv. **33**(1), 141–149 (2017)
2. Zadeh, M.K., et al.: Discrete-time modelling, stability analysis, and active stabilization of DC distribution systems with constant power loads. In: Applied Power Electronics Conference and Exposition, pp. 323–329. IEEE (2015)

3. Gecan, C.O., Chindris, M., Bindiu, R.: Power capability in low voltage DC distribution systems. Interdisc. Eng. **2**, 109–114 (2009)
4. Kakigano, H., Miura, Y., Ise, T.: Low-voltage bipolar-type DC microgrid for super high quality distribution. IEEE Trans. Power Electron. **25**(12), 3066–3075 (2010)
5. Mariscotti, A.: Methods for ripple index evaluation in DC low voltage distribution networks. In: Proceedings of the Instrumentation and Measurement Technology Conference, IMTC. IEEE, pp. 1–4 (2007)
6. Prabhakaran, P., Agarwal, V.: Mitigation of voltage unbalance in a low voltage bipolar DC microgrid using a boost-SEPIC type interleaved DC-DC compensator. In: Power Electronics Conference, pp. 1–6 IEEE (2017). Gallo, D., Landi, C., Luiso, M.: AC and DC power quality of photovoltaic systems. In: Instrumentation and Measurement Technology Conference, pp. 576–581. IEEE (2012)
7. Wang, M.H., et al.: Hybrid-DC electric springs for DC voltage regulation and harmonic cancellation in DC microgrids. IEEE Trans. Power Electron. **33**(2), 1167–1177 (2018)
8. Dey, P., Mekhilef, S.: Current harmonics compensation with three-phase four-wire shunt hybrid active power filter based on modified D–Q, theory. IET Power Electron. **8**(11), 2265–2280 (2014)
9. Lee, T.L., Wang, Y.C., Li, J.C., et al.: Hybrid active filter with variable conductance for harmonic resonance suppression in industrial power systems. IEEE Trans. Ind. Electron. **62**(2), 746–756 (2015)
10. Somlal, J., Rao, M.V.G.: Power conditioning in distribution systems using ANN controlled Shunt Hybrid Active Power Filter. In: International Conference on Smart Electric Grid. IEEE, pp. 1–5 (2014)
11. Beres, R.N., et al.: A review of passive power filters for three-phase grid-connected voltage-source converters. IEEE J. Emerg. Sel. Top. Power Electron. **4**(1), 54–69 (2016)
12. Kang, W., Zhang, L., Liu, C.: Output filter design method in current-source PWM converters. Trans. Chin. Electrotech. Soc. **27**(6), 83–89 (2012)
13. Yang, L., et al.: Second ripple current suppression by two band-pass filters and current sharing method for energy storage converters in DC Microgrid. IEEE J. Emerg. Sel. Top. Power Electron. **5**(3), 1031–1044 (2017)
14. Meehan, P., et al.: Varactor-based passive ripple filter with automatic tuning for low-noise power supply systems. IEEE Trans. Power Electron. **32**(6), 4741–4752 (2017)
15. Li, K., et al.: Novel load ripple voltage-controlled parallel DC active power filters for high performance magnet power supplies. IEEE Trans. Nucl. Sci. **53**(3), 1530–1539 (2006)
16. Bo, C., Zeng, X., Yao, X.: Three tuned passive filter to improve power quality. In: International Conference on Power System Technology, Powercon, pp. 1–5. IEEE (2006)
17. Wei, K., et al.: Research on the Matched DC Filter Design in the Power Accumulator Battery Testing System. In: International Conference on Electrical and Control Engineering (ICECE), pp. 4157–4160 (2010)
18. Fadloullah, I., Mechaqrane, A., Ahaitouf, A.: Butterworth low pass filter design using evolutionary algorithm. In: International Conference on Wireless Technologies, Embedded and Intelligent Systems (WITS), pp. 1–6 (2017)

Analysis for the Influence of Electric Vehicle Chargers with Different SOC on Grid Harmonics

Qi Sheng[✉], Minyou Chen, Qiang Li, Yingxiang Wang, and
Muhammad Arshad Shehzad Hassan

State Key Laboratory of Power Transmission Equipment and System Security and New
Technology, School of Electrical Engineering, Chongqing University, Chongqing 400044, China
290555446@qq.com

Abstract. In this paper, analysis for the influence of electric vehicle (EV) chargers on grid harmonics is conducted. The simulation model of the power distribution network with vehicle-mounted chargers is established, and the harmonic feature of the charger is analyzed. Considering different State of Charge (SOC) of the chargers and the relationship between harmonic current and initial SOC values of the EVs is established. To reduce the harmonic current caused by EV chargers, an optimization model of coordinated charging has been developed and the optimal solution is obtained by using the PSO algorithm. The validity of the proposed optimal charging schedule is verified through the simulation results.

Keywords: Electric vehicle · Harmonic current · Coordinated charging · PSO

1 Introduction

With the rapid development of electric vehicle (EV), the large number of grid connected chargers will result in the harmonic current into the electric grid [1]. It is necessary to study the influence of EV chargers on grid harmonics and take the corresponding measures to reduce the harmonic current.

The variation of the non-linear resistance was used to replace the variation of charging power in all periods [2]. The influence of the harmonics generated by EVs via charging to the grid was analyzed [3], and it was also pointed out that as the continual promotion of large-scale EVs, it needed to establish the management facility of large-scale EVs, and it could reduce the harmonic influence. The influence of the disordered charging for the EVs on power system was analyzed [4], and the corresponding solutions were performed, thus the power quality of the grid was increased.

To sum up, all the above research was done on the harmonic analysis with same initial SOC value for the EVs, and the high-frequency power vary circuit of the charger is mostly equivalent to the time varying resistor, the dispersing processing was also conducted. But the continuity and time-varying behavior of the charging curve for the battery power of the EVs were not exemplified.

In this current paper, the charger model of continual charging was established in Simulink. In addition, the charging process curve of the EVs was simulated more accurately. Afterward, the harmonic analysis was conducted on the charging process of EVs

© Springer Nature Singapore Pte Ltd. 2018
K. Li et al. (Eds.): ICSEE 2018/IMIOT 2018, CCIS 925, pp. 284–294, 2018.
https://doi.org/10.1007/978-981-13-2381-2_27

with different initial SOC, and the relation model between the SOC value of the EVs and harmonic current was fitted. Finally, the optimized charging model of orderly access for EVs was established, and it aimed to reduce the harmonic current based on above model.

2 Charger Modeling of EVs

2.1 Charger Model

The Fig. 1 demonstrates the structure of the high frequency charger. The three-phase bridge rectifier is used to rectifier the three-phase AC current. In addition, this current passes through the filtering circuit which is composed by capacitor and resistor. The DC-DC power converter is used to convert the power. Finally, the output power passes through the output filtering circuit to recharge the EVs as verified by [5, 6].

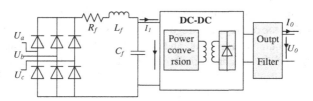

Fig. 1. The structure of the high frequency charger

The most widely used power batteries for EVs are lithium-ion batteries [7]. The built-in lithium-ion battery of MATLAB is taken as power battery of the EVs in this proposed paper. The model of the single charger is established in Matlab/Simulink according to the structure chart of the charger as shown in Fig. 2.

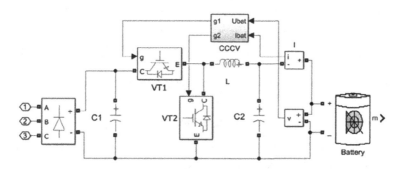

Fig. 2. Simulation model of EV charger

2.2 Buck-Boost Converter

It can be seen from Fig. 2 that two-way Buck-boost converter is used for the power conversion of the charger, and it can transform the output DC voltage to the ideal charging voltage [8, 9]. When the EVs are charged, the DC/DC converter works in the buck voltage-reduction mode. The switch VT$_1$ is works at the constant switch frequency, and the switch VT$_2$ maintains the cut-off state. In last, the power passes from the U_{dc} to the battery and required charging voltage or current can be obtained through adjusting the duty cycle of VT$_1$.

2.3 Charging Modes of the EVs

In this paper, the conventional charging method is used for charger. For controlling, two-phased charging control method is implemented. The charger is connected with the constant current in the first phase, and the charging voltage was maintained constantly in the second phase. When the current received the stop signal of charging, the EVs stopped the charging [10, 11].

The charge at constant voltage and current is achieved with the automatic switching mode and the control sketch as shown in Fig. 3. The current mono-cycle control is adopted for the phase of constant current for fast charging [12]. Afterward, the battery voltage V_{bat} reaches the reference voltage V_{ref}. The system is switched to double closed-loop control of the outer voltage loop and inner current loop. The voltage-loop output becomes the input of the current-loop after the PI adjustment. In addition, it is compared with the battery feedback current and triangle wave. The output signal will control by switch VT$_1$. The current will follow the reference voltage to maintain the constant voltage.

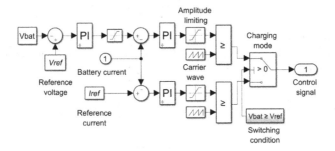

Fig. 3. Block diagram of constant-current and constant-voltage charge control

2.4 Validity Verification of the Charger Model

In order to verify the validity of the proposed model, a simple distribution model is established in Matlab/Simulink as shown in Fig. 4.

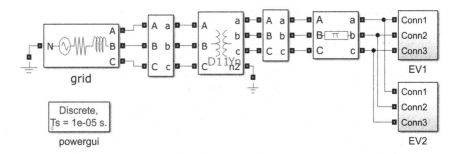

Fig. 4. Simulation model of charging station

The battery charging current Ibat and voltage Vbat waveforms are shown in Figs. 5 and 6 on the initial level of the SOC = 0%. These waveforms proved that the above charging control method of constant current and voltage has capability to run in the predefined manner.

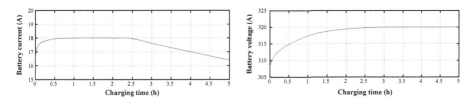

Fig. 5. Current curve of EV charge   **Fig. 6.** Voltage curve of EV charge

3   The Influence Analysis of the Initial SOC State on the Harmonic Current

When the number of EVs reaches a certain level in distribution networks, the corresponding harmonic current amplitude sizes are measured, and compared with the permitted value of harmonic current in the Power Quality Public Grid Harmonics. The obtained limit table is shown in Table 1. It can be seen from Table 1 that when the number of EVs increases to 20, the 5th and 7th harmonic currents exceed the permitted value. It indicates that they are more likely to exceed the standard limits.

Table 1. Amplitude limit of every harmonic current

Harmonic frequency	Harmonic current permissible value (A)	Harmonic current effective value (A)				
		1 EV	5 EVs	10 EVs	15 EVs	20 EVs
H 5	20	4.19	10.23	15.78	19.87	23.06
H 7	15	1.76	5.61	9.49	12.83	15.41
H 11	9.3	0.94	2.58	4.21	5.73	7.22

3.1   The Simulation Analysis of the EVs in the Same Initial State

The variation rule of the effective value for all harmonic currents is mainly analyzed in the charging process. The charging time in the simulation curve is uniformly set at 5 h to facilitate the comparative analysis and it conforms to the conventional charging time for EVs in actual life. The initial SOC value is taken as the distinction condition of the EVs. When the initial SOC is the same, the 5th and 7th harmonic currents generated by EVs of different number is firstly analyzed as shown in Fig. 7.

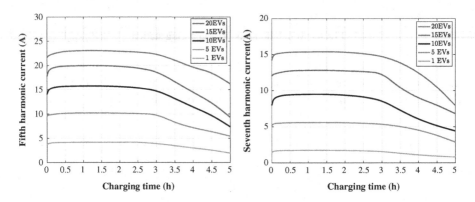

Fig. 7. Fifth and seventh harmonic current effective value

It can be seen from the above figures that when the charging number of EVs increases, the both 5th and 7th harmonic current values are also increased. However, it is not the algebraic sum of the harmonic current generated by all EVs in stand-alone condition. Therefore, it indicates that the harmonic currents are offset. The total change trend of all the harmonic currents is similar [13]. So, when multiple EVs of different initial SOC value are charged, the harmonic currents are also offset.

3.2   Simulation Analysis of EVs in Different Initial States

The 20 EVs are taken as the example and the simulation analysis of the charging is conducted in two different initial states which are given below:

(1) The initial SOC value of the 20 EVs to be charged at 0%;
(2) The 20 EVs are divided into 5 groups and 4 in each group. The initial SOC of the power battery in each group of EV is set as 0%, 20%, 30%, 50% and 80%.

No load is added after the charging. The simulation analysis on the variation of the effective value of harmonic currents is conducted in these two charging combination and the result is shown in Fig. 8.

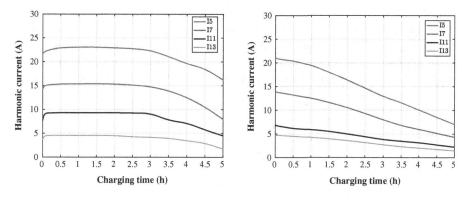

Fig. 8. Harmonic current change curve at the same and different initial charge

4   Optimization Model of the Coordinated Charging for EVs to Reduce the Harmonic Current

4.1   Optimization Model to Reduce the Harmonic Current

Based on the above simulation analysis on different initial SOC values of the EVs, the initial SOC of the EVs to be charged in the certain area. The purpose to reduce the harmonic current of the distribution network can be more economically realized on the basis of none adding extra harmonic governing device through controlling the orderly access of the EVs according to coordinating charging.

The overall change trend of the 5th and 7th harmonic currents is similar in the charging process. The 5th harmonic is taken as the example. The SOC data and harmonic current data of the single EV are obtained in the overall charging process based on simulation and the data fitting is conducted with the MATLAB curve fitting toolbox. In addition, the relation function between S_i of SOC and harmonic current I_h during the whole charging process of single EV is obtained from the following equation:

$$I_h(S_i) = \begin{cases} 4.164e^{0.00024S_i} - 0.4228e^{-0.64S_i} & (0 \le S_i \le 50) \\ -0.000197S_i^{2.088} + 4.922 & (50 < S_i \le 100) \end{cases} \tag{1}$$

If each EV is regarded as a harmonic source, then N EVs are multiple as harmonic sources. According to the superposition principle of the same harmonic for multiple harmonic sources and in consideration that the harmonic current researched in this paper is all effective value, the adopted superposition equation of the same harmonic on the ideal condition is as follows if the phase angle information of the harmonic component in the superposition equation is ignored:

$$I_h = \sqrt{\sum_{i=1}^{N} I_{h.i}^2} \tag{2}$$

Where $I_{h,i}$ is effective value of the hth harmonic current of the harmonic source i; I_h is the effective value of the hth total harmonic current.

The overall charging period of the EV is set at 5 h to facilitate the research and each hour is divided into 10 periods namely $t = 0, 1, 2, 3\ldots50$ with 51 points in the time. The total harmonic current generated by the charging of N EVs at the t point in time can be expressed as follows:

$$I_{h,t} = \sqrt{\sum_{i=1}^{N} (I_{hi,t}(S_{i,t}))^2} \tag{3}$$

Where $S_{i,t}$ is the SOC of the EVs in the tth point in time and N is the number of the EVs; $I_{hi,t}(S_{i,t})$ is the effective value of the harmonic current generated by the ith EV at the tth point in time. Because the $S_{i,t}$ of EV is increasing during charging and the $I_{hi,t}(S_{i,t})$ also changes with $S_{i,t}$. The value of $S_{i,t}$ variation in each charging period needs to be determined by SOC real time estimation.

Since the initial SOC of the EV is defined in the proposed paper. The rated capacity and charge current of the battery are also defined in the real time simulation. The following formula can be used to calculate the SOCs of the next charging time point by using the ampere-hour integration method combined with the open-circuit voltage method.

Since the initial SOC of the EV is predefined in this paper. The rated capacity of the power battery and the real time change value of the charging current are also implemented. So, the ampere-hour integration method combined with the open-circuit voltage method [14] which can be used to calculate the SOC of the next charging time point. The formula is as follows:

$$SOC = SOC_0 - \frac{\int_0^t KIdt}{Q_c} \tag{4}$$

Where SOC_0 indicates the initial SOC of the power battery; K is a constant related to temperature; I is the charge and discharge current of the power battery (the charge current is negative and the discharge current is the positive); Q_c indicates the power battery rated capacity and t is charging time.

Therefore, we can calculate the value of $S_{i,t}$ change at each charging time by using Eq. (4), and then take it into Eq. (3) to get the total harmonic current value produced by N EVs at time t.

To sum up, the maximum value of the 5th harmonic current generated by multiple EVs can be expressed as $max[I_{h,t}(S_{i,t})]$. If the maximum value tends to be the minimum, the overall trend of the total harmonic current generated by the charging is also towards the minimum. Therefore, by minimizing the maximum harmonic current generated by the EV as the objective function which is given below:

$$f = \min\left[\max\left[I_{h,t}(S_{i,t})\right]\right] \tag{5}$$

The initial *SOC* of each EVs is different and the time required for fully charging is different. The range of charge and the remaining charge time must be taken into account. The following technical constraints are established to check the capability.

(1) Initial electric quantity constraint:

The users often charge the EVs during 80% or below of the *SOC* according to the actual situation which is given as under:

$$0 \leq S_i \leq 80 \tag{6}$$

(2) Remaining charging time constraint:

Since the initial SOC_0 of EV is equal to S_i and the rated capacity of the battery Q_c is predefined. The *SOC* of the EV at the end of charging should be equal to 100% and the charge current $I = -I_t$ at time t can also be obtained from the simulation data. Assuming the end time of charging is t_e, ignore the influence of temperature and charge-discharge efficiency factor K and bring them into Eq. (4) to calculate the $T_s = t_e - t$. To ensure that the remaining charging time for an EV is greater than or equal to zero during the permitted period of time:

$$T_s = \frac{(100 - S_i) * Q_c}{I_{bat}} \geq 0 \tag{7}$$

4.2 Solution to the Optimization Model

Considering the nonlinearity of the objective function and the large solution space of the control variable, PSO is selected in this paper for the solution [15]. The *D*-dimension particle X_S of the population size m is constructed on the initial *SOC* of the EVs and the ith particle is as follows in Eq. (8):

$$X_{si} = (S_{i,1}, S_{i,2}, \dots, S_{i,D}) \quad i = 1, 2, \dots, m \tag{8}$$

The fitness function of the PSO is obtained by the following equation:

$$v_i^{t+1} = \omega_i^t + c_1 r_1 (p_i^t - x_i^t) + c_2 r_2 (p_b^t - x_i^t) \tag{9}$$

$$x_i^{t+1} = x_i^t + v_i^{t+1} \tag{10}$$

In the equation, c_1 and c_2 are the learning factors; r_1 and r_2 indicate the random number of the interval (0, 1); ω indicates the inertia weight factors; v_i^t and x_i^t are the speed and position corresponding to the ith particle in the tth iteration process; p_i^t and p_b^t are the personal best and the global best of the particle.

4.3 Analysis and Verification of the Optimal Solution

Comprehensively, the setting of various parameter values is as follows:

Population size $m = 100$; particle dimension $D = 20$, namely the total number of EVs to be charged in the charging station; learning factors $c_1 = c_2 = 1.5$; the maximum and minimum of the inertia weight are respectively $\omega_{max} = 0.9$, $\omega_{min} = 0.4$; the maximum iteration time is set at 200.

The optimization model is solved when the number of EVs to be charged at 20. The solution set of the optimal initial SOC for whole charging period is given below:

$$S = [2.15;73.70;68.24;44.93;63.24;74.12;57.65;78.93;72.96;1.63;$$
$$38.13;51.96;18.95;9.37;22.33;74.70;19.56;3.22;42.09;79.66]$$

The SOC value is set for the EV according to above optimization result and simulation experiment is conducted in the distribution network. The optimized change curve of the harmonic current is shown in Fig. 9.

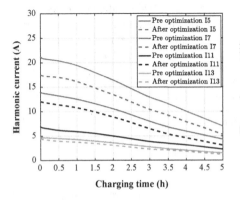
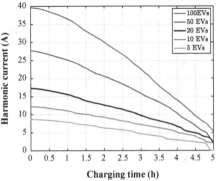

Fig. 9. Optimized harmonic current change curve

Fig. 10. The influence of optimization model on the access of large scale electric vehicle

It can be clearly seen from the Fig. 9 that the overall harmonic current generated by the charging in the orderly combination selected for the EV is much less than that in disordered charging. Therefore, it can satisfy the limit value of the harmonic current in the national standard.

4.4 Application of Optimization Model of Coordinated Charging

In actual charging, the number of EVs to be charged in the charging station on a large scale not only 20, but also can be solved by this optimization model. The EVs that accord with the optimal initial SOC can be selected for coordinated charging. In this way, the harmonic content injected into the power network can be reduced more economically without adding additional filter devices.

Based on the coordinated charging optimization model, the PSO algorithm is used to solve the optimal coordinated charging SOC of each EV when the particle dimension D is 5, 10, 20, 50, and 100 respectively. The optimized SOC of EV under different dimensions is introduced into the coordinated charging optimization model and the harmonic current variation curves at 51 charging points are simulated as shown in Fig. 10.

It can be seen more intuitively from the Fig. 10 that more number of EVs, the stronger reduction of the same harmonic current is generated and the more obvious the decreasing trend of the harmonic current. In addition, the harmonic current produced by the more large-scale EV to the later stage is even lower than the harmonic content produced by the smaller size EV. Therefore, the harmonic control effect of the coordinated charging optimization model will become more and more obvious when the size of the EV is expanding.

5   Conclusion

In this paper, the charger model of the EVs is established and charging control strategy for EVs at constant voltage and current is completed. It is also verified via simulation results that the charging mode of constant voltage and current can be realized in the established model.

The simulation analysis is conducted in the distribution network through the established charger model and the change curve of the harmonic current for EVs in different initial states is obtained. It is also obtained that the effect of the harmonic current can be reduced when the EVs are charged at different initial SOC. The optimization model of orderly access of the EV to reduce the harmonic current is established based on this and the model is solved through PSO algorithm. Finally the effectiveness of the control strategy to reduce the harmonic current is verified in this paper through the simulation experiment. At the same time, the optimization model is applied to show that the more number of EVs, the better the harmonic control effect of the coordinated charging strategy.

References

1. Zhang, J.: Design on high efficiency power DC/DC converter used by electric vehicle. Modern Instruments (2012)
2. Na, L., Mei, H.: Analysis on harmonics caused by connecting different types of electric vehicle chargers with power network. Power Syst. Technol. **35**(1), 170–174 (2011)
3. Sourkounis, C., Broy, A., Ni, B.: High power charging of electric vehicles in distribution grids. In: Power Generation, Transmission, Distribution and Energy Conversion, pp. 1–6. IET (2010)
4. Liu, X., Li, S., Yu, H.: Coordinated charging optimization mode of electric vehicles in the residential area. Trans. China Electrotech. Soc. **30**, 238–245 (2015)
5. Zhou, J., Ren, G., Chen, W.: Harmonic analysis of electric vehicle AC charging spot and research on harmonic restriction. Power Syst. Prot. Control **45**(5), 18–25 (2017)
6. Rahman, M.H., Xu, L., Yao, L.: Protection of large partitioned MTDC networks using DC-DC converters and circuit breakers. Prot. Control of Modern Power Syst. **1**(1), 19 (2016)
7. Guo, X.W., Kang, L.Y., Wen-Biao, L.I.: Research on SOC estimation based on SOH and off-line data segmented correction. Chin. J. Power Sources (2017)

8. Wang, M., Ye, T., Li, T.: Study of bidirectional DC-DC converters applied to energy storage system. Trans. China Electrotech. Soc. **28**(8), 66–71 (2013)

9. Tong, Y.B., Wu, T., Jin, X.M.: Study of bi-directional DC/DC converter. In: Proceedings of the CSEE (2007)

10. Qiu-Sheng, H.E., Lei, X.U., Xue-Xue, W.U.: Review of lithium battery charging technology. Chin. J. Power Sources (2013)

11. Liu, W., Wu, H., He, Z.: A multistage current charging method for Li-Ion battery considering balance of internal consumption and charging speed. Trans. China Electrotech. Soc. pp. 1401–1406 (2017)

12. Liu, Y.X., Wang, T.Y., Yang, Y.Y.: Modeling and simulation of electric vehicles' charge and discharge system. Power Syst. Prot. Control **42**(13), 70–76 (2014)

13. Liu, G.H., Wei, M.Y., Chen, Z.L.: Study on harmonics suppression mechanism of electric vehicle charging. Power Electron. **45**(12), 11–13 (2011)

14. Deng, T., Sun, H.: Research on real time estimation method of new SOC ampere hours integral for lithium ion battery. J. Chongqing Univ. Technol. **1**, 020 (2015)

15. Bing, Y., Wang, L., Liao, C.: Effects of uncertainty charging habits on electric vehicles' charging load demand and the charging load regulation. Trans. China Electrotech. Soc. **30**(4), 226–232 (2015)

Generation Capacity Planning with Significant Renewable Energy Penetration Considering Base-Load Cycling Capacity Constraints

Jingjie Ma, Shaohua Zhang$^{(\boxtimes)}$, and Xue Li

Key Laboratory of Power Station Automation Technology,
Department of Automation, Shanghai University, Shanghai 200072, China
eeshzhan@126.com

Abstract. Base-load cycling capacity (BLCC) shortage problem may seriously affect the integration scale of renewable energy. The ability to improve the BLCC only by operational dispatch of conventional plants is very limited. Therefore, it is critical to guarantee adequate BLCC at the capacity planning level. However, the BLCC have been ignored currently at yearly planning stage. In this paper, a yearly generation capacity planning model considering the BLCC constraints is proposed based on the screening curves method. With this model, an optimal mix of generation capacity can be obtained. Through dispatching conventional plants of the optimal mix, the BLCC constraint of each day in the planning year can be satisfied. Then, the impacts of cost parameters and renewable energy integration scale on the optimal mix are theoretically analyzed. Numerical simulations are presented to verify the reasonableness and effectiveness of the theoretical analysis.

Keywords: Significant renewable energy penetration
Base-load cycling capacity · Generation capacity planning
Screening curves method

1 Introduction

With the increasing shortage of fossil energy resources, intermittent renewable energy, notably wind power, is expected to play an increasing role to the sustainable development in the near future [1]. Because of the inverse peak-regulation characteristics in wind power output, large scale penetration of wind power will increase the daily peak-valley difference of net loads, which will result in base-load cycling capacity (BLCC) shortage problem [2, 3]. The BLCC shortage problem will pose an adverse impact on secure operation of power systems. The ability to mitigate the BLCC shortage problem only by operational dispatch of conventional plants is very limited [4, 5]. It is critical to guarantee adequate BLCC at the capacity planning level. However, as the BLCC constraint is generally considered in the daily operation in power systems, it has been ignored currently at yearly planning stage. As such, it is vital to meet the BLCC constraints in the planning level.

© Springer Nature Singapore Pte Ltd. 2018
K. Li et al. (Eds.): ICSEE 2018/IMIOT 2018, CCIS 925, pp. 295–305, 2018.
https://doi.org/10.1007/978-981-13-2381-2_28

Nowadays, many research works [6, 7] have focused on ensuring the BLCC by operational dispatch of conventional plants. These researches are short-term solutions with great limitations although they can improve the BLCC to a certain extent. In [8], an optimal capacity-allocation method was proposed for large-scale energy storage systems to relax peak-regulation. Ref. [9] proposed a capacity planning model based on screening curves method to describe the efficient plants portfolio. Ref. [10, 11] developed a new system planning model taking into account technical operational constraints such as the maintenance parameters and transmission interconnection. However, the BLCC constraints haven't been considered for power systems. Therefore, research gaps exist in yearly generation capacity planning considering BLCC constraints. This paper addresses the problem by screening curves method. Screening curves method [12, 13] is a useful approach to compute the optimal generation capacity for a target year.

Based on the screening curves method, a yearly generation capacity planning model considering the BLCC constraints is proposed in this paper. With this model, an optimal mix of generation capacity can be obtained. Through dispatching conventional plants of the optimal mix, the BLCC constraint of each day in the planning year can be satisfied. Then the impacts of cost parameters and renewable energy integration scale on the 'base-load' technology capacity and 'peak-load' technology capacity are theoretically analyzed. Numerical examples are presented to verify the reasonableness and effectiveness of the proposed model. The optimal mix with and without BLCC constraints are compared. The impacts of renewable energy integration scale on the optimal mix are examined.

2 Screening Curves Method with Renewable Energy Penetration

The screening curves method is a simple way to use annual load shape information and costs of competing power plant technologies to find a least-cost generation mix solution for a given load shape. The bottom half in Fig. 1 is the annual generation cost curve, the investment cost is its intercept and the operation cost is its slope. Let u_1 be the technology with the highest investment costs per capacity unit and u_3 with the lowest investment costs $(c_{inv,3} < c_{inv,2} < c_{inv,1})$. However, operating costs are highest for u_3 and lowest for u_1 $(c_{op,1} < c_{op,2} < c_{op,3})$. Then refer to u_1 as 'base-load' technology and to u_2 as 'intermediate load' technology and to u_3 as 'peak-load' technology.

The generation cost curve determines the optimal operating duration for each technology. The minimum cost is the lowest piece-wise linear function of firing hours (as shown in the red line in Fig. 1). The points of the intersections on the horizontal axis separate technologies, and the intervals of these points determine the annual firing duration of those technologies. The load-duration curve gives a one-to-one relationship between firing duration and generation capacity. Thus, the optimal generation capacity K_1, K_2, K_3 and the optimal generation quantity in a given year can be calculated.

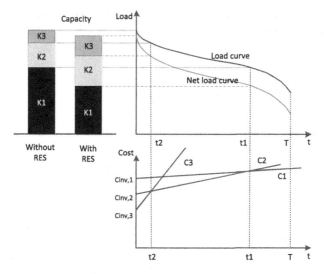

Fig. 1. Graphic method of the optimal mix for three technologies

With renewable energy penetration, it is economically mandated to feed-in renewables generation before considering any other generations. The net load $R(t)$ is defined as the initial load minus the renewables generation, can be estimated by:

$$R(t) = L(t) - P_{RES}(t) \tag{1}$$

where $L(t)$ is the load level at time t, $P_{RES}(t)$ is the output of renewables generation. The net load was rearranged in decreasing order to obtain the net load-duration curves. Figure 1 shows that after renewable energy penetration, the peak-valley load difference increases, which leads to a heavier pressure of base-load cycling. Also, the renewable energy penetration will change the load duration curve, which results in a different optimal mix.

3 Generation Capacity Planning with BLCC Constraints

3.1 BLCC Constraints

The BLCC adequacy of power systems is generally evaluated by BLCC in one day. The BLCC of a day can be defined as the minimum load minus the minimum output limit. Assume a power system with N conventional generation technologies. The total startup units' capacity of each day is equal to the maximum load of that day, i.e.

$$\sum_{i=1}^{N} K_i \mu_i(d) = R_{\max}(d) \quad d \in [1, 365] \tag{3}$$

where, K_i is the installed capacity of technology i, $\mu_i(d)$ is the ratio of the startup units' capacity to the installed capacity of technology i at day d. The minimum output limit of the startup units at day d is:

$$P_{Gmin}(d) = \sum_{i=1}^{N} K_i \mu_i(d) \eta_i \qquad (4)$$

where, η_i is the ratio of the minimum output to the installed capacity of technology i, $\eta_1 \geq \eta_2 \geq \ldots \geq \eta_N$. Since the cycling capacity of each technology is not the same, the different type of startup units will result in different minimum output limit. The minimum output limit of day d reaches its maximum, when the generation units are dispatched so as to minimize generation cost, i.e.

$$\max_{\mu_i(d)} P_{Gmin}(d) = \sum_{i=1}^{N} K_i \mu_i(d) \eta_i, \quad \mu_N(d) \leq \mu_{N-1}(d) \leq \ldots \leq \mu_1(d) \qquad (5)$$

The minimum output limit of day d reaches its minimum, when the generation units are dispatched in order to maximize BLCC, i.e.

$$\min_{\mu_i(d)} P_{Gmin}(d) = \sum_{i=1}^{N} K_i \mu_i(d) \eta_i, \quad \mu_N(d) \geq \mu_{N-1}(d) \geq \ldots \geq \mu_1(d) \qquad (6)$$

If the minimum load of day d is greater than $\max_{\mu_i(d)} P_{Gmin}(d)$, the system can be dispatched most economical at day d, and has a certain BLCC margin. If the minimum load of day d $R_{min}(d) \in [\min_{\mu_i(d)} P_{Gmin}(d), \max_{\mu_i(d)} P_{Gmin}(d))$, the BLCC constraint can be satisfied through dispatching conventional plants of the optimal mix at day d. If the minimum load of day d is smaller than $\min_{\mu_i(d)} P_{Gmin}(d)$, the BLCC constraint cannot be satisfied through dispatching conventional plants of the optimal mix at day d.

3.2 Generation Capacity Planning Model with BLCC Constraints

The efficient power system is defined by a minimization of total costs. The annualized investment cost of u_i is $c_{inv,i} K_i$. The annualized operating cost of u_i is $c_{op,i} Q_i$, where Q_i is the total energy of u_i. Formally, generation capacity planning with BLCC constraints is determined by the problem:

$$\min \ C(K_i) = \sum_{i=1}^{N} Q_i c_{op,i} + \sum_{i=1}^{N} K_i c_{inv,i} \qquad (7)$$

$$s.t. \quad K_i \geq 0 \quad \forall i. \qquad (8)$$

Take four technical types model as an example, an extension to n-technology case follows straightforward from the 4-technology case. The efficient energy (described by Eqs. (9)) and efficient capacities (described by Eqs. (10)) can be obtained by the screening curves method.

$$Q_4 = \int_0^{t_3} R(t)dt - t_3(K_1 + K_2 + K_3), \quad Q_3 = \int_0^{t_2} R(t)dt - t_2(K_1 + K_2) - Q_4$$
$$Q_2 = \int_0^{t_1} R(t)dt - t_1 K_1 - Q_4 - Q_3, \quad Q_1 = \int_0^{T} R(t)dt - Q_4 - Q_3 - Q_2 \tag{9}$$

$$K_1 = R(t_1), \qquad\qquad K_2 = R(t_2) - R(t_1)$$
$$K_3 = R(t_3) - R(t_2), \quad K_4 = R_{\max} - R(t_3) \tag{10}$$

where t_1, t_2, t_3 denoting the operating hours of u_2, u_3, u_4 respectively. The BLCC constraints are as follows:

$$K_1\mu_1(d) + K_2\mu_2(d) + K_3\mu_3(d) + K_4\mu_4(d) = R_{\max}(d)\ d = 1, \ldots, 365 \tag{11}$$

$$\mu_4(d) \geq \mu_3(d) \geq \mu_2(d) \geq \mu_1(d) \tag{12}$$

$$K_1\mu_1(d)\eta_1 + K_2\mu_2(d)\eta_2 + K_3\mu_3(d)\eta_3 + K_4\mu_4(d)\eta_4 \leq R_{\min}(d) \tag{13}$$

3.3   Solution Method

First select the maximum load $R_{max}(d)$ and minimum load $R_{min}(d)$ for each day of the planning year. Then rearrange them in a decreasing order of maximum load. $d = 1$ is the maximum load day of the year, i.e. $R_{\max}(1) = \max\limits_{d\in[1,365]} R_{\max}(d) = \sum\limits_{i=1}^{N} K_i$. Reoptimize the generation capacity from $d = 1$ to $d = 365$ according to the different BLCC constraint of each day. $K_i^d, i = 1, \ldots, 4$ is the optimal mix which satisfies the first d days' BLCC constraints.

The difference between the total capacity of startup units and total installed capacity of day d is: $\Delta P(d) = R_{\max}(1) - R_{\max}(d)$. If $\Delta P(d) < K_1^d$, the BLCC constraint of day d can be simplified to:

$$(K_1^d - \Delta P(d))\eta_1 + K_2^d\eta_2 + K_3^d\eta_3 + K_4^d\eta_4 \leq R_{\min}(d) \tag{14}$$

Construct the Lagrange function to solve the number of operation hour t_1^d, t_2^d, t_3^d. Then the optimal generation capacity for each technology type can be obtained by Eqs. (10). The Lagrange function can be written as follows.

$$\xi = c_{inv,1}R(t_1^d) + c_{inv,2}(R(t_2^d) - R(t_1^d)) + c_{inv,3}(R(t_3^d) - R(t_2^d)) + c_{inv,4}(R_{max} - R(t_3^d))$$

$$+ c_{op,1}(\int_0^T R(t)dt - \int_0^{t_1^d} R(t)dt + t_1^d R(t_1^d)) + c_{op,2}(\int_0^{t_1^d} R(t)dt - t_1^d R(t_1^d) - \int_0^{t_2^d} R(t)dt$$

$$+ t_2^d R(t_2^d)) + c_{op,3}(\int_0^{t_2^d} R(t)dt - t_2^d R(t_2^d) - \int_0^{t_3^d} R(t)dt + t_3^d R(t_3^d)) + c_{op,4}(\int_0^{t_3^d} R(t)dt \quad (15)$$

$$- t_3^d R(t_3^d)) - \beta^d (R_{min}(d) - R(t_1^d)(\eta_1 - \eta_2) - R(t_2^d)(\eta_2 - \eta_3) - R(t_3^d)(\eta_3 - \eta_4)$$

$$- R_{max}(1)\eta_4 + \Delta P(d)\eta_1)$$

where β^d is the Lagrange multiplier to condition (14). The Karush-Kuhn-Tucker conditions are:

$$\frac{\partial \zeta}{\partial t_1^d} \geq 0 \perp t_1^d \geq 0, \quad \frac{\partial \zeta}{\partial t_2^d} \geq 0 \perp t_2^d \geq 0, \quad \frac{\partial \zeta}{\partial t_3^d} \geq 0 \perp t_3^d \geq 0 \quad (16)$$

$$\frac{\partial \zeta}{\partial \beta^d} \leq 0 \perp \beta^d \geq 0 \quad (17)$$

Besides the complementary-slackness conditions, by assumption $t_1^d, t_2^d, t_3^d > 0$, conditions (16) give

$$t_1^d = \frac{c_{inv,1} - c_{inv,2} + \beta^d(\eta_1 - \eta_2)}{c_{op,2} - c_{op,1}}, \quad t_2^d = \frac{c_{inv,2} - c_{inv,3} + \beta^d(\eta_2 - \eta_3)}{c_{op,3} - c_{op,2}}$$

$$t_3^d = \frac{c_{inv,3} - c_{inv,4} + \beta^d(\eta_3 - \eta_4)}{c_{op,4} - c_{op,3}} \quad (18)$$

Condition (17) allows two possible solutions with respect to β^d: If $\frac{\partial \zeta}{\partial \beta^d} < 0$, β^d has to be zero by complementary slackness. At this point, the system have a certain BLCC margin, the BLCC constraint does not work, which will result in $t_1^d = t_1^{d-1}, t_2^d = t_2^{d-1}, t_3^d = t_3^{d-1}$. If $\frac{\partial \zeta}{\partial \beta^d} = 0$, $\beta^d > 0$ by complementary slackness, which will result in an increase of t_1^d, t_2^d, t_3^d.

If $K_1^d \leq \Delta P(d) < K_1^d + K_2^d$, the BLCC constraints can be simplified to:

$$(K_1^d + K_2^d - \Delta P(d))\eta_2 + K_3^d \eta_3 + K_4^d \eta_4 \leq R_{min}(d) \quad (19)$$

Similar to the above solution, introduce the Lagrange multiplier β^d to condition (19). Two possible solutions are given by complementary slackness: If $\frac{\partial \zeta}{\partial \beta^d} < 0$ (which means $R_{min}(d) > (K_1^d + K_2^d - \Delta P(d))\eta_2 + K_3^d \eta_3 + K_4^d \eta_4)$, $\beta^d = 0$. The BLCC constraint does not work, which will result in $t_1^d = t_1^{d-1}, t_2^d = t_2^{d-1}, t_3^d = t_3^{d-1}$. If $\frac{\partial \zeta}{\partial \beta^d} = 0$ (which means $R_{min}(d) = (K_1^d + K_2^d - \Delta P(d))\eta_2 + K_3^d \eta_3 + K_4^d \eta_4)$, $\beta^d > 0$ by complementary slackness. Correspondingly, $t_1^d = t_1^{d-1}$, $t_2^d = \frac{c_{inv,2} - c_{inv,3} + \beta^d(\eta_2 - \eta_3)}{c_{op,3} - c_{op,2}}$, $t_3^d = \frac{c_{inv,3} - c_{inv,4} + \beta^d(\eta_3 - \eta_4)}{c_{op,4} - c_{op,3}}$.

3.4   Effect of Cost Parameters and Renewable Energy Integration Scale

This section analyzed the effect of cost parameters and renewable energy integration scale on the 'base-load' technology capacity and 'peak-load' technology capacity.

The 'base-load' technology capacity is $K_1 = R(t_1)$ and 'peak-load' technology capacity is $K_4 = R_{max} - R(t_3)$. The derivative of K_1, K_4 with respect to any variable x are:

$$\frac{\partial K_1}{\partial x} = \frac{\partial R}{\partial t_1}\frac{\partial t_1}{\partial x}, \quad \frac{\partial K_4}{\partial x} = -\frac{\partial R}{\partial t_3}\frac{\partial t_3}{\partial x} \tag{20}$$

As $R(t)$ is strictly monotonously decreasing, derivatives of K_4 have the same sign as the derivatives of t_3 with respect to the same variable, derivatives of K_1 have the opposite sign as the derivatives of t_1 with respect to the same variable.

Without BLCC constraints, the operating hours of 'base-load' technology is $t_1 = \frac{c_{inv,1} - c_{inv,2}}{c_{op,2} - c_{op,1}}$, the operating hours of 'peak-load' technology is $t_3 = \frac{c_{inv,3} - c_{inv,4}}{c_{op,4} - c_{op,3}}$, which exhibits the independence of technologies that are not adjacent in the merit order.

After considering the BLCC constraints, the system becomes less economic to maintain the BLCC constraints, which will result in an increase of t_1, t_2, t_3. The increase of renewable energy will lead to a heavier BLCC demand, which will result in the reduction of 'base-load' technology capacity and the increase of 'peak-load' technology capacity.

4   Numerical Analysis

4.1   Data Assumption

The proposed method is applied to the data of a province in China. Figure 2 depicts the residual net load duration curves with 7%, 10%, 13%, 16% of the maximum load's wind power integration after the linearization fitting. And the black dotted line is the original net load duration curve with 10% of the maximum load's wind power integration. Table 1 shows the key parameters for five different conventional generation plants [9, 11].

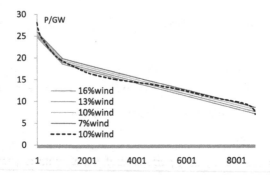

Fig. 2. The net load duration curves after the linearization fitting

Table 1. Key parameters for different types of plants

Parameter	Unit	Lignite	Hard coal	CCGT	OCGT	Oil
capitalized cost	k$/ MW·year	213.9	124.8	74.7	53.4	46.1
Variable O&M	$/MWh	8.6	23.4	43.3	60.9	84.0
Minimum output/installed capacity		0.60	0.50	0.35	0.25	0.20

4.2 Impact of BLCC Constraints on the Optimal Mix

Figure 3 depicts the impact of BLCC constraints on the optimal mix under 13% wind power integration. It can be seen that the 'base-load' technology capacity reduce and the 'peak-load' technology capacity increase after considering the BLCC constraints.

Figure 4 shows the impact of BLCC constraints on the BLCC adequacy of the planning year. Without BLCC constraints, the system can be dispatched most economical in 100 days, the BLCC demand cannot be satisfied through dispatching

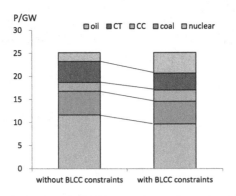

Fig. 3. Impact of BLCC constrains on the optimal mix

conventional plants of the optimal mix in 3 days during the planning year. After considering BLCC constraints, the system can be dispatched most economical in 178 days. And all of the 365 days' BLCC demand can be satisfied through dispatching conventional plants of the optimal mix.

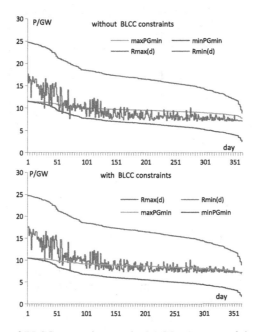

Fig. 4. Impact of BLCC constraints on the BLCC adequacy of the planning year

4.3   Impact of Renewable Energy Integration Scale on the Optimal Mix

Figure 5 shows the impact of renewable energy integration scale on the optimal mix with and without BLCC constraints. Without BLCC constraints, the 'peak-load' technology capacity increased 0.47%, the 'base-load' technology capacity decreased 3.82% as the wind power integration scale increased every 3%. With BLCC constraints, the 'peak-load' technology capacity increased 24.14%, the 'base-load' technology capacity decreased 9.98% as the wind power integration scale increased every 3%. It can be found that the change of wind power integration scale has a greater influence on the optimal mix after considering the BLCC constraints.

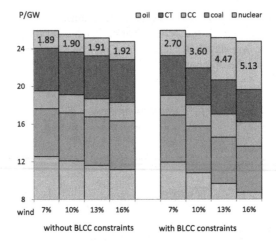

Fig. 5. Impact of renewable energy integration scale on the optimal mix

5   Conclusions

In order to guarantee adequate BLCC at the capacity planning level, a generation capacity planning model considering the base-load cycling capacity (BLCC) is proposed based on the screening curves method. With this model, an optimal mix of generation capacity can be obtained. Through dispatching conventional plants of the optimal mix, the BLCC constraint of each day in the planning year can be satisfied. Then, the impacts of cost parameters and renewable energy integration scale on the optimal mix are theoretically analyzed. Numerical examples are presented to verify the reasonableness and effectiveness of the proposed model. It is shown that: with the increase of renewable energy integration, 'peak-load' technology capacity will increase and 'base-load' technology capacity will decrease. Compared to the optimal mix without the BLCC constraints, the change of renewable energy integration scale has a greater influence on the optimal mix after considering the BLCC constrains. This work is helpful to determine an optimal conventional plants mix of a BLCC-constrained power systems.

References

1. Baldick, R.: Wind and energy markets: a case study of Texas. IEEE Syst. J. **6**(1), 27–34 (2012)
2. Troy, N., Denny, E., O'Malley, M.: Base-load cycling on a system with significant wind penetration. IEEE Trans. Power Syst. **25**(2), 1088–1097 (2010)
3. Batlle, C., Rodilla, P.: An enhanced screening curves method for considering thermal cycling operation costs in generation expansion planning. IEEE Trans. Power Syst. **28**(4), 3683–3691 (2013)

4. Coester, A., Hofkes, M.W.: E. Papyrakis.: An optimal mix of conventional power systems in the presence of renewable energy: a new design for the German electricity market. Energy Policy **116**, 312–322 (2018)
5. Babrowski, S., Jochem, P., Fichtner, W.: How to model the cycling ability of thermal units in power systems. Energy **103**, 397–409 (2016)
6. Xu, L., Ruan, X., Zhang, B., Mao, C.: An improved optimal sizing method for wind-solar-battery hybrid power system. Proc. Chin. Soc. Electr. Eng. **32**(25), 88–98 (2012)
7. Castronuovo, E.D., Lopes, J.A.P.: Optimal operation and hydro storage sizing of a wind hydro power plant. Int. J. Electr. Power Energy Syst. **26**(10), 771–778 (2004)
8. Yan, G., Feng, X., Li, J.: Optimization of energy storage system capacity for relaxing peak load regulation bottlenecks. Proc. Chin. Soc. Electr. Eng. **32**(28), 27–35 (2012)
9. Steffen, B., Weber, C.: Efficient storage capacity in power systems with thermal and renewable generation. Energy Econ. **36**, 556–567 (2013)
10. De Jonghe, C., Delarue, E., Belmans, R., D'haeseleer, W.: Determining optimal electricity technology mix with high level of wind power penetration. Appl. Energy **88**, 2231–2238 (2011)
11. Belderbos, A., Delarue, E.: Accounting for flexibility in power system planning with renewables. Int. J. Electr. Power Energy Syst. **71**, 33–41 (2015)
12. Zhang, T., Baldick, R., Deetjen, T.: Optimized generation capacity expansion using a further improved screening curve method. Electr. Power Syst. Res. **124**, 47–54 (2015)
13. Zhang, T., Baldick, R.: Consideration of existing capacity in screening curve method. IEEE Trans. Power Syst. **32**(4), 3038–3048 (2017)

A Multiple Model Control Method of Coal-Fired Power Plant SCR-DeNOx System

Jianhua Zhang[1(✉)], Bin Jia[2], Ben Zou[2], Xiao Tian[2], and Chunyao Liu[2]

[1] State Key Laboratory of Alternate Electrical Power System with Renewable Energy Sources, School of Control and Computer Engineering, North China Electric Power University, Beijing, China
jbj60509@126.com
[2] School of Control and Computer Engineering, North China Electric Power University, Beijing, China

Abstract. Nowadays, energy consumption problem and air contamination affecting the quality of our lives horribly is becoming more and more serious. Industrial emission issues have attracted much attention specially. As a crucial index, the denitration efficiency of Selective Catalytic Reduction (SCR) system, which is the primary way to control emission of NO_x in coal-fired power plant, is normally required above 80%. In this paper, Fractional Order Proportional Integral Differential based on Internal Model Control (IMC-FOPID) controller is introduced to control the emission of NO_x by implementing multiple model strategy. Compared with traditional PID controllers, the proposed control method in this paper is more effective.

Keywords: IMC-FOPID · SCR · Multiple model strategy

1 Introduction

Accompanied by the extensive economic development pattern of high pollution, high energy consumption and low efficiency, both energy depletion and air pollution are main factors to restrict sustainable development and ecological civilization construction all over the world. Emission of NO_x in power plants is a big threat to environment. Hence, it is urgent to develop an efficient, reliable and economical denitration technology to reduce the emission of NO_x [1].

Using Extreme Learning Machine (ELM) method to establish the relationship between boiler operation parameters and emission amount of NO_x, the emission of NO_x has been optimized in real time [2]. ELM is still being researched in industrial applications. The methods that combine feed water heater with steam ejector and change burner structure were proposed in [3, 4], respectively. Whereas, it is difficult to put them into practice. Designing burner based on gray box model aims at obtain a specific boiler structure merely [5]. An improved nonlinear model predictive controller was applied to control the emission of NO_x [6]. The FOPID controller proposed by

© Springer Nature Singapore Pte Ltd. 2018
K. Li et al. (Eds.): ICSEE 2018/IMIOT 2018, CCIS 925, pp. 306–313, 2018.
https://doi.org/10.1007/978-981-13-2381-2_29

Poblubny has five adjustable parameters and is more flexible than traditional PID controller [7]. Reference [8] presented a sliding mode control method to control the NO_x emission for a denitration system applied in thermal power units. Multiple model strategy, which has attracted much attention, is generally regarded as a feasible approach to dealing with complex systems. The characteristics of power plants are very complicated in terms of uncertainties, nonlinearities, time-varying and changing operating points. Therefore, combining the IMC-FOPID control strategy presented in reference [9] with the multiple model method, a multiple model IMC-FOPID controller is utilized to optimize NO_x emission of power plants in this paper.

The rest of this paper is organized as follows. In Sect. 2, an SCR-DeNO$_x$ system is briefly introduced. The main control scheme is then developed in Sect. 3. Consequently, simulation results are given in Sect. 4. Finally, some conclusions are drawn in Sect. 5.

2 Description of SCR-DeNOx System

At present, SCR denitration technology is most widely applied among many denitration methods. This method is characterized by explicit chemical reactions, no by-products and no secondary pollution. Correspondingly, it has some advantages in terms of high reliability, simple structure and high denitration rate (above 80%). The SCR denitration unit is usually installed between the economizer and the air preheater so that the catalytic reduction reactions occur in the suitable temperature range (300–400 °C). A diagram concerning a denitration unit of a 600 MW sub-critical unit in a power plant is depicted in Fig. 1.

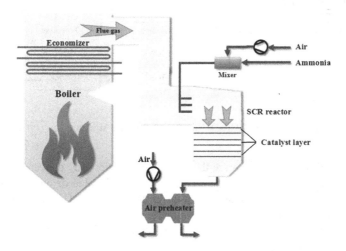

Fig. 1. SCR-DeNO$_x$ system process flow diagram

The chemical reactions occur under the effect of catalyst and dominant reaction insides is $4NO + 4NH_3 + O_2 \rightarrow 4N_2 + 6H_2O$, which achieves the objective of denitration mostly.

In the SCR-DeNO$_x$ system, there is a delay of the NO$_x$ measurement in the inlet and outlet of the SCR reactor. Therefore, the characteristics of the SCR-DeNO$_x$ system is complex in terms of large inertia and time delay. For the #1 unit of 600 MW power plant in Fig. 1, ammonia injection disturbance tests have been conducted under three typical operating conditions and corresponding transfer functions can be obtained by identifying dynamic characteristics according to experimental data [8].

3 Control Scheme

In this paper, we will present a kind of multiple model control strategy on SCR denitration cascade system. And some preliminaries are introduced as follows.

3.1 Multiple Model Strategy

In this paper, three local models are modelled for SCR denitration unit operating at three typical operating points corresponding to 350 MW, 450 MW, 550 MW load based on the idea of decomposition and synthesis. The cascade control method is adopted as the basic strategy of SCR denitration control system, in which outer loop uses IMC-FOPID controller and inner loop PI controller. The diagram of SCR denitration control system is shown in Fig. 2.

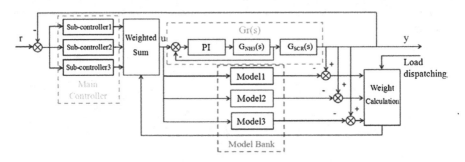

Fig. 2. SCR-DeNOx system control structure

As shown in Fig. 2, r and u are the set point of outlet NO$_x$ concentration and the output of the primary controller respectively. y is actual value of outlet NO$_x$ concentration, $G_{NH_3}(s)$ is the ammonia flow transfer function and $G_{SCR}(s)$ represents the transfer function of outlet NO$_x$ concentration.

3.2 IMC-FOPID Controller Design

FOPID controller has received considerable attention in the last two decades, which is more flexible than traditional PID controllers. Nevertheless, this advantage also implies that tuning of the FOPID controller can be much more complex because of five parameters that need to be tuned instead of three parameters in PID controllers.

Recently, many researchers have studied FOPID and proposed different tuning methods. For the sake of convenience of application and control, we apply the approach in
the literature [8] into tuning the parameters of FOPID controller for SCR denitration
control systems. The tuning procedure is roughly summarized as follows (Fig. 3).

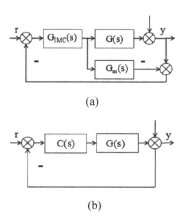

(a)

(b)

Fig. 3. (a) Sub-controller based on IMC or (b) traditional PID controller

Let $G_m(s)$ be the reference model of an linear time-invariant integer order system.
Step 1. Based on the IMC controller design, $G_m(s)$ must be factorized as follows:

$$G_m(s) = G_m^+(s)G_m^-(s) \tag{1}$$

where $G_m^-(s)$ is the non-singular part of $G_m(s)$, $G_m^+(s)$ stands for the singular part
which contains all time delays and right-half plane zeros, and its steady-state gain must
be equal to one.
Step 2. The IMC controller is specified as

$$G_{IMC}(s) = \frac{1}{G_m^-(s)} f(s) \tag{2}$$

where $f(s)$ represents a low pass filter with a steady-state gain of one, its form is

$$f(s) = \tau_c s^{a+1} (0 < a < 1) \tag{3}$$

where the time constant and non-integer are chosen by the phase margin and the
crossover frequency of the closed-loop by

$$a = \frac{\pi - \varphi_m}{\pi/2} - 1 \tag{4}$$

$$\tau_c = \frac{1}{\omega_c^{a+1}} \tag{5}$$

Step 3. The traditional feedback controller $C(s)$ can be indicated by [10]

$$C(s) = \frac{C_{IMC}(s)}{1 - C_{IMC}(s)C_m(s)} \tag{6}$$

The transfer function of PI controller in inner loop are $\frac{1}{0.4}\left(1 + \frac{1}{0.625s}\right)$ under three typical conditions. As the inner loop is tuned properly, the whole inner loop can be regarded approximately as a plant whose gain is one. Then let it cascade with $G_{SCR}(s)$ together. Then the combination becomes $Gr(s)$ shown in Fig. 2. Next, the primary controller can be designed in accordance with above-mentioned step 1 to step 3.

The usual form of $G_{SCR}(s)$ is:

$$G_m(s) = \frac{ke^{-\theta s}}{(1 + T_1 s)(1 + T_2 s)} \tag{7}$$

In this case, the time delay is approximated by

$$e^{-\theta s} = 1 - \theta s \tag{8}$$

Substituting the time delay approximation in $G_m(s)$ and using (2), the IMC controller is obtained by

$$C_{IMC}(s) = \frac{(1 + T_1 s)(1 + T_2 s)}{k(1 + \tau_c s^{a+1})} \tag{9}$$

Thus, the corresponding feedback controller is

$$\begin{aligned}
C(s) &= \frac{(1 + T_1 s)(1 + T_2 s)}{k(\theta s + \tau_c s^{a+1})} \\
&= \frac{1}{1 + \frac{\tau_c}{\theta}s^a} \frac{T_1 + T_2}{k\theta}\left[1 + \frac{1}{(T_1 + T_2)s} + \frac{T_1 T_2}{T_1 + T_2}s\right]
\end{aligned} \tag{10}$$

4   Simulation Results

In this section, IMC-FOPID controller is applied to every $Gr(s)$ in three typical operating conditions. As described in Fig. 2, the total output of the primary controller u is the weighted sum of u_i which corresponds to three typical operating conditions such that

$$u = \sum_{i=1}^{3} w_i u_i \tag{11}$$

Where w_i is the weight of u_i, its value is directly related to the quality of system switching. In practice, the weights of u_i under two operation points, which are close to the current load L, are not zero respectively. The weights can be calculated by

$$w_1 = \frac{|L - L_1|}{L_2 - L_1}; w_2 = \frac{|L - L_2|}{L_2 - L_1} \tag{12}$$

Where L_1, L_2 are two loads which are nearest the current load L. The experimental results of the unit load at operating point 1 (load 400 MW) and operating point 2 (load 500 MW) respectively are indicated as follows.

Figures 4 and 6 show the manipulated variables at 400 MW and 500 MW respectively. Figures 5 and 7 indicate the controlled output signal using PID cascade control

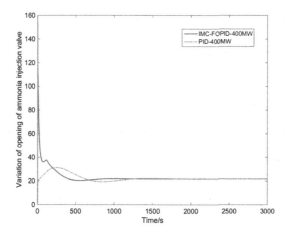

Fig. 4. Variation of opening of ammonia injection valve at 400 MW

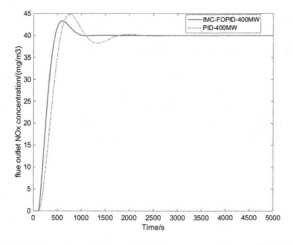

Fig. 5. Response of flue outlet NO_x concentration at 400 MW

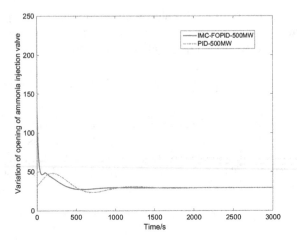

Fig. 6. Variation of opening of ammonia injection valve at 500 MW

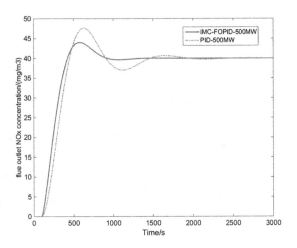

Fig. 7. Response of flue outlet NO$_x$ concentration at 500 MW

(dot-dash line) and proposed method in this paper (solid line) at 400 MW and 500 MW respectively. It can be observed that the response curve is smoother, the overshoot is smaller and response is faster than that under traditional PID cascade control.

5 Conclusion

Considering the coal-fired power plant SCR denitration system, IMC-FOPID controller based on multiple model strategy is proposed in this paper. The feasibility of this scheme has been proved by experimental results. Meanwhile, the proposed control method can achieve better control quality than the traditional PID controller. The proposed control system plays important role in ensuring economic and safe operation of SCR denitration system of a coal-fired power plant. In practice, SCR denitration systems usually operate at varying operating conditions, therefore, the proposed control strategy should be extended to deal with SCR denitration systems operating over a wide range in further research.

References

1. Ding, L., Liu, C., Chen, K., Huang, Y., Diao, B.: Atmospheric pollution reduction effect and regional predicament: an empirical analysis based on the Chinese provincial NO_x emissions. J. Environ. Manage. **196**, 178–187 (2017). https://doi.org/10.1016/j.jenvman.2017.03.016
2. Tan, P., Xia, J., Zhang, C., Fang, Q., Chen, G.: Modeling and reduction of NO_x emissions for a 700 MW coal-fired boiler with the advanced machine learning method. Energy **94**, 672–679 (2016). https://doi.org/10.1016/j.energy.2015.11.020
3. Chen, W.X., Zhang, S.P., Li, B.X., Liu, M., Liu, J.P.: Simulation study on 660 MW coal-fired power plant coupled with a steam ejector to ensure NO_x reduction ability. Appl. Therm. Eng. **111**, 550–561 (2017). https://doi.org/10.1016/j.applthermaleng.2016.09.104
4. Ma, L., et al.: Effect of the separated over-fire air location on the combustion optimization and NO_x reduction of a 600 MW FW down-fired utility boiler with a novel combustion system. Appl. Energy **180**, 104–115 (2016). https://doi.org/10.1016/j.apenergy.2016.07.102
5. Zhao, H.R., Shen, J., Li, Y.G., Bentsman, J.: Coal-fired utility boiler modelling for advanced economical low-NO_x combustion controller design. Control Eng. Pract. **58**, 127–141 (2017). https://doi.org/10.1016/j.conengprac.2016.10.005
6. Stadlbauer, S., Waschl, H., Del Re, L.: SCR ammonia dosing control by a nonlinear model predictive controller. IFAC Proc. Vol. **47**, 3018–3023 (2014). https://doi.org/10.3182/20140824-6-za-1003.02497
7. Poblubny, I.: Fractional-order system and $PI^\lambda D^\mu$ controller. IEEE Trans. Autom. Control **44**, 208–214 (1999). https://doi.org/10.1109/9.739144
8. Fu, J.Q.: The application of sliding mode control in the thermal power units denitrification control system. North China Electric Power University (2016)
9. Maâmar, B., Rachid, M.: IMC-PID-fractional-order-filter controllers design for integer order systems. ISA Trans. **53**, 1620–1628 (2014). https://doi.org/10.1016/j.isatra.2014.05.007
10. Vinopraba, T., Sivakumaran, N., Narayanan, S.: IMC based fractional order PID controller. IEEE ICIT. **49**, 71–76 (2011). https://doi.org/10.1109/icit.2011.5754348

Communication Network Planning with Dual Network Coupling Characteristics Under Active Distribution Network

Zhiqiang Fu[1], Xue Li[1(⊠)], Dajun Du[1], and Sheng Xu[2]

[1] Shanghai Key Laboratory of Power Station Automation Technology,
Shanghai University, Shanghai 200072, China
13167032368@163.com, lixue@i.shu.edu.cn
[2] School of Electronic and Information Engineering, Nantong Vocational
University, Nantong 226007, China

Abstract. A novel communication network planning method is proposed by considering the relationship between optical fiber communication network and power grid and the topological stability of communication networks. Firstly, the minimum spanning tree is used to generate the shortest power grid topology in term of the minimum expense of initial power grid. Then, for dual network (i.e., power grid and communication network) coupling characteristics, considering the constraints of network looping rate and invulnerability, an economic planning model is established and further solved by using the particle swarm optimization (PSO) algorithm. Finally, a 29-node system is employed to confirm the effectiveness and feasibility of the proposed method.

Keywords: Communication networks · Power grid
Active distribution network · Topology stability · PSO algorithm

1 Introduction

To solve energy shortage and environmental degradation problems, renewable energy has been rapidly developed [1, 2], where a new type of distribution network "active distribution network" is proposed [3, 4]. This requires flexible network structure and active control management, so the grid planning problem becomes a key issue for active distribution networks.

There exist some grid planning methods. For example, branch exchange method [5] is proposed to make the original radial form a loop and then break another branch to open the loop. The optimal network structure is optimized by genetic algorithms [6]. The graph theory [7] is employed for the distribution network planning, and an improved minimum spanning tree method is proposed by considering the investment costs and operating costs of the line.

The above mentioned planning methods mainly focus on the planning problem of power grid. There is short of research on the planning of communication network under active distribution network [8]. However, the current active distribution network has deeply integrated the communication network. Only when the communication network

© Springer Nature Singapore Pte Ltd. 2018
K. Li et al. (Eds.): ICSEE 2018/IMIOT 2018, CCIS 925, pp. 314–323, 2018.
https://doi.org/10.1007/978-981-13-2381-2_30

has good reliability, the whole current active distribution network can run smoothly and safely. Therefore, it is necessary to study the communication network planning problem.

To solve the communication network planning problem, the minimum spanning tree is firstly used to generate the shortest power grid topology in term of the minimum expense of initial power grid. Considering the constraints of network looping rate and invulnerability, an economic planning model is established and further solved by using the particle swarm optimization (PSO) algorithm. Finally, the effectiveness and feasibility of the proposed method are verified by a 29-node distribution network.

2   Communication Network Model Under Active Distribution Network

Before the planning of optical fiber communication network, a physical power network need be generated. To minimize the cost of power network planning, the initial span is generated using the minimum spanning tree. Then the communication network planning model is established by considering loop rate and network invulnerability.

2.1   Power Network Model

A real power network topology can be abstracted as a graph of points and edge sets [9], where the weight of the edge is defined as the cost required building the edge, and the sum of all edge weights represents the total cost in the whole topology graph. To minimize the total cost, the physical power network construction cost function is expressed as:

$$F_{d-\cos t} = \min \sum_{i=1}^{m} \omega(u, v) \tag{1}$$

where u and v represent the vertex of the topology of power grid, $\omega(u, v)$ represents the weight and m represents the number of vertices. To solve this problem, the minimum spanning tree method is employed to get the network topology as follows:

Step 1: Enter the grid node coordinates, where the vertex set is V and the edge set is E.
Step 2: Initialization $E_{new} = \{\}$ and $V_{new} = \{x\}$. In the minimum spanning tree to generate the physical network topology, where $E_{new} = \{\}$ is the set of edges and $V_{new} = \{x\}$ is the point set, and x is any node in the set (starting point).
Step 3: In the edge set E, select the edge $\langle u, v \rangle$ with the smallest weight, where u is the element in the set V_{new}, and v is not in the set V_{new}. Add v to the set V_{new}, and add $\langle u, v \rangle$ to the set $E_{new} = \{\}$. Repeat this step until $V_{new} = V$.

Using the above procedure, the power network topology is obtained and denoted by V_{new} and E_{new}.

After the topology of power grid is obtained, the model of optical fiber communication network need be established based on the structure of the graph, network construction cost and the constraints of network looping rate and invulnerability.

2.2   The Model of Optical Fiber Communication Network

Network construction cost of optical fiber cable is expressed by

$$C = \sum_{i=1}^{m} e_i w_i \tag{2}$$

where C is network construction cost, w_i is construction cost of the ith cable line, m is the number of optical fiber lines to be selected, and e_i is

$$e_i = \begin{cases} 1, & \text{The i}^{th} \text{ cable is selected} \\ 0, & \text{The i}^{th} \text{ cable is not selected} \end{cases} . \tag{3}$$

After network construction cost function is constructed by (2), network reliability constraint is then analyzed. It is represented by the node loop rate in optical fiber communication network [10], which is given by

$$P = \frac{v_{cycle}}{n} \tag{4}$$

where P is the node loop rate and the value is the ratio of the number of looped nodes and the summed points in the network, and n is the total number of nodes in the communication network, and v_{cycle} is the number of looping nodes (i.e., the nodes forms the loops).

After communication network reliability is constructed by (4), network topology reliability constraint is then analyzed. It is represented by the network invulnerability, i.e.,

$$K(G) = \frac{\sum_{i=1}^{m} D(i)}{\sum_{i=1}^{m} D_{full}(i)}. \tag{5}$$

where $\sum D_{full}(i)$ is the sum of the degrees of importance of all nodes in the graph of the fully connected network, and $\sum D(i)$ is the sum of the degrees of importance of all nodes in the real topology graph, and m is the number of nodes.

The node importance $D(i)$ is given by

$$D(i) = \frac{S_i}{l_i}, \tag{6}$$

where S_i is the edge weight, l_i is the degree of node position importance, which is given by

$$l_i = \frac{1}{m} \sum_{j=1, j\neq i}^{m} l_{ij}, \tag{7}$$

$$S_i = \sum_{(i,j)\in B_i} \frac{1}{\omega_{ij}}. \tag{8}$$

For the node i, after setting the distance between the edges directly connected to node i as the distance value of the shortest line in the topology, l_{ij} is the shortest path distance between nodes i and j. ω_{ij} is the distance connected by nodes i and j if they are directly connected, otherwise it is unlimited. So S_i is the larger, then the closer the node is to the surrounding nodes, the more important the position in the network is.

The paper is concerned with the constrain of the network invulnerability and loop rate. Loop rate is not less than 70% and invulnerability is not less than 0.3.

3 Joint Planning Model of Power Grid and Communication Network

A communication planning model is obtained by the coupling of communication network and power grid.

The relationship between the power grid and the communication network is shown in Fig. 1. The upper layer is the planning model of power grid. Then, the lower layer optimizes the communication network based on the upper model, and the communication network cost value F_c is transferred to the upper layer.

In the above model, the optical fiber cost F_c is divided into two parts: (1) The supporting facilities for laying optical fibers, such as towers, and the cable channel;

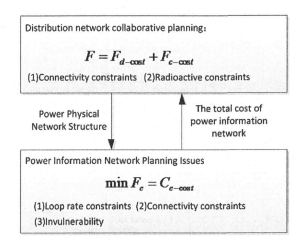

Fig. 1. Communication network planning model with dual network

(2) The optical fiber cost. The optical fiber laid along physical network can save the cost of constructing the tower and excavating the cable ditch. However, when the communication network is laid along physical network, it may increase the distance of fiber laying. Therefore, how to lay the communication network need to be optimized.

According to communication network, if there is a path from node i to node j, and this path exists in the power grid, calculate the total cost of laid along the power grid (not include the cost of towers or digging cable ditch) $Cost\_1$, and the total cost $Cost\_2$ of direct connection node i and node j. Compare $Cost\_1$ and $Cost\_2$, select the smaller value as the topological edge of the communication network.

4   Solution of Active Distribution Network Collaborative Planning Model

The upper layer is physical network planning by taking into connectivity and radiation account. The lower layer is communication network planning by considering invulnerability and loop rate constrains. Physical power grid is obtained by the minimum spanning tree, which is stored in an adjacency matrix [11]. The lower layer is solved by hybrid PSO and Floyd algorithm, and the specific solution process is shown in Fig. 2.

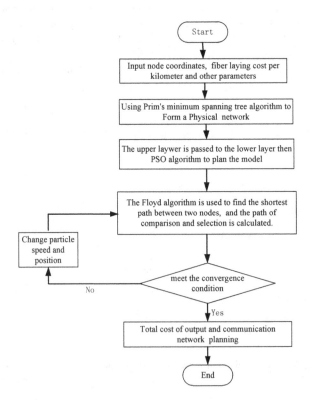

Fig. 2. Planning flowchart of communication network model

5 Simulation Results

5.1 Simulation Introduction

The case used for communication network planning is a 29 nodes system as shown in Table 1. The installation cost of the optical fiber with supporting facilities is 0.42 million dollar per kilometer, and the cost per kilometer of the grid along the distribution network is 0.33 million dollar, and the substation node is equipped with optical fiber. Communication network planning, the substation node number is "1, 7, 14, 20, 27". The loop rate is defined as not less than 70% and the invulnerability not less than 0.3.

Table 1. The coordinates of the node

Node	X axis coordinates	Y axis coordinates
1	1.976	1.09
2	1.056	1.026
3	0.48	1.304
4	1.928	1.798
5	0.196	1.076
6	3.64	0.474
7	0.524	0.914
8	2.876	1.808
9	0.184	1.602
10	1.008	1.586
11	0.664	1.822
12	3.36	0.904
13	0.548	0.43
14	0.916	0.182
15	3.424	1.192
16	2.856	0.182
17	2.488	0.272
18	3.272	1.738
19	2.876	1.56
20	3.112	1.394
21	2.348	0.112
22	2.128	0.334
23	3.3	0.474
24	3.44	1.49
25	2.304	1.556
26	1.172	0.354
27	2.388	0.506
28	2.944	1.196
29	3.616	0.718

5.2   Result Analysis

The physical power grid generated by the minimum spanning tree as shown in Fig. 3, and the initial grid of the communication network generated by the substation nodes is shown in Fig. 4.

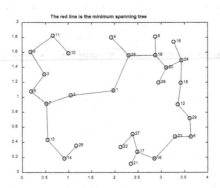

Fig. 3. Initial physical grid (Color figure online)

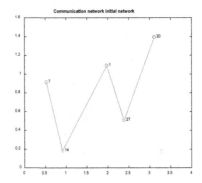

Fig. 4. Initial communication network grid

According to the initial communication network in Fig. 4, the communication network model solved by PSO algorithm, which meets the loop rate and network invulnerability constrain. After each particle is selected by the edge, the Floyd algorithm is used to find the shortest path between two points on the physical network shelf, as shown in Fig. 5, the shortest path of the 14–17 nodes on the physical shelf. The green nodes (i.e., 1, 7, 14, 20, and 27) are the substation nodes, and the others are ordinary load nodes.

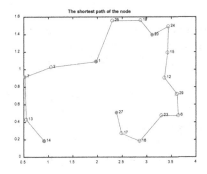

Fig. 5. 14–17 the shortest path of the node (Color figure online)

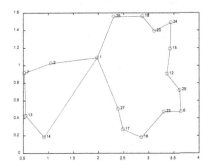

Fig. 6. Planned communication network

The topology is selected by calculating cost of optical fiber laying along the physical network and the supporting facilities. The total cost of the network is 162.3 dollar. The topology of the communication network planning is shown in Fig. 6, and the mapping of physical network and communication network is shown in Fig. 7.

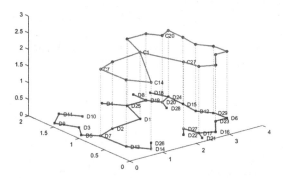

Fig. 7. Two-layer network coupling diagram

To ensure the loop rate, it can be seen that the fiber node 1 and node 14 are directly connected in Fig. 6. If the communication network is laid along 1-2-7-13-14 nodes, the loop rate only 60%. Then, to reduce the economic costs of communications network planning, node 7 and node 14 are laid along physical network by comparing Fig. 4 with Fig. 6.

After considering the loop rate and invulnerability constrain, the communications network invulnerability improved from 0.2738 to 0.4413. The importance of nodes is shown in Table 2, and the higher the value, the lower the degree of importance. Case 1 is the initial communication network, and case 2 is the importance of the nodes obtained by the PSO algorithm. The importance of nodes is significantly reduced as is in Table 2.

Table 2. Node importance indicator

Node	Case 1	Case 2
7	1.934	3.423
14	3.219	3.541
1	1.534	5.587
20	1.560	1.716
27	0.725	3.235

6   Conclusions

In this paper, a communication network planning model in the active distribution network is established by taking the coupling characteristics into account, and the model is solved by hybrid PSO and Floyd algorithm. The experimental results of a 29 nodes distribution network show that: (1) Considering the coupling of physical networks and communication networks, the communication network planning cost can effectively reduce; (2) The communication network invulnerability can be effectively improved by considering the loop rate and invulnerability constrains.

Acknowledgments. This work was supported in part by the national Science Foundation of China under Grant No. 61773253, and project of Science and technology Commission of Shanghai Municipality under Grants No. 15JC1401900, 14JC1402200, and 17511107002. This work was also supported in part by the Funds of Nantong Applied Basic Research Plan (GY12017015) and Qing Lan Project of colleges and universities in Jiangsu province.

References

1. Jiang, L., et al.: Growth in wind and sun: integrating variable generation in China. IEEE Power Energy Mag. **13**(6), 40–49 (2015)
2. Koutsoukis, N.C., Georgilakis, P.S., Hatziargyriou, N.D.: Multistage coordinated planning of active distribution networks. IEEE Trans. Power Syst. **33**(1), 32–44 (2018)
3. Samuelsson, O., et al.: Active distribution network — demonstration project ADINE. In: Innovative Smart Grid Technologies Conference Europe, pp. 1–8. IEEE (2010)

4. You, Y., et al.: Technology and its trends of active distribution network. Autom. Electr. Power Syst. **36**(18), 10–16 (2012)
5. Bi, P.X., J, L., Zhang, W.Y.: Improved branch switching method for distribution network reconfiguration. Proc. CSEE **21**(8), 98–103 (2001)
6. Ramirez-Rosado, I.J., Bernal-Agustin, J.L.: Genetic algorithms applied to the design of large power distribution systems. IEEE Trans. Power Syst. **13**(2), 696–703 (1998)
7. Zhou, B.X., Liu, X.Y.: Topology analysis method of distribution network based on network graphics and its application. Autom. Electr. Power Syst. **27**(16), 67–70 (2003)
8. Pu, T.J., et al.: Analysis and application design of multi-source collaborative optimization scheduling architecture for active distribution network. Autom. Electr. Power Syst. **40**(1), 17–23 (2016)
9. Cheng, K.Q., Li, S.W., Zhou, J.: Evaluation method of network invulnerability based on edge weight. Comput. Eng. Appl. **46**(35), 95–96 (2010)
10. Shi, Y., Guo, S.Y., Qiu, X.S.: Immune algorithm based route planning method for power communication network. J. Beijing Univ. Posts Telecommun. **2**, 14–17 (2014)
11. Ma, W.Y., Mao, G.W.: System hierarchy division based on graph theory and matrix theory. J. Lanzhou Jiao Tong Univ. **28**(6), 150–154 (2009)

Author Index

Printed in the United States
By Bookmasters